HISTORY AND THE CONSTRUCTION OF THE CHILD IN EARLY BRITISH CHILDREN'S LITERATURE

How did the "flat" characters of eighteenth-century children's literature become "round" by the mid-nineteenth? While previous critics have pointed to literary Romanticism for an explanation, Jackie C. Horne argues that this shift can be better understood by looking to the discipline of history. Eighteenth-century humanism believed the purpose of history was to teach private and public virtue; by creating idealized readers to emulate. Eighteenth-century children's literature, with its impossibly perfect protagonists (and its equally imperfect villains) echoes history's exemplar goals.

Exemplar history, however, came under increasing pressure during the period, and the resulting changes in historiographical practice—an increased need for reader engagement and the widening of history's purview to include the morals, manners, and material lives of everyday people—find their mirror in changes in fiction for children. Horne situates hitherto neglected robinsonnades, historical novels, and fictionalized histories within the cultural, social, and political contexts of the period to trace the ways in which idealized characters gradually gave way to protagonists who fostered readers' sympathetic engagement. Horne's study will be of interest to specialists in children's literature, the history of education, and book history.

Ashgate Studies in Childhood, 1700 to the Present

Series Editor: Claudia Nelson, Texas A&M University, USA

This series recognizes and supports innovative work on the child and on literature for children and adolescents that informs teaching and engages with current and emerging debates in the field. Proposals are welcome for interdisciplinary and comparative studies by humanities scholars working in a variety of fields, including literature; book history, periodicals history, and print culture and the sociology of texts; theater, film, musicology, and performance studies; history, including the history of education; gender studies; art history and visual culture; cultural studies; and religion.

Topics might include, among other possibilities, how concepts and representations of the child have changed in response to adult concerns; postcolonial and transnational perspectives; "domestic imperialism" and the acculturation of the young within and across class and ethnic lines; the commercialization of childhood and children's bodies; views of young people as consumers and/or originators of culture; the child and religious discourse; children's and adolescents' self-representations; and adults' recollections of childhood.

Also in the series

The Writings of Hesba Stretton
Reclaiming the Outcast
Elaine Lomax

Public School Literature, Civic Education and the
Politics of Male Adolescence
Jenny Holt

The Nineteenth-Century Child and Consumer Culture
Dennis Denisoff

Conceptualizing Cruelty to Children in Nineteenth-Century England
Literature, Representation, and the NSPCC
Monica Flegel

History and the Construction of the Child in Early British Children's Literature

JACKIE C. HORNE

ASHGATE

Published by
Ashgate Publishing Limited
Wey Court East
Union Road
Farnham
Surrey, GU9 7PT
England
www.ashgate.com

Ashgate Publishing Company
Suite 420
101 Cherry Street
Burlington
VT 05401-4405
USA

British Library Cataloguing in Publication Data
Horne, Jackie C., 1965–
History and the construction of the child in early British children's literature. – (Ashgate studies in childhood, 1700 to the present)
1. Children's literature – 18th century – History and criticism. 2. Children's literature – 19th century – History and criticism. 3. Children's stories, English – History and criticism. 4. English fiction – 18th century – History and criticism. 5. English fiction – 19th century – History and criticism. 6. Literature and society – Great Britain – History – 18th century. 7. Literature and society – Great Britain – History – 19th century. 8. Didactic fiction, English – History and criticism.
I. Title II. Series
823.5'099282–dc22

Library of Congress Cataloging-in-Publication Data
Horne, Jackie C., 1965–
  History and the construction of the child in early British children's literature / by Jackie C. Horne.
    p. cm. — (Ashgate studies in childhood, 1700 to the present)
  Includes bibliographical references and index.
  1. Children's stories, English—History and criticism. 2. Children—Books and reading—Great Britain—History—17th century. 3. Children in literature. I. Title.
  PR830.C513H67 2011
  823'.08729099282—dc22

                                                                    2011001047
ISBN 9781409407881 (hbk)
ISBN 9781409407898 (ebk)

Printed and bound in Great Britain by the
MPG Books Group, UK

To Keith, for love and a library card

Contents

List of Figures

Acknowledgements

Unlike Robinson Crusoe, who spent the majority of his island sojourn alone, I have had much good company during my research and writing adventure. First, I would like to thank the organizations that have supported my work: The Children's Literature Association, through its Hannah Beiter Graduate Student Award and its Best Article of the Year Award; the Mitzi Myers Memorial Fund, for awarding me a fellowship to conduct research at UCLA; the Spencer Foundation, for a Graduate Research Grant in Education; the Brandeis Women's Study Program, for a Sagan Grant for Graduate Work in Women's Studies; the Brandeis University English Department, for an Advanced Teaching Fellowship and for honoring me with the Milton Hindus Memorial Endowed Dissertation Fellowship; and the Center for the Study of Children's Literature at Simmons College, for offering me a post-doctoral Fellowship. The confidence in my scholarship shown by each of these organizations, as well as their financial support, made much of the research for this book possible.

For quick responses to questions and requests for information, provoking intellectual debate, and continual goodwill, I thank participants in the three academic listservs that continue to inform my thinking and my work: the Victoria list; the Eighteenth Century list; and the Child Lit list. I also wish to thank the many librarians who have helped me in my quest to track down hard-to-find children's books: Jeff Rankin, Dan Slive, and the staff at Special Collections at the UCLA Library; Laura E. Wasowicz at the American Antiquarian Society; and the librarians in the Phillips Reading Room at Harvard's Widener Library.

I also wish to thank my teachers, mentors, and fellow graduate students at Brandeis University for their insights, challenges, and intellectual support. I am grateful to the participants in Brandeis's Spencer Foundation Education Seminar 2003-2004, in particular, to Joyce Antler and Sharon Feiman-Nemser, for giving me the amazing opportunity to discuss my work and receive support from scholars outside the field of English. I thank Robin Feuer Miller, for sharing her thoughts on children's literature with me; Govind Sreenivasan, for his insights into European intellectual and religious history; John Burt and John Brereton, for giving me both a pragmatic and a theoretical grounding in rhetoric and composition; Mary Baine Campbell, for her unwavering support of my teaching; Sue Lanser, for her advice and intervention during a crucial period during the writing process; and Laura Quinney, Paul Morrison, Jeff Nunokawa, Michael T. Gilmore, and Tom King, for their intellectual rigorousness and their confidence in me as a scholar. The students who entered the English Ph.D. program with me continue to inspire me; I would particularly like to thank Lori Davis Perry, for her early friendship and support, and Emily Bernhard-Jackson, dissertation dyad partner extraordinaire.

My teachers and later colleagues at the Center for the Study of Children's Literature at Simmons College helped me to navigate the transition from a career in publishing to one in academia. Thanks to Gary Oakes, the epitome of collegiality; Kelly Hager, fellow devotee of Victorian children's literature; Becky Thompson, a model of the intellectual as activist; and Lowry Pei, who helped me to recognize the teaching skills I did not know I had. My largest debt is to Susan Bloom and to Cathryn Mercier; I will be forever grateful to you both for your many leaps of faith on my behalf.

Special thanks are due to the readers who engaged deeply and often with earlier versions of this manuscript. I thank Beverly Lyon Clark for sharing her wide knowledge of children's literature with me, and for giving me the confidence of her unwavering support. I am grateful to John Plotz for the depth of his intellect, the breadth of his knowledge of contemporary critical literature, and for his continual challenges to push my thinking, and my writing, farther than I ever thought they could go. Finally, I wish to thank Susan Staves for taking me, and my unconventional project, under her wing, even in the midst of her impending retirement. I am continually amazed by how much she knows, not just about literature, but about history, about art, about politics, about life. I feel deeply grateful, and deeply honored, that she has been willing to share even a small fraction of that knowledge with me.

I cannot imagine that this book would ever have been completed without the humor and friendship of the inhabitants of my own local island: my Traymore Street neighbors. Our Wednesday night dinners and our mutual babysitting have given me both the time to work on this book and much needed respite from it. Thanks in particular to Sarah Queen, for giving me a kick in the pants at the right time; to Anita Wagner, for sharing information about negotiation strategies; to Roger Michel, for his photographic advice and his acerbic wit; and to Nicole and Tom Hammond, Erin Hanley, David Weinstein, Norbert Hoffman, David McMahon, and especially Anne Marie Michel, Trey Peck, and Jessica Boyatt, for laughter, encouragement, and support. And thanks, of course, to the kids: Hannah, Sam, Sebastian, Thomas, Ben, Alex, Avery, Maggie, and Violet.

Heartfelt thanks to Dan Brenner, for helping me to see and move beyond the limitations of my own personal island.

Finally, I wish to thank my family. Jane and Floyd Smith have been a seldom acknowledged, but always deeply appreciated, source of support over the past 25 years. My parents, Ken and Rhoda Horne, gave me the confidence to pursue my dreams by always taking it for granted that I would, without question, achieve them. My daughter, Maddie, who has been with me only a little longer than this book, continues to be a source of joy, even though she is certain that *The Lightning Thief* is far more fun to read than anything I could write. Most importantly, I wish to thank my partner, Keith, for his unwavering support of my intellectual and professional pursuits, his silly jokes, and for continuing to believe that I did not marry him *just* to get a Harvard Library card. May life with you continue to be an "awfully big adventure."

Introduction:
Setting off on an Exemplary Adventure

> The study of history seems to me, of all other, the most proper to train us up to private and public virtue.
>
> —Henry St John, Lord Viscount Bolingbroke,
> *Letters on the Study and the Use of History* (1735)[1]

> Before you begin the following Sheets, I beg you will stop a Moment at this Preface, to consider with me, what is the true Use of Reading; and if you can once fix this Truth in your Minds, namely, that the true Use of Books is to make you wiser and better, you will then have both Profit and Pleasure from what you read.
>
> —Sarah Fielding, "Preface" to *The Governess:*
> *or, The Little Female Academy* (1749)[2]

If you ask a twenty-first century historian "why study history?" you are likely to hear several different, but related, responses. Study history to find out the truth about the past. Stretch your understanding of what it means to be human by encountering the differences between people of times gone by and people of the present. Learn to see how social structures and ways of thinking shape human subjectivity. Begin to imagine the future by studying the patterns of the past. Anyone who has taken a class in history, or read a contemporary work about the long-ago, would not find such answers surprising.

Yet if you were to give the same answers to an early eighteenth-century reader posing the same question, he (or, more rarely, she) would be likely to look at you with confusion or even scorn. For, as the above quote from Lord Bolingbroke, from his widely popular *Letters on the Study and the Use of History*, suggests, educated Enlightenment thinkers took it for granted that the purpose of reading history was not only intellectual, but also moral: to "train us up to private and public virtue." Though Bolingbroke phrases his assertion as a personal pronouncement, his understanding of the purpose of history was one widely shared by both writers and readers of history during the neo-classical period in England. Unlike twenty-first century readers of history, eighteenth-century readers focused not on the differences, but on the similarities, in human behavior across historical time. Such readers typically learned "public and private virtue" by reading histories that featured the stories of exemplary men of the past, men whose virtuous behavior

---

[1]   Bolingbroke, Henry St John Lord Viscount. *Letters on the Study and Use of History* (1735). ELIOHS: Electronic Library of Historiography. Web. July 5, 2006. Letter II, 177.

[2]   Fielding, Sarah. *The Governess: or Little Female Academy*. London: A Millar, 1749. London: Pandora, 1987, *xiii*.

they themselves could emulate, or whose vicious behavior they could shun, whether such men had lived in classical Rome, Renaissance Italy, or medieval England. As Mark Salber Phillips, in his engaging analysis of eighteenth- and early nineteenth-century history writing, *Society and Sentiment*, reminds us, the assumption that "a reader who is confronted with effective representations of the ideal will be moved by a spontaneous desire for emulation—or, in the case of vicious example, by an equivalent feeling of abhorrence" (126) was central to eighteenth-century humanist teaching.

The conception of history as exemplum was not a temporary odd aberration of Enlightenment thinking, but a tradition with long historical roots, roots dating back to the classical period. As George Nadel explains, using historical figures as moral *exemplum* was common practice among Roman writers. Teaching by example, the Romans felt, was far more effective than teaching simply by precept (a method associated by Romans with unpopular Greek philosophizing). Roman rhetoricians even went so far as to argue that *exempla* were not merely persuasive, but "irresistibly implanted motives of right conduct" (Nadel 298). Plutarch's *Lives*, the most popular classical reading from the sixteenth to the nineteenth century, provided both the clearest justification for exemplary biography, and the most accomplished example of it.

Though competing conceptions of history emerged subsequent to the Roman model (Christian providential history, for one), what Nadel terms the "Exemplar Theory of History" proved the dominant model in the writing of secular European history from the Roman period until the nineteenth century. Writing history not to explore difference, but to find what Leo Braudy terms "timeless maxims of political behavior," the eighteenth-century historian sought to uncover "the uniformities of moral and political truth to bring himself and his reader into a point of view that transcends the present moment" (15, 17). This "instrumental view of history" continued to hold sway throughout the eighteenth century in England, as the sentiments of Bolingbroke, writing in 1735, find their echo in the 1783 arguments of Hugh Blair, Chair of Rhetoric and Belles Lettres at the University of Edinburgh: "As it is the office of an Orator to persuade, it is that of an Historian to record truth for the instruction of mankind. This is the proper object and end of history" (*Lectures on Rhetoric and Belles Lettres*, qtd. in Phillips 14).

Arguments such as Bolingbroke's and Blair's, arguments that pointed to the moral purpose of creating and studying history, find their echo in justifications for another type of literature, a literature just beginning to emerge in eighteenth-century England: the genre of juvenile fiction. The opening words of the Preface of Sarah Fielding's 1749 children's novel *The Governess; or The Little Female Academy*—"the true Use of Books is to make you wiser and better"—could easily be substituted for those of Blair, or of Bolingbroke, and vice versa. Such justifications for writing for children were not confined to Sarah Fielding's work, the first full-length English-language novel written for young people; they appeared in the majority of volumes published for children in Britain during the eighteenth century. And such claims of teaching morals through exemplar were not restricted only to the eighteenth-century women authors typically labeled "moral tale" writers. Even John Newbery, whose publications were famously set in opposition to the morally-focused writings of the "cursed Barbauld Crew" by Charles Lamb, demonstrates in the prefaces and dedications of his children's books (both through imitation and parody) his adherence to the key Enlightenment belief in the power of literary exemplars to teach morality. For example, the title page of Newbery's first children's book, *A Little Pretty Pocket-Book* (1744) satirically replaces the moral exemplar character with purchasable goods, claiming that merely playing with the accompanying Ball and Pincushion "will infallibly make Tommy a good Boy and Polly a good Girl" (cited in Townsend, *Written* 15), while in his company's more famous publication, the anonymous *The History of Goody Two-Shoes* (1765), the idealized actions of Margery Meanwell, a.k.a. Goody Two-Shoes, have led to her very nickname becoming synonymous with someone whom modern-day readers would term a morally smug, self-righteous prig. Despite his reputation for publishing books free from the didacticism of the "Barbauld Crew," even the playful Newbery does not stray far from the eighteenth-century exemplar model of character construction.

As Edward Augustus Kendall asserts in his dedication to *Keeper's Travels in Search of his Master* (1798), the goal of leading the reader toward virtuous behavior is one shared not only by other types of overtly moral writing—"fable … song, … admonition … reproof"—but also by the most highly-regarded prose genre of the Enlightenment: "history" (qtd. Bator, *Masterworks* vol. 4, 192). Thus, I would suggest, eighteenth-century children's literature may be better understood by placing it not in the context of the genre of the novel for adults, but rather in the genre with a more similar purpose and function: the genre of history.

Scholars of eighteenth-century literature may object at this point, arguing that exemplarity featured prominently not only in the field of history, but also in novels for adults in this period. Why link books for children to history, when a more natural link is to fiction for their elders? In *Before Novels: The Cultural Contexts of Eighteenth-Century English Fiction*, J. Paul Hunter notes the presence of exemplarity in novels written for adults, arguing that "novels had at their center a concept of imitation and evitation" (281–2). Allen Michie, in his examination of the reception histories of Richardson and Fielding, agrees, noting that the general reading public in eighteenth-century England "believe[s] morality is the reason novels exist in the first place" (73). While Clara Reeve's assertion in *The Progress of Romance* (1785) that Fielding "painted nature as *it is*, rather than as *it ought to be*" would suggest praise to twenty-first century readers, for Reeve and many of her eighteenth-century peers, who preferred morally exemplary characters over ordinary, flawed ones, her comment points to a far different value judgment: a belief that Fielding's novels are "much inferior to *Richardson's* in morals and exemplary characters" (Reeve, qtd. Michie 57, 76).

Challenges to the necessity, or even the usefulness, of ideal exemplar characters in novels, however, began far earlier in fictions for adults than they did in fictions for children. Such challenges can be seen as early as the 1740s, in the debates between Fielding and Richardson and their proponents. And by the end of the century, Richardson's novels, though still praised for their morality, were no longer appealing to a large general readership; overt didacticism and exemplary characters were no longer the norm in novels for mature readers. As Sir Walter Scott wrote in his defense of Fielding's *Tom Jones* in *Lives of the Novelists* (1821–1824), "The professed morality of a piece is usually what the reader is least interested in" (qtd. Michie 103).

During the eighteenth and early nineteenth centuries, novels written for adults were often considered both morally suspect and of markedly lesser literary status than histories, in part because of their early rejection of idealized characters in favor of flawed ones.[3] As Terry Lovell notes, adults who read novels in the period often did not want to own them, not only because of their high cost but also because of their low cultural status (50–51). Circulating libraries of the period featured many novels for adults, but very few for children, M.O. Grenby points out; this fact, when linked with the evidence of marginalia in children's books from the period that demonstrates the "extreme pride that children felt in possessing their own books" (Grenby, "Adults Only?" 26), paradoxically suggests that while novels for children may have cost less than those for adults, they may have held a higher cultural status than the much maligned novels consumed by their elders.

Authors of eighteenth-century fictions for children rarely attempted to validate their own writing by linking their work to a genre as suspect as the adult novel, or to enter into debates about whether real or ideal characters were best suited to their productions. Exemplarity in history and in children's literature also differs from that in the novel for adults, at least according to Hunter's definition of the genre; his list of 10 characteristics of the novel includes both "subjectivity" and "empathy and vicariousness," an empathy that "give[s] readers a sense of what it would be like to be someone else, of how another identity would feel" (24). Such subjectivity and empathy came far later to the genre of history, and likewise to the genre of children's literature, than it did to the novel for adults. Modeling their works as much on, if not more after, works of exemplary history than on novels intended for adults, Enlightenment children's writers not only sought to instruct, but also took it for granted that in writing morally idealized protagonists, what many twentieth-century literary critics often denigrated as "flat" or "one-dimensional" characters, they were deploying the most effective method for fostering exemplarity in their young readers.

From Flat to Round in Children's Literature

> One general leaning, however, may be observed; it is the growing tendency to select the subject of the imaginative literature of children from matter closely approaching their own experiences, instead of widely apart from them. Modern

---

[3]   See Ferris and J. Paul Hunter for more detailed discussions of the relative status of the genres of history and the novel.

stories are mostly written about modern children and modern men and women. This sort of child's fiction is not new, but it assumes a different form from that which it had in earlier times; it is more familiar, more true to nature, less didactic, and gives employment to a higher range of ability. Above all, it is more introspective and sentimental.

—William Caldwell Roscoe, "Fictions for Children" (1855)[4]

The Enlightenment vision of idealized exemplar characterization continued to play a role in fiction written for children far into the nineteenth century. But by the twenty-first, it had become a given that "round" characterization is better than "flat," and that a review which labels a new book "didactic" means the kiss of death. When, and more importantly, *why* did this dramatic shift away from idealized exemplar characterization occur?

Most historians of children's literature date the "when" to the opening decades of the nineteenth century (although debates about the precise date continue to roil; more about this in Chapter 1). As William Caldwell Roscoe (grandson of William Roscoe, author of the famed children's poem *The Butterfly's Ball*) observes in an 1855 essay on the history of English children's literature, the most notable change over the course of a half-century of books for children is how mid-Victorian fiction features "matter closely approaching their own experiences," rather than material "calculated to elevate and instruct" (30). Such "matter," Roscoe explains later in his essay, refers not only to the events of a story, but, most strikingly, to the construction of the child characters within it. Eighteenth-century children's literature, he explains, featured idealized protagonists created to exemplify virtues to be adopted and vices to be shunned:

> a good boy is a good boy, and a bad boy is a bad boy; the former attains to riches and honour, and in conjunction with a lovely partner, to a high state of domestic felicity; the vices of the latter turn upon him at every corner in life with a malignant perseverance of persecution that affords the most remarkable illustration of the doctrine that virtue is the only happiness, and ultimately lead him to the gallows. Thither he is accompanied by the tears of the virtuous associate of his early years, whose last triumph of discipline consists in refusing to tell a lie to save his unhappy friend. (30)

Writing from the vantage point of the mid-nineteenth century, Roscoe can be certain that his descriptions of a boy so good he would not tell a lie to save his friend from hanging will evoke not a desire for emulation in his intended audience, but instead to ridicule and scorn. By 1855, Roscoe could safely assume that his readers no longer shared the Enlightenment humanistic assumptions that would lead an author to uphold such "priggish" behavior for admiration and emulation. For Victorian readers of children's literature, like readers today, expected their

---

4   William Caldwell Roscoe, "Fictions for Children." *Poems and Essays by the Late William Caldwell Roscoe*, ed. Richard Holt Hutton. London: Chapman and Hall, 1860. First published in *The Prospective Review*, February 1855. Reprinted in Salway, 29.

books to feature "modern" characters, characters marked by their similarities to themselves—"familiar," not "didactic," and, above all, "introspective" and "sentimental," marked by emotion. By mid-century, the "flat" character common in the eighteenth-century had, in the majority of books for children, given way to the "round."

Although the "when" is easy to identify, the "why" is far more tricky to pinpoint. Many writers of histories of English-language children's literature avoid the issue entirely by choosing to label earlier works for children "not really children's literature" because of their flat, didactic character depictions. Others, while granting the generic label to earlier fictions, sidestep the need to explain generic differences by judging their authors unskilled; if they had only been better writers, such critics assert, they would have written well-rounded, rather than flat, characters and would have shunned the didactic impulse inherent in one-dimensional character construction.[5] But as Deidre Shauna Lynch so trenchantly points out in regard to adult fiction, early eighteenth-century readers did not have the same expectations about fictional characters we have today; it was not simply a case of poor writing, of "round characters inside flat characters all along, signaling frantically to get out" (123) that led authors to construct characters that we would deem one-dimensional. Eighteenth-century readers expected to assess characters not on the depths of their psyches, but rather on their legibility, their outward characteristics. The flat but outwardly legible character, rather than the round and internally legible one, was the one such readers were trained to expect and respond to. To understand literature of this period, we must read such characters on their own terms, rather than viewing them simply as faulty precursors to later, and because more "round," better constructed characters.

Other historians point to changes in literature for adults to account for the shift in children's literature character construction. Such critics typically assume a simple cause-and-effect relationship between the rise of literary Romanticism, with its new construction of the child in poetry for adults, and the new type of character depiction in literature written for children. More historically-minded critics, in turn, suggest that the rise of Evangelicalism, with its emphasis on emotion rather than reason, played a role in the shift. Both explanations have their merits, but they do not tell the full story behind such a dramatic shift in the construction of character.

Scholarship of the past two decades, much of it building upon the work of Mitzi Myers, has rightly rejected earlier critics' dismissals and denigration of eighteenth-century children's texts, and has begun to explore such texts for their ideological, historical, and aesthetic practices. Yet few have typically explored beyond the givens of literary Romanticism and/or Evangelicalism to explain the shift in character construction from eighteenth-century texts to Victorian-era works. Those critics who have (primarily in article, rather than book-length works) have been indebted to the relatively new field of childhood studies, and in particular to

---

[5]   See Humphrey Carpenter; Summerfield; Goldstone; Townsend; Muir; Hazard.

historians of childhood, who examine and analyze both the actual child in history and the ideas about childhood that existed at different times in the past. A brief outline of this recent work, particularly that focusing on the period during which the round character began to displace the ideal in literature for children, can begin to give us a clearer picture of the historical and cultural shifts in this period that contributed to the abandonment of the ideal exemplar character in favor of a new type of character construction.

The Child, Historical and Ideological

Children and childhood became of major concern to historians only during the last half of the twentieth century. Much of the early debate in the field focused on taking issue with Philippe Ariès's purported claim[6] in his groundbreaking work *Centuries of Childhood* (1962) that there was no such thing as childhood before the early modern period. Medieval historians argued that the emergence of childhood occurred during the Middle Ages (Hannawalt; Shahar); others argued for the seventeenth century (Stone). Most recently, historians have even argued that the "real" child did not emerge until the early twentieth century (Zelizer; Steedman). Such differences suggest that what is at stake has less to do with anything demonstrably "real" about childhood and everything to do with how each historian defines what it means to *be* "a child."

Only in the past 10 to 15 years have historians begun to shift away from debates about *when* a universal childhood was discovered and toward an understanding that childhood in *every* period is a social construction. Finding "real childhood" in the past can be difficult, such work reveals, if historians look only for a childhood that matches contemporary understandings of what childhood, by nature, is. But when historians remove their contemporary blinders, and look instead at how people of the period perceived childhood, in ways that may differ markedly from our own understandings, childhood becomes legible in a way previously unnoticed. Such a shift in the historiographic approach to the study of childhood has led contemporary historians to examine what social, political, economic, and intellectual changes may produce a shift from one period's construction of childhood to another's, rather than focusing on when a "real" sense of childhood emerged (Heywood; Müller; James and Prout; Cunningham *Childhood, Invention*, and "Review").

What then, was childhood like for actual children in Western Europe before the eighteenth century, when a separate literature for children first emerged? And how did childhood change during the time when this literature was in its infancy? Historians of childhood have focused on childhood and work, childhood and religion, and childhood and demographics in an attempt to give us a picture of a lived childhood far different from the one we take for granted today.

---

[6] A mistake in translation, argues Cunningham ("Review" 1196).

Before the eighteenth century, the majority of children in Western Europe worked. The bulk of the population lived an agrarian existence, and children were typically involved in farm chores from an early age. Medieval children as young as seven were sent away from home to work as servants or as apprentices, to learn skills not attainable at their own homes, although taking up regular work was more common for those in their early teen years (Orme 306–9). Children's early introduction to work continued to be the norm well into the early modern period; as Colin Heywood notes, "the majority of families sought work for their children as a matter of routine," both to keep them from the sins of idleness and sloth and to contribute to the family's financial well-being (121).

The nature of children's work began to change, however, during the eighteenth century. Increasing urbanization and industrialization led plebian children (by the early nineteenth century increasingly referred to as "working class") away from work supervised by their families or neighbors, and towards work in factories, often supervised by unfamiliar adults. The shift from an agrarian to a capitalist market economy also led to an increase in the professional and business classes,[7] with a concurrent change in their children's work. Rather than shift in setting, however, the work performed by these children shifted in kind. With their fathers' professional work adding markedly to the family's income, such children no longer needed to contribute financially to their families in order for the family unit to survive. By 1815, while the majority of the population (more than 70 percent) still relied on the physical labor of both its adults and its children for its support, the 2 percent that formed the aristocracy and landed gentry, and the 15 percent whose family heads owned businesses or engaged in genteel professions (Frost 3), could afford to detach its sons and daughters from the realm of work. Thus, while plebeian children increasingly went to labor for unfamiliar adults, genteel children became increasingly likely not to work for pay at all outside the home until their late teens or early twenties, with girls rarely working for pay at all. Before this period, the majority of children had typically begun to integrate themselves into the adult world of labor at an early age; in contrast, during the eighteenth century, and increasingly in the nineteenth, the gap between the adult world of work and the childhood realm of dependence increased for genteel children (Kertzer xv). Throughout European history, childhood had been regarded as different from adulthood, but the economic changes brought on by the shift from an agrarian to a market capitalist society created a much larger gap between the experiences of

---

[7]   Members of the professional and business classes have typically been labeled "middle class" by literary scholars of the eighteenth century and the Victorian period. Recent historical work, however, suggests that such a label may be premature when applied to England before the passage of the 1832 Reform Bill. Thus, I prefer to use the terms "gentry," "genteel," or "business and professional classes" when referring to those families whose fathers worked but did not have to perform physical labor to maintain their families economically. See my earlier essays on the work of Agnes and Catharine Strickland ("The Power of Public Opinion" and "Settler Dreams") for an in-depth discussion of the reasoning behind this choice.

the two groups during this period, as well as a gap between the experiences of the children of the laboring classes and those of the gentry.

Religious changes also influenced European cultural beliefs about childhood, particularly in England after the adoption of Protestantism as the state religion. For a Catholic baby, baptism signified a cleansing; baptized babies were thus deemed innocent, free of original sin. But for Protestants, who gained increasing power and influence in England during the sixteenth to eighteenth centuries, baptism held no such promise; even the youngest child was believed to be tainted by the stain of Adam's fall from grace. Puritan families in particular felt a deep urgency to teach their children about sin and the necessity of faith, instruction that took place in part through reading the Bible. Teaching the child to read thus became a religious duty for the faithful Protestant parent (Cunningham, *Invention* 66). Many of the most popular early works of literature for children, such as James Janeway's *A Token for Children* (1672) and John Bunyan's *A Book for Boys and Girls* (1686), were written by Puritans to point children to the path of salvation (Demers and Moyles 42–4).

Protestant faith also asserted an individual's direct relationship with God, rather than a relationship mediated by a priest, as in Catholic doctrine. This belief placed additional responsibilities upon parents, and upon fathers in particular. As Hugh Cunningham notes, "It was a commonplace of the time that fathers stood in relation to their families as the king did to the country and as God did to humanity as a whole. Their rule was expected to be absolute, but just. Obedience to paternal rule had to be enforced" (*Invention* 67). Families thus began to become more child-centered, with parents, rather than priests, ever-more responsible for the correct religious upbringing of their children. While the period from the seventeenth to the twentieth century witnessed a longterm secularization of attitudes toward children and childhood, the late eighteenth and early nineteenth centuries saw a resurgence of Protestant Christianity and its claims on the child (Cunningham, *Children* 61), a resurgence that played a key role in the substance and form of literature for youth produced in this period.

Historians point not only to religious transformations, but also to immense demographic shifts that occurred during the eighteenth century, particularly in England, to explain changes in the experiences of actual children. Before this period, high birth rates coupled with high mortality rates characterized Europe; little effort was made to avoid pregnancy after marriage. Parents had young children throughout their lives; mothering thus was often equated with childbearing more than childrearing. During the nineteenth century, however, with the advent of improved living conditions and a new focus on personal and public hygiene, mortality rates for children decreased, leading to a dramatic increase in population, particularly in England, from 10.9 million in 1800 to 40.8 million in 1910 (Kertzer xxi, xi). English birth rates did not slow until the mid-nineteenth century, which meant that during the opening decades of the 1800s, the population grew increasingly younger. With the proportion of children in the population exploding, increased attention to children and childhood followed as a matter of course.

John Gillis argues that this demographic shift led to a concurrent shift in the understanding of the role of the mother, away from motherhood as child*bearing* and toward motherhood as child*rearing*. Bearing the largest number of children no longer signified good mothering; instead, mothers were now judged on how well they cared for those children they had (31–47). Such a shift in the conception of motherhood also led to an increased focus on the child.

Political and social forces led to marked changes in the condition of actual children in Western Europe during the eighteenth and early nineteenth centuries, widening the gap between child and adult and making genteel English families in particular far more child-focused than they had been in the past. Unsurprisingly, Europeans' *ideas* about childhood simultaneously underwent major shifts during this period. James A. Schultz, analyzing texts of Middle High German, suggests that medieval Europeans believed that the way one treated a child did not affect how that child would develop into an adult; instead, it was more commonly believed that one could see the future adult in the traits of the child. Schultz argues that these texts show us a construction of childhood far different than our post-Enlightenment, post-Romantic one: "While we know that natural development means constant change, MHG writers know that the nature of the individual is stable. While we know that experience affects children in ways that are profound and immutable, MHG writers know that the effects of experience, even the most disruptive experience, are superficial and reversible" (255). Such beliefs, Schultz argues, were not unique to Medieval Germany; similar views can be found in ancient Greek and Roman texts (255).

Schultz also suggests that Middle High German texts demonstrate that childhood was generally thought of as a time of deficiencies, rather than a time of positive attributes, and thus a time when children aspired to adulthood rather than longed to remain children (246–51). Karin Calvert makes a similar claim in her study of the material culture of early American childhood, arguing that colonial parents found their children to be "rather inadequate creatures, terribly vulnerable to accident and disease, irrational and animalistic in their behavior, and a drain on the family's resources and energy" (75). Material culture produced for children in this period, Calvert asserts, demonstrates parents' desire to force their children to develop rapidly, to "push them into the adult world as quickly as possible" (76).

This view of children as both fixed and inadequate began to shift by the late seventeenth century as philosophers and educators began to assert that children could be shaped and molded by their environments. John Locke, with his espousal of the child as a *tabula rasa*, with no innate ideas, in *An Essay Concerning Human Understanding* (1690), gave voice to changes already well underway in Europe about the ability of adults to influence the man or woman that the child would ultimately become. Locke also attempted to popularize another cultural shift, one that increasingly recognized the individuality of children. Children were not all the same, he argued; they each have their "various Tempers, different inclinations, and particular Defaults," and thus each must be taught according to his or her "natural Temper" (qtd. Cunningham, *Children* 64). The idea that childhood has stages and that each child is unique would take more than a century to become conventional wisdom, although progressive writers in the wake of Locke, such as Abbé Pluche (in his nine-volume set of encyclopedias, *Spectacle de la nature* [1732–1751]) would follow his lead in stressing the importance of gearing pedagogy to "the individual child's personality, temperament, and interests" (Koepp 162). In his influential pedagogical novel *Émile* (1762), Jean Jacques Rousseau agreed with Locke's ideas about childhood individuality, yet took issue with Locke's emphasis on the adult's role in teaching the child, believing that no child should be formally educated before the age of 14. Rather than being a blank slate, a child was born with innate talents and abilities that would emerge naturally, without any prodding from adults; in fact, adults were only too likely to corrupt the naturally innocent child, Rousseau asserted. By the beginning of the nineteenth century, German and Swiss philosophers and educators, particularly Johann Gottfried Herder, reinterpreted Rousseau's construction of the child by replacing the metaphor through which it was articulated. Instead of comparing the child to untouched, pristine nature, as did Rousseau, Herder drew upon the stage-theory of history recently developed by Scottish philosophers, viewing children as similar to archaic mankind, who would proceed orderly through several stages of development—from savagery to civilization—as did human societies. By switching the metaphor through which childhood was viewed, Herder allowed educators to once again insist on the importance of the adult's role; rather than corrupt interlopers into childhood's pristine forests, adults could now be viewed as more highly civilized beings ready to help less developed children/savages progress into social beings (Kümmerling-Meibauer 185–6).

The increased focus on the malleability of the child also led to changing ideas about the child's economic role. Educators began to argue that because children were so impressionable, education should extend longer, increasing the time when the child of the professional or businessmen remained separated from the economic life of the family. Throughout most of the nineteenth century, children of working-class families continued to contribute to their families' finances through work inside and outside the household, with many children working in paying jobs by the age of seven. But during the same period, gentry children shifted from being an economic asset to a financial liability to their families, emphasizing their role as dependents of the family unit (Frost 31; Cunningham, *Children* 85). As more and more families moved from the working to the gentry class (from 15 percent of the population in 1815 to 25 percent in 1900 [Frost 3]), their children, once valued for their contribution to the family coffers, became increasingly valued for their sentimental, rather than their economic, role in family life.[8]

While childhood had not always been seen as a time of dependency, at least for older children, traditionally it had been viewed as a time of deficiency. Rousseau, in addition to urging changes in pedagogy, was also one of the earliest writers to

---

[8] See Zelizer for an account of how the ideology of the "economically worthless child" trickled down to (or was forced upon) the working classes.

take issue with such a belief, which dated from the medieval period. Rousseau argued that rather than being a time of lack, in many ways childhood was the *best* time of life, a period adults could and should look back on with nostalgia. He also asserted that a child should have the right to be a child, rather than be forced to become an adult as soon as possible, and insisted that children had the right to be happy:

> What is to be thought, therefore, of that cruel education which sacrifices the present to an uncertain future, that burdens a child with all sorts of restrictions and begins by making him miserable, in order to prepare him for some far-off happiness which he may never enjoy? (*Émile*, Book II, 50).

Such a belief in the value of childhood, and in the idea that childhood may be characterized by a special understanding that is lost once the transition to adulthood occurs, found its greatest articulation in the work of the Romantic poets, in particular in the poems of William Wordsworth.

Such new beliefs about the nature of childhood, when combined with the increasing focus on privacy and comfort that characterized the genteel lifestyle, shifted the focus of the family inward, resulting in the development of a more child-centered, affectionate family during the period (Cunningham, *Children* 62). Cunningham notes that it is difficult to know whether the rise in written references to parental affection for children "reflects anything more than a tendency to give written expression to such feelings, and to the survival of such writings," but does posit that a concurrent rise in complaints about overindulgent parents suggests that such affection may be a new development in European parenting during the seventeenth and eighteenth centuries (58). Other historians tend to agree with Cunningham, arguing that a rise in affection between parents and children is characteristic of this period.

By the middle of the nineteenth century, then, a new ideology of childhood had developed, one vastly different from the one that characterized pre-Enlightenment Europe. This construction of childhood can be distinguished by its three core concepts, according to Cunningham: a commitment to the idea that children should be reared in families; a new belief that the way a child was brought up would dramatically affect the adult that child would one day become; and an acknowledgment that children should have rights and privileges of their own. Children and childhood were granted more importance than they had had in the past, as signaled by the increased belief in the importance of early education, a growing interest in the way children learn, a heightened concern for the salvation of the child's soul, and a sense that childhood was the best, rather than the worst, time of life (*Children* 41). The Enlightenment thus emerges as "the point of transition to a world expecting adult lives to be shaped by childhood experiences and, at the same time, looking to childhood as the repository of values held in high esteem" (Cunningham, "Review" 1207).

Historians of children's literature have pointed to some or many of the above social, cultural, and ideological changes in European understandings of childhood during the eighteenth century to explain the birth of children's literature as a genre. With childhood increasingly being seen as something distinctly different from adulthood, with children forming a greater percentage of the population as a whole, with the child granted rights and privileges distinct from the rights and privileges inherent to humans in general, and perhaps most importantly, with the Protestant focus on the need to educate the young taking hold in the wider culture, the development of a literature specific to this new being, "the child," seems almost inevitable. Why this literature should begin with ideal exemplar characterization might also be answered by this history—with its genesis in religious training, and with a focus on shaping and molding newly pliable youth, such literature took for granted the truism of eighteenth-century humanist teaching: that effective representations of the ideal would provide the sharpest spur to readerly emulation.

Such a history also gives partial answers to the question of why the literature gradually began to turn away from such ideal exemplar models in favor of "round" character development during the early nineteenth century. A more child-centered family; motherhood valued more for quality over quantity, more for childrearing and less for childbearing; the burgeoning conception of childhood as a series of developmental stages; the rise of written accounts of parental affection for children—each, in all likelihood, contributed in part to this gradual literary shift.

Another contributing factor can be found in the work of recent literary critics of the novel for adults. Such critics have attempted to account for the shift from flat to round character construction in such fictions by examining the use to which readers might put different types of fictional characters, particularly in their attempts to accommodate the eighteenth-century's increasingly complex commercial society. Lynch suggests that the rapidly expanding print market, which threatened to blur class lines by democratizing reading, turning elite literary culture into its opposite through mass circulation, led to the development of new strategies of reading that created a desire for "deep" rather than shallow or flat characters:

> Since *deep* truths can so easily be represented as knowledge inaccessible to all but a few, the private reading could supply a means of restaging the stratification of society. The act of sympathetic rereading, of constructing and identifying with a character's point of view, could appear a means of forestalling the process whereby the mass circulation of elite culture threatens to turn into its opposite. (146–7)

Instead of regarding the shift from "flat" to "round" as a formal, and natural, development of the novel for adults as a genre, then, Lynch asks us to see the development of character interiority as a historically-specific shift, a resistance to the democratization inherent in England's burgeoning market culture. Rather than simply being a reflection of the rise of a bourgeois individualism, as claimed by Ian Watt in *The Rise of the Novel*, Lynch inverts the relationship, arguing that "at the turn of the nineteenth century characters became the imaginative resources on which readers drew to make themselves into individuals to expand their own interior resources of sensibility" (126).

Can a similar argument about the rise of Romantic self-culture be made in regards to literature for children? Did children, like adults, feel anxiety in the face of increasingly complex commercial society, and turn to books to make themselves into individuals? Eighteenth and early nineteenth-century children's books rarely feature scenes of children shopping (Maria Edgeworth's "The Purple Jar" a notable exception); in fact, the nineteenth-century construction of the child depended in large part on the separation of the child from the corrupting influences of the marketplace. Yet as Dennis Denisoff suggests, Victorian adults understood that children, because of their purported openness to influence and formation, were "the most accessible context through which consumerism … could become the driving force of cultural identity" (6). If late eighteenth- and early nineteenth-century elite readers felt anxieties about the democratizing force of mass literacy on their own behalf, it seems more than likely that such anxieties would be all the greater when their progeny were considered. Children themselves may not have felt such anxieties, but the parents, guardians, authors, and publishers who cared for and catered to them are likely to have felt them on their youngsters' behalf, and have created and purchased literature that would assuage such anxieties accordingly.

Lynch's explanation for the shift from flat to round characters in novels for adults resonates, but her analysis of how the shift actually occurred leaves something to be desired. In attempting to tease out a more detailed account of the transition as it occurred in fiction for children, I have discovered it of far less use to follow links between adult novels and works for youth than to connect juvenile works to a genre already in possession of the elite literary status that Lynch suggests novels of interiority were attempting to claim: the genre of history. For the changes in the way history was conceived and written during the late eighteenth and early nineteenth centuries had a profound influence on the writing of literature for children, particularly in the changing construction of the child within that literature.

Recent collections such as those edited by Anja Müller and by Andrea Immel and Michael Witmore have begun to tease out the myriad ways that such changes in the *idea* of the child impacted the actual child in history, examining changes in legal, medical, artistic, literary and other domains to which children were subject. But only a handful of literary critics have begun to apply the recent work of historians of childhood (both actual and ideological) to the fascinating works of literature produced for children during the opening decades of the nineteenth century, a period when newer models of childhood both challenged and coexisted with older discourses, pulling the literature in multiple, often conflicting, directions. None, to my knowledge, have articulated the key relationship between Enlightenment exemplar history and idealized exemplar character construction in children's literature. More importantly, no critic has yet connected the striking changes in historiography during the opening decades of the nineteenth century to subsequent changes in the practice of writing for children. A more complex explanation of the "why" behind the shift from flat to round characterization in literature for children, and from texts that wore their didacticism on their sleeves to those that emphasized entertainment over morality, can be found, I will argue, by exploring the connections between the writing of history and the writing of children's literature. Thus, in the section that follows, I will take what appears to be a detour away from children and their literature to explain and explore the changes that occurred in the field of history writing during the period 1790–1830. But the diversion is a temporary one, for, as we will see, the changes disrupting the norms of historiography also had a similar, if later occurring, impact on the writing of literature for children.

From Exemplarity to Identification in Historiographical Practice

[History] gives us, and only it can give us, an extended knowledge of human nature;—not human nature as it exists in one age or climate or particular spot of earth, but human nature under all the various circumstances by which it can be affected. It shows us what is radical and what is adventitious; it shows us that man is still man in Turkey and in Lapland, as a vassal in Russia or a member of a wandering tribe in India, in ancient Athens or modern Rome; yet that his character is susceptible of violent changes, and becomes moulded into infinite diversities by the influence of government, climate, civilization, wealth, and poverty."
—Anna Barbauld, "On the Uses of History,"
A Legacy for Young Ladies (1826)[9]

To know [men of classical Rome] truly, we must not content ourselves with viewing them from a distance, and reading them in abridgment. We must watch their minutest actions, we must dwell upon their every word. We must gain admission among their confidents [*sic*], and penetrate into their secret souls.
—William Godwin, "Of the Study of the Classics" (1797)[10]

As James Chandler and Mark Salber Phillips both argue, the exemplar theory of history came under increasing pressure during the late eighteenth and early nineteenth centuries, challenged, and ultimately supplanted by, what later historians have come to term "historicism." The challenge to classical exemplar history, which assumed human uniformity, rather than difference, across time, had its roots in several sources. One source was the newly emergent stadial theory of the Scottish Enlightenment. Writers such as Adam Ferguson and John Millar crafted sociological accounts of the natural evolution of civilizations, accounts that challenged the uniformity of human behavior by suggesting that different societies could exist at different "stages" at the same point in time. Adam Smith (in the influential *Wealth of Nations* [1776]) described the history of a nation in the context of its progression through four economic stages of civilization (hunting/gathering; pastoral/nomadic; agricultural/feudal; and commerce/manufacturing). Each of these economic stages

---

[9]   123–4.

[10]   In *The Enquirer: Reflections on Education, Manners, and Literature*, 37.

necessitated specific and quite different political and social structures, and could exist at one point in time but in different geographical locations.

Smith's "stage theory" gained prominence during the 1790s, when technological developments, social changes, and political revolutions in America and France, changes which were increasingly understood as "radically restructuring human relations over time," led historians to acknowledge the impossibility of a universal moral exemplarity across the boundaries of period (Chandler, "History" 355). Thus, the historicism that emerged in the early decades of the nineteenth century broke radically from that of the past; rather than viewing historical actors as exemplars of universal moral lessons, romantic historicism envisioned the past as radically other from the present. No longer viewing the past as a repository of timeless human virtues, historians began to envision history as a process, one characterized by asymmetrical and uneven, though uni-directional, development. Human subjectivity, perhaps even human morality, should not be understood as uniform across time, such thinkers began to argue, but rather as constructed by historically-specific conditions. Writers of history for adults would draw upon this new belief to construct a far different type of history for their readers, one in which history's moral utility no longer played a primary role. As we shall see in the following section, however, writers for children took far longer to accept the abandonment of history's (and fiction's) moral utility, and the ideal exemplar character most often used to model it, than did those writing for an adult audience.

Stadial theory did not produce the only pressure on historiographical practice in the period. Though an emphasis on rational thought is often regarded as the key characteristic of the Enlightenment period, the late eighteenth century is when the concept of sympathy, in the guise of sensibility and sentiment, came to dominate philosophical, religious, and political discourse. And as Phillips argues, the rise of sentimentalism played "an enormously important role" in suggesting that we read history not only, or even primarily, to discover morally exemplary role models, but rather, "to experience a sense of the evocative presence of other places and other times" (28). Intriguingly, proponents of sensibility initially grounded their justifications precisely on its abilities to strengthen the moral faculties, an argument with which writers of children's literature certainly sympathized.

The impact of sentimentalism in mid and late eighteenth-century Europe was widespread, its presence felt in art, philosophy, politics, and literature. Sensibility found its most influential literary articulation in the novels of sensibility published during the third quarter of the eighteenth century, works such as Rousseau's *La Nouvelle Héloïse* (1761), Laurence Sterne's *A Sentimental Journey* (1768), Goethe's *Die Leiden des jungen Werther* [*The Sorrows of Young Werther*] (1774), and Henry MacKenzie's *The Man of Feeling* (1771), works that featured not the exemplary men of epic, romance, or classical history, but the ordinary (if highly sensitive) men of the novel. Throughout the eighteenth century, however, literary sensibility had its critics, those who doubted its proponents' claims that its readers could vicariously strengthen their moral faculties not by reading about morally exemplary characters or figures from history, but rather by reading and sympathizing with the suffering of others. Criticism came from all points on the political spectrum, from the radical Mary Wollstonecraft in *The Vindication of the Rights of Woman* (1792) to the conservative Hannah More, whose early praise in her 1782 poem "Sensibility" soon gave way to a more skeptical attitude in her *Strictures on the Modern System of Female Education* (1799) and her novel *Coelebs in Search of a Wife* (1808). Rather than fostering a habit of benevolence, as its proponents claimed, such critics believed that novels of sensibility would only create a state of dreamy or excited passivity in their readers, a passivity that would lead not to social sympathy, but enervating isolation, or, for women, a susceptibility to sexual license. Issues of gender also played a role in literary sensibility's downfall. While early in the eighteenth century, emotionally motivated benevolence was considered a manly trait, sensibility increasingly became associated with the feminine; the "man of feeling" increasingly became regarded as effete by century's end. Even many of its proponents began to repudiate their heroes of sensibility; "Be a man and do not follow me," Goethe argued in verses prefixed to later editions of *Werther* (qtd Todd 134). By the late 1770s, "sensibility" as a positive literary term gave way to the pejorative "sentimentality": an affected, debased overindulgence in feeling for its own sake rather than as a catalyst to performing good works for the benefit of others. Poets of the Romantic era would largely turn away from sentimentalism's interest in forging sympathetic connection, choosing instead to celebrate "an unsentimental belief in the power of a single human mind" (Todd 136).

Yet the influence of sentimentalism, and the sympathy characteristic of the sensibility that purportedly embodied it, continued to register in many aspects of late eighteenth- and early nineteenth-century British culture, including, as Phillips argues, in historiographical practice. Historical accounts, which, in the eighteenth century, relied on an air of "aloof generality" to dignify and validate their status, gave way during the nineteenth to less distanced narratives, narratives that sought to bring readers closer to the experiences they related (Phillips 26). Historians began to foster such closeness by opening up their narratives, describing not only linear political events, but also the subjective experiences of individual people of the past. In depicting the "inward dimensions of an individual life," nineteenth-century historians sought to engage their readers by fostering sympathetic connections between the people they described and the people for whom they wrote (276). Thus, the humanist assumption that modeling exemplarity through idealized portraits gradually began to give way to the sentimentalist belief that "characters and experiences more ordinary than ideal" might prove more effective at "foster[ing] habits of benevolence" (Phillips 126–7). The best role models, sympathy suggested, would not be those who embodied the highest ideals, but rather those more like their readers, those with whom a reader could forge an emotional bond, those with whom they could *identify*. The goal of evocation, which, during the eighteenth century, featured most prominently in the minor historical genres of biography and memoir, had, by the 1840s, become a central tenet of all historiographical practice. While the moral dimension of such evocation would not always be at the forefront in works aimed at an audience of adults, writers for children would soon come to embrace evocation and identification as new and powerful tools to deploy in their continuing crusade to shape morally responsible young readers.

Changing Historiography, Changing Children's Literature

> Her intention is, by this means, to excite a laudable curiosity for works of History and Biography, which, it is presumed, will be read with more diligence, and recollected to better effect, when they are combined with that species of individual attachment awakened in a sensible child towards a person of his own age, actuated by his own motives and affections.
> —Barbara Hofland, "To the Reader,"
> *Adelaide, or, The Intrepid Daughter* (1823)[11]

The opening decades of the nineteenth century served as a time of transition in the writing of history for both adults and for children, a transition from moral exemplarity to emotional evocation. The transition occurred more slowly in writing for children than for adults, however; as Nadel notes, by 1800, while classical exemplar history had largely disappeared from adult histories, it was still commonly found in textbooks for young people: "only for the education of children [could] the justification of the study of history in terms of its moral utility … be plausibly upheld" (314). And what was true for children's histories was also true for the majority of children's fiction. Long into the nineteenth century, novels written for children continued to justify their existence in introductions or prefaces that claimed that what followed was not only designed to "entertain," but also to "instruct." Fictions constructed to teach morals overtly to young readers continued to flourish in the opening decades of the nineteenth century, written by authors such as Sarah Trimmer, Maria Edgeworth, and the Evangelical writer Mary Martha Sherwood. But as history, the genre children's literature often linked itself to in order to justify its existence, began to change in reaction to new demands for emotional evocation, so, too, did literature for children gradually begin to open itself up to new possibilities. As in works of history for adults, the implausibly perfect or irretrievably evil character of children's literature came under increasing pressure from the new generic dictate of creating emotional sympathy between character and reader. Thus, even in the early nineteenth-century moral fictions by Trimmer, Edgeworth, and Sherwood, we can begin to see signs of what we today term "round" characterization. And by the mid-nineteenth century, with the publication of the work of Charlotte Yonge, flat characters designed to model moral exemplarity appeared far less often in novels for children than round characters designed to improve readers via a different means, the evocation of identification and emotional connection.

---

[11]   iii.

Though historians and critics of early children's literature writing before the 1980s often noted significant differences between eighteenth-century and nineteenth-century literature for children, their focus was less on a shift in characterization than on a shift in purpose. Such writers typically denigrated the overt didacticism of eighteenth-century fictions for children, contrasting it unfavorably with the nineteenth-century novels that, in their view, focused less on instruction and more on entertaining their young readers. Praising the influence of literary Romanticism, with its focus on the innocence, rather than the sinfulness, of the child, such critics applauded the "new" children's literature for its celebration of imagination (constructed as inherent to childhood), and often ridiculed eighteenth-century texts' focus on rationality (constructed in eighteenth-century children's texts as the culmination of the transition from child to adult). Because Romanticism presents an image of childhood far more familiar to contemporary readers than that found in eighteenth-century fictions written for young people, much of the pre-1980s history of children's literature told a story of progress, with the refreshing breeze of Romanticism liberating child readers from repressively didactic eighteenth-century moral tales by way of imaginative fantasy novels of the Victorian "Golden Age." Historians of early British children's literature simultaneously constructed the shift from flat, one-dimensional characters prevalent in eighteenth-century children's fiction to what they termed more "realistic" child characters in nineteenth-century juvenile works as a liberation of the child (protagonist and reader) from repressive Enlightenment moralists by liberated, Romanticism-inspired artists. Like Roscoe before them, such critics could simply not imagine that characters whom they found to be goody-goodies, "shocking prigs," and "stuck up formal chits" could appeal to any real child reader (Roscoe 36). With no knowledge of the prevalence of exemplarity in pre-Victorian history, the beliefs about reading character held by eighteenth-century readers, or of the relative newness of the concept of reader identification during the late-eighteenth and early nineteenth centuries, historians and critics often read earlier texts against our current standards for evaluating the effectiveness of literature for children, judging earlier works as deficient because they could not recognize the aesthetic principles that undergirded them, and praising those that seemed to bear the mark of a progressive Romantic ideology of the child.

In her work on Maria Edgeworth and other Georgian moral tale writers for children, Mitzi Myers was the first to complicate this explanation. Taking issue with those who would dismiss early juvenile literature because its depiction of the child is "unrealistic," Myers began, in the late 1980s, to point to the constructed nature of our own contemporary view of childhood, arguing that we see childhood through a Romantic lens: "the Romantic lens we habitually look through is a culturally conditioned ideology, a tissue of assumptions, preferences, and perspectives, and not a trans-historical, universal body of truth about childhood" ("Little Girls" 135). Myers's work has paved the way in the last 15 years for a handful of critics to begin to explore the children's literature written by the most popular eighteenth- and early nineteenth-century women who wrote for children, women such as Sarah Trimmer, Hannah More, Maria Edgeworth, and Mary Martha Sherwood. Such literature drew upon a far different ideology of the child than that promulgated by the Romantic movement.

But even when today's critics describe or analyze such works, the contemporary assumption that writing about "realistic" characters is more interesting than writing about ideal ones, or that sympathetic identification, rather than moral exemplarity, is the goal, can often creep into the discussion. Writing in 1997, in an essay on domestic discord in Victorian children's novels, Jan Mark recognizes that moral exemplarity is a key characteristic of earlier British children's fiction— "Early children's fiction, as a vehicle for moral instruction … relied heavily on the presentation of a serene and stable environment in which parents and elders functioned as exemplars" (133). Yet she also reads such literature with twentieth-century blinders when she asserts that a dysfunctional family in a story entitled "The Punishment of Wilfulness" "is far more stimulating to write—and read— about than the ideal home" more common to eighteenth-century children's fiction (134). For Mark, it is not a shift in ideology, but simply the "pleasures of creating children's fiction" that "override the urge to instruct in these early authors," leading them to depict less idealized families. Similarly, in her essay on women writers for children in the late eighteenth century, Norma Clarke misreads the function of exemplarity, assuming that young readers are asked to identify completely with ideal protagonists: "the writers of moral tales pitched their textual efforts at producing ideal little children. … Successful products of their teaching would imitate the perfect adults who teach them, lisping morally unimpeachable homilies" (101). Eliding the child *within* the book with the child *outside* the book, Clarke assumes that writers want young readers to identify with their idealized protagonists; if such identification is successful, readers will in turn become "ideal little children" like those in their fictions. But if we consider literary protagonists not as characters with whom readers are asked to identify, but rather as exemplary models that children, imperfect humans that they are, can strive to emulate but can never completely equal, our interpretation of the cultural work these texts undertake changes significantly.

As M.O. Grenby has recently suggested, "It is tempting to argue that as the eighteenth century went on, the child at the centre of this new culture of childhood became increasingly 'real,' deposing the two-dimensional, idealised child who had been the subject of earlier philosophies, curricula and children's books" ("Introduction" 315). It is a temptation to which he urges us not to succumb, and during the past five years, more critics have been heeding his warning. Yet even sympathetic critics often find it difficult not to yield to the temptation to read with historical blinders on. Clarke's assertion that although "serious scholarly work on the women of this period is now appearing … there is still a great gap to be filled and much thoughtless repetition of old stereotypes to be undone" seems just as true today as it did when she wrote it in 1997 (93). Critical work that discusses early children's literature within the framework of an understanding of eighteenth-century exemplarity is certainly one of the gaps worthy of exploration.

Additionally, while scholarly work has appeared in the past decade on eighteenth-century children's book writers, and work on Victorian-era writers continues apace, little work has been done on texts written in the gap between these two periods. With the exception of work on the now-canonical Maria Edgeworth, Hannah More, Anna Barbauld, and Sarah Trimmer, and Dennis Butts's work on Barbara Hofland, Romantic and early Victorian-era writers for children have largely gone unread. Almost no critical work has been done on the authors whom F.J. Harvey Darton, in one of the earliest histories of children's literature, *Children's Books in England* (1932), terms the "Early-Victorian favourites": those who published after the rise of the moral tale but before the onset of mid-Victorian Golden Age fantasy. Books by the most popular authors of this period, such as Barbara Hofland, Agnes and Catharine Strickland, Ann Fraser Tytler, and Frederick Marryat, rarely conform to neat generic categories, one reason why critics may have overlooked them (212). With children's literature histories typically organized around genre, and emphasizing the emergence of, or shifts in, forms of literature for children—the fantasy, the domestic story, the school story, the adventure tale—it is hardly surprising that a period characterized by, in Darton's terms, "an apparent lack of central impulse" proves disappointing or of little interest (212). Yet to understand how children's literature made the transition from idealized moral exemplar to sympathetically engaging characterization, it is vital to study the messy, conflicted texts that struggled to negotiate the often contradictory demands of the old exemplar character and the new, emotionally evocative one.

Myers attributed the dismissal of the pre-Victorian children's book authors to the issue of gender. The majority of the books published for children during the eighteenth and early nineteenth centuries were written by women; critics and historians (typically male) demonstrated gender bias in their wholehearted focus on male writers and their dismissal of female authors, Myers asserted ("Little Girls Lost" 135). Yet such dismissals might also be attributed to the dictates of twentieth-century genre study. Until quite recently, and particularly in the field of children's literature, literary critics focusing on studies of genre worked to discover and describe distinct and enduring formal characteristics, characteristics that remained constant despite changes in social and political circumstances under which any given text was written. But as Richard Maxwell and Katie Trumpener note, "[t]he Romantic novel is a genre in transition during an era of transition" (5). Characterized less by a "unifying artistic sensibility than it is by a spirit of experimentation" (Maxwell and Trumpener 1), British fiction written during the opening decades of the nineteenth century did not cohere enough to warrant its analysis under the older rubric of genre study. This lack of coherence, when linked to the critical veneration of the poetry produced by British authors during this period, suggests why the fiction of the opening decades of the nineteenth century received scant critical attention during the twentieth.

But genre study in adult literature has taken a more complex turn at the beginning of the twenty-first century; overturning assumptions about the unity and fixity of genres, critics now explore the uneven development of generic change, looking at instabilities, at generic mixtures and overlaps, and at a text's historical context, rather than its universal and enduring genre characteristics. Instead of dismissing texts as uninteresting because they fail to conform neatly to distinct genres categories, contemporary genre study takes such a lack as the sign of deeply significant instabilities—as genre in the process of becoming.[12] Only within the past 10 years has this shift in the conception of genre study begun to open up a space for critics to approach the Romantic novel written for adults without apologizing for its inadequacies.[13] And such work has yet to be undertaken in the field of fiction for children during the opening decades of the nineteenth century.

It is with such a conception of genre study in mind that I began to search out and read novels written for children during the period 1800–1840. In particular, I began to become intrigued by the adventure novels—tales of children stranded on deserted islands, or subject to the vicissitudes of the historical past—novels that struck me as being quite different from the adventure novel that I had come to know from my reading of Victorian children's literature. Initially, I envisioned my project as a straightforward genre study, one that would identify the conventions of adventure novels written before the rise of the "real" adventure novel for boys during the Victorian period. I had intended to analyze how these earlier, primarily woman-authored texts differed from, or in some cases served as the precursors of, Victorian adventure texts that functioned to construct a masculinity suited to the nineteenth-century British imperial project. I expected to find that pre-Victorian adventure fictions depicted a far different construction of gender than did their later Victorian counterparts.

Challenges to gender proprieties did appear in many of the texts I read, and the construction of gender has become one of the focuses of my analysis. Particularly in the novels penned by women, adventure proves the perfect form in which writers can mount protests against constructions of femininity that grew increasingly constraining during the opening decades of the nineteenth century. The woman-authored robinsonades, histories, and romances that I analyze deploy and laud literary forms coming under increasing attack for being overly feminine; protest the period's increasing marginalization of fatherhood; allow their girl characters to speak up, and speak against, patriarchal authority; and challenge the naturalness of gender roles by demonstrating how societies in the past constructed femininity differently than does their own.

---

[12]   See Maria Nikolajeva's "Children's Literature as a Cultural Code" for one articulation of such an approach.

[13]   As an example, note the recent addition of *The Cambridge Companion to Fiction in the Romantic Period* to Cambridge University Press's *Cambridge Companions to Literature* series, books that present introductions to "major writers, artists, philosophers, topics and periods" for student readers ("Cambridge Companions"). Though the series began more than two decades ago, in 1986, it was only in 2008 that a volume on early nineteenth-century fiction was deemed necessary or relevant.

But the more I read, the less I came to believe that early juvenile adventure must, by its very form, challenge dominant discourses of gender relations, or even that the form must necessarily engage in the discourse of gender relations at all, at least beyond the degree that any text of any period both reflects and constructs the masculinity and femininity of its times. As previous critics have demonstrated, British Victorian adventure novels for boys worked as a genre to construct a very specific type of masculinity, one that functioned to support the British imperial project. Yet earlier adventure texts do not cohere around a distinct set of gender ideologies; some uphold quite conventional gender roles, while others value certain aspects of contemporary femininity and masculinity while undermining others, the combinations shifting with each new text one reads. The link between genre and gender simply did not seem to hold.

And unlike Victorian adventure novels, which, in addition to their uniform construction of masculinity, cohere around other clear genre conventions, the earlier books I read did not seem to embrace as clear a set of formal principles, at least not to the extent that a genre-based argument might be convincingly posited. In fact, experimenting with conventions—whether they be conventions of gender, of literary form, of the construction of character—rather than conforming to them, seemed to be almost all that these texts had in common with one another.

That experimentation, then, and the social, cultural, and political contexts that helped to shape it, soon became the idea around which the study began to cohere. In particular, I became fascinated by the ways in which each of these texts experimented with question of character construction. Wondering why such experimentation seemed more common in adventure stories and in historical fiction than in the more popular domestic tale of the period led me to investigate early nineteenth-century historiography, and to the intriguing discovery that many of the changes I was observing in adventure novels for children held striking similarities to those occurring in the realm of history writing for adults. Thus, the project took on an entirely new direction, one that attempted to connect these two seemingly disparate types of writing, to demonstrate how the changes in one field of literature could so influence the writing in another.

The book that has taken shape in the wake of this research does not pretend to be a comprehensive survey of literature for children written in Europe, or even in England, during the opening decades of the nineteenth century. Instead, it focuses tightly and specifically on individual books, reading and analyzing those that struck this author as being of particular interest in tracing the shift from morally idealized to emotionally evocative characterization. In particular, it focuses on books that might, using a broad generic definition, be termed "adventure" stories—books in which characters are shipwrecked, à la Robinson Crusoe, on deserted islands, or in which they are subject to the turbulent political and military events of the distant past through fictionalized histories or historical fictions. Just as Phillips first noticed signs of shifting exemplarity in the field of history in the "lesser" genres of memoir and biography, I, too, found signs of the shift in children's literature in genres that, during the opening decades of the nineteenth century, were not as highly valued as the domestic moral tale. Setting their tales outside of the domestic sphere, early nineteenth-century authors found in the deserted island and in the distant past places in which they could safely experiment with new types of character construction, types that might seem threatening in a more realistic sphere. Ironically, the emergence of "realistic" characters can most easily be seen in the "unrealistic" genres of the robinsonade, the fictionalized history, and the historical romance.

Yet if the authors I examine chose different settings and different models of character construction than their contemporaries who chose to write stories set in the domestic sphere, they shared, I argue, a central purpose with such writers: to convince their child readers to model their behavior after the characters about whom they read. For while the ideal exemplar character grew increasingly out of favor during the period this book examines, the goal of modeling exemplarity was never far from the minds of the authors who wrote the books in which this shift occurred. Historians and critics have typically linked the shift away from exemplar characterization toward what they term "realistic" character development to a simultaneous shift away from didacticism; yet I will argue that the first shift is entirely compatible with the goal of teaching children moral lessons. Instead of placing exemplarity and realism in binary opposition, I suggest, a more fruitful avenue may be to consider the contiguities between these apparently dissimilar types of juvenile character construction. In analyzing early juvenile adventures, I have come to see the ways in which both constructions of the child—the "ideal" child (whether perfectly good or perfectly bad), and the "ordinary" child (i.e., the psychologically nuanced, the sympathetically flawed)—attempt to create a bond between reader and protagonist, a bond which functions to foster a desire for emulation. Rather than read a shift away from ideal characters as a sign of juvenile fiction's increasing "reality," and hence a "freer" child, then, we might more productively interpret the gradual increase in depictions of child interiority as the sign of a historically specific effort to foster an exemplarity altogether continuous with that found in earlier literature. Authors writing for children deployed both "ideal" and "ordinary" character construction with the same goal: to persuade their readers to emulate their characters' correct behavior. The real difference lies not in authors' aims, I suggest, but in their means of achieving them.

Experimenting with Exemplarity in the Genre of Adventure

This book is structured as four chapters, each of which explores the shift from exemplar to sympathetic identification in a different type of adventure story. Chapter 1, "The Emergence of the Ordinary: Parents and Children on the Deserted Isle," traces the emergence of a new construction of childhood in a type of castaway story far different from the paradigmatic model of Defoe's solitary Crusoe: the family robinsonade. Stranding their children on deserted islands not alone, but with a parent or parents, the authors of such family robinsonades use the island as the ideal space for experimenting with a new construction of the child, one characterized not as an idealized exemplar, but as a combination of good and bad qualities: what I have chosen to call the "ordinary" child. Once the construction of the child shifts away from the ideal to the ordinary, a space emerges for the inclusion of childhood emotion in its depiction. No longer relegated to the realm of the evil, or constructed as the irrational impulse that comes between a child and rational decision-making, emotion emerges as the central means by which authors persuade their readers of the "ordinariness" of their youthful protagonists, and foster sympathetic identification between them and their texts' readers. Intriguingly, this emergence of the "ordinary" child depends in large part on a concurrent change in the construction of the character of the parent. Fictional parents still remain a center of moral authority, but their reaction to the misbehavior of their children changes markedly over the period. Only when a parent can take pleasure in his or her child, in addition to acting as his or her moral guide, can a truly "ordinary" depiction of childhood emerge.

Chapter 1 traces the emergence of emotion in the depiction of parent and child characters, the concurrent anxiety about the challenges to parental authority that the inclusion of such emotion presents, and the differing methods four authors use to contain such anxieties. It does so by examining four early juvenile robinsonades, two written by continental writers, two by Englishwomen. I open with an analysis of Johann David Wyss's *Der schweizersche Robinson*, first published in English under the title *The Family Robinson Crusoe* in 1814, one of the earliest works of children's literature to depict the emotional pleasure a parent can take in his children. Such emotional pleasure must never be allowed to threaten the authority of the patriarchal parent, however; take pleasure in your children, Wyss admonishes parents, but never at the expense of your own authority, a markedly gendered message. In contrast, Frenchwoman Jeanne Sylvie Mallès de Beaulieu, in *Le robinson de douze ans* (1818), translated into English as *The Young Robinson* (1825), takes issue with the patriarchalism of Wyss's argument, asserting instead that emotion itself is the only foundation upon which parental authority can be built. Writing in the sentimental, rather than the realistic, mode, a mode increasingly associated with the feminine in the period, Mallès de Beaulieu continually constructs empathy between child and parent as the ultimate goal in parent-child relations. Yet the lengths to which such empathy leads the child—to the erasure of any desires and beliefs of the child that do not coincide with those of the adult—makes Mallès de Beaulieu's emotionally-based construction of the parent-child relationship as problematic for later English writers as was Wyss's valuation of authority over emotion. The final two sections of this chapter explore British family robinsonades published after Wyss's and Mallès de Beaulieu's, and in many ways in conversation with them: Barbara Hofland's *The Young Crusoe* (1828) and Ann Fraser Tytler's *Leila, or The Island* (1839). Both Hofland and Tytler struggle with the same anxieties about emotion, agency, and authority as did their earlier counterparts. Yet neither wholeheartedly embraces one end of emotion/authority feminine/masculine binary, as did the Frenchwoman and the

Swiss parson. Rather, each attempts to deploy emotion to forge a stronger bond between fictional child and parent, a bond that in turn makes the child more open to the parent's authority. Yet this new form of disciplining the child (protagonist and reader) simultaneous opens up new spaces for resistance, resistance that each text cannot help but acknowledge. Rather than functioning only to neutralize or contain such resistance, as did the novels of Wyss and Mallès de Beaulieu, the novels of Hofland and Tytler call their readers' attention to contradictions inherent in constructing a discourse of parental authority linked to sympathetic engagement, creating a child subjectivity aware of ambivalences, contradictions, and subtleties. That Hofland's protagonist is a boy and Tytler's a girl highlights the role gender plays in constructing such subjectivities.

Not all authors, however, would find the new construction of the ordinary, emotional, sympathetic child as congenial as did Hofland and Tytler. In Chapter 2, "Deadly Islands: The Function of Death in the Juvenile Robinsonade," I examine another sub-genre of the robinsonade, one that delves deeply into the problems that sympathy poses. In the "deadly island" robinsonade, a major character (or characters) dies rather than prospers upon the isle. Instead of functioning as a testing ground upon which a new vision of sympathetic exemplary can be articulated, the deadly island registers the difficulties such a vision presents when faced with competing constructions of childhood also (re)emerging during the early decades of the nineteenth century: the inherently sinful child of Evangelical discourse, and the inherently innocent child of Romantic poetry. Attempting to reconcile these three vastly different visions of childhood proves the central concern of two juvenile deadly island robinsonades: Frederick Marrayat's *Masterman Ready* (1841–1842) and Jefferys Taylor's *The Young Islanders* (1841). Marryat deploys death to contain the possibility that the mischievousness of the "ordinary" child may in fact be a sign not of ordinariness, but of latent Evangelical sinfulness. Taylor, despairing at the possibility of ever reconciling three such contradictory constructions, turns away from the promise of sympathetic connection to the horrors of the Gothic to compensate for the failure. That these failures occur with male, but not female, protagonists suggests that masculinity provided particularly difficult challenges to such attempts at reconciliation.

In Chapter 3, "Engaging Histories: Fictionalized History for Children," I shift from the robinsonade to another genre in which experiments in exemplarity also featured: the realm of history. I analyze three works of history for children that attempt to address the problem of traditional history's inability to engage its youngest readers by experimenting with three major changes in history writing for adults. Jefferys Taylor, Agnes Strickland, and Harriet Martineau deploy these changes—a shift away from exemplary role models toward identification with "ordinary" figures of history; the inclusion of information about the material lives and internal feelings of historical actors (the new "social history"); and a newfound awareness of the radical alterity of the past—creating in the process an experimental hybrid form that I have termed "fictionalized history."

Taylor allows *The Little Historians* (1824) of his three-volume history to write the story of England's past themselves, to deeply humorous, and thus deeply engaging, effect. But laughter is not Taylor's only goal; under the guidance of a wise father, the little historians learn what "counts" as history, a lesson that must be learned anew given the pressures placed upon the genre by the expansion of history's audience and the demands for sympathetic engagement such an expansion brought about. In contrast, Agnes Strickland works not to police the borders of history, but to expand them. In *Tales of Illustrious British Children* (1833), Strickland combines real historical events with imagined dialogue and imagined historical children, inviting her young readers to identify with the children of the past. Drawing on the new social history, Strickland encourages her readers to forge a bond of sympathy with the children of history, both by explaining how they must have felt, and by describing the physical, material conditions of their lives. In so doing, Strickland disrupts the dictates of "real history" laid out in *The Little Historians*, replacing a masculine, linear, political history with a feminized, sentimental vision of history as a field of social relations. Harriet Martineau, of a far more radical political cast than either Taylor or Strickland, replaces history's tradition goal of conveying exemplary role models with a new purpose: suggesting to children what might happen in the future of their own society by analyzing how radical change occurred in a society of the past. In *The Peasant and the Prince* (1841), Martineau examines the recent past (Revolutionary France), experimenting with historical fiction only to abandon it in favor of social history in her attempt to create sympathetic understanding not only between child readers and those of the past, but between middle-class readers and their upper-class and working-class compatriots. As with sympathy between fictional parent and child, sympathy between reader and historical actor has not only its benefits, but also its dangers, dangers that each of these three authors struggle to articulate and to contain.

The book concludes with a consideration of the intersection between changes in historiographical practice and the construction of gender, in particular, the construction of girlhood, during the opening decades of the nineteenth century. Chapter 4, "'Men in Petticoats' and Girls in Pants: The Construction of Femininity in Early Historical Romance and Fiction for Girls," explores the rise of what Miriam Burstein describes as "gender anachronism": a new late eighteenth-century awareness that women in different times and in different societies may have been subject to different moral and social standards than contemporary women, standards which may have shaped their behavior accordingly. Before the late eighteenth century, British writers of women's history celebrated their subjects' timeless virtues rather than their historically-specific circumstances; readers of such histories thus sympathized across time and space to identify with idealized exemplary models presented by the women of the past (*Narrating* 12). But the rise of social history, which insisted on the importance of depicting everyday life and the inner world of feelings rather than just the political and military events of a nation or state, made such universalizing discourses, and the bond of sympathy they promoted, increasingly difficult to maintain.

Women who wrote historical fictions and romances for girls in the early nineteenth century increasingly drew upon this concept, which might better be termed "gender chronism" than Burstein's "gender anachronism." Gender chronism suggests that certain actions, thoughts, and beliefs considered to be outside the realm of the feminine could in fact exist in a woman—but only at a specific moment and a specific place in historical time. By placing their girl protagonists in the past, writers such as the anonymous author of *The Beautiful Page* (1802), Barbara Hofland (in *Adelaide, or, The Intrepid Daughter* [1823]), and Agnes Strickland (in *Alda, or the British Captive* [1841]) allow them to act in ways deemed unacceptable by the domestic ideology that emerged in the eighteenth century, and that came to dominate British discourse by the mid-nineteenth. The past thus becomes a place of fantasy, a space in which the restrictive gender codes of domesticity give way to a field of gender possibility. That Hofland's novel, which expressed the most anxiety about this transgression of gender, proved the most popular, while Strickland's, which embraced it most enthusiastically, was greeted by lackluster sales (and concluded with the death of its protagonist), suggests the fears that such a vision of gender chronism presented to readers of the early nineteenth century, particular when promulgated in books intended for girls. Sympathizing with a heroine who acts according to gender norms not your own could prove a deeply transgressive act for a girl reader, particularly when such a heroine embodies characteristics typically reserved for the realm of the masculine.

Many of the novels that I discuss in the following pages have rarely, if ever, been read by historians or critics of children's literature. Those who have read them tend to discuss them only in the context of large overviews of the past, and in light of broad arguments about the development of the field. When characterized only by their broadest outlines, many of these works do fit comfortably within the established narratives of the history of early children's literature—a move from didacticism to amusement; a focus on religion at the expense of entertainment; above all, a refusal to engage in the political issues roiling the society in which they were written. If my readings of these books appear to be lengthy, particularly to readers unfamiliar with them, I offer as excuse my discovery that attempts to discuss them in a few paragraphs led both to distorting simplification and reductive reiteration of the dominant narratives that have shaped the field for much of the past 200 years. Many of these novels may appear strange, deficient, even unworthy of such detailed attention, especially when read with current-day aesthetic standards in mind. Yet only when we look at such texts in detail, and set them in relation to the cultural, historical, and aesthetic standards of the times in which they were written, can we begin to recognize their innovativeness, their attempts to intervene in cultural and intellectual debates of the period, and the impact they had on later writing for children. Just as nineteenth-century historiography urged historians toward more proximate norms of distance in their writing, so, too, do I urge readers to move closer to these texts of the past. Look closely, and with sympathetic eyes, as you explore the uncharted territory of exemplary adventure, and witness a genre in the process of becoming.

Chapter 1
The Emergence of the Ordinary:
Parents and Children on the Deserted Isle

The "Real" of Literary Historians

Most twenty-first-century historians of childhood are careful to note that it is easier to study ideologies of childhood than it is to study the lives of real children of the past. But twentieth-century literary critics writing about the history of children's literature did not have the informed historical accounts of childhood that we now have today. Thus, like the early historians of childhood, they, too, often looked for signs of the child in the literature of the past based on their own ideas of what they viewed to be a natural, universal understanding of childhood. Whenever they found such a sign, literary historians typically deployed the term "real" or "realistic" to mark its appearance. But what, precisely, did the word "real" mean to such critics? How did they know a "real" child from an unreal one?

Looking closely at the detailed discussions of characters who are granted the title "real" in such histories, we can begin to tease out the assumptions that twentieth-century critics rely on when adjudicating between the "real" and the "unreal." Surprisingly, what one familiar with accounts of the "inward turn" in adult fiction of the late eighteenth century might assume would be the primary characteristic of "realism" in literature for children of the same period—the introduction of character interiority—is rarely mentioned by critics when discussing the advent of the "real" in books for the young. Perhaps twentieth-century critics, brought up in the wake of E.M. Forster's *Aspects of the Novel* and its lauding of round characters, simply take interiority so much for granted as a component of the "realistic" that they assume there is no need to focus on it in a critical work. Before moving on to a discussion what critics *do* focus on when they discuss the real, however, the shift in the depiction of character interiority seems worth articulating. In eighteenth-century texts, child characters rarely have interiority; narrators describe their actions, and give readers definitive explanations for the motives that incite said actions. Character is conveyed through external behavior; a character's thoughts and emotions are always conveyed secondhand, focalized through the lens of the narrator, if they are mentioned at all by these texts. Such constructions of character are typically labeled "flat" by twentieth-century historians of children's literature, but we would be more historically accurate if we labeled them "exemplary." As discussed in the Introduction, such exemplar character construction would have been quite familiar to eighteenth-century readers, both in the fictions and in the histories they read. Thus, the characters that twentieth-century critics would denigrate as being "flat" would not just be expected, but praised, by eighteenth-century readers, for such character construction was central both to historical discourse and to the juvenile novel that shared its purpose of molding moral readers.

The shift from "flat" to "round," or, writing from a historically-informed point of view, from exemplary to what we might term "ordinary," began in the late eighteenth century, but did not become the norm until well into the nineteenth. During this period, authors began to construct characters whose importance lies not only in their actions and behaviors, but also in their thoughts and feelings. Fictions for children gradually begin to show readers what is happening inside the heads of their child characters, and to show this directly rather than at one remove. Instead of a (obviously adult) narrator telling us what a child character did, and why a child character did it (she was good, he was bad), readers more often hear the thoughts of the child character directly. In juvenile novels of the early nineteenth century, the inside view is typically subject to comment by a narrator who makes value judgments about character's thoughts; later in the century, character's thoughts are more often given directly, with the narrator making an appearance infrequently (typically at the most ideologically fraught moments in a text). Thus, the psychologically "round" character of the child emerges.

Such a shift toward interiority in the construction of character in fiction for children aligns quite neatly with the actual and ideological shifts in childhood that eighteenth and early nineteenth-century Europe witnessed. A similar "inward turn" occurred in novels for adults at the end of the eighteenth century, a turn that has been much commented on by literary critics. But for historians of children's literature, this shift toward interiority is so taken for granted that it is rarely discussed directly. Many point to it indirectly, by denigrating the didactic tendencies and "preachy and wearisome passages" of pre-Victorian children's literature (Townsend 44). More common are passages that equate the "real" not with interiority, but with a particular kind of action, one that would in earlier literature for children be held up as a negative example of the exemplary: bad behavior. For example, in his discussion of Susan Warner's *The Wide, Wide World* (1850), John Townsend opines "… although virtuous friend Alice is a bloodless figure, human nature breaks in, in the shape of a bad girl, Nancy, who says it is no use trying to teach her to be good" (60); in his later discussion of Alcott's *Little Women* (1868), he writes, "Already that is not the real Jo; the Jo we remember is the one who does … unladylike things. … *Little Women* marks … an increased truth-to-life in domestic stories, with children seen as people rather than examples of good and bad" (Townsend 62).

Again, as they did with signs of the "real," other historians see this shift toward bad behavior in juvenile literature occurring earlier than does Townsend. Jackson points to 1839's *Holiday House*—"it introduced a sprightliness in its young characters, most notably Laura Graham, who with her brother, Harry, tumbles regularly into mischief" (232)—while Avery and Kinnell point even earlier, noting of Mary Ann Kilner's *The Adventures of a Pincushion* (ca. 1780), "Charlotte's violent and entirely understandable reaction" to an argument with her sister over toys "is shown much more as the natural outcome of a squabble than as the kind of wicked or aberrant behaviour frowned upon by Puritan writers. … This is a normal children's quarrel which takes full account of natural aggression and stubbornness" (54). Behaving badly, whether in 1868 or 1780, seems to be the defining mark of the "normal," "natural," or "realistic" for historians of children's literature.

But bad behavior itself cannot function as the sole marker of the realistic child, for bad children also commonly appeared in eighteenth-century texts. Child characters in both eighteenth- and in nineteenth-century fiction behave poorly: they argue, yell, cause damage to property, hit, punch, pull hair, and speak rudely to their adult caretakers. What marks the true difference between the exemplar characters of earlier literature and the "real" characters of literature in the newer vein is not only the way that their protagonists act, but also how the adults around those children *re*act to their behavior. Take, for example, Avery and Kinnell's description of an early Maria Edgeworth novel: "Less tolerable is the hero of *Frank* (1801), just enough of a real boy to show an insatiable curiosity about his surroundings, but painfully accommodating to his tiresome parents" (56). A second change is required in order for a text to qualify as "realistic," such critics imply, a change not in the child characters, but rather in the characters of those "tiresome parents": adults within these texts must react differently to the misbehavior of their fictional children. When praising the "real," historians focus less on the remarkable shift from outside to inside, as do critics of adult literature, than they do on the shift in how the outside was perceived and valued.

Butts calls attention to this difference in his discussion of the actions of the children in Sinclair's *Holiday House*, a book often termed the first Victorian children's novel: "their grandmother and uncle are remarkably forgiving. … The degree of toleration shown towards the children is truly astonishing … the gentle humor of Uncle David, when the children organize a disastrous tea-party or damage a table, is unexpectedly appealing" ("Beginnings" 83). Butts echoes Jackson's earlier comments about the book, in which she numbers the adults' changing reactions to the misbehavior of the children, as one of the novel's key innovations (232, 236). While critics such as Myers, and Avery and Kinnell, remark on the "realistic" actions of their child protagonists, they fail to discuss a concurrent sympathetic *re*action on the part of the adults in the texts they examine, suggesting that this second characteristic of the "real" comes later in the period than does the first.

It is not only the adult characters within the novels that register a shift in response to child behavior; the authors who create them and the narrators who tell their stories have also changed how they respond. For example, Townsend notes of Frederick Marryat's 1836 novel, "The most likable aspect of *Mr Midshipman Easy* is the presentation of the hero: the author mocks Jack Easy's youthful waywardness but at the same time sympathizes with it" (45). Similarly, Darton links the appearance of the "charming and lenient old grandmother" and the "nice funny uncle David" within *Holiday House* to the author who created them: Catherine Sinclair "knew and understood real children … and that in her own mind … she reconciled her staid primness in adult conduct with her complete abandonment of all constraint for the young" (220, 221).

Finally, the responses of the new fictional parents and authors/narrators to childhood misbehavior requires a far different response from *readers* of the books in which they appear. The appearance of such adult presences marks a significant shift in how young readers were intended to respond to the characters within their texts. Rather than see them as exemplary figures, ideals towards which they, imperfect human beings as they are, could strive to emulate but could never actually completely embody, readers were now being asked to *identify* with the characters in their texts, to construct a bond through sympathy with what is now being constructed as "natural," rather than evil, misbehavior. The biggest shift in the construction of character in children's literature of the early nineteenth century, then, may be less the creation of fictional interiority per se, than a specific interiority marked by the child's "natural" inclination to misbehave, a textual interiority that simultaneously constructs a readerly interiority that "sympathizes with it" as does the narrator of *Mr Midshipman Easy*.

In eighteenth-century juvenile fictions, adults typically fear fictional children who misbehave—they signal a failure of parenting, the intrusion of sin, a threat to stable society. Unsurprisingly, then, authors of such fictions often craft untimely deaths for their "evil" misbehaving characters, as a punishment for the threat they pose. But by the Victorian period, misbehavior is far more likely to be seen as natural, forgivable, even, I would argue, amusing and pleasurable—if it is kept within strict boundaries.[1]

The Emergence of the Ordinary

The mischievous literary child did not emerge, fully formed, like Athena from the head of Zeus. Instead, the shift from the exemplary to the ordinary proceeded in fits and starts, with some narrators condemning the new construction even while they depicted its actions with sympathy, others embracing it but tempering its threat through the addition of sentimental discourse, and still others rejecting it altogether. Some literary historians suggest that this new construction enters through the back door as it were, through publishers' appropriation of denigrated folk and fairy tale material, previously deemed worthy of only chapbook publication aimed at the plebian class. The characters in such tales, while constructed just as "flatly" as the characters in earlier moral tales, do behave in ways that often make misbehavior appealing. Yet if the shift had its birth pangs in the realm of the fairy tale, its development is to be traced more clearly in novels written for genteel children

---

[1]   In her article on civility books for children, Margaret Higonnet provocatively suggests that a shift from manuals of proper conduct pre-French Revolution to those focusing on misconduct post-Revolution may have been inspired by the "momentary glimpse of the child perceived as a potentially active citizen, capable of taking political action" in the overtly politicized French children's literature written during the French Revolution (131). Nineteenth-century conduct books (both French and English), unlike their predecessors, contain a "double message": conform to the rules, but take pleasure in the exuberance of the depictions of transgressiveness.

in the experimental period of the opening decades of the nineteenth century. We can find its roots in late eighteenth and early nineteenth century domestic tales, as Mitzi Myers has argued, but its first shoots and leaves would have to emerge in quite a different setting—not in the familiar domestic or moral tale setting of house and home, but rather in a place that attempts to create a hybrid of the fantastic and the domestic—the deserted island of the robinsonade.

The deserted island proves a perfect setting in which authors can explore and experiment with this new construction of the ordinary, mischievous child and of the tolerant, playful adult. Free from the judgment of society and peers, the deserted island, like the Lockean child, provides a blank slate upon which authors can imagine and inscribe different versions of parenthood and adulthood. In this chapter, I will explore the ways in which writers of juvenile robinsonades during the opening decades of the nineteenth century began to experiment with depicting non-ideal child characters, and discovered a concomitant need to craft parent characters who viewed the behavior of such children as natural rather than sinful. In particular, I will explore the rise of emotion in these books. The novelty of such child figures often stems from the depiction of their emotions, rather than just their behavior. Previous historians suggest that in depicting child protagonists who feel, and who often feel emotions which, under a Puritan vision of childhood, would be considered signs of inherent evil—fear, anxiety, anger, desire—nineteenth-century writers for children liberated the child from the heavy didactic hand of its moral tale predecessors. But, as I will argue, writers who deployed non-ideal constructions of childhood were still centrally concerned with exemplarity; they simply changed the means by which they hoped to achieve it. By making their child protagonists less ideal, more "ordinary," juvenile writers believed they would create a sense of identification in their readers, an identification which would in turn foster a stronger reader desire to accept the text's moral messages than the older, ideal model could in a period increasingly characterized by the importance of sympathetic engagement with the other.

Writers also strengthened the motivation to exemplarity by adding emotion to their depiction of their protagonists' parents. While parents in eighteenth-century juvenile novels had served as dispassionate, rational teachers, parent characters in children's literature of the opening decades of the nineteenth century gradually begin to display emotions in their interactions with their children. In particular, such characters become humanized through depiction of the pleasure they take in being a parent, in observing and interacting with their children. Intriguingly, only by first granting parents the right to take pleasure in, rather than simply reprimand or teach, their child protagonists can these protagonists be granted textual subjectivity. I am not making a historical argument, *pace* Philippe Ariès, Lloyd de Mause, and Laurence Stone, that actual parents did not love or take pleasure in their children prior to the nineteenth century; work by historians Linda Pollock, Nicholas Orme, and others convincingly disproves such historical claims. Rather, I am interested in exploring when the idea of parental pleasure first begins to appear in literature intended for children, and what function it serves in the project of fostering exemplarity. The depiction of parental emotion plays a key role in humanizing the parent, and thus, I will argue, strives to make that parent's authority more acceptable, more appealing, both to the children within the text, and to the children outside it during a historical period in which family affection became increasingly common in real and discursive families.

But texts often suggest ways of reading far different from the intentions of their authors, and the advent of emotion in the depiction of parents and children does not come without anxiety. For if, as John D. Morillo argues in regards to adult literature in the neoclassical and romantic periods, talk about shared, universal feelings, feelings which pointed to a universal human nature, provoked anxiety because of its disturbing potential to level British social distinctions, so too, I would suggest, do emotions have the potential to break down the relationship of authority between parent and child (2–3, 223). Incorporating emotions opened the door to multiple types of child agency, agency simply not available under the older model of ideal exemplarity. The authors who penned such experimental work during this transitional period struggled, I argue, to embrace an emotionally complex construction of the child while warding off the threat to their authority posed by the myriad types of child agency that such a construction grants.

I explore this double tug—towards emotion on one hand, back towards authority on the other—by examining a curiously prevalent subset of the robinsonade genre: stories in which a child spends at least part of his or her time on a deserted island not alone, but in the company of a parent. The deserted island, a place apart from society, presents a safe space for authors to experiment with the potentially volatile, disruptive creation of emotion in their child and parent characters. During their island sojourns, both children and parents learn not just how to behave, but, more importantly, how to feel—how to forge a bond of emotional connection between parent and child. For authors of children's literature, such bonds ideally function to make parental authority more compelling, and foster a desire in the reader to model his or her own behavior after that of the child who listens to his or her emotionally connected parent within the text. But even while such bonds function to enforce parental (and thus, authorial) authority, they inadvertently open up new possibilities for child agency, particularly in allowing the child to talk, and in some cases, to talk back, to parental authority. In analyzing the texts that follow, I hope to trace the pleasures inherent in both resisting and succumbing to the siren call of parent-child emotion, both for the child within the text, and for the reader without.

The Pleasures of the Patriarchal Father: Emotion and Authority in Johann David Wyss's *The Family Robinson Crusoe* (1812–1813, 1814)

Both the earliest and perhaps most famous family robinsonade is that of Johann David Wyss, the eighteenth-century Swiss parson who penned stories of a family shipwrecked together on a deserted island for the entertainment and instruction of

Fig. 1.1   "The first family robinsonade": the Swiss Family Robinson on
              the point of shipwreck. Courtesy of the UCLA Charles E. Young
              Research Library Department of Special Collections.

his own children. Wyss wrote his collection of stories in the 1790's, and intended his audience to be his family alone. But his son, Johann Rudolf Wyss, convinced of the utility of the tales, later persuaded his father to allow him to edit and shape them into a novel; the book was published in Zurich in 1812–1813 under the title *Der schweizersche Robinson, oder der schiffbrüchige Schweizerprediger und seine Familie. Ein lehrreiches Buch für Kinder und Kinder-Freunde zu Stadt und Land.* We know the book today by the title of its second English edition translation, *The Swiss Family Robinson*. But the novel made its first appearance in English under the title *The Family Robinson Crusoe: or, Journal of a Father Shipwrecked, with his Wife and Children, on an Uninhabited Island*, published in two volumes in 1814 for the Juvenile Library of M.J. Godwin and Company.[2] The book's popularity led to myriad other transliterations, adaptations, and new translations published in English throughout the nineteenth century[3], but to explore the shift from exemplar to ordinary character construction we must return to the book's first English-language version.

The Juvenile Library translation unfolds, like Defoe's *Robinson Crusoe*, as a journal. As Kevin Carpenter notes, the central figure in the story is the writer of that journal, the unnamed father, who, like the elder Wyss himself, was a parson.

---

[2]   The Godwin's choice of Wyss's text for translation seems unsurprising, as the novel's progressive pedagogical program aligns neatly with William Godwin's own. Note his championing of ordinary rather than exemplary character construction, and his belief that identification is the main goal in juvenile reading, in the preface to his *Bible Stories*:

> The old books described the real tempers and passions of human beings. Their scenes were often supernatural and impossible, but their personages were of our own species. The modern books on the other and abound in real scenes, but impossible personages … [t]heir young people are all so good, and their old people so sober, so demure, and so rational, that no genuine interest can be felt for their adventures.… Everything is studied and attended to, except those things which open the heart … and enable him to put himself in imagination into the place of his neighbour, to feel his feelings, and to wish his wishes. (iii–v).

Imagination is not simply a good in itself, Godwin asserts; its importance lies in its ability to foster identification in the reader, which in turn provides the "ground-plot upon which the edifice of a sound morality must be erected" (v).

[3]   For a comprehensive discussion of the complex publishing history of English language editions of Wyss's novel and its sequels, see Martin Green's chapter on the book in *The Robinson Crusoe Story* (65–78). Green attributes the initial Godwin translation to William (perhaps with help from his future son-in-law, Percy Bysshe Shelley), although later Godwin biographers grant the laurels to Mary Jane, a skilled translator who worked with children's book publisher Benjamin Tabart before marrying Godwin (Green, *RCS* 77; Scrivener 144).

The Godwin edition includes three black and white engravings credited to "H. Corbould del" and "Springsguth SC." H. Corbould refers to Henry Corbould, a well-regarded book illustrator whose later work including illustrating Homer, Milton, Shakespeare, and Byron's *Don Juan* and *The Book of Poets*; the "del" names him as the designer or delineator of the illustration, while "SC" refers to to the engraver (the one who *sculpsit*, or "sculpted" or "made" it), Samuel Springsguth.

Carpenter goes on to suggest that the father whom the narrative views as exemplary is anything but to a modern audience:

> ... the father [is] probably the harshest, most opinionated, intolerant, insensitive and pompous parent-figure in children's literature. This learned killjoy is endowed with near-absolute wisdom, not to mention his profound knowledge of natural history, geometry, carpentry, wine-making, tannery, medicine, weaponry and Bible-exegesis. Most markedly, at the beginning of the story, is the way he comes down heavily on his sons' natural exuberance (impatience, he calls it), particularly when they make a discovery he has not planned them to make. (41)

Since Wyss's story is one of the few children's texts from the early decades of the nineteenth century to have remained consistently in print to this day, Carpenter feels free to judge its narrator by contemporary standards for how a parent in a children's novel should behave. But when we set the first English translation into its historical context, and examine closely its depiction of the father/child relationship, something surprising is revealed: the father, far from being a killjoy, is vitally interested in the pleasures of the adult/child relationship, in a way vastly different from that of parent characters in other English-language children's literature of the period.

The Preface to the novel, written by Johann Rudolph, echoes contemporary English-language moral tale texts by emphasizing the utility of these stories: "The following work has for its main purpose to be of use to children" (Wyss v). But unlike earlier writers, who viewed their moral lessons as applicable for all audiences, Wyss immediately qualifies and contracts the potential audience, both by age and by class: "... it is not all children for which it can pretend to be adapted, but only ... such as have acquired that portion of instruction that is given from the age of eight and 14 years in most of the primary schools in the large towns, and even in the villages" (v). Clearly, Wyss's differentiation between different ages of children is linked to the emergence during the mid-eighteenth century of clear distinctions between children's developmental stages, suggested by Rousseau and seen in England in both child-care manuals such as William Cadogan's *Essay upon Nursing and Management of Children from their Birth to Three Years of Age* (1748), and James Nelson's *Essay on the Government of Children* (1753), and in lesson books for children such as Anna Barbauld's *Lessons for Children from Two to Three Years Old* (1778), and Ellenor Fenn's *Fables in Monosyllable* (c. 1783), advertised as 'suited to children from four to six years of age' (Avery and Kinnell 50–51). In this recognition of the differences between children, differences that make some texts suited to children of one age but not of another, lie early hints of what will later emerge in juvenile fiction: a shift from the ideal to the individualized in the depiction of children. One ideal will not serve the needs of children of different ages, or from different classes. Such a view is in striking contrast to the ideal depiction of children in the majority of eighteenth-century juvenile fiction. Such works, Patricia Demers notes, emerged from a catechetical tradition, one whose goal was not to depict children as they were, but to provide exemplary portraits as models for correct (and incorrect) moral behavior (*Heaven* 140). "Superhuman paragons" and the "bad [who] stay bad" are the hallmarks of such writing; as Demers notes, "most instructive storytellers stayed loyal to the model of the pious exemplar and the principle linking virtue and happiness" (128, 129, 131).

In his preface, Wyss describes what his father was trying to achieve in his depiction of his child characters, something rather different from the catechetical exemplars of contemporary moral fiction:

> The purpose he [the elder Wyss] had in view was to amuse, to instruct, and to fashion the character of four sons borne to him by an exemplary woman: in doing this, he conceived the idea of faithfully pourtraying these four children in correspondence with the germs of character he had already remarked in them. He made them act and speak, exactly as they were accustomed to act and speak in the *ordinary* train of their lives .... (vii, italics added)

Just as the preface argues that there are differences between the children of its potential audience, so too will the novel portray child characters who are different from each other, with individual characteristics and habits. Thus, *The Family Robinson Crusoe* stands as one of the earliest examples in English-language juvenile literature in which child characters are depicted not as simply good or evil, but as nuanced, psychologically distinct individuals—in a style that twentieth-century critics of children's literature would label "realistic."

To detach such depictions from the value-laden baggage that has typically accompanied the term "realistic" in written histories of English children's literature, I would like to propose a switch to the term "ordinary," a word that the translator of Wyss himself uses. While the "ordinary" character may come closer to a real life human child than an ideal character does, it is important to emphasize that the ordinary character is just as much a construction as is the ideal character. What is held up as ordinary differs across time and place just as much as what is deemed ideal does; thus, as critics, we must interrogate the construction of ordinariness just as we would the construction of the ideal exemplar.

Ordinary character construction differs from ideal exemplar character construction in four important ways. First, the age of the ordinary child character matters; unlike ideal children, whose actions are upheld or denigrated no matter what their age, ordinary children can and do act differently depending on how old they are. When first introducing his children to the reader, Wyss's father narrator is careful to include each son's age; each child's behavior, such information suggests, stems in part from the age and developmental stage that child currently occupies. Anna Letitia Barbauld, with her four-volume *Lessons for Children* first published in the 1770s, created the first reading books to recognize the differing needs of different-age children; Maria Edgeworth extended Barbauld's insights in creating developmentally distinguished fictional characters in the stories found in *The Parent's Assistant* (1796) and *Practical Education* (1798). Wyss, writing during the same decade as Edgeworth, might, along with Edgeworth, be one of the first writers to craft child characters whose actions differ depending on their ages in the genre of the novel for children.

Second, the ordinary child has both good points and bad points, talents and flaws; the combination of both make for unique, individual characters. Wyss's narrator indicates this when he lists the family members in order of their departure from the sinking ship. The eldest, Fritz, "between 14 and 15 years of age, a handsome curl-pated youth full of intelligence and vivacity" (I. 22), can be haughty and bossy, but also proves himself brave during the family's island adventure. Ernest, 12, "of a rational reflecting temper, [is] well informed, but somewhat disposed to indolence and the pleasures of the senses" (I.22), while 10-year-old Jack is a "light hearted, enterprising, audacious, generous lad" (I. 22). Jack's temper is "less docile" than those of his brothers' (I. 141), but he provides much entertainment to the family through his love of jokes and play.

While the narrator's description of the elder boys suggests something new in character depiction, his words about Francis, the youngest at six, point to an older concept of childhood. Describing Francis as "full of the happiest dispositions, but whose character was not yet pronounced" (I. 22), the narrator echoes the idea that the child has an inborn nature that is gradually revealed as the child moves closer to adulthood, an idea noted by James Schultz in the medieval German texts he analyzed (252). Simultaneously, however, the text goes on to show its investment in the ideology of character change and growth; while each child may have a propensity toward a particular fault, parental training and guidance can mitigate that fault's tendencies while helping the child enhance positive character traits. Here we see a paradigm shift about the depiction of child characters in the middle of becoming.

Before exploring the third and fourth characteristics of ordinary character construction, it is first necessary to consider the ways that ideal exemplarity continues to echo within the midst of the ordinary. For *The Family Robinson Crusoe* is clearly not ready to abandon the ideal exemplar mode altogether; in fact, as Johann Rudolph explains, despite his father's desire to depict the "ordinary train of their lives," he found it necessary to "strengthen ... or [make] more prominent whatever of excellence or frailty he found in them" (vii). By shifting from strict to exaggerated mimesis, Wyss believes, the exemplary function of ordinary character construction can be strengthened: "by this means he should render their faults the more displeasing to them, and alarm them the more with the consequences that might result, and that he might render sound judgment and integrity more lovely in their eyes (vii–viii). The elder Wyss's goal, then, is not simply to entertain his young listeners (and later, readers); it is to convince them of the "loveliness" of good behavior. The best way to do this, he believes, is not by abandoning exemplarity altogether, but by making the exemplary more enticing, more pleasurable, by making the characters who embody it more ordinary than ideal. Wyss's explanation for why his father chose to set his tales on a deserted island could equally be applied to his father's decision to construct ordinary rather than ideal characters: "To give children an interest in the studies they pursue, it is necessary to excite their curiosity, and to give them a wish to learn. The lessons of morality and science that are then interspersed will then be read with pleasure, and devoured with avidity" (x).

Such ideas suggest the influence on Wyss of the rich debates taking place in Germany, Switzerland, and France on the purposes and practices of pedagogy during the mid- to late-eighteenth century. John Locke, in his *Essay Concerning Human Understanding* (1690) and *Some Thoughts Concerning Education* (1693), was one of the earliest proponents of using play in teaching, but the educational reform debate shifted to the continent in the eighteenth century with the publication in Paris of Jean Jacques Rousseau's "scattered thoughts and observations" on educational theory, *Émile, ou l'education* [*Emile, or on Education*] (1762). Though initially denigrated, Rousseau's ideas on developmental stages of childhood, the innate goodness of the child, and the need for a child to learn through the senses rather than through rote book learning soon spread throughout Europe; despite Rousseau's disdain for public schooling, many subsequent continental school reformers cited Rousseau as a formative influence. These include German Johann Bernard Basedow (1724–1790), founder of the Philanthropin (1774), an experimental school which children were educated in a friendly and gentle manner rather than with the severe discipline common in earlier days; Joachim Heinrich Campe (1746–1818), a later director of Basedow's school (and author of the first robinsonade written for children, *Robinson der Jüngere* [1779]); Immanuel Kant (1724–1804), whose open support of Basedow's project and comments on education in his philosophical writings indicated his reformist sympathies; and educational reformer Johann Heinrich Pestalozzi (1746–1827), whose own experimental schools in Switzerland, founded on the principle that successful education depended on providing a child with security and genuine affection, soon drew acolytes from other continental nations. Incorporating pleasure into the pedagogical project, such educators believed, would lay a far firmer foundation for success than mere rote learning, enforced by strict discipline, ever could.

The precise nature of the pleasure that his father's text offers, Johann Rudolph suggests, lies in a concept that we today take for granted, but one which was novel for the children's literature of his time: identification. As the son explains, "His own children were especially delighted at finding themselves brought forward as the personages of this imaginary history, and transported to the scene of a distant ocean" (xiii). Later, when describing how his father decided to publish the tale beyond the family circle, he elaborates: "one of the personages, who is brought forward as a child during the course of this narrative ... felt in his own person the deep interest and lively pleasure which the story excited, and recollect[ed] how many lasting advantages he had himself derived from the use of this book" (xiii). In order to convince a child of the desirability of moral behavior, one must first incite curiosity about that behavior; the best way to incite such curiosity is not, Wyss suggests, through ideal moral exemplar alone, but by inciting a desire to model exemplarity by first meeting a child on his own ground, by depicting characters with whom he, in his struggles with temptation and character flaws, can identify. This concept of character identification, an identification fostered not through the intellect but through the emotions, thus becomes the third characteristic of ordinary character construction.

Intriguingly, though Wyss constructs his boy characters as ordinary, he is loathe to extend this construction to the opposite sex. Wyss himself had no daughters, and his "anxiety" to "paint his family just as it was" prevented him from "introducing girls in his uninhabited island," Johann Rudolph reports (ix). Yet if we read *The Family Robinson Crusoe* with Felicity Nussbaum's analysis of domesticity, sexuality, and colonization in mind, we can see that there is another reason for banning girls from the deserted island which extend beyond the simply mimetic. As Nussbaum argues, eighteenth-century European travel literature often linked "climate and sexual desire to define a temperate, civilized Europe that possesses the sexual constraint necessary to engage in the work-discipline productive of political liberty and civic virtue, in marked contrast to the libidinous and indolent torrid zones" (Nussbaum 10). The introduction of younger girl characters to a tropical desert island, Wyss asserts, "would have spoiled the integrity of his painting: several other motives may easily be conceived" (Wyss ix). Those "several other motives" are left to the imagination of the [adult] reader here, although a scene later in the novel—during which eldest son Fritz enthusiastically asks why they, like Biblical patriarchs, might not "cause a great nation to descend from [our] loins," and his father has "not now time to answer"—suggests one possible reason. The presence of girls, particularly girls who are not ideal moral exemplars, might call into question the binary contemporary European discourse was at pains to construct between the chaste, domestic European woman and the sexualized, and hence uncivilized, woman of the torrid zones, thus troubling not only the project of shaping young male characters, but of shaping a Western European identity that would justify the colonial project.

But Wyss knew that his book "could not be without utility to children of the softer sex," and hence envisions the mother character, described by the narrator as "exemplary," as the model for any girls who may happen to read his book (ix). Her character hearkens back to earlier models of character depiction in children's literature, depictions structured by the dictates of the ideal rather than the ordinary. The unnamed mother embodies the exemplar, although more along the lines of an exemplary femininity than an exemplary morality: "in delineating his wife he should present to them a model of the power given to the female sex over the happiness of their families, both as wives and mothers" (ix). The mother character thus serves as the model of an exemplary domesticity, warding off the threat of torrid sexuality by being unmarked by the faults that characterize her sons.[4]

---

4   Unlike the mother in later translations and elaborations of the novel, however, Wyss's mother is far less docile and in need of protection. She speaks up to gently criticize her husband when he lectures too long, laughs when he ignores her stories, and takes physical risks, albeit with some reluctance. Comparing this mother figure to her construction in later translations, elaborations, and, of course, the Disney film version would be a project worth further investigation.

Wyss may be willing to depict boys who have faults, but portraying a mother constructed in a similar manner, or bringing girl characters into contact with such boys, might lead to pleasures of a kind no juvenile author of the early nineteenth century can admit.

In suggesting that readers identify with, rather than idealize, their fictional protagonists, Wyss again echoes the innovations of Maria Edgeworth, whose story characters were, Mitzi Myers claims, "every nineteenth-century youngster's imaginary playmates" ("Reading Rosasmund" 61). Yet there is a final type of pleasure that seems original to Wyss himself, a pleasure that serves as what I am arguing will prove the final characteristic of ordinary character construction: the pleasure of parenthood. We can see indications of a shifting role for the parent right from the Preface's opening sentence: Not only is his father's work to be of "use to children," Johann Rudolph asserts; it is also to be of use "to the friends of children" (v). Just as he defined his view of "child," Wyss explains precisely what he means by the term "friends of children":

> I do not by the friends of children particularly understand that class of individuals who are engaged in philosophical researches, theories, and experiments on the subject of education; but such fathers, teachers, and others, who delight to employ their attention on the youthful mind; who observe with pleasure the actions and discourses of children; who reflect naturally and without any preconcerted system upon their faculties, dispositions, and characters; who find themselves prompted to infuse useful knowledge into them through the medium of conversation …. (vi)

"Friends of children," who are always men (for Wyss mentions only fathers, not mothers or other women, when describing this group) must "delight to employ their attention on the youthful mind," "observe with pleasure the actions and discourses of children," and "reflect naturally" (v). In order to qualify for the sobriquet, then, an adult must not simply instruct a child in correct behavior, or religious and moral principles, as in earlier juvenile fiction: he must take *pleasure* in such instruction. Intriguingly, then, this fourth characteristic of ordinary character construction lies not in the depiction of the child, but in the depiction of the parent; a parent must feel *pleasure* when interacting with his or her child. Parental emotion evoked by the child thus becomes a key component of ordinary juvenile character construction.[5]

In Wyss's construction, parental pleasure lies not in the interaction with the child, but in the observation of it, the attention focused on it. Despite Wyss's objection to formulaic scientific theorems, he has no objection to the scientific method: making a child into an object of study. For, as Bettina Kümmerling-Meibauer notes, in the wake of Rousseau's reconstruction of the child, adults

---

[5]   It is worth noting the one major continuity between exemplar and ordinary character construction: such characters remain members of the genteel class, the smallest (17 percent in 1815, according to Frost) but most influential proportion of the English population.

began to view children as "unknown beings," beings to whom they had to adopt "an observer's position ... in order to fathom their character[s]" (185). We see Wyss's pastor father taking up just such a position in regards to his four sons. At the same time, however, that the friend of children is taking pleasure in what is specifically childlike in the children he observes, he must also simultaneously be working to change precisely what gives him pleasure. For to observe the "actions and discourses of children" suggests that such discourses are far different from those of the adult; in order to achieve the goal to "improve," to "infuse useful knowledge" into the child, then, one must change that child, that object of pleasure, into an adult. This second goal, however, has pleasures of its own. The next section of this chapter will explore the different pleasures on offer in Godwin's translation of Wyss's text, both for the adult narrator within the book, and for the English child reader outside it.

The first, and least surprising, type of pleasure that the parson father of *The Family Robinson Crusoe* takes in his boys is pleasure in their good behavior. For example, he is "well satisfied" when Fritz stands his ground rather than fleeing after hearing an unexplained menacing noise (53), and when Fritz makes a sagacious pronouncement, the father replies "That is an excellent remark, my boy, said I, and gives me more pleasure than a hundred crowns would do" (68). The nature of this pleasure is twofold. First, it is the pleasure of being listened to, of being accepted as a moral guide. Second, it is pleasure not in childhood, but in a maturity that leaves childhood behind: "I am well pleased to find you beginning to estimate things according to their real value and usefulness, instead of considering them as good or bad, like children, upon feeble views" (68).

A second type of pleasure in the father/son relationship emerges when children use their reason to figure out the solution to a problem. For example, after the father expresses his inability to think of a way to move the animals from the shipwreck to the island, Fritz devises the idea of fashioning life jackets for them. After experimenting and discovering that Fritz's plan is sound, the father is so pleased that he exclaims "Victory!" and hugs his son "with delight" (129). This pleasure, like the pleasure in correct moral behavior, both reinforces the father's authority as a teacher, and suggests pleasure in seeing the child turning away from the childish toward adult rationality.

Yet there are also many moments in the text where the father takes pleasure not from observing good behavior or rational thought in his children, but from noticing a gap between the competency of his child and his own knowledge or skills, a gap that leads to comical mistakes. Examples of this third type of parental pleasure include a scene in which Francis mistakes soup cakes for glue, for which he earns the doubly-valenced nickname "little blockhead" from his father (29), and a scene in which Jack attempts to subdue a lobster: "having observed how I held it to avoid the gripe, he laid his own hand on it in exactly the same manner; but scarcely had he grasped it, than he received a blow on the face from the lobster's tail, which made him lose his hold, and the animal fell to the ground. Jack again began to bawl out, while I could not refrain from laughing heartily" (31). Here, the adult narrator's pleasure lies in recognizing the gap between the abilities or knowledge of the child and those of himself, and in savoring the greater mastery, as well as the comical pratfalls that a lesser mastery leads to.[6]

There are also many moments, however, when the narrator father enjoys an almost vicarious pleasure in watching or anticipating what culture has labeled as "particularly childlike" emotions, emotions that he as an adult is no longer supposed to feel. After Father and Fritz return from an exploring expedition laden with animal discoveries, he muses, "I had sufficient time for amusing myself with the idea that we should arrive at our home with something of the appearance of keepers of rare animals for show. I enjoyed in foresight the jubilations of our young ones when they should see the figure we made" (89). And when Fritz is supposed to be helping craft a sail, the father relates

> He soon after brought me a small streamer, which he had cut from a piece of linen, and which he entreated me to tie to the extremity of the mast, and he appeared as much delighted with the streamer as with the sail itself. ... I could not withhold a smile at vanity like this, in such a situation as ours; it gave me too an opportunity of observing the operation of this prominent feature of human nature, in a lad of 14 years of age. I myself took great pleasure in seeing the little streamer floating on the air, and in the respectable appearance of our machine altogether." (120–21)

Instead of correcting what to a moral tale writer would have been a grave fault (vanity), the father takes pleasure in seeing it in his son. And his son's pleasure gives him leave, it seems, to enjoy a vain pleasure himself, despite the fact that he is an adult, not a child. There is a clear difference between adult and child, as the father's words "Do you then, my son, said I, take your materials for a model from your admirable mother, who never fails to make allowance for the buoyant spirits so natural to youth" indicate (68). Yet just as clearly, there are times when a parent doesn't simply "make allowance" for what is childlike, waiting for the chance to change it, but instead takes an active pleasure in observing, perhaps even participating vicariously, in it.[7] Catherine Sinclair's 1839 novel *Holiday House* is usually credited as being the first English-language juvenile novel in which adults allow children to be naturally mischievous, and in which readers are allowed to

---

[6]   Erica Fudge argues that for early modern philosophers, laughter was a key quality in differentiating humans from non-humans. For such philosophers, true human laughter is not simply bodily (for a purely bodily response would put it into the category of the animal); instead, true laughter emerges when the mind and body interact, when the mind sees an "exterior failure" and its own success (26). Such laughter seems at the heart of the response Wyss's narrator father to the failings of his children.

[7]   There are, to be sure, moments in this text where what a contemporary reader would term mischievous behavior is deemed wrong and corrected by the boys' father. At some of these moments, however, there is often a hesitation, a breakdown of the clear bad-behavior-leads-immediately-to-chastisement model found in other juvenile novels of the period.

take pleasure in that mischievous behavior, yet we see something remarkably similar occurring in Godwin's translation of Wyss, nearly 25 years earlier.

Yet even while Wyss's text acknowledges the real pleasures a father can take in his sons, it is simultaneously fearful of where those natural childlike mischievous tendencies might lead. Thus, a pattern emerges that is repeated throughout the novel, one in which an initially playful type of mischief leads inevitably to a far graver sin, a sin that the older, wiser father must condemn and correct. For example, in the abovementioned lobster episode, Jack, angered by his lack of mastery, attacks the lobster and kills it; likewise, Fritz grows angry when the family dogs attack his captured agouti, and beats them, unable in the moment of passion to recognize either the instinct that motivates the animals nor the likely results of his abuse of these protectors of the family. "When he had grown a little cool, I seriously remonstrated with him on his violence of temper," the narrator reports, remonstrations that occur and reoccur throughout the novel (43). Adults may be free to take pleasure in watching the actions of their children, the text suggests, yet such pleasurable actions almost inevitably lead to other, more extreme and less appealing actions, actions which require the parent to shift from an observing role to that of the moral guide and disciplinarian far more common in literature of the period.

Adult pleasure is also rudely interrupted at moments in the text when children make any sign of attempting to cross the clear demarcation line between adult and child, by assuming an authority or decision-making power reserved in this text for the exemplary father. Carpenter's earlier observation, suggesting that the father's displeasure at his son's natural exuberance comes to the fore at moments when "they make a discovery he has not planned them to make" is certainly warranted. For example, when Fritz proposes without prompting the idea of making a new rudder for the boat, his father decides on a different plan to address the same problem (121). But when, as discussed earlier, father first solicits his son's advice on how to solve the problem of getting the animals from ship to shore, his pleasure at his son's ingenuity is unbounded. I cannot but help having a sneaking suspicion that the father is not quite as much "at a loss" at thinking of a solution to this problem as he proclaims, and that he is using the opportunity to test his son's reasoning abilities against his own (129).

In fact, the pleasures of being an observer, though important, may be less than the pleasures of being an authority figure. Whenever the father's authority is questioned in this text, it is reasserted, even to the point of aggression, as the following conversation between the father and Fritz, which occurs after their discovery of a gourd tree, demonstrates:

> These rinds serve them [the natives] to keep their food and drink in, and sometimes they even cook their victuals in them.
> Oh, father! it must be impossible to cook their victuals in them; for the heat of fire would soon consume such a substance.
> I did not say the rind was put upon the fire.
> How droll! Pray how are victuals to be cooked without fire?

> Nor did I say that victuals could be cooked without a fire; and my meaning was, that there is no need to put the vessel that contains the food, upon the fire.
>
> I have not the least idea of what you mean; there seems to be a miracle.
>
> So be it, my son. A little tincture of enchantment is the lot of man. When he finds himself deficient in intelligence, or is too indolent to give himself the trouble to reflect, he is driven by his weakness to ascribe to a miracle, or to witchcraft, what is, most likely, nothing but the most ordinary operation of art or nature.
>
> Well, father, I will then believe in what you tell me of these rinds.
>
> That is, you will cut the matter short, by resolving to swear on the word of another; this is an excellent method for letting your own reason lie fallow. Come, come, no such idleness; let me help you to understand this amazing phenomenon. (62–3)

When Fritz disagrees with the pronouncement of his father, he is immediately told he is wrong. But instead of explaining why directly, the father takes pleasure in extending the game of "who knows why?" There is certainly an element of playfulness here in the father's behavior, an attempt to entice his son into thinking of the right questions to ask to gain the information he wants. But there is also a distinct edge of aggression against the child in this process; by continually enticing his son to make further mistakes, the father not only proves just how wrong Fritz's initial questioning of parental knowledge must be, but forces his son to performatively demonstrate the inferiority of his own knowledge.

If questioning a father's knowledge disrupts pleasure, then assuming any type of parental role towards a sibling proves even more disturbing to the narrator. The father's deepest moments of displeasure stem not from scenes in which his children misbehave, but from those scenes when a child, by criticizing one of his brothers, attempts to usurp the role of authoritative parent. For example, when Fritz objects to being teased "maliciously" by younger brother Jack, his father extends his criticism not just to the comment at hand, but to what he sees as its larger implications for his authority: "Your reflections on their faults, which, thanks be to heaven, are such as do injury to none, *give me no pleasure*; I am aware of their existence without the aid of your observations, and I beg you will leave to me the task of correcting them" (89, emphasis added).

Anxiety about the possibility of role reversal, about the parent being pushed aside and turned into the child, is felt not just by the character of the father, but also by Johann Rudolph himself. In the preface, Johann Rudolph expresses a similar anxiety about the reader's judgment of his and his father's book. Children will not read prefaces, he asserts, but *friends of children* will; he will account for the story's origin in the hopes that "In such a detail they will perhaps find motives for indulgence, if not for approbation, and will proceed to the work itself with less severity of analysis and criticism" (vii). Here Johann Rudolph fears that the text that he shaped out of his father's stories will be turned into the object of scrutiny, the "child" that the "friends of children" will turn their attention to. Just like the father narrator, Wyss does not want to be turned into the object of the gaze, one whose authority might then be questioned or doubted; instead, he wants to gain approbation, indulgence, for his text, just as for the child within it.

Yet the preface continues to express anxiety about the authority of its writer. Wyss refers to himself in the third person, as the "editor," an editor who distances himself from both his own father and the text's narrator by suggesting he does not have scientific knowledge and cannot confirm the facts in the story. Despite vouching for the author by asserting that he relied on good sources, the editor ultimately returns authority not to the text, but to the adult outside it, asking that parents and teachers who give the book to young readers correct any errors that the passage of 20 years (the time between the book's writing and its publication) may have introduced. "In reality," Wyss concludes, "it is very rarely, and perhaps never, proper that children should read by themselves; few indeed are the individuals in those tender years that are not either too indolent, too lively, or too capricious to employ themselves usefully upon this species of occupation" (xvi). Wyss's text may argue for a new level of indulgence toward children, and acknowledge the pleasure a parent may take in mischievous child behavior, but ultimately such indulgence must always occur under the watchful eyes of a parent. For children to read even a text as morally correct as *The Family Robinson Crusoe* by themselves not only makes for a potentially useless occupation, but also deprives the parent of the deeply pleasurable role of being the one in charge.

For Wyss, father and son, then, the pleasure the parent takes in observing and interacting with the child must never be allowed to threaten the patriarchal authority which structures both this text and the culture in which it was written. A father's power as a parent ultimately stems not from the emotional bonds he creates with his children, they believe, but from his position as family patriarch. Emotions that reinforce such a position (laughing at a child's lack of ability, smiling at a child's learning what the parent wishes to teach) can be comfortably incorporated, yet those that challenge it (anger that exceeds boundaries established by the father, jokes which call the father's knowledge or authority into question) must be immediately countered. Though it is Fritz who expresses the desire to emulate the Biblical patriarchs, it is truly the narrator himself who sees himself in the role; adding emotion to the depiction of the father tempers his authority only to make it all the more compelling.

Adopting the narrative role of patriarch becomes more difficult for the writers who followed in Wyss's footsteps with their own versions of the family robinsonade. For each of the novels to which I turn now were written not by a man, but by a woman. Unable to picture herself in the role of authoritarian patriarch, each writer turns to a model of parent-child relations grounded not in the power of command, but in the power of connection. For these authors, emotion, increasingly being held to be the special province of the female sex with the rise of domestic ideology in the opening decades of the nineteenth century, proves a far more compelling method for establishing reader identification, and for fostering reader emulation, than does Wyss's insistence that emotion must be held in check by authority. Yet each writer, in her own way, struggles with the same issue—how to reconcile the need for maintaining parental authority in the face of the destabilizing potential of child and parental emotion—that confronted the far less emotionally-invested Wyss.

Sentimentality and the Ordinary Child: Jeanne Sylvie Mallès de Beaulieu's *Le robinson de douze ans* (1818, 1825)

Wyss's family robinsonade proved popular not just in England, but also in France, where it was translated as *Le Robinson Suisse* by Madame de Montolieu, an established children's book author. Martin Green suggests that the novel proved particularly appealing to the French, perhaps because of the culture's "emphasis on family loyalty and family sentiment" (76). But not all French*women* were happy with Wyss's patriarchal vision of the family, and in 1818, a quite different re-imagining of Defoe's castaway story appeared for French children. Jeanne Sylvie Mallès de Beaulieu's juvenile robinsonade, *Le robinson de douze ans: histoire intéressante d'un jeune mousse français, abandonné dans une île déserte* (published in Paris in 1818, translated into English by "F.L." in 1825)[8] follows Wyss's model in constructing her child protagonist along the lines of the ordinary character as established by Wyss: a boy of a specific age, with both good and bad qualities, one with whom readers are invited to identify through engagement of their emotions and through observing the pleasure that his parents take in him. But

---

[8]   The Bibliothèque nationale de France online catalog lists 35 French language editions of Mallès de Beaulieu's novel published between 1818 and 1923, suggesting that the novel was one of the most popular titles for children in nineteenth-century France. The book was translated into German (1820), Dutch (1829), and was published in Brussels in French (1825), but surprisingly, only two British editions appear to have been in published, both in 1825. Issued under the title of *The Young Robinson*, this English-language translation was published by H. Holloway of Lambeth and H.R. Thomas of London, publishers of such little renown that they do not even appear in Philip Brown's *London Publishers and Printers c. 1800–1870*. The translation proved more popular in America, where three separate editions, each under the title *The Modern Crusoe*, were issued by different publishers (Boston's James Loring in 1827; Hartford's Silas Andrus & Son in 1855; and New York's Kiggins & Kellog in 1857). The English-language quotations used in this chapter are taken from the 1827 American edition, which appears to be a reprint of the English edition, as it includes the translator's preface by "F.L."

This translation follows the original French quite closely. As the implied translator of *The Young Robinson/The Modern Crusoe* is not, using Emer O'Sullivan's terms, an amplifying or reductive narrator, or one who drowns out the narrative voice of the source text, but rather one who mimics the implied narrator of the original, I have not added French quotations from *Le Robinson de douze ans*.

The early English-language editions contained no illustrations, but the French edition copy held by the UCLA Children's Book Collection, with a title page marked "Vingtième edition," includes "de gravures imprémées en deux couleurs."

she takes each of these four aspects of ordinary character construction in different directions than did Wyss.

While the English edition of the novel was deemed by the *Monthly Critical Gazette* as "written in the true spirit and style of the elder *Robinson*" (qtd. in Carpenter 102), it seems to follow more closely the pattern identified by Andrew O'Malley in his study of abridgments of Defoe's novel. O'Malley argues that chapbook abridgments of *Robinson Crusoe*, intended for plebian readers, focus on action and adventure, while abridgments published in book form for children emphasize the domestic aspects of the tale ("Crusoe at Home"). In particular, Mallès de Beaulieu has serious questions to raise about the gender roles of the domestic family as constructed in both Defoe's original and Wyss's recasting, questions with particular resonance when read in the context of rapidly changing laws about the family instituted during the French Revolution and the Napoleonic period. *Le robinson de douze ans* also points to connections between gender and genre by demonstrating the inability of the realistic mode to simultaneously forge parent-child connection *and* maintain parental authority.

At first blush, Mallès de Beaulieu's tale hews quite closely to the contours of *Robinson Crusoe*'s plot. After 12-year-old cabin-boy Felix, the sole survivor of his maiden voyage, arrives on his deserted island, he closely follows the model of Defoe's protagonist: he explores his domain, builds a shelter, domesticates animals, and cultivates land. He even makes a companion out of a native other. Yet the nature of his relationship with this native other, as well as the relationship Felix has with his family before he leaves for the sea, is far different from that depicted by Defoe.

In juvenile robinsonades, as in contemporary juvenile fantasy, protagonists are typically banished to a space outside of everyday reality in order to learn something, in order to grow and change, to mature. In the case of Defoe's Crusoe, as Ian Watt notes, "Defoe himself gives two main explanations for Crusoe's solitude. At times Crusoe feels he is being punished for irreligion; at others for his filial disobedience in leaving home" ("Robinson Crusoe as Myth" 313).[9] In the opening pages of the novel, Defoe emphasizes the second explanation. His "Propension of Nature" is to disobey his father:

> My Father ... had design'd me for the Law; but I would be satisfied with nothing but going to Sea, and my Inclination to this led me so strongly against the Will, nay the Commands of my Father, and against all the Entreaties and Perswasions of my Mother and other Friends, that there seem'd to be something fatal in

---

[9]   In his later *Rise of the Novel*, Watt goes on to argue that neither explanation is the true one; what is really at stake in the argument between Crusoe and his parents is a disagreement about "whether going or staying is likely to be the most advantageous course materially: both sides accept the economic argument as primary" (*Rise* 65). Although the economic argument is certainly important, as much subsequent criticism of the novel demonstrates, issues of filial duty are still certainly at play in the opening of Defoe's work.

> that Propension of Nature tending directly to the Life of Misery which was to
> befall me. (5)

Crusoe may ignore his mother's "Entreaties and Perswasions," but his real sin is
in going against both the Will and the Commands of his father. A child's resistance
to patriarchal authority, rather than a child's inability to connect to the feelings of
a parent, proves the true problem.

Defoe does bring in the potential for child/parent sympathy when he describes
Crusoe's reaction to his father's entreaties. Crusoe is "sincerely affected with this
Discourse" of his father's, and resolves to stay home; "But alas! a few Days wore
it all off," and he is soon once again dreaming of the sea (7). That there might be
potential for the child/parent bond of sympathy to be reciprocal—that a parent
might understand the emotional motivations of the child—is not even considered.
For although Crusoe is affected, at least temporarily, by the emotions of his father,
his parents are not moved by his emotional pleas. When he entreats his mother to
intervene with his father, she refuses, emphasizing that if there is any connection
through emotion to be made, it is he, not his father, who should make it: "how I
could think of any such thing after such a Discourse as I had had with my Father,
and such kind and tender Expressions as she knew my Father had us'd to me" (8).
Defoe's depiction of parent/child relations echoes that of many Protestant writers
of the late medieval period, writers who regarded the relationship of parents to
children as "mirroring that of king to subject and God to humanity. The universe
was framed on principles of rule and obedience. Children might deserve care, but
they were bound to serve, to listen, and to obey" (Orme 83).

During the opening chapter of Mallès de Beaulieu's retelling of Defoe's tale, it
appears that her protagonist, Felix, must be cured of a similar tendency as Defoe's
Crusoe: disobeying patriarchal authority. Yet, as indicated by her protagonist's
surname (Francoeur, or frank/open heart), Mallès de Beaulieu sees the real
problem as quite different than that asserted by Defoe; rather than focusing on the
child's lack of strict obedience to patriarchal authority, she emphasizes instead
the child's lack of an empathetic emotional connection with his parents.

The novel opens with the depiction of a man far different from either Defoe's
unfeeling father or Wyss's rational parson. Louis Francour, returning from war,
has a "feeling heart," one that "sighed for those tender ties, which, in honouring
the man with the title of husband and father, bestow on him, in the bosom
of a beloved family, all the happiness he is capable of enjoying in this world"
(5–6). The text immediately grants him such a family, a marriage soon followed
by the birth of a son. Such domestic relationships prove "propitious"; Francour
père was "always satisfied and joyous" and "wished that all around him should
feel pleasure," especially his wife (6). He also takes pleasure in his baby son,
holding him and lulling him to sleep with old war songs. While the pleasures
taken by Wyss's parson father in his sons are often focused on the rational, and
are curtailed when they edge into other, more dangerous areas, M. Francour's
parental pleasures focus predominantly on the emotional, indicating a shift toward

greater parental emotion and pleasure in the construction of ordinary protagonists in Mallès de Beaulieu's text.

Such a focus on a father's pleasure in family life signals a new emphasis on sentiment in the construction of the French family, an emphasis that first emerged from French Enlightenment thought during the eighteenth century. James Traer suggests that such new ideas might have remained those of a few elites if not for the French Revolution. In its goal of creating a more ideal society, the legislators of the French Directory made drastic changes to the laws governing family and marriage (16). Under the ancien régime, the father, standing in his family as the king to the State, had both legal and physical power over his wife and children. Fathers had the right to manage the property of their wives and children, and could punish them physically or by confining them without legal review (15). But, as Claudie Bernard notes, "la Révolution assaille non seulement la puissance du Roi-pére, mais celle due Pére-roi" (19). During the period of the Directory, multiple decrees were enacted that pointed to a far different construction of the family; instead of being built around an authoritative father, this new family "emphasized the role of sentiment in family life and sought for women and children greater dignity, liberty, and equality with men" (Traer 137–8). Rather than using marriage to advance a family's political or social goals, marriage increasing came to be viewed as an institution in which individuals could and should find self-fulfillment and happiness. New laws granted young men and women greater freedom in choosing a marriage partner, legalized divorce, granted all children equal rights of inheritance, lowered the age of majority for both young men and women, and created provisions for legal adoption (Traer 16–20). They also granted women greater rights in parental decision-making by abolishing the *lettre de cachet*, a document that under the ancien régime allowed a father (but not a mother) to incarcerate "rebellious" children, including those who refused to marry the people he had chosen for them, or to pursue the career he had selected for them. The creation of a family also court gave women increased rights over the supervision of their children (Traer 138). All of these laws pointed to a drastically different conception of marriage and family life than the one that had governed ancien régime ideology.

Under Napoleon, however, the Directory's view of the family, as signified by the institution of new family law, came under increasing suspicion. Divorce in particular acquired a symbolic link to the Terror and the excesses of the Republic, and the drafters of the new French civil code sought to curtail it, as well as other rights focusing on individual freedom and greater rights for wives and children within the family (Traer 167–8). While some aspects of the revolutionary construction of marriage survived in the Civil Code of 1802 and 1803, "most provisions of the code governing internal organization of the family abandoned the principle of equality or relative equality of family members for one authority. Almost every article concerned with family relationships reinforced the authority of the husband and father" (Traer 189–90). Wives were once again instructed to obey their husbands and to follow them wherever they moved; they could no longer plead in court, or govern their own property without the consent of their husbands. Divorce remained, but was now subject to restrictions that emphasized the husband's and father's rights at the expense of the wife's. And a father's (but not a mother's) right to confine recalcitrant children was reinstated (Traer 190). The family, the key to the social stability of the State, was once again under the father's rule.

Le robinson de douze ans, written shortly after the defeat of Napoleon at Waterloo, attempts to intervene in these debates about the construction of the family in post-Revolutionary France, overtly challenging gender proprieties of French society. With the reinstatement of the monarchy in 1815, Frenchwomen might anticipate an even greater restriction of rights granted them under the Directory than had occurred under Napoleon. While the new conception of the family in the Revolutionary period had not granted women the right to vote, its focus on the happiness of spouses and the importance it placed on how children were raised gave new "importance and dignity" to the roles of wife and mother within the domestic circle, granting each the right to "affection, equality, and respect" (Traer 138–9). Mallès de Beaulieu's text attempts to leverage this new respect by offering an implicit argument against a potentially more conservative return to the patriarchal, authoritarian ancien régime construction of the family.

To do so, Mallès de Beaulieu draws upon the construction of the ordinary child established by Wyss, but makes significant changes to it. Like Wyss's boy protagonists, *Le robinson de douze ans*, Felix Francoeur, is constructed along ordinary lines, with both good and bad characteristics. While "[h]is memory and capacity filled his good parents with joy," his "extreme heedlessness and giddiness" and "a quarrelsome disposition, which often procured him a beating" from his schoolmates cause his parents unease (8). Despite the opening pages' construction of father Francoeur as an affectionate husband and father, the text initially suggests that the only way to check such natural tendencies in a recalcitrant child lies in asserting ancien régime patriarchal authority: "Felix would have been a very bad boy if the fear of his father had not restrained him" (8). M. Francoeur's "wise severity," however, is "but too much counteracted by the excessive tenderness of his mother," the narrator informs us (8). Maternal "excessive tenderness" is initially denigrated, pointed to as a fault; as the novel progresses, however, its task will be both to demonstrate the fallibility of paternal authority and to recuperate emotionally-based maternal connection.

For patriarchal authority lasts only as long as a patriarch, and Mallès de Beaulieu kills off Felix's father when Felix is eight. As a result, Felix is "entirely set free … from that salutary restraint so necessary to such a disposition as his. From that time he gave himself up entirely to his love of pastime and diversion, neglected his studies, and disregarded the gentle reproofs of Susan [his mother]" (8). The new Napoleonic Civil Code might decree that "the wife owes obedience to her husband," but it could not force a child to obey his mother. Although title IX of the code, on "*Puissance paternelle*" ("Paternal Power"), asserted that children were subject to the control of both mother and father, it also decreed that a "father alone exercises this control during marriage" (French Civil Code Book I, title IX). The Code's "reassertion of paternal control," which had been limited by earlier revolutionary legislation, now included a father's right to have a child whose conduct caused "grievous dissatisfaction" arrested and confined for up to a month (Censer 147; French Civil Code Book I, title IX).

The widowed Susan Francoeur does not pursue or even appear to consider such an option when faced with her rebellious son. Rather than celebrating newly reinstituted fatherly rights, the text proceeds to hold up as central the very maternal tenderness that it initially condemned. Like Defoe's Crusoe before him, Felix develops a craving to go to sea, sneaking away from home to play in the nearby seaport, but the reaction of his parent is far different than Crusoe's: "Poor Susan, weeping and disconsolate, told her son, that he would break her heart" (9). But Felix is not yet open to understanding or empathizing with the emotional life of a parent, even to the degree that Defoe's Crusoe had; he flippantly replies "she would do well to accustom herself to these things, because that, as soon as he was old enough, he was determined to embark on board the first ship that would receive him" (9). Unlike Crusoe's parents, however, who sever their emotional connection to their rebellious son, Felix's mother insists on maintaining it, despite her son's recalcitrant behavior. Susan finds Felix another father figure, his godfather, a sea captain, who agrees to take him on board his ship. "Mr Sinval will supply the place of your father; he will watch over you, and accustom you to that subordination so necessary in every situation of life" (10), Susan asserts.

Yet submission to patriarchal authority is not at the heart of the conflict between mother and child, at least in the mind of Susan, as her speech to Felix before he departs reveals:

> My son ... you have by your conduct added a thousand poignant griefs to those already inflicted by the loss of your father. A spirit of disobedience has taken hold over your mind; you have braved the authority of your mother, and formed the resolution of abandoning her; but what would become of you if I had not been careful to make proper arrangements for you? ... My heart trembles at the many dangers you will there be exposed to; I pray Heaven to protect you, and to avert from you the punishment threatened to disobedient children. (10)

Braving the authority of a father may mean disobeying his decrees, but disobeying the authority of a mother means disregarding the bonds of emotional attachment between mother and child, "abandoning her," severing the bonds of "tenderness" that she has worked so hard to construct. By inflicting "a thousand poignant griefs," Felix disregards the feelings of his mother in favor of his own; yet a mother will never do the same—she will continue to "make proper arrangements" for her child, and will "pray to Heaven to protect" him. In refusing to resign herself to God's will, Susan presents a striking contrast to Defoe's patriarch, who "said with a Sigh, That Boy might be happy if he would stay at home, but if he goes abroad he will be the miserablest Wretch that was ever born" (8).

A reader could be forgiven for expecting that once Felix arrives on ship, the naval authority of the sea captain will reassert the necessity of a "wise but severe" patriarchal authority in curbing Felix's faults. Instead, the text once again demonstrates the limitations to which patriarchal authority is prone. Susan may have thought she was making "proper arrangements" for Felix by placing him under the protection of his godfather, but Captain Sinval doesn't share the same "wise severity" of M. Francoeur: "[Felix] was very much caressed by his godfather, whose heart he had gained by his attentions and his engaging manners. His frolics amused Mr Sinval; and when he had deserved punishment, he extricated himself by some merry conceit, and in exciting laughter he disarmed anger" (15–16). Sinval takes pleasure in a (god)child's behavior in a way similar to that of Wyss's narrator-father; yet, unlike Wyss's patriarch, Sinval does not know where to draw the line between mischief and sin, encouraging bad behavior by taking pleasure in the "merry conceit" of his charge. And so, because of his connection to the Captain, Felix gains power over the other boys on board ship, becoming a "tyrant" from whom they cannot gain redress because of the Captain's prejudices in his favor. A patriarchal vision of parental authority, as instituted in the Napoleonic Code, proves ineffective when a patriarch lacks the rationality and sense of Wyss's pastor father. The text symbolically rejects such a vision of patriarchal authority a second time when Captain Sinval is swept overboard during a fearful storm.

The same storm leads to the shipwreck that strands Felix alone on his deserted island. Intriguingly, at this key point in the text, the third person narration shifts abruptly to Felix's first person account. Such a shift aligns Felix more closely to the original Robinson, whose story unfolded through the eye of "I." Yet it also points to the inability of a first-person narrative to convey the family dynamics so important to the novel's pre-shipwreck scenes. The first-person creates a far-stronger sense of identification between reader and protagonist, a goal central to the emerging construction of the ordinary child protagonist. But in this text, such reader identification must be delayed; identifying *too* strongly with Felix's longing for the sea would make it more difficult for readers in the opening scenes to understand Susan Francoeur's point of view, an understanding vital to the text's championing of parent-child empathy. In order for readers to find Felix's lack of family feeling troubling, they need to be outside his point of view, distanced, looking at his actions from one remove. In the pre-shipwreck scenes, Felix may be able to sympathize with his mother, but he cannot yet empathize; he cannot understand the situation from the parental viewpoint. He thinks of the pleasure he will take when he returns home; his mother thinks only of the pain their separation will cause (12). The lesson of empathy, which Felix will learn during his years on a deserted island, is already being taught to the reader through the use of the third-person in the novel's opening chapters.

In shifting to the first person once Felix arrives on the island, Mallès de Beaulieu suggests that it is now important for readers to identify with her protagonist. Initially, such identification is fostered not only through the use of the first person, but also through the mode of realism. Following the Crusoe pattern, Mallès de

Beaulieu spends the first few island chapters, which cover four years in Felix's life, recounting in realistic detail how Felix builds a home, domesticates animals, and plants crops. Literary critics writing of Defoe's novel often connect such descriptions to British imperialism; in an early example, James Joyce argued that

> [t]he true symbol of British conquest is Robinson Crusoe, who, cast away on a desert island, in his pocket a knife and a pipe, becomes an architect, a carpenter, a knife grinder, an astronomer, a baker, a shipwright, a potter, a saddler, a farmer, a tailor, an umbrella-maker, and a clergyman. He is the true prototype of the British colonist, as Friday (the trusty slave who arrives on an unlucky day) is the symbol of the subject races. (24–5)

But Mallès de Beaulieu, unlike Defoe, was not writing in England during the first wave of British colonial exploration, but in France in 1818, at the end of what historians term France's first colonial empire. Before the French Revolution, the country had controlled colonies in Canada, Louisiana, the West Indies, and India, but after Napoleon's defeat in 1815, only the West Indian sugar islands and some scattered African and Asian posts remained under French control. Rather than use realistic descriptions of Felix's cultivation of the island to symbolize French colonial power or identity, as did Defoe and many nineteenth-century English writers of children's adventure novels who followed his model, Mallès de Beaulieu instead uses such descriptions to encourage readers to identify more closely with Felix than they did in the opening pages of the novel. By hearing directly of his setbacks and accomplishments, and his reactions and feelings to the same, readers are asked to change their feelings toward Felix, away from regarding him as an unreformable villain and toward sympathizing with his plight.

At this point in Defoe's narrative, when Crusoe has developed his island into a "manor," it all becomes threatened by the intrusion of the mysterious footprint, a threat that is later neutralized (or contained) by the domestication/subordination of the native Friday and the slaughter of the cannibalistic savages who attempt to sacrifice a captured European. Felix, too, once he has established himself on the island, encounters a native presence. But the purpose of this encounter is not an imperialistic one, but instead one that allows Felix, and through him the reader, to experience the very emotions that his own mother felt. During one day's exploration, Felix espies three canoes manned by copper-skinned people. Far from coming to the island to kill and eat "the inhumane feastings," as were Defoe's natives (129), these "poor creatures" are the pursued: "two enormous fishes, or rather sea monsters" overturn the last canoe and devour its two adult occupants. An object floating by the canoe evokes Felix's "ardent desire" and "my heart, which beat violently, seemed to announce some happy event" (152). For, like Felix, there is a survivor from this second natural disaster: "An infant, beautiful as the day, was sleeping tranquilly in [the basket]; its complexion was tawny, and it appeared to be about a year old" (152). Here we have the fourth aspect of ordinary character construction—parental emotion—but with a difference, one that insists that readers not just observe the parent taking pleasure in her child, but that the child character and reader feel the emotions of a parent.

For Felix's emotions, rather than his actions, are the focus of this initial meeting: "My extreme surprise may be conceived, but it is impossible to give an idea of the excess of my joy" (152). The tawny child immediately becomes not Crusoe's "my Savage," but "my child, my little boy" to Felix, who takes pleasure in it that is both physical and emotional: "the little innocent opened its eyes and smiled on me. I bestowed thousands of kisses on it" (152); "My heart danced with joy; my mind was filled with a thousand projects, all of them having reference to the child" (153); "I will love him, and he will love me; this is a happiness which I should not have dared to hope for: I shall no longer work for myself alone, and my labours will become a hundred times more interesting." (154). Unlike Crusoe, who is motivated first by the desire to "get me a Servant" and only second by the thought of "perhaps a Companion or Assistant" (158), Felix is motivated by a wish for a reciprocal relation of love: "Hitherto my hands had been employed, and my mind had not been idle, but my heart wanted some object to which it might attach itself, and I now found it, and enjoyed, in anticipation, the friendship which my dear Tommy would have for me; wholly engrossed by him, I had a right to look for that return of affection which would constitute my happiness" (159). It is almost as if Felix has learned, simultaneously with the reader, to develop emotional sympathy for another.[10]

The relationship between Felix and Tommy is not a vision of a master/servant relationship, as is the relationship between Defoe's Crusoe and Friday. Nor is it an enactment of a father/son relationship, despite Tommy's designation of Felix as "Papa." Instead, the text depicts a mother/son relationship, with Felix cast in the maternal role. Felix must care for the child as a mother: he washes him (in water that he's warmed by exposing it to the sun the day before); crafts a cradle made comfortable with skins and moss; feeds him with pap (in imitation of the women of his own country); and develops a plan for his future education. The bulk of Felix's narrative description of Tommy focuses, however, not on his or the child's actions, but rather on how the actions of the child make him, acting in the role of mother, *feel*: "all his motions appeared peculiarly graceful, and I beheld him with delight" (156); "intoxicated with my happiness ... I invented some games to amuse my dear little child and to make him laugh, which always gave me fresh delight" (157); the child is "this object of my tender affection and sweetest hope" (157–8). The level of emotional description here is in marked contrast to that displayed by

---

10   This difference between Defoe's and Mallès de Beaulieu's narratives can also be seen in the contrast between the name given to Crusoe's native, and the one given to Felix's. Crusoe writes, "I made him know his Name should be *Friday*, which was the Day I sav'd his Life; I call'd him so for the Memory of the Time; I likewise taught him to say *Master*, and then let him know that it was my name" (161). Felix gives his charge a European name (Tommy in the English translation; Tomy in the original French), and is overjoyed when the boy, after several months, begins "to stammer some words; the name of 'Papa' already struck my ear, and made my heart palpitate with joy" (161).

Fig. 1.2   "Felix thanks God for bringing him Tommy, a child to mother."
            Courtesy of the UCLA Charles E. Young Research Library
            Department of Special Collections.

Wyss's narrator father, whose emotions towards his children are always tempered by what he sees as his more important role: to teach. They are even greater than those of the emotionally invested but wisely severe M. Francour.

In fact, the emotions here are so excessive that critics may cavil that Mallès de Beaulieu's depiction of emotional tenderness on the part of a 16-year-old boy/man is unrealistic, that it is simply a fantasy. This seems to me to be precisely the point: Mallès de Beaulieu's construction of the perfect child is not one who submits to the all-knowing authority, however playfully constructed, of a patriarchal father, as in Wyss's fantasy (or a more severe one, as envisioned in the Civil Code of Napoleon), but rather one who adopts the all-loving emotion of what is constructed in this text as a maternal subjectivity. To portray such a child, the mode of realism is not adequate, Mallès de Beaulieu suggests; rejecting as too constraining the realism of Wyss's robinsonade, Mallès de Beaulieu replaces it with the heightened realism of the sentimental novel.

As Dana D. Nelson points out, one key argument emerging from recent feminist work on the sentimental tradition is that "sentimental novels can—and should—be read in terms of psychorealism" (177).[11] By embracing the mode of sentimentalism, Mallès de Beaulieu thus follows the course taken by many women writers during the eighteenth and early nineteenth centuries, writers who including elements from an earlier, feminine romance tradition even while they embraced aspects of domestic realism in an attempt to come closer to the truth of eighteenth- and early-nineteenth-century women's psychological lives. As Deborah Ross argues, including elements of both romance and realism allowed women writers to "set alternative realities side by side ... permit[ing] them to comment on each other. As a result they revealed large gaps between what women wanted, what they had a right to demand, and what they were likely to receive—especially in love and marriage" (Ross 10). If we substitute "especially in motherhood" for the final phrase in Ross's construction, we come closer to understanding the psychological and cultural work being done by Mallès de Beauleiu's text—resisting the Napoleonic Code's construction of paternalistic parenthood, and asserting the primacy of a maternal parenthood constructed on emotional connection.

We can see this resistance reflected in the depiction of Felix's parenting style. Luckily for Felix, Tommy appears to have a disposition far less troublesome than Felix's was as a child. But even so, Felix's model as a parent is not the indulgent Captain Sinval; nor is it a patriarchal authoritarianism, as laid out in the "Paternal Power" section of the Napoleonic Code. Instead, Felix takes both of his parents as role models: "I prevented all his wants, but granted nothing to his caprices.

---

[11] Nelson's observation stemmed from her review of recent feminist work on early American sentimental literature, but similar work on sympathy and sentiment in British literature of the same period, and in the Victorian period, by such scholars as Adela Pinch, David Marshall, and Audrey Jaffe suggests that the same point can apply to British works as well.

If he asked by expressive gestures for any thing which I ought to refuse him, an unripe fruit for example, or a tool by which he might be hurt, his cries or tears would not obtain it for him; convinced of their unutility, he shed them only when he was in pain; I then sought for their cause with tender solicitude, and either succeeded in relieving or in diverting them" (162). Such a pedagogical approach aligns Felix with the ideology of Rousseau, with its emphasis on learning through experience. Yet its Rousseauvian aspects are tempered by the emotions that drive Felix's actions. Felix is strict, as was his father, but does not take pleasure in asserting his power of the child, or in reveling in his greater mastery, as did Wyss's parson. Instead, his actions focus entirely on Tommy's welfare, and on caring for his charge with the "tender solicitude" characteristic of his mother's parenting. For his efforts, Mallès de Beaulieu rewards her protagonist with the son he himself should have been: "I was the object of [Tommy's] most tender attachment; he was never so happy as with me, and as soon as I called him, he quitted every amusement to run into my arms" (163).

Yet becoming a parent himself is not enough to make Felix "perfectly happy," or to earn him rescue from the island. Two years of parenting bliss pass in the span of a few sentences, until we get to the real crux of the matter. For while Felix terms his companions (child, dog, parroquet, goats) a "family," it is clear that there is one family member noticeably lacking: a mother. For while Felix may be able to mother Tommy, he cannot mother himself: "It was only the remembrance of my mother that prevented my being perfectly happy; without that, I should neither have regretted the world, nor have desired to quit my solitude" (167). Immediately, a storm blows up, ready to fulfill his wishes. Felix cannot help the floundering ship forced near his island by the storm; he hears the ship's canons, but "they were heard only by a boy, who was unable to render assistance" (168). The narrative here repositions Felix, not now a "Papa" but instead a "boy"; this shift prepares the reader for the upcoming shift in his role, from parent back again to child.

Through an unbelievably providential twist of plotting fate, a mother arrives. But not just any mother: Felix's own mother is shipwrecked on the very island that provided a safe haven for her son. In recounting the episode, Felix once again focuses on his feelings:

> At the affecting sound of this voice, I experienced the most violent emotion; it recalled to my mind a very tender remembrance. I considered attentively the features, disfigured by sorrow and fear, THEY WERE THOSE OF MY AFFECTIONATE MOTHER, the palpitations of my heart left little room for doubt. Divided between joy, grief, and compunction, I remained speechless and was near fainting. Susan perceived my paleness. 'God protect my preserver,' cried she, and starting from my arms, made me sit at the foot of the rock, and returned me those cares I had liberally bestowed on her. (171)

Emotions, pleasant, painful, and most of all, felt in the body, are at the heart of this passage. "Violent emotion" leads not to excess, as was hinted at in the reproachful characterization of Susan's emotional indulgence at the opening of the novel, but rather to "tender remembrance," a vision of an "affectionate mother"—violent emotion tamed by love of the maternal. While it might be tempting to read Felix's "near fainting" as a negative sign of feminization, or perhaps infantilization, the ending of this passage asks us to move beyond viewing emotion as feminine weakness; instead, emotion here leads to connection, to reciprocal care: Susan "returned to me those cares I had liberally bestowed on her." Becoming a parent and bestowing care is not enough to reform Felix, suggests this text; a true parent-child relationship is one in which the care, and the pleasures such care can give, are mutual.

As Adela Pinch notes in her work on the epistemology of emotion, the late-eighteenth and early-nineteenth centuries are often thought of as a period when people "increasingly learned to claim their emotions as the guarantors of their individuality." Yet Pinch's analysis also reveals "a concomitant tendency to characterize feelings as transpersonal, as autonomous entities that do not always belong to individuals but rather wander extravagantly from one person to another" (3). For Mallès de Beaulieu, this "extravagant wandering" appears to be the desired goal, a goal to be fostered through the experience of parenting. Felix's feelings for Tommy pass magically to his mother: "she pressed the poor child to her heart, and I saw that she participated in all the sentiments with which he had inspired me" (175). Holding the baby, Susan feels what Felix feels; by reading about the baby, and Felix's feelings towards him, readers are likewise invited to open their arms to extravagantly wandering parental emotion.

The remainder of Mallès de Beaulieu's text appears to endorse a vision of the parent-child relationship as one of mutuality, of parental empathy for the child, and child empathy for the parent. And yet, because the narrative point of view remains Felix's, in the first person, readers have far more access to Felix's feelings for his mother than Susan's for her son. During Felix's time with Susan on the island, Mallès de Beaulieu emphasizes the need for Felix not simply to sympathize with, but to empathize with the emotions of his mother.[12] In another strange inversion of the child/parent roles, Felix (and through him, the reader) frequently plays the role of observer of his own mother/child during their time together on the island, a role that not only gave great pleasure to, but also threatened the authority of Wyss's patriarchal narrator. But for Mallès de Beaulieu, such pleasure is comforting, not anxiety-provoking: "I frequently left my cookery to enjoy the pleasure of looking on her during her slumber; the refreshment of sleep had spread over her cheek a rosy tint; her features regained their sweetness, and I contemplated with delight the beloved countenance of my mother, nearly such as I had seen it formerly" (172–3).

---

[12]   David Marshall points out that during the period "sympathy" encompassed the meanings we currently associate with both "sympathy" and "empathy" (*Surprising*, 3). I use both terms because our current sense of the difference between them—sympathy as the sharing of another's feelings, empathy as a heightened form of sympathy, one which suggests an additional sense of identification with and understanding of the other—is important to my argument.

Looking upon his mother as a mother would upon her infant in a cradle, Felix's observation places him not in the role of patriarchal authority but of maternal caregiver. Mallès de Beaulieu's texts offers the deepest kind of wish fulfillment for a mother reading this story to her child: the fantasy that her child truly loves her in the same way, to the same degree, that she loves that child.

Felix also merges with his mother by recounting to us the story of how she came to be on the island. "I shall here take up the recital of Susan, and in nearly the same words she herself made use of; the lively interest I took in it engraved it deeply in my memory," he informs the reader (178). The story unfolds in quotations, as if Susan were telling it herself, but her words are written by Felix; writing his mother's story in the first person, Felix once again crosses the boundary between parent and child. His mother's experience is "engraved … deeply in his memory," but transformed, made his own, for the words are not exactly hers, only "nearly the same." Once again, Mallès de Beaulieu indulges in a fantasy of a child living the emotional life of a parent: in her tale, the Lockean "blank slate" of the child is not engraved with moral or factual instruction, but with the emotions of a parent. For the story that "Susan" tells is one of emotions, rather than just actions: "weeping," "grief," "shock," "my unhappy existence," "extreme agitation," "excessive debility," "anguish," "haunted" are the words and phrases she uses to describe her situation after Felix's departure. In ventriloquizing his mother, emotions that once belonged to her are again experienced by Felix, and through him, by the reader. Mallès de Beaulieu calls on emotion as the means by which her readers can identify not only with Felix, but, like Felix himself, to identify with his mother.[13]

In only one respect does Felix not share all with his mother. Felix may have immediately recognized Susan after her arrival on the island, but Susan cannot trace the outlines of her 12-year-old son in the now manly adolescent before her. Felix, fearing "it would have been dangerous to make myself known to my mother, in her present weak state; she would have been unable to support the excess of joy this discovery would have occasioned," keeps his identity a secret (171). Despite the imperative to connect, some emotions are too risky to share, the text suggests. Simultaneously, however, protecting his mother from the dangers of emotion allows Felix (and the reader) to experience another pleasurable emotion: knowing

---

[13]   In his analysis of eighteenth-century French theorist Abbé Du Bos, David Marshall casts doubt on the idea that eighteenth-century readers believed that the suffering of fictional characters could move the reader to the same extent that real-life suffering does. Du Bos suggests that when readers confront an artistic representation of suffering, they are moved, but not truly afflicted, for the awareness of the illusion of art contains the emotion of the spectator (in this case the reader) (20–3). Catherine Gallagher suggests the opposite is true in her analysis of Hume's *Treatise of Human Nature*: "Because they were conjectural, suppositional identities *belonging* to no one, they could be universally appropriated. A story about nobody was nobody's story and hence could be entered, occupied, identified with by anybody" (168). My analysis of reader identification in Mallès de Beaulieu aligns more closely with Gallagher's than with Marshall's reading.

a delicious emotional secret. "In the midst of the enjoyments I had procured for my mother, sighs often escaped her bosom: she thought of her dear Felix; he was near her, and she knew him not" (176). If Felix were to empathize completely with his mother's grief, he would only wish to assuage it; but here sympathy rather than empathy is at play. Sympathizing, rather than empathizing, with his mother's grief, Felix (and the reader) can derive pleasure from it, for sympathy allows for a subject and an object, rather than the merging of the two demanded by empathy. Only when emotion goes too far—Susan faints on her son's 18th birthday—must the pleasures of sympathetic anticipation be given up, and Felix's true identity revealed. The pleasure of anticipation can only be enjoyed when the object of it is not in danger; as soon as that line is crossed, then the anticipation must be given over, and replaced by connection: "The excess of joy suspended all the faculties of the tender Susan; she leaned her head on my bosom, and a flood of tears relieved her heart" (195).

Once all impediments to the emotional union of Felix and his mother are removed, the novel can conclude. Five pages after he reveals his true identity to his mother, Felix informs the reader that "Providence had … determined to restore us to the society of our fellow creatures, and was even then preparing our deliverance" (200); deliverance follows in the next (final) chapter. The novel itself ends with a description of the virtuous life Felix, his mother, and Tommy adopt once they return to France (charity, economy, contentment with their station in life), and a list of improving admonishments to the youthful reader, echoing many a moral tale of the era. But it is clear that the text's primary message lies in the first characteristic of their home: "enjoying domestic tranquility, we make all who surround us partake of our happiness" (216). The real moral of the story is the need to overturn the older model of parent-child relationship that the new Napoleonic Code hearkens back to, and that the reestablishment of the monarchy threatens to reinstate: one built on authority and obedience to a father. Instead, *le Robinson de douze ans* urges that such a construction be replaced by one that emphasizes emotional connection between parent and child, in particular the emotional connection of a mother and a son. In Mallès de Beaulieu's formulation, the child must not just observe, but more importantly, must empathize, must *feel* the same emotions that his parent does. By breaking down the boundaries between parent and child, by demanding that the child partake of the emotional pleasures of the parent, Mallès de Beaulieu points to the possibility that such empathy can extend beyond the boundaries of the family, to encompass "all who surround us."

To say that the novel's conclusion is improbable is an understatement. But rather than read this improbability as a fault, we would do better to consider its ideological implications. Deborah Ross suggests that improbable endings to women's novels were not signs of their authors' lack of skill, but rather a sign of their works' social critique: "It was only by trying to make happy endings believable within the confines of realism that the injustices of life could be exposed. To be truly useful to women, the romance ending had to look like the anomaly it was. This exposure could ultimately help reveal where society was falling short of its own proclaimed ideals" (Ross 164). The too-happy-to-be-believed ending of Mallès de Beaulieu's robinsonade, I would suggest, points to the shortcomings of post-Revolutionary France's construction of motherhood.

But while *Le Robinson de douze ans* protests the marginalization of emotionally-invested motherhood, it also suggests the limitations of such a model in the quest to construct a new model of literary child subjectivity. Such an all-encompassing bond between parent and child may be deeply appealing both to the mothers reading Mallès de Beaulieu's novel aloud, and to the children to whom they read. Yet by refusing to acknowledge that important differences may exist between parental and child desires, by collapsing the boundaries between parent and child, by "making" others, including the young reader, identify with and partake of maternal happiness, Mallès de Beaulieu limits the agency granted to the child both within and outside the book. The desire of the child to maintain some distance between himself and his mother arises in Felix's suppression of his true identity; such desire itself is in turn repressed by the text's insistence that all-subsuming empathy of the child for the parent is the only way to allow emotions into the parent-child relationship in texts for children without endangering the adult authority such texts imply by their very existence.

In Wyss and Mallès de Beaulieu, then, British authors who would adapt the family robinsonade for English audiences inherited two vastly different models for reconciling emotion and authority. In their later robinsonades, both Barbara Hofland and Ann Fraser Tytler would struggle with the same anxieties about emotion, agency, and authority that characterized the works of Wyss and Mallès de Beaulieu. But instead of deciding the matter all in favor of patriarchal authority, or of maternal connection, as did Wyss and Mallès de Beaulieu, both Hofland and Tytler choreograph an intricate dance between the two poles of this apparently binary opposition.

The Rise of Emotion in British Children's Literature

Although both *The Family Robinson Crusoe* and *The Modern Crusoe* were popular in England during the opening decades of the nineteenth century, neither was written by a British author. The emotional content that plays such a prominent role in each would take a little longer to make its first appearances in English-authored robinsonades for children. M. Nancy Cutt suggests that emotion first arises in British children's literature in tracts penned by Evangelical Christians in the opening decades of the nineteenth century. These books replaced the "Rule of Reason" common in eighteenth-century children's books with the "Rule of Religion" (*Ministering* 18). Before the rise of Evangelicalism, emotion in religion was typically viewed negatively, as "enthusiasm, that feeling of God within the mind feared since the English Civil War for empowering idiosyncratic, antisocial, and antiauthoritarian persons" (Morillo 5). The "enthusiasm" of the participants in the French Revolution only strengthened the connotation of emotion that threatened the stability of both governments and individuals (Mee 1–19). Given early juvenile literature's focus on creating moral, social adults out of what some might view as idiosyncratic, antisocial, and antiauthoritarian children, it is hardly surprising that its authors wished to avoid anything that smacked of potential disruption of the social order.

The delay might also stem from the less enthusiastic embrace of English educators of the doctrines of Rousseau when compared to continental educational reformers. Though some English educational theorists and writers for children, such as Maria Edgeworth and Thomas Day, adopted aspects of Rousseau's ideas, European educators such as Armand Berquin, Mme d'Épinay, and Mme de Genlis proved more open to Rousseau than were many of their English counterparts. The citation of Rousseau by pedagogues and deputies of the post-Revolutionary French government also very likely gave reactionary Englishmen and women pause (Bloch 1), as did the religious beliefs of other continental educators. For example, German educational reformer Johann Basedow's urging that denominationally-based religious instruction be replaced by the teaching of a universal natural morality drew the ire of the influential English children's book writer Sarah Trimmer, who denounced attempts to institute universal education based on undenominational, rather than Church of England doctrine ("Mrs Trimmer"). Early nineteenth-century educational debates, Alan Richardson argues, focused more on social aims than on pedagogical reform. Andrew Bell and Joseph Lancaster each promoted a monitorial system of universal education, a system that advocated the principles and discipline of factory production to instruction and classroom behavior. Such enterprises focused as much on inculcating "industrious" habits and moral behavior in working class pupils than in providing them with a rudimentary education (*Literature* 87–100). The affection, warmth, and pleasure characterizing Swiss and German pedagogical reform plans took far longer to seep into such an inhospitable climate.

Sentiment first makes an entrance into British children's literature via pathos, Cutt suggests, in particular through Evangelical revision of the juvenile martyr tale. In their earliest manifestations (as James Janeway's *A Token for Children* 1671 and 1672), martyr tales for the young featured faceless, emblematic children as role models. But in the hands of Evangelical authors, such characters "came to life": before their early deaths, they were depicted living interesting, and Cutt suggests, "realistic" lives (*Ministering* 19–20). Reading novels by Evangelical writers such as Lucy Cameron (*The History of Margaret Whyte*, 1799) and Mary Martha Sherwood (*The History of Little Henry and his Bearer*, 1814), one might want to qualify Cutt's claim to "realism" in the depiction of these child characters, or at least differentiate them from the "ordinary" character construction I discuss here. Readers may hear more detail about Margaret and Henry's lives than they would have seen in earlier tract literature, but the characters of Margaret and Henry are no less exemplary than their tract protagonist predecessors. What is really different about these Evangelical characters is the way readers are asked to feel for them as they die. Evoking pathos in their readers, such novels first make their readers feel for the characters in their stories, in the hopes that they then will act like them by becoming more religiously devout. Though Cutt does not state this explicitly, this shift seems to suggest that Evangelical authors were thinking along the same lines as Wyss and Edgeworth: that child readers would be more likely to want to model their behavior after a character's if an author could bring readers to respond emotionally to said character, rather than relying solely on a rationally-constructed model of exemplarity.

Once English Evangelical writers of the first two decades of the nineteenth century had recuperated pathos for the cause of religion, English writers of fiction for children felt freer to incorporate other types of emotion into their non-Evangelical texts. Cutt points to the 1820s as the period when "the expression of emotion by the young was coming into favour" in British novels for children (*Ministering* 23).[14] But this increase in emotion did not signal a new, unproblematic emancipation of the child from didactic exemplarity. Rather, as in Wyss and Mallès de Beaulieu, it represented a newfound belief by British authors that ordinary characters—characters of a specific age, with individualized good and bad characteristics, negative and positive emotions, and parents who took pleasure in them—would better serve the goal of inspiring emulation in readers than would idealized ones. By showing protagonists' emotions, and, perhaps even more powerfully, by showing parents' feelings towards their fictional children, juvenile authors of the period hoped to create a stronger sense of identification between their readers and their characters, an identification that would in turn create even more powerfully, rather than free readers from, the exemplarity imperative.

We can see both the heightened level of emotion, and the way such emotion functions to promote exemplarity, in two popular juvenile family robinsonades written by British authors from this period: Barbara Hofland's *The Young Crusoe, or the Shipwrecked Boy* (1829) and Ann Fraser Tytler's *Leila: or, The Island* (1839). Hofland has received surprisingly little critical attention for an author who was second only to Walter Scott in the number of novels she published during the period 1800–1829 (Garside 42). Tytler, thought not as productive as Hofland, almost equaled her in popularity with her three novels about her young shipwrecked protagonist, Leila. Both novelists created their own versions of the robinsonade; in them, both, like Wyss before them, strive to construct "ordinary" child characters, characters that experience both positive and negative emotions. But they both reject the authoritarian patriarchal model that characterizes Wyss's narrator, working instead to forge a model of parent-child connection similar to

---

[14]   Intriguingly, in the one example that she cites to support this trend, Grace Kennedy's *Anna Ross* (1823), Cutt focuses not only on protagonist Anna's emotions, but also on the emotions of the adults who surround her: "Those who are genuinely concerned about her give vent to emotion: kindly Uncle Ross, angry that she will not remain in his household; her jubilant country cousins; her tearful, affectionate Aunt Mary" (24). Once again, the granting of emotional subjectivity to child characters is deeply enmeshed with the granting of emotions to the parents or adults who care for them.

that found in Mallès de Beaulieu's highly sentimental text. That both take a father, rather than a mother, as their parent figure points to the different construction of fatherhood in early nineteenth century England than the one reemerging during the same period in France. It also suggests that British authors wished to extend what in Mallès de Beaulieu seemed a particularly maternal emotion into the realm of the fatherly. Yet such an extension proves far more fraught, as both Hofland and Tytler write in a mode far more closely aligned to the realism of Wyss and Defoe than the sentimentalism of Mallès de Beaulieu.

Once could argue, in fact, that the emotion used to humanize the fathers in these texts works to impose their authority over their children all the more firmly. Richard Brodhead's theory of "disciplinary intimacy" is apt in this regard. Drawing on Foucault, Brodhead argues that the emergence of emotion as a key component of parent-child relationships in the popular literature of America in the 1830s and 1840s is part of a broader shift away from an older disciplinary model of social regulation, one focused on public displays of corporal punishment. In the new model, which Brodhead links to the emergence of an American middle-class, socialization takes place not through bodily punishment, but through emotional disciplining: by personalizing disciplinary authority and sentimentalizing the disciplinary relationship, by "enmeshing the child in strong bonds of love," this new type of authority forces its subjects to internalize its "imperatives and norms" (20). Many British parents of the same period still relied on physical punishment, particularly of boys, assuming that "firm correction was a sign of their love for their children and certainly not abusive" (Frost 25). Yet a shift toward emotional discipline also begins to make its appearance in genteel British households during the early years of the Victorian period, a discipline focused on the emotions of love and guilt rather than the pain of physical blows (Frost 26).

Brodhead, like many critics who draw on Foucault, acknowledges that these new forms of discipline may present new types of freedom to the subjects they are meant to control. Yet, also like many Foucauldians, Brodhead mentions such freedoms in an aside, preferring instead to focus on the hegemonic force of this new discourse of disciplinary intimacy. Yet each new move to discipline a subject unintentionally opens up new avenues of resistance, avenues that are equally important to trace and analyze.

Hofland and Tytler deploy the mode of literary realism to create emotionally involved parents, and thus to align their child protagonists (and child readers) with parental values and norms. But by deploying dialogue to construct child protagonists, rather than relying solely on narrators as did earlier juvenile fiction, literary realism opened up a space for child agency by allowing child protagonists to talk. Emotionally-connected parents may have more power over their children, but as these texts inadvertently demonstrate, their children also have more power over them. Brodhead notes that the "tutelary seraphs" of popular American domestic fiction "become, in theory at least, unlimitedly controlling" (21). "In theory" is key here: for the theory itself proposes a totalizing force not borne up by these texts. Seldom as totalizing as it would imagine itself to be, such a drive to control may be more reflective of an adult fantasy of wish-fulfillment than of any parent-child relationship in practice, real or literary.

Emotion and the Child's Voice: Barbara Hofland's *The Young Crusoe* (1829)

"Dear papa," said little Charles Crusoe to his father, one morning, "do you think that our family is any way related to the famous Robinson Crusoe?"

—Barbara Hofland, *The Young Crusoe*[15]

From the very opening of Barbara Hofland's juvenile robinsonade,[16] readers immediately know that they are in far different territory than in Defoe, Wyss, or Mallès de Beaulieu. Hofland's text includes all four of the characteristics central to "ordinary" character construction: we know the age of young Charles, our protagonist (10 at the beginning of the tale; 14 by its end); we hear of his good and bad character traits; we come to identify with him by witnessing his emotions; and we watch his parents take emotional pleasure in him. Yet the ways in which Hofland implements these four characteristics proves quite different from those of Wyss and Mallès de Beaulieu. Instead of the first person adult narration of Defoe and Wyss, or the shifting narration of Mallès de Beaulieu, we are firmly in the third person common to earlier eighteenth-century juvenile moral fiction. Yet it is a third person different than that found in earlier moral tales: instead of opening with a narrated family history, or a value-laden description of its main character,

---

[15] Page 1.

[16] Hofland, one of the most popular authors of juvenile literature in the opening decades of the nineteenth century, published primarily with John Harris and A.K. Newman, although the prolific author had relationships with other major London publishers such as Vernor and Hood and Longmans. Anthony King Newman, a former apprentice of William Lane, the founder of the Minvera Press, became Lane's partner and then took over the press after Lane's death in 1814. Though Minerva was known primarily for its Gothic romance novels, the Press also issued occasional books for young readers. Newman dropped the Minerva Press name during the 1820s, and continued to be Hofland's main publisher of juvenile fiction well into the 1830s.

The Newman edition contains only a frontispiece, designed by E. Burney and engraved by Samuel Springsguth, depicting Mr Crusoe's native servant discovering Charles; the choice of such a scene suggests that Newman hoped to evoke the original Robinson Crusoe story rather than to accurately depict the rather more domestic and emotional tale Hofland actually wrote. Newman's illustration decision seems to have worked: with WORLDCAT listings of 13 editions published by Newman and other, later publishers, *The Young Crusoe* appears to be one of the strongest-selling titles of this popular early Victorian author. Dennis Butts reports that although there are no available records of the size of Newman's printings, initial editions of between 1000 and 2000 copies (the size of the initial printings of Hofland's children's books with Longman) are likely, with reprints in the 250-copy range. The illustration reprinted in this volume is from the title page of the 1833 Harper edition.

Hofland's novel opens with dialogue, and cedes the first words of her novel to her child protagonist.[17]

In relying primarily on dialogue to introduce her main characters during the opening chapters of the novel, Hofland situates her story not in the realm of Mallès de Beaulieu's heightened sentimentality, but in the realm of the mimetic domestic tale pioneered by Maria Edgeworth in the 1790s, the mimetic form that Wyss would emulate. But ordinary character construction takes a different form in Hofland's text than it did in Wyss's. In *The Family Robinson Crusoe*, the most common emotion used to make the child characters seem ordinary is anger or frustration. The four boys constantly chafe at one another, grow jealous of the others' achievements, or express scorn for the others' efforts or ideas. In contrast, Hofland's Charles becomes ordinary for us not through the childishness of his anger, but through the warmth of his connection to his father. While Hofland's use of dialogue clearly reflects the influence of Maria Edgeworth, the popular author of moral tales during the turn of the century often credited with introducing more lifelike child dialogue to juvenile literature, Edgeworth's focus on rational exchange between parent and child is tempered in Hofland by the addition of love. "Dear papa" are the first words we read; such words of endearment are used often throughout the novel not only by Charles when referring to his father, but also by Mr Crusoe when referring to his son. So great is Mr Crusoe's attachment to Charles, that, despite his rational desire to give his son the benefit of an English education, he allows his emotional desires to take precedence: he "could not at this period bring himself to part with the only comfort which remained to him" and keeps Charles with him in India while his mother and sister return home (6). The emotional connection so lacking between Mallès de Beaulieu's Felix and his mother is not at issue here; Charles and his "dear father" come to life through Hofland's portrayal of their emotional bond of affection. The work that Mallès de Beaulieu's text struggled so hard to complete—to foster a bond of emotional connection between parent and child—is now taken for granted in Hofland's construction of the ordinary child.

Yet while dialogue functions to display performatively the affection between parent and child, it also opens up the potential for disruption of the parent-child hierarchy of authority. Despite Mr Crusoe's response to Charles's question, a long disquisition on the reasons why *Robinson Crusoe* the novel is not "real," Charles cannot bring himself to disregard the "love" and "admiration" that led him to desire a familial connection with Defoe's shipwrecked sailor. He politely, but firmly, informs his father of his decision: "I am much obliged to you for telling me

---

[17]   In "Reading Rosamund Reading," Mitzi Myers suggests that Maria Edgeworth was the first British writer for children to create child protagonists "who speak in a juvenile voice" (60). While the dialogue in Edgeworth's tales certain served as a model for Hofland, Edgeworth rarely gives the first, or the last, word to her child protagonists ("The Purple Jar" being an intriguing exception); nor do they speak to their parents with anywhere near the freedom that Hofland's main character does.

all this, papa; but if you won't think me too childish, I shall choose to believe it all true, the same as I used to. I love Robinson Crusoe dearly" (3). A commitment to portraying the ordinary child through dialogue means including those moments when children resist parental teaching.

Hofland, like Wyss, is concerned to contain child agency when it conflicts with parental authority. But the method that Hofland's parents use to deal with child resistance is much less coercive than that of Wyss's narrator—the Crusoe parents never ridicule childish decisions or thoughts, or ask question after question until their child is backed into a corner. Instead, Mrs Crusoe smiles at Charles's "enthusiasm" for Robinson Crusoe, and responds to it in a way that suits her own purpose, telling him that "he would never do for a Robinson Crusoe" whenever he shirks work, exercise, or relies on the servants to do things for him that he should be doing himself (5). Emotion, here in the form of "enthusiasm," is not to be "repressed"; instead, the "sensible and affectionate" parent will first react with pleasure to it, then employ logic to turn it to "a good account" (5). Such parenting methods suggest a shift toward the "disciplinary intimacy" identified by Brodhead. They also reflect, and participate in the project of constructing, a model of discipline that eschewed routine beatings, one focused instead on "bending and moulding" the child. During the nineteenth century, such a model would eventually displace the authoritarian model of discipline typically employed by English fathers before the eighteenth century. John Tosh argues that this new model, based on "influence" rather than "authority," "required not decisive intervention, such as fathers had traditionally supplied, but the application of carefully graded emotional pressures, subtly attuned to the character of each child." Such moral suasion was "widely assumed to be beyond the capacities of a working father" such as Mr Crusoe, and were best assumed by a woman ("Authority" 52; *Man's Place* 91). Here, Hofland challenges such gender proprieties by assuring readers that such emotionally-attuned parenting belongs not just to the realm of a mother, but also to that of a father.

What most interests me about this passage, however, more than the adult Crusoes' parenting technique, is how readers come to know of it. Hofland does not only perform her pedagogy, by showing her parents turning Charles's emotions to good account, as is common in Maria Edgeworth tales; instead, her omniscient narrator grants her child reader access to the thoughts of her adult characters. In Mallès de Beaulieu, we are told by the narrator of the mother Susan's thoughts and feelings; in Hofland, by contrast, readers are granted access to the interiority of Mrs Crusoe. Such access is brief, but comes at particularly significant moments in the text. Most of the narration in this text is focalized through Charles's point of view. But every so often, passages like the one above intrude, passages in which we see the thought processes of adults, most often of Charles's father. What are the implications of such narrative interruptions for the young reader? Instead of working to make a reader identify with the child protagonist—one of the goals of ordinary exemplarity—such asides instead pull readers away from identification with the child, aligning the reader instead with the parent. In fact, what is happening here on a formal level is parallel to the ideological work being performed by the text as a whole: to demand that Charles within the text, and the young reader outside the text, forge a connection to the parent, and through that connection, to the parental point of view.

In Wyss, as in Edgeworth, such a connection is typically forged primarily through rationality: once parents explain, and the child understands their reasoning (either by accepting the authority of the parent, as in Wyss, or experimenting to test the logic, as in Edgeworth), the child then learns to align him or herself with the parental point of view. But for Hofland, like Mallès de Beaulieu, rationality is not enough: connection can be ensured only by combining rational understanding with emotion. We can see this at work in the following two passages, each of which grant the reader access not only to Mr Crusoe's rational thoughts, but also to his emotions:

> Mr Crusoe, aware that young minds cannot be long exercised on any painful subject, without injury to those energies necessary for their health and activity, urged the boys to prepare some food, and spoke with a cheerfulness he was far from feeling, but which had soon the happiest effect on his young companions. (28)

> Mr Crusoe felt his heart sink, as he perceived the impossibility (even if they could make a boat of sufficient magnitude to put out to sea) of launching it from such a shore. He yet thought, if ever they were so happy as to attain this power, it must be from this spot that they should go, and he examined it with great anxiety, from this consideration. (29–30)

In both of these passages, the reader is asked to switch allegiances for the moment, identifying not with Charles but with his father. In the first passage, such a switch asks young readers to take Mr Crusoe as a model for behavior, to speak with a cheerfulness they are far from feeling whenever they may be faced with adversity. In the second, readers are asked to feel with Mr Crusoe, to sympathize with his sinking heart and his anxiety; such shared feelings bind the reader, like Charles, more closely to this adult moral guide. Emotional identification leads to emulation, to valuing the adult point of view, here for the reader, and in the text for Charles.

Yet allowing young readers to see not only the rational thoughts, but also the emotions, of the adult authority figure within the text may have unintended consequences, particularly if the reader refuses the invitation to identify with the adult. What happens if, while reading the above passages, a reader identifies with Charles, rather than with Mr Crusoe? In the second passage, readers become aware of the fallibility of the adult; the father who once appeared to have all the answers, who could guide his son rationally and reasonably out of any predicament, shares the same anxiety, the same fears, as the child he is supposed to teach. His authority, no longer omnipotent, becomes open to suspicion. In the first passage, readers can be left with the startling realization that not all the emotions parents express reflect what they feel inside. Charles may be innocent of the knowledge that his father can manipulate him by feigning feelings, but after reading this passage, the innocence of the child reader can no longer be guaranteed. Depicting the emotions of a parent from the inside, then, does not only bind the child (within and outside the text) more closely to that parent; it also contains the potential to distance the child from the parent, by undercutting parental omnipotence.

Hofland, then, must make her readers forget the potential for destabilizing hierarchies that access to parental emotions creates. To do this, she ratchets up the emotional intensity of her story: first, by shipwrecking Charles and his father; then, by mysteriously spiriting Mr Crusoe away, so that Charles is left on the island alone. Mallès de Beaulieu taught emotional connection by emphasizing pleasure: after Felix tastes the joy and delight of parenting his young charge Tommy, he can then understand and forge a connection with his own mother. But Hofland suggests that the better teacher is sorrow. When Charles discovers that his father is gone,

> The sorrow, the very agony of Charles, now knew no bounds. He had lost his father, who was to him his whole world: his desolation and misery was beyond any thing that we can conceive a child to suffer—there is not one of my young readers that could have forborne to cry, if they had seen him thrown on the ground, weeping and wailing for very anguish: he was weak and ill, and had no one to nurse and comfort him; he loved his father with the tenderest affection, and he was torn from him, he knew not how; no human being was left on this desolate island, save him now perishing in the cold grave: his situation was desperate and hopeless, beyond all other situations of misfortune and wretchedness. (46–7)

That the narrator here steps back into a rare direct address to the reader ("there is not one of my young readers that could have forborne to cry") highlights the importance of emotion in this passage: instead of being asked to condemn Charles for giving in to his feelings, readers are instead invited to share in his suffering, to feel the pain of a connection to a father severed. That such a separation is "beyond all other situations of misfortune and wretchedness" indicates the stakes of the parent-child connection for Hofland. Forcing both Charles, and through him, the reader, to suffer the loss of a loving father, Hofland overwhelms doubt with loss. Fears of breaking the parental bond overcome any doubt about its efficacy or worth.

Of course, suffering functions not only to connect child to parent; echoing the suffering of Christ, it invokes a spiritual dimension. Susan Naramore Maher is certainly right to read the novel as a Christian allegory: "Hofland constantly reminds us of the thin line dividing life and death, salvation and damnation. Life on a desert island emblematically dramatizes all human life, from childhood on; we are all assailed, she suggests, we are all stranded, unless we accept the shelter of Christian principles" (153). On the level of overt author intention, it seems clear that for Hofland, what Charles' abandonment is meant to teach him is how to grow stronger in Christian faith. During his seven months on the island, there is little that is pleasurable for Charles. Instead, he is beset by physical crises, crises that inevitably lead to spiritual crises. He is petrified by an enormous fish, threatened by a nest of snakes, and nearly burns to death when the door of his cave catches fire during the night. Each peril leads him initially to despair:

God has abandoned him. But each then leads to greater faith, a new resolve to trust in God.

Yet something else of interest happens during these testing scenes: Charles doubts not only his spiritual father, but also his earthly father. In each episode, his setbacks lead him to think that perhaps Mr Crusoe really did abandon him on purpose. But each ends with Charles's rejecting such a thought and instead imagining new scenarios to explain his father's disappearance: he's been captured by pirates; he's drowned; he was pulled out to sea and rescued by a ship that couldn't turn back. Despite any potential evidence to the contrary, the text continually insists that Charles must have faith in his father, must repress any doubts he may have about him.

Hofland's novel thus addresses anxieties about the shifting role of fathers in early Victorian England. As John Tosh notes, since the Reformation, English fathers had been responsible for supervision of the spiritual and moral welfare of all household members, including children; mothers, because of their lesser virtue as females, played a supporting but secondary role. But the rise of sensibility in the late eighteenth century led to a shift in the British understanding of gender, one which concurrently influenced the construction of fatherhood and motherhood. During this period, a new vogue for interpreting male and female behavior in terms of the nervous system rather than the older Galenic humours model arose. While humoural biology viewed men and women as different in degree (with women as markedly inferior), it saw them as the same in kind. In contrast, the new nervous system model viewed women as fundamentally different from, rather than simply inferior to, men. In particular, the new system suggested that females had finer sensibilities than males, an attribute that allowed women to read and understand the feelings of others more easily than could men. This difference in ability soon suggested a difference in moral influence, with women, not men, newly cast in the role of moral guide (*Man's Place* 43–4).

In Mallès de Beaulieu's earlier robinsonade, the challenge to gender proprieties lay in the text's championing of motherhood and its rights. But in Hofland's texts, such a challenge stems from the novel's championing of emotional fatherhood. For by the 1830s, the rise of the moral stature of women, and particularly of mothers, had led to a concurrent decrease in the stature of fathers in England. As Tosh notes, "The elevation of the Angel Mother cut the moral pretensions of men in the home down to size, and their significance as parents was correspondingly diminished" (*Man's Place* 47). By the Victorian period, Claudia Nelson suggests, most fathers played "the part of a concerned onlooker" where their babies and young children were concerned, with their major familial responsibility seen as provider rather than moral or spiritual guide (*Family Ties* 46–7). Colin Heywood suggests that the Victorian father became a "second parent" (106), a view with which Hugh Cunningham concurs: by the 1830s, "fathers were relegated to a subordinate position" when it came to childrearing (*Children and Childhood* 69) (54). Hofland's text, written in the decade before the consolidation of this gendered domestic ideology, thus attempts to mediate cultural anxieties

Gimber del.et sculp

Fig. 1.3   "Charles and Mr Crusoe give thanks to God for reuniting father and son." Courtesy of the author.

about English fatherhood in a period when the role of father was just beginning to be eclipsed by that of mother.[18]

The unusual structure of Hofland's robinsonade reflects the text's investment in challenging consolidating constructions of nonemotional fatherhood. Unlike most robinsonades, Hofland's does not build to the climax of a final rescue. In fact, more than a third of the novel takes place *after* Charles leaves the island, and focuses not on Charles's story, but on the story of Mr Crusoe and his struggles to find his son after being rescued, delirious with illness, by Dutch seamen. Maher interprets this formal feature allegorically, suggesting that Charles's rescue "equates with

---

[18]   Hofland experienced anxieties about fatherhood firsthand: her own father died when she was a baby; her first husband died only four months after the birth of their second child; and her second husband gave her no children but fathered a son out of wedlock whom Hofland raised as her own (Butts, *Mistress* 2–4). Recuperating a personal vision of positive fatherhood, as well as a newly-imperiled cultural construction of fatherhood, can both be considered goals of Hofland's text.

spiritual deliverance for both father and son"; Mr Crusoe's refusal to listen to those who would persuade him to give up his quest make him an emblem of God the Father refusing to forsake Christ, his son" (Maher 154). Yet to read the novel's shift to the point of view of the parent only allegorically is to miss the way Mr Crusoe's story functions to deny the growing marginalization of British fatherhood, and to assert that the emotionally-connected moral parent could appear not only in female, but also in male guise.

An allegorical reading also fails to show how Mr Crusoe's suffering at the loss of his son aligns the child reader more closely with text's adult point of view. Every action, and every feeling, recounted by Mr Crusoe works to affirm the central role, the primary emotional bond, that Mr Crusoe has for his son. The only words he is able to utter to the Dutch seamen who rescue him from the island are "my son, my son" (148); he imagines situations which could lead to his son's survival, even while his companions attempt to quench all his hopes; nothing is "capable of diverting him from that one painful object which engrossed them" (Charles) (157). The narrator even goes so far as to tell the readers how they should feel about Mr Crusoe's plight: "all of our young readers will be aware, that, at this time, he was in a more deplorable state than Charles, as to his feelings, though the actual situation of the poor boy was apparently so much worse" (157). That God is the center of the universe may be this text's overt message, but it simultaneously assuages the adult father's anxiety that he is no longer the center of his son's.

Hofland's text also indulges the child reader's fantasy that he or she is the center of his or her father's universe. This, after all of the suffering that has come before, is surely one of the pleasures that Hofland's text has to offer its child readers. A second pleasure is that of spending pages and pages after the rescue being comforted, along with Charles. The reunion of parent and child is not only marked by strong emotions, but by physical contact, contact that by this period is becoming increasingly reserved for the realm of the maternal. As Tosh notes, while fathers were encouraged to play with their children, they were discouraged from developing emotional bonds with their sons: "too great an emotional closeness with sons would undermine their self-reliance and moral autonomy, that manly independence which was expected to be evidence by the age of 12 or so" ("Authority" 58). Charles, 14 by this point in the narrative, is well beyond the age when a boy was expected to eschew physical and emotional displays. Yet his reunion with his father redounds with both: "Mr Crusoe, who, pale and trembling, scarcely able to endure the joy and the fear of this awful scene, now took him in his arms, and holding him to his heart, thanked God for the possession of a gift so much beyond his hopes" (133); "Charles … was so entirely content, so perfectly happy, as he laid in the arms of his father" (134); we see Charles "sink down at the feet of Mr Crusoe, lay his head in his lap, and draw the shawl, in which he was arrayed, over his face, to hide the transports, or the tears drawn from him by the novelty of his situation" (144). Though Charles heeds the doctor's advice to ask his father no questions, "there was one thing he could not deny himself, which was that of closely nestling to his father, and either holding him by the hand or the clothes, as if he feared to lose him for a moment" (144–5). The pleasures of such physical contact are hard to reconcile with an allegorical reading of the novel. Instead, they are better understood in terms both of their rejection of the emerging construction of fatherhood and of managing the parent-child emotional bond. By returning Charles, and through him, the reader, to an almost infantile state of pleasure in physical contact with the parent, the text functions both to reject the detached construction of fatherhood and to suppress any doubts it may have inadvertently raised about the authority of said parent by depicting fatherly emotion.

During the course of the journey back home to England, Charles demonstrates that he has learned the lesson he was meant to learn: he is now in full compliance with his father's wishes. The text demonstrates this in particular through its discussion of Charles's future profession. Under the older, patriarchal model of fatherhood, fathers often chose their sons' careers, ushering them into the family business or drawing on patronage networks or kinship ties to establish them in suitable careers (Davidoff and Hall 331–2). But as occupations proliferated, patronage declined, and entry into public service and the professions grew increasingly dependent on competitive examinations or specialized training, fathers saw their power to choose their sons' professions and facilitate their access to them decline during the course of the Victorian period (Tosh, *Man's Place* 115–16). Rather than registering the beginnings of this decline, Hofland's text invokes the older patriarchal model. After Charles shows his knowledge and character during a storm, a passenger assumes that the boy will want to pursue a seafaring life. Charles, though he rejects this assumption, tells the passenger "I am much too young to determine on any thing, seeing I have a father who will determine for me" and " I shall certainly express no wish to my father on the subject, until my education is much farther advanced, and I may be supposed to have better reasons for choice than I can have now'" (178, 79). But his father hears of the conversation, and asks Charles what future he has in mind. Charles's desire to go into the church, rather than to sea, demonstrates that he's learned the second lesson of the text: to value what early in the text Mr Crusoe had termed the "comforts of social life," and, additionally, the spiritual life, over a life of solitary adventure (4). While this valuation of the social can be read positively, as a feminizing force, it also must be acknowledged that in this text, it is aligned with the authority of the adult, rather than the desire of the child; Charles initially desired to lead a life of adventure, similar to the one led by his hero, the literary Robinson.

Charles's choice of profession also indicates the text's rejection of what increasingly would become the norm for male work during the Victorian period: a splitting of work away from the home. In the past, for the majority of men, work and home had been in the same location, with little clear separation between the two. But over the course of the nineteenth century, beginning in the 1820s and growing exponentially after the transport revolution of the 1840s, ever-increasing numbers of men worked and lived in different places. Such splitting of work from home, Tosh argues, was a key component in the development of Victorian domestic ideology, with its focus on the moral Angel mother and breadwinning provider father (*Man's Place* 13–17). Some professions, however, were able to maintain the home/work connection, notably the clergy. By choosing the clerical life, Charles is not only able to embrace his father's values; he is also able to embrace a lifestyle in which a work-at-home father could maintain his role as family authority.

This episode about Charles's choice of profession also reveals a third lesson that the boy must learn about strong emotion: it is best kept within the family. Rather than extending exponentially to encompass "all who surround us," as in Mallès de Beaulieu's text, Hofland's novel teaches its readers that emotion is acceptable only when confined to the family circle. Charles was reluctant to tell of his professional wishes for fear of being ridiculed; while his father initially questions his emotion ("You seem to me, Charles, to have a greater dread of ridicule, than I should expect from a boy of your good sense in other respects"), he ends by telling Charles that he prefers a timid son to the exalted hero/conceited coxcomb that would result from openly displaying his emotions for public consumption. Such a display occurs during their journey home, when their ship stops to view the tomb of Buonaparte, and Charles disagrees with a fellow passenger's pity for the ex-emperor's isolation. His emotional description of a true solitary life makes his listener cry out in wonder, deeming him "absolutely eloquent" and "really quite poetical" (172, 173). Such attention is anathema to Charles, and he "hastened away to conceal his emotions" (173). In 1828, strong feeling may be appropriate for the father-son bond, but it cannot be extended into the public realm. The text's call for boys to restrain public emotional displays signals a growing trend, one that would find its fullest expression in the mid-Victorian period: an insistence that men repress their emotions to avoid appearing feminine, an insistence that would grow ever more strident as gender identities grew increasingly dichotomous in the decades to follow (Tosh, *Man's Place* 47, 189).

Simultaneously, however, the construction of an ordinary child character allows the reader, not a member of the Crusoe clan, access to the emotions of this fictional family. Ordinary character construction thus plays a compensatory role in Hofland's text, warning the child against displaying emotions in public on one hand, while offering the child access to the very emotions it would deny the reader—the private emotions of those outside his or her family—with the other.

The final pages of Hofland's text appear to argue that the strong emotion evoked by family ties should, in the maturing adolescent, be transferred away from the family, and redirected toward God. As in more overtly Evangelical tract fiction, strong emotion can function to reinforce piety; strong feelings can be re-channeled into religious belief. We see such a re-channelling taking place at several places in the novel. For example, after Charles has been rescued and is reunited with his mother, he becomes so happy that "he could not contain the overflowing of his thankfulness; and he retired to the room he had quitted, that he might, unseen, pour out his full heart to God, in prayer and praise" (191). Emotion is not bad, but strong emotion must be redirected toward the spiritual, rather than to the earthly, sphere if it is to be experienced safely by the male adolescent.

Yet even while Hofland's text works to contain and re-channel strong familial emotion, to insist that the child mature into an adult, it simultaneously continues to desire that the child remain a child, to feel the way a child feels. During his time on the island, Charles's pet parrot initially chants "Don't be a child" whenever Charles has doubts or despairs. But after Charles "matures," and decides to "meet the exigencies of his case like a man," he retrains the parrot to say, "Don't despair, my dear boy" instead, "both because the words reminded him of his papa, and taught him his duty" (53). While the text emphasizes the "don't despair" portion of the new saying, its second half seems equally significant: it urges Charles not to grow up, but to remain a "dear boy," to maintain his emotional connection to a nurturing father.

Thus Hofland continues to value, even to exalt, the father-son emotional bond, a bond that deflects the "don't be a child" of the text's overt didactic message of maturity. During his time on the island, Charles

> frequently got a long stick, and wrote, or made figures, on the smooth sands near the shore; and as his thoughts were always wandering after his father, his writing generally consisted of letters addressed to him; and many an epistle, full of tenderness and good feeling, was, day after day, washed away by the returning waves which passed over it.

> One morning, as he was going to take his station in the tree, he remarked that every word was obliterated, except "Dear papa."—"Ah!" said he, "those two words remain yet; they are the last words on the sands, and I dare say they will be the last words I shall ever utter. I remember reading in history, that Queen Mary said "*Calais* would be found written on her heart;" and if the thing were possible, "dear papa" would now be written on mine. (126)

An allegorical reading of this passage would insist that "dear papa" simply represents God the father, with the word of God written on the child's heart. Yet the text's concluding moments, with their continued focus on the earthly father-son bond, suggest that the message of piety that the text is overtly attempting to convey simultaneously allows the reader to continue to indulge in earthly, rather than spiritual, feeling. When Charles gives gifts to his mother and sister upon his return to England, his father jokingly observes that he "did not remember that Charles had given him any thing." Charles responds, "Oh! fie, papa—ever since the day my mother left us in India, your kindness and daily attention to my comfort, said continually, 'my son, give me thy heart,' and you must know and feel, that you had my *whole* heart" (194, emphasis in original). If Charles' "*whole* heart" is with his father, then what can be left for God?

Charles' future as a clergyman is left in doubt by the novel's final plot twist: an uncle Robinson has died, and will leave his estate to Charles if the boy will add "Robinson" to his name. Charles is reminded of how remembrance of his "old friend, Robinson Crusoe" helped him during his months on the island, but now, instead of the enthusiasm of boyish love he once felt for

Defoe's protagonist, Charles now terms him "poor Robinson" (195). Hofland's novel may assert that Charles cannot love both Robinson Crusoe and a father "dearly"—the one standing for solitary adventure, the other for social and familial bonds—but one surely can love both an earthly father and a spiritual one with equal emotional fervor. The pleasures of both loves are infinitely superior, both to solitary adventure and to potential doubts about the wisdom and authority of an emotionally open parent.

Talking Herself into Subjectivity: Ann Fraser Tytler's *Leila, or the Island* (1839)

> Annie … has had a note from Mr Hatchard her publisher as to a new edition of 'Leila in England;' and as we get a treat of ices and cakes at Grange's in Picadilly for every new edition, we paid a visit there on Saturday, and enjoyed our treat much. There is something very delightful in this mixture of literature and confectionery. We rejoice at the increasing moral influence of Miss Tytler's celebrated works, and rejoice also in the ices and cakes.
>
> —from a letter by Patrick Fraser Tytler, brother of Ann Fraser Tytler[19]

Repressing emotion in the context of the domestic is not of great concern to Hofland; in her novel, family feeling may be redirected towards God, but it can also be indulged in on earth. But when the robinsonade protagonist is an ordinary girl, rather than an ordinary boy, emotion becomes more dangerous, more in need of overt repression, redirection, control. The final robinsonade that I will consider in this chapter, Ann Fraser Tytler's *Leila, or the Island*,[20] is simultaneously

---

[19]   Quoted in Burgon, 326.

[20]   Tytler's novel was initially issued by John Hatchard, the Evangelical Tory bookseller who published the *Reports of the Society for Bettering the Condition of the Poor* and whose bookshop served as a meeting ground for members of the Clapham sect (Laver 12–14). *Leila* went through at least eight editions between 1839 and 1875, according to WORLDCAT listings; an 1879 edition states "13th edition" on its title page. *Leila* also proved popular in the United States, with at least five editions issued by Boston, New York, and Philadelphia publishers. Its sequels, *Leila in England* and *Leila at Home*, were also reprinted multiple times by Hatchard. Although Tytler was surely not as well-known as the earlier Evangelical writer Mary Martha Sherwood, the printing history of her *Leila* books points to a level of popularity similar to that of her contemporary, Barbara Hofland.

In *Children's Books in England*, F.J. Harvey Darton dates *Leila* 1839 (117), as does the DNB in its listing for Tytler's father, Alexander Fraser Tytler (1378). But in *Children's Literature: An Illustrated History*, Dennis Butts gives the publication date as 1833 (98), as does *The Osborne Collection of Early Children's Books 1566–1910* (St John 315). There are no copies of an 1833 edition listed on WORLDCAT; the earliest edition is listed as 1839. That edition included only a frontispiece illustration, but later editions were more lavish: for example, the Boston-based publisher Crosby, Nichols, Lee & Co. bound the book in purple paper with a gold-embossed spine, and included several black and white engravings by J.W. Orr, one of the most important engravers in nineteenth-century New York.

the novel most invested in depicting parental emotion, and in insisting on the necessity of controlling the child's. Intriguingly, despite this urge to repress the extravagant emotions of the child, Tytler's novel features the protagonist with the most individuality, and the most agency, of all of the characters we have yet encountered in the family robinsonade. Allowing juvenile emotion to enter the literary scene requires new methods to discipline the child, yet these methods unintentionally open up a space for a new type of resistance.

Tytler's novel, the earliest British robinsonade for children that features an ordinary girl as its protagonist, differs from the boy-centered robinsonade in significant ways. Departing from the male model presented in Defoe's *Robinson Crusoe*, Tytler eschews the classic pattern of abandonment and self-reliance that later becomes the normative trope in the male-authored juvenile adventure story, and that plays a large role in the earlier robinsonades we've explored. Leila Howard, Tytler's protagonist, is not stranded by herself, nor is she stranded with a group of other children. Instead, she is shipwrecked with two responsible adults: her nurse and her father. Physical survival is not a central problem for Leila and her caretakers, as it was for Felix and Charles, and even to a certain extent, Wyss's family; there are no wild animals that attack them, and food and shelter are fairly easy to come by. And while Leila's father, Mr Howard, plants crops, readers are only told this, never shown it; conquering the land, bringing a wild untamed island under cultivation and control, is simply not of interest to Tytler. Finally, Tytler's characters never encounter, never mind prove their superiority to, a native other.

But if Tytler's novel is not performing the same cultural work as later Victorian adventure stories for boys, its ideological messages are congruent with such cultural work, Susan Naramore Maher argues. Leila may not conquer the land, or a native other, Maher argues, but she does struggle mightily to conquer herself; by learning to curb her impulsiveness and restrain her emotions, she simultaneously learns to embrace the "filiative order": a God-centered creation, a father-centered family, each with a naturalized subtext of female subservience (Maher 155). Espousal of such a filiative order, Maher suggests, paves the way for later Victorian adventure tales and their "promotion of social order, imperial politics, and missionary objectives" (157).

Certainly, the broad outlines of Tytler's plot conform to a reading such as Maher's, which suggests that the construction of the ordinary child, particularly a girl child, can be easily appropriated for ideological gender work. For Leila is, like her family robinsonade predecessors, a character constructed after the new "ordinary" model. We are told Leila's age (eight), and we learn that she has strengths and weaknesses that are particular to her. As Mr Howard explains to Leila (and the reader), Leila's unique fault is her overindulgence in strong emotion: "She was a child of naturally quick temper and strong sensibility; but he had taken infinite pains to teach her to subdue her feelings" (29); her strengths include her energy, her good humor, and her openly expressed love for her father. The text invites readers to identify with Leila through depictions of her emotions, and to be persuaded of her ordinariness by witnessing the pleasure her father takes in her.

Leila unfolds as a series of loosely connected pedagogical dialogues between Leila and her father; the only "adventures" that occur are those that test Leila's religious and moral growth. The overt message of the text insists that Leila must learn to curb her major weakness, excessive emotion, by placing her trust in religion: "Leila, you are forgetting yourself; be composed, my love; put your trust in God"; "You should pray to God, Leila, that he would enable you to get over that impatience of temper, which is your greatest fault"; "I am sorry to be obliged to punish you, my child; but it is my duty to endeavour in every way to check this impatience of temper, which may lead you into the most frightful faults" (30, 49–50, 77). As Deborah Gorham describes her in *The Victorian Girl and the Feminine Ideal*, the exemplary woman/girl of the Victorian period would "be pure, gentle, and self-sacrificing. Possessing no ambitious strivings, she would be free of any trace of anger or hostility" (4). While both sons and daughters were taught the principles of self-sacrifice, this message was stressed more for girls than for boys; ironically, even while emotions grew increasingly associated with the feminine, and disassociated with the masculine over the course of the nineteenth century, girls were simultaneously thought more capable of self-renunciation than were boys (Gorham 19, 4–5). While it would not reach its full flowering until the mid-Victorian period, idealized femininity had begun to influence middle-class ideology by the 1830s, when *Leila* was written. Gorham argues, in fact, that the daughter might make for a better Angel in the House than the wife, for her childishness and asexuality were real, rather than culturally constructed. Idealized girlhood, then, would prove to be a major component in the development of Victorian domestic ideology.

Tytler's novel thus masks the larger gendered cultural work that it undertakes by making Leila's individual, particular faults align with those of larger cultural fears about girls and emotion in circulation in the period—that the angry girl child might call into question the naturalness and inevitability of the idealized girl vision. The emergent construction of ordinary girlhood posits that if a girl reader identifies with Leila, and also finds that she shares some of what are constructed as Leila's individual, particular negative characteristics, then said reader may be more likely to embrace the message of change than if the text asserted that these are faults general to *all* girls.

Maher's reading of *Leila* sees the embrace of a "filiative order" as the dominant ideology in Tytler's text. Such an interpretation, I would argue, misses the ambivalences inherent in the innovations to ordinary character construction that Tytler's text introduces. For reading Tytler's novel only to confirm its conservative agenda is to miss the ways in which the construction of the ordinary girl implicitly disrupts the very filiative order it is explicitly working to affirm. In order to see these disruptions, I would suggest, one must listen to Leila's talk. Unlike the child protagonists in the novels earlier in this chapter, Leila's voice, expressed in abundant dialogue, differs markedly from those of the adults around her, not only in content, but also in style. When Leila speaks, we know immediately that it is her, and not her father, or her nurse, even if Tytler fails to add a narrative nametag. Tytler's stylistic innovation in creating individualized dialogue for the child, and for the adults who surround her, adds an additional detail to the depiction of the "ordinary" child, a detail that functions to bind her reader ever more closely to what appears to be a "realistic" character and to the ideological message that that character is intended to convey. Yet at the same time, Leila's "talk" calls into question the very filiative order the text is at pains to model through its construction of an ordinary child character.

We must also listen, I would argue, to Leila's father. In her depiction of Mr Howard, Tytler expands upon the model hinted at in Hofland; readers are granted far more access to the private thoughts, and emotions, of this father than to any of the parents of the earlier robinsonades. This access purportedly works, as in the case of Hofland's Mr Crusoe, to bind the reader more closely to the parent's authority. Simultaneously, and perhaps inadvertantly, I would argue, it also destabilizes the same authority it works to reinforce.

Unlike earlier pedagogical fiction by Mary Wollstonecraft, Sarah Trimmer, and other women writers, which Mitzi Myers and other critics have praised for its depiction of mother-teachers who, in their roles as powerful authority figures, served as significant and empowering role models for women, *Leila* features no mentoria figure. Instead, Tytler creates a mentor; Leila's teacher is not her nurse, or her mother, who died soon after her birth, but rather her father. Instead of teaching the child to invest in emotional connection to a father by removing the father from the child, Tytler reverts back to Wyss's model, with the mentor father taking the opportunity to teach his child during their stay on the deserted island. Surprisingly, despite his sex, Mr Howard often seems less of an authority figure than those earlier distant, all-knowing mothers and teachers, or than Wyss's patriarchal narrator, in large part because of the emotional life Tytler grants him. Tytler appears to have modeled Mr Howard on her own brother, the historian Patrick Fraser Tytler, who, with his three children, came to live with her after the death of his wife in 1835 (Burgon 232). As Ann Fraser Tytler describes him, their own father, Lord Woodhouselee, thought his children "all perfection," and showed them "unlimited indulgence" (qtd Burgon 20). Brother Patrick resembled their father in his ability to become his own children's "playmate, in relaxing his mind, by bringing it down to the level of their merriment" (qtd Burgon 21). But he also felt that overindulgence in emotion was a "weakness": in a letter written from school, the boy Patrick noted, "I scarcely believe there was a single letter which I received from home over which I did not shed tears. You see I conceal nothing, however unfavorable to myself: and yet, what will you not say against this weakness?" (qtd Burgon 64). As a parent, Patrick Tytler was an involved father, one who "delighted in [his children's] society to a far greater extent than most parents" (Burgon 231); the death of his wife may have allowed him to play a more active role in their lives than that of many other fathers during this period, one in which the role of the mother was beginning to eclipse that of the father (as discussed in the previous section). But unlike his own father, who never found fault with his "perfect" offspring, Patrick Fraser Tytler actively sought to shape his children, in particular teaching them habits of religious devotion. Yet he sought to temper such moral and religious training, rejecting the austere religious severity he was taught at school in favor of pleasure, benevolence, and emotional connection. As he noted in a written prayer addressed to God:

> And thus, whilst I keep my heart and conscience clear from every vicious pursuit, I may yet never despise or forsake that innocent enjoyment which even in this world Thou hast so abundantly provided for those that love thee. Enable me to show to my companions, to every one with whom I am concerned, that true Religion increases, instead of taking away cheerful enjoyment, by assuring us that we are happy under the approving smile of a most benevolent Father. (qtd Burgon 67)

Tytler's novel begins not with the child, but with the adult, and with the adult's emotions, emotions that echo many of brother Patrick's views. Fearing Leila dead after their arduous trip via raft from the ship to the island, her father cries, "O that I too had perished!" (6). Though we may feel that such a reaction is only natural, an early nineteenth-century religious reader would instantly recognize that Mr Howard's wish, which both devalues life by longing for death, and devalues God by not submitting to his will, is sinful. Though Mr Howard immediately regrets his rash outburst, and asks God for forgiveness, readers know from his very first words that he is not perfect. Yet at the same time, his emotional outburst humanizes him in a way unheard of in earlier mentoria tales. In earlier moral and religious fictions, it was not uncommon for the faults of adults outside of the family or school to be noted and used as a means of instruction, but rarely if ever were mentor figures characterized as flawed in any way, as Tytler's Mr Howard is. In his performance of emotional attachment to his child, Mr Howard is far closer to Hofland's Mr Crusoe than to mentoria figures of earlier fiction, or of the patriarchal authority of Wyss's pastor father.

We saw in Hofland's Mr Crusoe the emergence of parent interiority in the juvenile robinsonade: readers were, in brief asides, granted access to the thoughts and emotions of the parent character. In Tytler's novel, parental interiority is not confined to brief moments; instead, readers are frequently inside the head of Mr Howard. We see him not just from the outside, a distant authority figure offering instruction and admonishment to his daughter. Instead, Tytler's narrator gives us access to his thoughts, thoughts that demonstrate not only his piety (although they certainly do this), but also his doubts, his struggles. For example, the narrator tells us that while Mr Howard is grateful for the bounty of the island after being stranded there for a year, "still there were many moments of deep depression for which he severely chid himself" (159). Readers often hear of his "melancholy thoughts," his "deep anxiety" (41). While Leila's father is clearly depicted as the authority figure throughout the novel, he is no longer the inaccessibly perfect instructor of earlier didactic fiction, or of the Wyss robinsonade; by opening up Mr Howard's mind to her readers, and demonstrating that in thought if not in deed he, too, at times has difficulty living up to the precepts he wishes to impart

Fig. 1.4   This illustration of the opening scene presents a calm, contained Mr Howard, hardly a father wracked by "the deepest despondency" described by the text. Courtesy of the author.

to his daughter, Tytler humanizes patriarchal authority by granting it interiority, subjectivity, individuality.

Placing us inside the head of Mr Howard has a second, more surprising effect. Because much of the narrative is focalized through Mr Howard, readers are not always looking at Leila, the book's main character, directly; we're looking at Leila through the eyes of Mr Howard. And there is a clear sense that Mr Howard takes real pleasure in this looking, a pleasure that the reader is invited to share. In many instances, Mr Howard takes pleasure in looking at Leila while she prays, or participates in other religious devotions. But at others moments in the novel, Mr Howard's pleasure is connected first to the physical, and only secondly to the spiritual. Much of his pleasure stems from gazing at the beauty of his daughter, a beauty that Tytler, clearly influenced by the Romantic construction of the child, almost always links to images of nature: his sleeping daughter "lay like a summer rose, in dreamless sleep. He looked at her in silent thankfulness" (61); later that morning, "it was pleasing to see the white hens flocking round Leila … eagerly picking up the food she had prepared for them" (62).

If Mr Howard only took pleasure in the sight of a passive Leila, or a Leila ensconced in the domestic, his looking would fit in well with Maher's argument that Tytler's text functions to enforce a filiative order. But Mr Howard takes pleasure in Leila's *active* beauty as well: "He awoke strengthened and invigorated, and found Leila standing by his side—no longer the pale Leila of the day before, but blooming as a rose, and sparking with intelligence" (18). And "Leila darted out into the open air, and in her turn stood laughing at her papa; the wind blowing her luxuriant hair all about her blooming face, and threatening every moment to lift her light figure from the ground" (45). When Leila responds to a bower he has built for her, Mr Howard "was almost as happy as his child; her pure joy was balm to his heart, and he watched her in silent gratitude as she flew from one spot to another in all the restlessness of delight" (91). While the main thrust of the novel is suspicious of Leila's abundant physical energy, and works to make Leila leave her childhood behind by containing and repressing her "willfulness" and emotional extravagance, a clear counter-discourse values the pleasure that an adult takes from looking at and listening to the emotional, energetic, ordinary child, even to the point of setting the child as "next to" God in importance. For when Leila asks her father "What am I to you, papa?" he replies, "When your beloved mamma was taken from me, it was your infant smiles, my child, next to the consolations of my heavenly Father, that first spoke peace to my sad heart" (128). By suggesting that the child has something of value to offer to the adult, Tytler differs from the stance taken by earlier didactic writers, following instead in the footsteps of the Romantics. But by simultaneously insisting that the adult still has much to teach the child, Tytler also rejects the reifying tendencies of the Romantic construction of childhood, even while she adopts aspects of that Romantic child in her depiction of the pleasure-giving Leila.

While readers can only experience the pleasure of Leila's physical presence at one remove, through Mr Howard's perceptions, they can experience several other types of pleasure more directly, without Mr Howard's mediation.

First, they can take pleasure in Leila's misbehavior. Intriguingly, such misbehavior is rarely depicted directly; instead, readers hear about it after it has occurred, when Leila tells her father about her misdeeds through dialogue. This pleasure differs significantly from that in Wyss, where the events are told to the reader by the adult father narrator, and both the reader and the narrator typically laugh *at* the child, when the child makes a mistake and then suffers the consequences (Jack being nipped by the lobster, or being pricked by a plant yet again after refusing to believe his father when he tells him of its dangers). With Leila's misbehavior, in contrast, the reader is not invited to feel superior to Leila, but rather to identify with her. While Mr Howard may find her story a "sad, sad account indeed" (52), readers are far more likely to laugh and sympathize with Leila than chastise her when they hear the girl, in her own voice, tell of snatching the spectacles off her nurse's nose, or making a face at nurse when she is not looking, or wishing to throw sand at the woman. The text always insists that Leila repent her bad behavior, that she confess it to her father and acknowledge her fault. Yet by allowing us to hear Leila directly and extensively, without a mediating judgmental narrator (as in Wyss or occasionally Hofland) or through the eyes of a judgmental parent (as in Mallès de Beaulieu or occasionally Hofland), Tytler's text simultaneously opens up a space for reader identification with and sympathy for such misbehavior. By allowing the child to tell her own story, Tytler also allows the reader to laugh, to take pleasure in the childish reactions her text is working so hard to discipline.

In fact, the main pleasure that Leila inspires, both in Mr Howard and in readers, stems from her stories, her words, her "talk." Perhaps the most surprising thing to a modern reader coming to Tytler's text with the expectation of finding a repressive tale of a girl being trained to be meek and silent in her pious, submissive duty to patriarchal authority is the fact that Leila rarely stops talking. And the pleasures associated with Leila's talk are multiple.

Within the text, Mr Howard, like the narrator of *The Family Robinson Crusoe*, often takes pleasure in the religious sentiments spoken by his child, particularly as he notes their growing complexity and religious conviction over the course of their year on the island. Yet, as was the case with his looking, the pleasure that Mr Howard receives from listening to Leila is often separate from religion. Leila's bodily energy is mirrored in her talk; just as her body continually "bounds" ahead of her father when they are out walking, so too does her conversation, as the following example, a brief excerpt from the first extended dialogue between Leila and her father, demonstrates:

> "Do you know now, papa?"
> "Yes, I think I can guess."
> "O no, papa, you are not to guess, I am to tell you. Well, you see—but are you listening?"
> "Yes, my love, I am listening"
> "Then don't look so melancholy, dear papa, for it is a funny story. Now I will tell you—but where was I?"
> "You were in a pink silk quilt, Leila, I think."
> "Yes, so I was, papa; and now I am glad, for you are laughing again." (21)

Mr Howard laughs, and his laugh has multiple sources: pleasure in the headlong energy of a child, unable to stay focused on what she is supposed to be speaking of; pleasure in having greater knowledge than that child; pleasure in having their roles temporarily reversed (he is not to guess, she is to tell him); and perhaps most importantly, pleasure in being distracted from his "melancholy" thoughts. Throughout the novel, there is a clear tension between Mr Howard the moral instructor, who tells Leila that being so easily distracted is a "bad habit" that she "must endeavor to get the better of" (48), and Mr Howard the father, who cannot help but be distracted himself by the distractions of his daughter. That Tytler is not condemning Mr Howard for the pleasure he takes in Leila's discourse is made clear by the differing reactions her talk inspires in Mr Howard and in Nurse, who, the narrative asserts, is far less of a role model for a good teacher than is Mr Howard. In response to one of Leila's meandering stories, Nurse replies, "O Miss Leila! It would confuse any body's head to hear you run on in this way!" (135), while Mr Howard tells her "Get along, you little fairy … I am sure it would make any one smile to hear you run on in this way" (110–11). That second "any one" includes the reader as surely as it does Mr Howard.

If Tytler's text presented Leila's talk solely as an object of pleasure for an audience, be that audience her father within the text, or the reader outside of it, it could hardly be suggested that the novel presents a more liberating construction of childhood than earlier moral or religious fiction for children. In fact, as I have argued about a text contemporaneous with Tytler's, Catherine Sinclair's *Holiday House*, constructing the child as a performer for the entertainment of adults can in fact be *more* repressive ("Punishment"). But in Tytler's narrative, Leila's talk is not just entertaining; it actually grants her a certain degree of agency, in three important ways.

The first is that Leila, through her talk, actively elicits stories from those around her. "Tell me" becomes the most common phrase Leila utters throughout the novel: "Now papa … tell me all your travels and all your discoveries, as you promised, and begin at the very beginning" (145); "O, papa, do not stop, tell me more about them" (95); "But now, nurse, I have told you a story, and surely you would tell me something you did when you were a little girl" (178). While Mr Howard and Nurse occasionally resist Leila's requests, far more often they do "tell her" what she asks to hear. Leila, then, is not just the passive recipient of the stories the adults think are necessary to her spiritual development, but the active elicitor of stories that *she* wants to hear.

Of course, Nurse, and particularly Mr Howard, like Hofland's Crusoe parents before them, work to "turn" Leila's desires to "good account": each strives to shape the stories that Leila requests into tales meant for her improvement. For example, when Leila asks her father to tell her how the ants built the enormous anthill she has found, he attempts to turn her curiosity into a lesson: "They do it, Leila, by the most constant patience and industry; they are never a moment idle … they are not like some little girls who used to tire sadly when they had long frills to hem … You must now try to resemble those little ants, and patiently pursue your task till you have made it perfect" (95–6). Leila, though she acknowledges his point, quickly asks another question about the ants, neatly pushing her father to turn his moral lesson into a lecture on natural history, which to Leila is "as wonderful as a fairy tale" (97). If, as Donelle Ruwe has suggested, the tutor in Rousseau's *Émile* has "an almost sinister ability to educate Emile through anticipating his questions and controlling his environment," while later pedagogical mentoria such as the mother in Sarah Trimmer's *An Easy Introduction* are more direct and less manipulative ("Guarding" 10), Mr Howard by comparison often seems to be simply following along in the wake of his daughter's talk.

Eventually, though, most conversations between Leila and her father come around to Mr Howard's point. But while Leila usually acknowledges the value of the lessons her father is working to teach her, there are moments in the novel where she actively resists them, moments in which neither her father's reason nor his religious convictions can convince her to change her mind. A case in point is her sentimental view of animals. Throughout the narrative, Leila thinks about animals as if they were people, expressing sympathy for captured animals and dismay at the thought of animals being eaten—all sentiments at odds with the Christianity that Mr Howard wants to impart to his daughter. When Leila puts words into the mouths of fledgling birds, her father upbraids her: "Now, Leila, don't let your imagination run away with you" (82). But instead of agreeing, Leila modifies her story, and maintains her point: "Well, papa, I mean that they understood—for they did understand, papa" (82). And when Leila wants to feed the young birds, because she feels that "it is cruel in them to eat the poor worms and flies" (83), Mr Howard tries to change her mind, both by appealing to the religious belief in the natural hierarchy of God's creatures, and by trying to validate her emotions yet subsume them to reason. Yet Leila once again takes the conversation off in another direction, and Mr Howard's point is never conceded.

The narrator suggests that Mr Howard's method of educating his daughter, which is characterized by "sympathy" and "forbearance," will in the end bring her to adopt his way of thinking more effectively than an authoritarian enforcement of rules and regulations would (100). Like Hofland's Mr Crusoe before him, Mr Howard deploys the "influence" rather than the "authority" model of parenting. Intriguingly, as noted earlier, such a model was deemed more appropriate to mothering than to fathering, particularly in the mid-Victorian period. But here, as in Hofland's robinsonade, the style is shown to be within the abilities of a caring father, particularly if his wife has been written out of the plot. Though Tytler is clearly drawing on the true-life model of her own brother with his children, her text might also be responding to the first of what would be a series of legal decisions restricting the traditional rights of fathers to exert power over their wives and children that were passed by Parliament over the course of the nineteenth century: the 1839 Custody of Infants Act, which allowed women separated from their husbands to petition for custody of children under seven, and access to children under sixteen. Claudia Nelson notes that the passage of this Act and it subsequent extensions, which came earlier than those Acts granting wives control over their own money (the Married Women's Property Acts of 1870, 1881, and 1893), points to the relatively low standing fatherly influence held in the period, at least as compared to the more culturally dominant vision of the father as breadwinner (*Invisible* 112).

Tytler's narrative, like Hofland's before her, thus takes issue with the trend to push aside fathers and replace them with mothers as the primary influence in a child's life. Neither Leila's mother, whom the narrative has killed off before it began, nor Nurse, whose class position makes her a poor mother-substitute, can provide the combination of discipline and emotional connection that a patriarchal father influenced by the new focus on emotional connection within the family is able to give. Throughout, the text makes it is clear that readers should agree with Mr Howard, rather than with Leila, at those times when Leila resists his instruction. Yet by allowing emotion to enter the parent/child relationship, her texts also opens up a space for resistance to parental instruction, not only for Leila, but for the reader as well. Such opportunities for resistance register in the text's reluctance to show Leila accepting her father's point of view in all cases, as would be common in earlier didactic fiction for children.

The final pleasure I'd like to discuss is that of the verbal and physical affection displayed both by child toward parent, and parent toward child. As in Hofland's robinsonade, Tytler's father often uses terms of endearment when he talks to his child, calling her "my love" and "my dear child." In *The Young Crusoe*, however, the physical affection between Charles and his father emerges only after they suffer the pain of separation; it seems a temporary indulgence, one that will likely lesson once Charles has become less afraid, less tentative at being back in society. But in Tytler's novel, there is no separation, and the physical affection between Leila and her father is a constant throughout the story. Leila often sits on his knee when she talks to him; Mr Howard embraces her, or catches her to his breast; she climbs up on his bed and hangs around his neck (47, 57, 155, 122). As Leila tells her father, physical affection can lead to spiritual connection: "When you are kissing me, and looking at me so kindly, then I love God more for keeping you alive to kiss me, and to be so good to me" (88). As Deborah Gorham notes, the Victorian idealization of girlhood presented in art, literature, and conduct writing was "most fully expressed" by portraying that girl's relationships with other members of her family, especially its male members. The daughter's relationship with her father featured most often in such portrayals. Two common tropes of the period consisted of the ideal daughter in the "serene and happy home," who provided "gentleness and cheerfulness" in a domestic setting that gave him respite from the ugly and sullying realm of business, while the ideal daughter in the family under stress provided moral and emotional support (38). Leila, it seems, plays both such roles simultaneously.

Yet the close physical and emotional relationship that Leila has with her father is also a source of anxiety in this text, as it was not in Hofland's. As the narrator reports, "Nothing delighted her so much as to get upon his knee, and have him all to herself" (44). Leila herself tells her father, "I like so much when I sit upon your knee, and you tell me plans, and chat with me a great deal; and I am so glad here, you know, nobody will come to disturb us" (47). Knee-sitting in particular seems to indicate trouble; as M. Nancy Cutt notes, when Mary Martha Sherwood made revisions to *The Fairchild Family* between 1818 and 1822, she revised a scene in which a young Fairchild girl sits upon the "coachman's knee" to have the girl perch on the housemaid's instead (*Mrs Sherwood* 76). Such changes, Cutt suggests, point to the beginnings of what would be later become a Victorian insistence on strict propriety.

While sitting on a father's knee is not quite the same as sitting on a coachman's, both hint obliquely at sexuality, something a good Victorian daughter was supposed to know nothing about, never mind feel. Fears of impending knowledge of sexuality seem to underlie a more benign disagreement between parent and child in the novel: whether rescue is longed for or resisted. Throughout the novel, Leila insists that she is happy to remain on their deserted island, and has no wish to continue their journey on to England, for her relationship with her father is enough to satisfy her emotional needs: "I like you to have all my pleasures, both my great pleasures and my little ones, for you are my papa, and my friend, and my every thing" (127). And indeed, many Victorian daughters whose mothers died took on the role of "deputy wife," as Claudia Nelson terms it, providing their fathers not only with companionship and moral uplift, but also with managerial expertise for his home, and even surrogate mothering for his younger children (*Family Ties* 87). Yet Tytler's text worries that the degree of emotional closeness Leila expects and demands from her father might push her beyond the boundaries of the ideal girl, one who consistently sacrifices herself for her family/father and who accepts her subordinate role without demanding anything from him in return. Being a father's "every thing" might be acceptable for an eight-year-old girl, but this text is intent upon making the child grow up, and the child, especially the girl child, cannot take her father as her sole emotional resource. Both Mr Howard and nurse consistently desire to leave the island, to interact with others beyond the family circle. When nurse tells her that she misses having a "sociable cup of tea" with her friends back in England, Leila mistakenly believes that "sociable" means sweet (135); it is clear that when nurse tells her that "No, Miss Leila; you don't understand me the least" that not only Leila's vocabulary misunderstanding is at stake. The parrot that Leila almost squeezes to death with affection could equally stand in for Mr Howard, for his dictate, "Leila … you must restrain your affection" could equally be applied to himself (142). While the overt educative message of the text is for Leila to grow spiritually by learning to control her anger, it also becomes clear that she also must restrain her affection for her father, and look outside of the father-child bond for emotional connection. Unlike in Hofland's text, in *Leila*, containing emotion within the family becomes a problem when the family is a father-daughter pair, for the threat of forbidden sexuality hovers over the relationship. Thus, the text ultimately insists that Leila extend her emotional life beyond the family circle.

How does Leila learn this lesson? Not surprisingly, through the arrival of another person on the island. During a storm, another ship is wrecked, and

Mr Howard finds a small girl washed ashore. Yet the connection between the two girls is fleeting: "an almost imperceptible shade of colour tinged her check: it deepened into a faint flush; she opened her blue eyes,—they appeared to rest on Leila for a moment: she seemed to smile. It was an angel's smile—the heavy eyelids closed, her pulse had ceased to beat" (205). Instead of the early death of the protagonist common in the juvenile martyr tale, Tytler here displaces death onto another child character. The girl, Clara, functions as a spiritual messenger, promising not only the delights not only of heaven, but also the potential for emotional connection to others outside of the family.

The same suffering that led Charles to maturity thus also leads Leila. And, like him, she must pass through a stage of intense emotion before leaving childhood behind. After Clara's death, "Leila strove hard to be composed, and the violence of her first emotions seemed to have passed away; but still her papa could not prevail upon her to leave for any length of time the object of her deep interest" (206). When they bury Clara, Mr Howard continues to insist that she restrain her emotions: "Leila, my child … there must be no violent emotion … let me see you command yourself; endeavour to raise your thoughts from earth to heaven" (210). Yet Leila, despite the lesson of Clara's death, still cannot keep her grief in check: "Leila struggled with emotion; but when he closed the book, and all was over, she threw herself upon the grave, and wept such tears as she had never wept before" (211).

And so, Tytler adds another emotional crisis for Leila to deal with, one with a "depth of suffering which touched her far more nearly" (211): the illness of her own father. During this crisis, Mr Howard wants to talk to Leila about the possibility of his death; when she protests, he tells her: "Leila, dear child, at this moment you are increasing my illness; all emotion must be avoided; if you are able to command yourself, I will go on, but if not, you must leave me, dearest, to nurse's care" (212). The text makes an all too obvious link between Mr Howard's recovery and his daughter's ability to "command" herself. At the height of his fever, Mr Howard warns Leila that he might not recognize her; it immediately happens:

> "Who are you?" he said. "You are not Leila." The affrighted child burst into an agony of tears.
> "No," he continued, "you are not Leila—my Leila never weeps, she is always smiling.
> In a moment Leila's tears were dry. (216)

Of course, once Leila finally passes the test of emotional restraint, Mr Howard's fever subsides. Only emotional restraint can ensure continued emotional bonds between a father and a daughter, the text insists, for such emotional restraint guarantees a similar sexual restraint.

The text makes Leila perform such emotional restraint throughout its final pages, emotional restraint that typically leads Leila to give up her most powerful source of agency: her talk. When her father recounts the story of discovering Clara, "Leila looked up at her papa's agitated countenance, and forbore all further questions" (208). And during her father's recovery, "Leila began to give him an account of what had taken place the evening before, but checking herself, she said, 'But we will not talk of it now, papa, for it may make you ill again'" (218). The narrator tells us directly that Leila has matured:

> But there was a change in Leila: her extreme childishness had passed away; she was equally attentive to her numerous pets, yet seemed less entirely occupied by them; and though always cheerful and often gay, a shade of seriousness would sometimes pass across her face. ... She never now expressed the hope that they might continue always on the island. (219–20)

Leila has learned the two lessons that the text has set out to teach: expressing *too much* emotion, and valuing family attachment to the detriment of other social ties, cannot be allowed. Thus it is not surprising that immediately after Mr Howard's physical, and Leila's emotional, crises are over, a rescue ship sails into the island harbor.

Yet while insisting that Leila is different, that she is more mature, that she has left emotional extravagance behind, the text simultaneously insists that she is the same child it worked so hard to change:

> Still the happy forgetfulness of youth was hers. No sooner had she turned round the point of rock, and the cave came into view, with her pretty garden brilliant with flowers, and all the happy birds and animals which flew to meet her, than for a moment all remembrance of their banishment was forgotten, amid the thoughts of her pleasant home. (220)

During the novel's final pages, Leila continues to exhibit strong emotion. After a potential rescue ship turns away without seeing them, "Leila threw herself into her papa's arms, and wept upon his breast" (225); when saying goodbye to Clara's grave: "here the emotions with which she had been struggling gave way to a burst of grief" (229). Even the adults take part in the emotional display when they leave the island: "Mr Howard and Leila were too much agitated to speak; nurse wept and laughed by turns" (230). Our final image of Leila is one marked by emotion: "A little girl stood there [on the boat] in eager expectation; she seemed another Clara, but not so pale. Leila sprang forward, and in a moment they were clasped in each other's arms" (231). Clearly, the text is as deeply invested in continuing to display emotion as it is to curb it. That readers are equally invested in such contradictory dictates is evident not only from the popularity of Tytler's novel, but from the two multiply–reprinted sequels the novel inspired. Leila has grown up, has reached the end of her story, at the end of this novel; yet her story "continues," allowing readers to indulge in the fantasy that maturity is a permeable boundary, one that a literary protagonist can cross and re-cross for the pleasure of the reader.

This double imperative—to grow up, but remain a child; to restrain emotion, but also express it—suggests that instead of the "disciplinary intimacy" model of Brodhead, we might be better served by a theory specific to children's literature in analyzing the emergence of emotion in parent-child relationships in the juvenile fiction of early nineteenth-century Britain. In his provocative article "Pleasure and Genre: Speculations on the Characteristics of Children's Fiction," Perry Nodelman argues that what gives him (and, he suggests, both adult and child readers) pleasure in reading the best children's literature is the way in its texts "pleasurably pull" him in two opposite directions: toward identifying with the protagonist, but simultaneously toward feeling superior to him or her; toward celebrating maturity but "in a way that causes me to question the completeness of its wisdom" (4). *The Tale of Peter Rabbit*, *Anne of Green Gables*, *Charlotte's Web*, *Treasure Island*—all reenact the "story of innocence joyfully indulged and then sensibly transcended"; the repetition of this story throughout the canon of children's literature returns readers over and over again to the position of innocence, the dictates of "growing up" acknowledged but endlessly deferred. The children's texts that Nodelman draws upon to support his theory are primarily from the twentieth century, with a few late Victorian texts added. But the double pull that Nodelman describes can also be found in much earlier, seemingly monovocal didactic literature, such as *Leila* and *The Young Crusoe*. Nodelman argues that the pleasures that such double-message texts hold need not be guilty ones, as a "disciplinary intimacy" reading would insist. Instead of papering over ideological contradictions in order to keep subjects ignorant of ideology's deficiencies, these texts instead draw attention to such contradictions, and thus create a child reader aware of ambivalences, subtleties, inconsistencies (13). As Hofland and Tytler's texts make abundantly clear, the roots of such a complex, multi-sided child subjectivity lie not only in the imaginative fantasy literature of the Victorian Golden Age, but also in the experimental didactic adventure novel of the earlier nineteenth century, a genre explicitly invested in experimenting with the new literary construction of the "ordinary" child. Offering both "moral influence" and "ices and cakes," robinsonades such as *The Young Crusoe* and *Leila* allow readers to indulge simultaneously in the pleasures of both.

Chapter 2
The Failure of the Ordinary: The Function of Death in the Family Robinsonade

The Lords day before that in which she died, a Kinsman of hers came to see her, and asking of her, whether she knew him, she answered; yes, I know you, and I desire you would learn to know Christ: you are young, but you know not how soon you may die; and O to die without a Christ, it is a fearful thing: O redeem Time, O Time, Time, Time, precious Time! Being requested by him not to spend her self: she said, she would fain do all the good she could while she lived, and when she was dead too, if possible; upon which account, she desired that a Sermon might be Preached at the Funeral concerning the preciousness of Time. O that young ones would remember their Creator!

> —James Janeway, "Of one eminently converted between
> Eight and Nine years old, with an account of her
> Life and Death" in *A Token for Children* (1672)[1]

"How many are you, then," said I,
"If they two are in heaven?"
Quick was the little Maid's reply,
"O Master! we are seven."

"But they are dead; those two are dead!
Their spirits are in heaven!"
'Twas throwing words away; for still
The little Maid would have her will,
And said, "Nay, we are seven!"

> —William Wordsworth, "We Are Seven" (1798)[2]

As we saw in Chapter 1, during the opening decades of the nineteenth century British writers of children's robinsonades experimented with creating a new type of child subjectivity, a subjectivity grounded not in idealized religious or moral exemplarity but in the ordinary workings of daily life. This shift from idealized to ordinary characterization did not, as previous critics have suggested, indicate a more liberated construction of the child in juvenile literature, but instead registered a broader cultural shift in the way literature for children modeled the exemplary. Rather than present idealized characters for readers to emulate, as was common

---

[1]   Example I.23. Quoted in Demers and Moyles, 47.
[2]   *Selected Poems and Prefaces by William Wordsworth*, ed. Jack Stillinger, 49–51.

in eighteenth–century history and in fiction for children, early nineteenth–century writers increasingly began to believe that the best way to encourage readers to accept their didactic messages was to first foster a bond of emotional identification between readers and characters. Such a bond would be far easier to promote if their texts' characters had the same faults, foibles, and emotions as did their juvenile readers, authors increasingly came to believe. But while such writers as Barbara Hofland and Ann Fraser Tytler may have hoped that by deploying ordinary characters, their readers would accept their didactic messages without question, the coding of behaviors that would once have been labeled "sinful" as "ordinary" in their works opened up a space for readers to take pleasure in such behaviors even as they imbibed the texts' surface message to transcend them.

Contested Visions of Childhood

While early literature of adventure for children may be notable for its increasing engagement with a construction of child protagonists we might call "ordinary," two very different constructions of childhood would emerge from other British literary genres of the early nineteenth century. The rise of the Evangelical movement during the first half of the century, both within the Church of England and in dissenting religious sects, led to a reassertion of the Augustinian construction of the child as born in original sin. Like Hofland and Tytler, evangelical authors for children, in particular the immensely popular Mary Martha Sherwood, moved away from featuring paragons of virtue as protagonists, creating main characters who had flaws as well as characteristics worth emulating. But they simultaneously insisted that the childish anger, fear, jealousy, and greed their main characters experienced were signs not of a mischievous nature inherent to the ordinary child, but of sin. As M. Nancy Cutt notes in her discussion of Sherwood's *The History of the Fairchild Family* (part I 1818), for the Evangelical, there are no little sins; evil is absolute, without gradation (*Mrs Sherwood* 65). Though Sherwood's novel features parents as loving and attentive as those in the novels of Hofland and Tytler, there is no laughing at, or taking pleasure in, childish misbehavior in the works of the Evangelicals in this period.

A third, far different construction of childhood simultaneously emerged from the pens of the lauded adult poets of the early nineteenth century. In the works of Charles Lamb, Thomas de Quincey, Hartley Coleridge, and, in particular, William Wordsworth,[3] a new type of exemplary child began to appear, a child depicted not within the context of an ordinary emotional family life, but rather as a being apart. Rejecting both the Lockean construction of the child as a morally neutral blank slate, and the newly reasserted Evangelical view of the child as one born in original

---

[3]   Many critics would place William Blake in this group as well, pointing in particular to his *Songs of Innocence* and *Songs of Experience*. But as Judith Plotz persuasively argues, the Victorians who later drew on Blake's binary to valorize innocence failed to acknowledge the critique of innocence that pervades Blake's work (xv).

sin who must be disciplined for its own salvation, the early Romantic poets instead drew upon and expanded Rousseau's construction of the inherently virtuous child of nature. As described by Judith Plotz, this new "Romantic child" became the "sanctuary of valuable but socially endangered psychic powers—idealism, holism, vision, animism, faith, and isolated self-sufficiency" (13). In the hands of Wordsworth and other first generation Romantic poets, the Romantic child came to represent the inherent creative powers that the adult poet must reclaim in order to create art, powers that emerge in an all-sufficing solitude. As both Plotz and Alan Richardson demonstrate, the child in Wordsworth's poetry is a multi-valenced creature, but the idea of the Romantic child in the broader culture came to be linked with a far narrower set of characteristics. As Richardson describes it, the Romantic child appears "Edenic, natural, and asocial" ("Childhood" 122). Bettina Kümmerling-Meibauer emphasizes the "more direct relationship to transcendence" of European Romantic childhood, a transcendence characterized by both positive qualities— creativity, imagination, and contemplation—and negative ones—isolation, longing, melancholy, and premonitions of death (186–7). Such characteristics, particularly the Romantic child's innocence, solitariness, and inherent connection to nature, emerge in striking contrast to those of the Evangelical child. Rather than in need of teaching by adults, as in the Evangelical model, the Romantic child could serve as exemplar to them; as James Holt McGavran poetically notes, "the adult's eyes are filled with light from the [Romantic] child" (7).

Isolating the child in nature, rather than enmeshing it within social institutions of school, state, and family, Plotz suggests, allows the Romantic poets to construct the child as an emblem of fixity rather than of growth or change (24). Rather than the developmental (and, as I have argued, the multi-vocal) construction of childhood to be found in the children's adventure novels written by British women in the period, the Romantic child who appeared in much of the adult poetry by men did not change, did not grow; "unmarked by time, place, class, or gender ... represented as in all places and all times the same," the "Child" became fixed, reified, essentialized (Plotz 5). Intriguingly, the Romantic child thus may have more in common with the idealized exemplar characters of eighteenth-century moral literature than with the ordinary, multi-valenced child emerging in contemporaneous literature for children.

Yet despite their similarities, the Romantic child and the idealized exemplar child differ markedly in one respect: death. The child of religious exempla, such as Sarah Howley, the girl described by James Janeway in the first epigraph to this chapter, or her descendent, the child of early nineteenth-century Evangelical fiction, such as Mrs Sherwood's Little Henry (*The History of Little Henry and his Bearer*, 1814), typically must die in order for the true power of her or his exemplary message to take hold of the reader. The child of Romanticism, in contrast, does not die; in fact, the very fixity of its construction serves as a buffer against death. If the child cannot change, cannot grow, then the child cannot die; even if the physical body no longer exists, the transcendent "Child" remains: "We are seven," not five.

In some ways, the Romantic construction of childhood, rather than the Evangelical one, seems better suited to the genre of the robinsonade, with its focus on the solitary castaway who returns triumphant at novel's end, having conquered his island and survived its attempts on his life. Defoe's novel was, after all, the only book Rousseau would allow his fictional Émile to read before the age of 12. As Martin Green notes, an "upward curve of adventure, optimism, and expectation ... directed outward, to achievement and self-confidence" characterizes the typical robinsonade (80). Yet such an "upward curve" necessitates not only the protagonist's success against nature and natives while on the island, but also his (or her) triumphant rescue and return to civilization at novel's end. Death may be dealt out to the disloyal sailors who, in robinsonade after robinsonade, abandon their ships and their helpless passengers in an attempt to save their own lives, or, particularly in later Victorian stories for boys, to the aggressive and often cannibalistic natives who threaten or attack shipwrecked Europeans. Yet European Robinsons must return, alive and prosperous, if the robinsonade is to conform to the pattern of the Crusoe story as laid out by Defoe and his followers, rather than remain in nature, as in the Romantic construction of childhood. This is particularly true of the juvenile robinsonade; children's literature from the Victorian period onward constructs its child, and that child's literature, as characterized by hope rather than by despair.

So what is one to make of juvenile robinsonades in which Evangelicalism invades the island in the form of death? Rejecting both a Romantic ending, which would allow the child to remain in the island idyll, and an ordinary child ending, which would return the child to civilization triumphant, the evangelically-tinged robinsonade deals death rather than life. In Frederick Marryat's *Masterman Ready* (volume I, 1841; volumes II and III, 1842), often accorded the status of the first "real" juvenile adventure story in histories of children's literature, the death of the title character provides the novel's climactic scene, while in Jefferys Taylor's *The Young Islanders* (1842), death is a running leitmotif, the narrator's fellow shipwrecked schoolmates dying off alone or in groups in almost every chapter. In each of these two juvenile robinsonades, I will argue, death is deployed in an attempt to interrogate the three seemingly opposed constructions of the child— the Evangelical child, the Romantic child, and the ordinary child, who embodies both positive and negative traits—at play in children's literature of the period. For, as Roger Cox notes of the ideologies of childhood in the early decades of the nineteenth century, "[w]e are faced ... with competing discourses that claim different histories and define themselves as much by opposition to other sets of ideas and beliefs as to their own intrinsic logic" (76). Hugh Cunningham echoes this idea, arguing that "[b]oth in attitudes to childhood and in behaviour towards children we are confronted at every turn by ambivalences and contradictions" (*Children* 62). In Marryat, death functions to defuse such ambivalences and contradictions, to contain the possibility that the mischievous ordinary child may turn out not to be the father of the wise poet, Wordsworth, but rather of that other powerful cultural construction of Romanticism: the passionate, irreligious rebel,

Lord Byron. For Taylor, in contrast, death signals an inability to reconcile three such opposing constructions, and a resultant despairing turn toward the excesses of the Gothic to compensate for the failure.

The Ordinary Child as Father to the Man: Frederick Marryat's *Masterman Ready* (1841–42)

Frederick Marryat, a former captain in the Royal Navy, wrote best-selling sea stories for adults during the 1820s and 1830s. When the public taste began to shift away from tales of nautical derring-do towards social realism, Marryat's friend, Charles Dickens, supplanted him as the most successful novelist in England (Pocock 172). Sales of Marryat's books for adults waned accordingly, and Marryat soon decided to turn his talents to a different market: the juvenile novel. His first book for children, *Masterman Ready*,[4] a re-envisioning of Wyss's *Swiss Family Robinson* written at the urging of his own children, proved a commercial success, and Marryat continued to write for juvenile readers throughout the remainder of his life. Most histories of children's literature credit Marryat with being the father of the juvenile adventure story, although, as Margery Fisher points out, Marryat's popularity with young readers stems far more from his adult sea novels than from the more didactic *Masterman Ready*, a novel that has

---

[4]   Marryat's novel has a long publishing history. Several of Marryat's novels for adults had earlier been published by Longman, one of the largest and most respected publishers in early nineteenth–century London; when Marryat turned to writing for children, the company continued to publish his works. Initially issued in three separate volumes by Longman, the parts of *Masterman Ready* were subsequently published together as one novel. Kevin Carpenter lists a reprint edition in 1842 by H.G. Bohn (Carpenter 105), but this edition does not appear in the database WORLDCAT, or in the British Library's listings; the earliest London reprint WORLDCAT lists is 1851, by the original publisher, Longman, which suggests that though the initial printing may have been larger than those of most children's books, given Marryat's fame, the novel was not, at least initially, popular enough to warrant multiple reprintings. The 1841 edition contains no illustrations; the illustration included in this volume was taken from the 1853 New York Appleton edition.

The publisher H.G. Bohn, who made his name in the market by purchasing the copyrights of remainders and republishing and selling them at lower prices, began to reissue *Masterman Ready* in 1854 (four later editions listed on WORLDCAT); the cheaper edition appears to have brought Marryat's novel to a wider audience, increasing his once waning popularity. Upon his retirement, Bohn sold his stock of new books to Bell and Daldry (later George Bell), which issued the novel in 1867, and in six later editions (as listed on WORLDCAT). Multiple publishers reprinted Marryat's novel during the period 1870–1900. American publishers appeared to publish more editions during the earlier period than British publishers; Appleton issued 12 editions between 1841–1883. Multiple German translations were published during the nineteenth century; the book has also been translated into 11 other languages.

far more in common with earlier juvenile moral literature than most historians of children's literature would have us believe (37).

Although Marryat's novel has many similarities to the robinsonades discussed in Chapter 1, it differs in two significant ways. First, although it, too, features a family—the Seagrave father, mother, and four children are cast away together on a South Seas island—Marryat's novel includes an additional character: Masterman Ready, the pious, knowledgeable seaman who provides both the survival skills and moral compass for the hapless stranded family. And, unlike earlier juvenile novels, which eschew the confrontation with the native other that formed the climax of Defoe's novel, the climax of Marryat's novel is an attack on the castaways by "savages" in volume III. Besieged, the family is slowly dying of thirst, the water that was to have tided them through any attack having been surreptitiously drained away before the arrival of the natives by six-year-old Tommy Seagrave, who, in his naughtiness, preferred an easier method of collecting water than hauling it from the family well. Masterman Ready takes it upon himself to sneak out of the protected fortress in order to replenish the water supply. His mission appears successful; he reaches the palisades with his prize. Yet just as he is about to enter, Ready is attacked. William, the eldest Seagrave boy, shoots and kills his native assailant, but Ready has already been mortally wounded. Although Marryat returns to the Defoe pattern by having the captain of the Seagrave's ship return just in the nick of time to rout the natives and rescue the Seagraves, his inclusion of the death of his title character tempers the triumph of the novel's denouement.

Why must Ready die? Critics have put forth several possible reasons. Martin Green cites the novel's embrace of a "severely evangelical ethos," an ethos that "runs counter to the spirit of adventure," and cites the death of Ready as the most "exceptional" characteristic of an ethos which he is clearly puzzled to find in the midst of a robinsonade (88, 89). Joseph Bristow concurs, although he labels the impulse moralistic rather than evangelical; linking the novel to earlier children's literature, he describes it as "a didactic tract rooted in eighteenth-century children's literature, designed to provide moral sustenance to the young reader" (94). But he also points to an imperial context: the final confrontation with the natives after nearly three volumes of little to no real "adventure" functions as the return of the "repressed 'others' of Marryat's colonized world"; only a violent encounter can bring this adventure-less novel to an end (101). Claudia Nelson echoes the didactic arguments of Green and Bristow, arguing that "the project of influencing the elders must be undertaken not only wordlessly but lifelessly, when Ready's sacrifice of his life for the family leads Mr Seagrave to exclaim that 'by his example, sinful as I must ever be, I have become, I trust, a better man'" (*Boys* 15). Thus, Ready's death functions not only as the "ultimate self-effacement" but the "ultimate influence—and clearly one depends on the other" (*Boys* 15). Ready also must die, Nelson argues, because his Christian piety simply makes him too good for the world of adult men that characterizes civilization outside the island; the evangelical ideal is ill suited to the masculine life of commerce and market. Nelson's analysis also implies a class component: the Seagraves's desire to include Ready as a part of their post-island domestic household would entail a dangerous crossing of class boundaries, a crossing that can be countenanced in the liminal space of the deserted island, but not in the world of the larger social order.

All of these interpretations are intriguing, but they do not explain what to me is the most curious part of Ready's death: his dying words to the elder Seagrave brother, William. The last words we hear from the sailor, with the exception of his call to the family to take leave of them, are "Poor little Tommy; don't let him know that he was the cause of my death" (III.124). Ready gives no explanation for this dying wish, and it seems strikingly at odds with the purported didactic intent of the text. If Tommy is to learn from his mistakes, then is it not necessary that he be made aware of them? Mr Seagrave certainly thinks so, at least initially, exclaiming as the elder members of the family gather to discuss the momentous events of the day, "It adds much to my regret ... that his life should have been sacrificed through the thoughtlessness of one of my own children; what a lesson it will be to Tommy when he is old enough to comprehend fully the consequences of his conduct!" But when William informs his father of what readers already know—"That he must not know, papa, ... one of Ready's last injunctions was that Tommy was never to be told of it. He made me promise"—Mr Seagrave readily concurs: "His last wishes shall be religiously attended to, my dear boy" (III.128).

Why must the secret of Ready's death be kept from Tommy? Not just now, but forever? And why must the secret, paradoxically, be known all too well by the child reader outside the text, even while it is kept a secret from the child within? To answer these questions, we must turn to the way in which Marryat's text constructs the six-year-old Tommy. For while Claudia Nelson is surely correct to locate the novel's "center" in the "instinctive bond between the pious and elderly title character and 12-year-old William" (*Boys* 14), the connections between the pious sailor and the "naughty" Seagrave sibling that lie at its periphery can lead us to see the intriguing return of a different repressed "other," the venturesome, rebellious child who was the father of the pious man Ready.

As in much didactic fiction for children, Marryat's novel includes an early, brief description of its main characters, setting out their defining traits. The other Seagrave children rate fairly offhand comments: the sole girl, Caroline, is described only by age, while baby Albert is noted to be "a fine strong little fellow" in addition to being not yet a year old (I.14–15). William, the novel's main child character, rates a few more phrases: "the eldest, a clever steady boy, but, at the same time, full of mirth and humor" (I.14). Throughout the three volumes of the novel, William proves himself over and over to be "a clever, steady boy," but any mirth or humor he might possess are rarely depicted during the rest of the book. William's younger brother, six-year-old Thomas, is similarly described in dual terms: "a very thoughtless but good-tempered boy, full of mischief, and always in a scrape" (I.14); but, as in the description of William, half of the terms do not play out in the course of Marryat's text. Tommy is perpetually getting into scrapes, but rarely would a reader be tempted to term his temper "good." Maurice-Paul Gautier terms him an "enfant terrible," but suggests that as such he is more realistically portrayed than the rather flat William ("Tommy, l'enfant terrible, aura une présence aussi grande et peut-être plus vraisemblable en maintes occasions que William, son frère aîne" [II.176]). Taken together, however, the two brothers form a dual mirror for the book's main protagonist, the profoundly pious Masterman Ready, a religious man with a less than spotless past.

Before turning to Ready, I want to explore the nature of Tommy's purported "realism," the nature of his scrape-prone behavior. Early in the novel, readers are treated to a long description of Tommy's penchant for mischief. When the Seagraves's ship, bound for Australia from England, stops at the Cape of Good Hope, Mr Seagrave and the boys go ashore and visit a botanical garden, which includes a den of captured lions. Tommy teases the caged lions, throwing stones at them while the others are distracted by stories told by their guide. When Tommy gets too close to the bars, one lion springs and roars at him; Tommy stumbles and falls out from the lion's reach. After roaring himself and being scolded by his father, Tommy keeps "a most respectful distance" from all the other caged creatures; "He wouldn't even go near to a Cape sheep with a broad tail" (I. 25).

In this scene, designed to highlight the character of mischievous Tommy, multiple discourses of the child are at play, discourses that sit uneasily together in the same passage. Tommy's conduct, tinged with aggression and violence, harkens back to an earlier model of the child as characterized by original sin, a model that had recently reemerged in the early decades of the nineteenth century in the juvenile fiction of Mary Martha Sherwood, her sister Mrs Cameron, and other evangelical writers. The scene's conclusion, with Tommy learning from his mistake to "keep a respectful distance" from the other animals, suggests a Lockean belief in the ability of the child to learn from experience. As Tommy "roars" alongside the lion, he is linked with nature, and with the savage, echoing the constructions of the child as uncivilized, savage (a positive trait) found in the writings of Rousseau. And the hint of humor of the final line of the passage—"He wouldn't even go near to a Cape sheep with a broad tail"—suggests an invitation to the reader, if not to the adults within the text, to laugh at the behavior of the mischievous child, an invitation that points to a different construction: a combination of the naturally innocent Romantic child with the naturally-mischievous ordinary child. If we can and should laugh at such behavior, it cannot be truly bad, truly sinful, and may even be a source of pleasure for the more mature onlooker.

This passage also introduces two patterns that will characterize each recurrence of Tommy's misbehavior throughout the novel. First, Tommy's action stems from the fact that adults are not watching over the boy. So interested are they in a story being told, they do not pay attention to a boy who they know is prone to getting into trouble. There is a separation between adult and child, a separation unlike that seen in earlier family robinsonades; the child and adult may be in the same physical space, but their minds are occupied by different objects. The novel marks this separation as an inevitable, yet deeply regrettable result of the emergent construction of the ordinary mischievous child. Second, while the passage ends with the idea that Tommy learns from his mistake, the idea of learning from one's mistakes is repudiated over and over during the course of the novel, as Tommy repeatedly misbehaves, and as his misbehavior leads to ever more serious and dangerous consequences. Despite the hopes of earlier rational moral writers, for Marryat the child is, by definition, *not* able to learn his lesson; Tommy's inability to do so leads directly to Ready's death.

Tommy's misbehavior is portrayed in 18 separate scenes in the novel, a number that indicates their importance as a secondary running plot throughout the book. During the novel's first volume, one is initially tempted to read Tommy's actions as comic relief, actions which mitigate the tension of the struggle to survive the storm and subsequent shipwreck. In one farcical scene, Tommy grabs a basin of hot pea soup, spilling it over his sister; Juno, the children's nurse, slips as she rushes to Caroline's aid, falling on the terrier, who bites her. In another, Tommy fires a musket supposed to be used only to signal trouble, causing Ready anxiety and fear but ultimately no danger. And when the family is walking to a new home site on the opposite side of the island, Tommy's whining that he is tired leads older brother William to carry him "pickaback," a distraction which leads William to lose sight of the trail markers and delay the family's arrival by several hours, with one child after another setting off on a crying jag, a chorus of comic discontent. Martin Green clearly wants to read Tommy, the "liveliest and naughtiest of the Seagrave children" in a positive light, but ultimately finds such a reading untenable: "Tommy has caused alarms and mishaps throughout the book, but because he is so lively, the reader remained sure that he was to be forgiven—indeed, preferred—according to the conventional morality of fiction. But the plot forces us to take even children's naughtiness judgmentally, puritanically" (80). The "conventional morality of fiction" to which Green refers—a preference for the mischievous rather than the well-behaved child—has as long history in literature for adults, in comic novels and plays such as Fielding's *Tom Jones* and Richard Brinsley Sheridan's *The School for Scandal*, and in the preference for younger sons in the Old Testament and in folklore. But preference for the scapegrace is just beginning to emerge in literature for children at the time when Marryat is writing. Although such characters made frequent appearances in his novels for adults, Marryat finds it hard to fully embrace this convention in his work for children.

We can also see Marryat's unease with the emergent vision of the Romantic child, a vision that is characterized by its association of childhood with imagination, an association that often provokes a longing in the adult for a childhood now lost. One day, Tommy is planting some stones; when his mother asks what he is doing, he tells her "I'm playing—I'm making a garden." When his mother protests that planting stones won't make anything grow, he replies, "I know that ... but I'm making believe, because I have no seeds." Again his mother protests, saying "But you said you were sowing seeds, Tommy, and not stones." Tommy replies, "Well, I pretend, and that's the same thing" (I.157). Mrs Seagrave, unappreciative of her child's urge to imagine, focuses instead on the lack of precision in his utterance: pretending is not the same, she insists, as really planting seeds. She then attempts to turn the conversation into a moral lesson. Yet Tommy resists

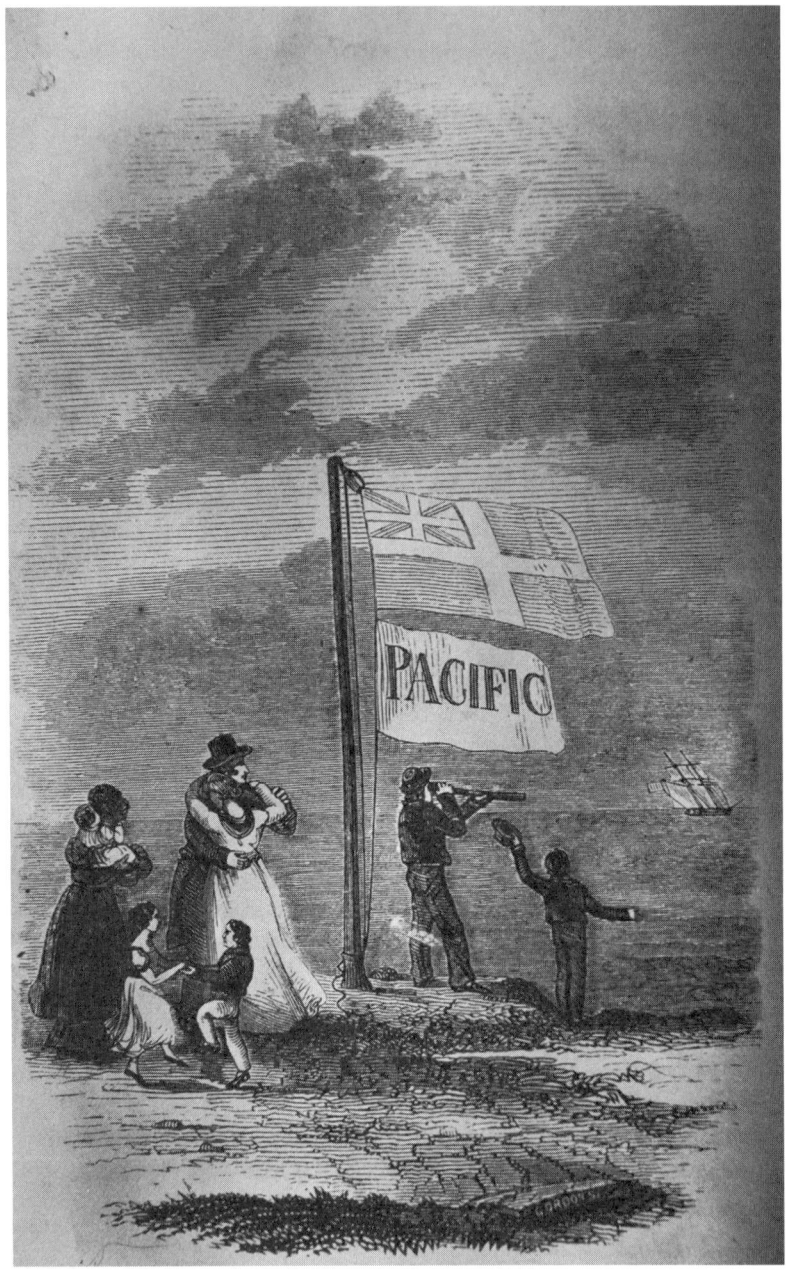

Fig. 2.1   "Mischievous Tommy frolics with his sister while the rest of the Seagrave party looks anxiously toward a possible rescue ship." Courtesy of the author.

her efforts, turning every comment she makes back to his own concerns: "You should never eat anything that is not given to you" leads Tommy to reply "I like cocoa-nuts; why don't we have some to eat? There's plenty there upon the trees" (I.157–8). One might be tempted to feel that Marryat is criticizing the parenting of Mrs Seagrave here, objecting to her lack of engagement in her child's imaginative life; yet the balance of the scene focuses on Tommy's aggressive behavior, not on condemning his mother. Clearly, the adult Seagraves have little tolerance for a Romantic vision of childhood, one that constructs the child as by nature imaginative and then celebrates the creative power of that imagination.

Tommy's character connects in many ways to an Augustinian vision of the child as characterized by original sin. Many of Tommy's mishaps stem from his greed, in particular his desire for food: dropping his mother's thimble into the soup in an attempt to scoop out an early taste; stealing eggs from the henhouse before they can be collected for the entire family's use; choking on a bone because he eats so quickly. A fear of bodily desire, constructed here as a child's desire for food, characterizes much evangelical writing for children in the period. Tommy's resistance to work, and his aggression not only towards animals (throwing stones at the lion, kicking a goat, killing beetles, teasing a crayfish) but also toward his sister (he puts a cinder into her hand and burns her; he threatens to shoot her when she would tell the adults he is playing with the forbidden firearm) also points to an inherent original sinfulness rather than to a playful mischievousness.

Yet if Marryat is not ready to embrace the Romantic child, neither is he entirely comfortable with a vision of the child as original sinner as constructed by evangelical discourse. When his mother chastises Tommy for teasing a goat, she tells him "It is very wrong of him to do so, especially as he is told by his father and me that he ought not. Good children always obey their parents, but Tommy is not a good boy." Tommy immediately takes exception: "You said I was a good boy when I learned my lesson well this morning," he retorts. When his mother answers "Yes, but you should always be good," Marryat allows Tommy the last word: "I can't always be good … I'm very hungry, I want my dinner." (I.160). In older brother William, Marryat sets forth a portrait of a child who can "always be good," yet in this passage Marryat clearly sympathizes with the impossibility of perfect behavior. Marryat's fantasy child, William, is an ideal child, yet this fantasy is continually interrupted, troubled, and contested by the return of the repressed ordinary child, with its bodily urges and selfish desires.

Marryat's construction of Tommy draws upon evangelical constructions of the child, but it departs from that construction in its ultimate judgment of Tommy's behavior. Instead of insisting that such behavior must be eradicated, rooted out, replaced by better values, the novel, with its repeated pattern of misbehavior after misbehavior, suggests that Tommy *cannot* change, that such behavior is not sinful, but only natural—for a child. Although the Seagraves and Juno often upbraid Tommy for his deeds, Masterman Ready, the moral compass of the novel, does not. Instead, he consistently explains Tommy's behavior as a natural result of his being a child. For example, after Ready must brave shark-infested waters to retrieve

Tommy, who has set himself adrift in the sailboat, he exclaims to William, "How much mischief may be created by a thoughtless boy! However, one can't put old heads on young shoulders, and so Master Tommy must be forgiven" (III.75). And at the novel's climax, when Tommy's stealing of the water has endangered not only himself, but also his entire family and Ready, Ready explains to William, "A child does not reflect upon consequences, Master William, nor could we possibly foresee that his using up the water could have created such misery. It was an idle trick of his, and whatever may be the consequences, it still can be considered as such and nothing more" (III.105). Explicitly rejecting the idea that Tommy's behavior stems from sin, Ready replaces the explanatory power of original sin with a different construction of the child: irrational, thoughtless, unable to "reflect upon consequences." In so doing, Marryat rejects not only the evangelical construction of the child, but also the construction that characterized the child of the rational moralists who wrote juvenile fiction in the early decades of the century, a child who could use reason to learn from life's experiences. In traditional Catholic doctrine, the age of reason is seven. But Evangelical and moral writers for children often featured younger protagonists (five of Janeway's 13 pious children were four or five; Sherwood's Little Henry is five or six; Edgeworth's Rosamund is "about seven" in "The Purple Jar"), believing that even young children could be taught to reason, and/or to recognize the sinfulness of bad behavior. Marryat here seems far more influenced by Rousseau, who, in *Émile*, identifies 12, rather than seven, as the age of rational thought.

Why is Ready so sympathetic to Tommy's bad behavior? In part, the novel suggests, because it is so similar to his own behavior as a child. For, as we learn from the "History of Old Ready," told by the sailor over the course of multiple chapters during volume II, Tommy's childish actions are in many ways a mirror image of his own. "Mine was a proud nature when I was a child," Ready tells the entire family as they listen to his story over the course of a season of rainy evenings; "I could not bear that any boy should do what I could not; and I often ventured so rashly, that I might do more than other boys dared to do, that it was a wonder, as everyone then said, that I had not lost my life a hundred times" (II.21). Just as Tommy is continually endangered by his mischievous behavior—almost killed by falling cocoanuts, nearly choking to death on a bone, within a hair's breadth of being swept out to sea in a runaway boat—so too was the young Ready.

Joseph Bristow suggests that Tommy offers a "glimpse" into the text's resistance to its own puritanical message, a message that insists both that "children are naturally unruly" and that they "must learn the error of their ways." Ready's inset narrative—"almost in spite of itself"—asserts that "boys are independent at heart, in nature rebellious, and competitive in spirit. They are 'venturesome.' Adventure characterizes boyhood" (100). Bristow argues that the lack of real adventure in Marryat's novel is the result of the erasure of all "traits of incorrigible boyhood" that Ready's back-story tells. Yet Bristow is incorrect when he suggests that Ready's incorrigibility ceases as soon as he joins the navy and leaves childhood behind; Ready goes on to tell the Seagraves a tale of repeated mistakes, missteps, and ill-judgments that extend far into his adult life. Though he vows to change his ways after the death of his mother, he, like Tommy, is soon back pursuing his own selfish wants, indulging his own bodily desires. After inheriting £2000, he spends profligately (£100 in only 10 days); after purchasing part of a ship, and becoming its captain, he foolishly sails home from a trading expedition without waiting for a naval escort, nullifying the insurance and losing his entire investment when his ship is captured by the French. He begins to embrace Christianity, but then rejects his teacher, a Scottish seaman, when the man's religious exhortations become a thorn in his side in rebuking his pride, vanity, and self-indulgence. Only after being imprisoned by the French, and losing all his money, does Ready truly convert, and become the overtly pious exemplar that we, and the Seagraves, have known him as from the start of the novel.

Ready's behavior is not the only example in the text of adults, rather than children, behaving badly. In fact, Ready's inset history is riddled with adult men in positions of authority who abuse the child and adult Ready. His godfather, Mr Masterman, after whom he was named, cheats him out of his fortune and provides no support to his widowed mother after the death of Ready's father, the man's business partner; the captain of his first ship is verbally and physically abusive; a Dutch farmer who captures him and his friends after they flee imprisonment in South Africa is equally brutal, beating the boys and whipping the other workers and slaves. As Gautier notes, "... la présence des adultes s'accompagne toujours de violence. ... Nous sommes frappés par le contraste entre le comportement des jeunes et celui de leurs aînes." (II.181). This is certainly true in Ready's inset narrative; yet on the island, it seems to be just the reverse. The more telling contrast is between the adults of the world beyond the island, and those upon it; compared with the outside world, the island is an idyll of caring adults, while violent, abusive behavior appears not in the adults, but in the child.

Ready's death, his self-sacrifice, then, can be read symbolically as an attempt not only to rid the world of adult sinful behavior, but also to consign and confine such behavior to the safe space of childhood. For it is not the child who learns from the Christ-like self-sacrifice of the Christian martyr Ready; instead it is the adult male. Mr Seagrave is far from the violent, aggressive adult males who intervene in Ready's childhood and young adulthood, yet he was wont on occasion to lament his fate and distrust in God's protection. Significantly, such scenes are the only times in the novel when Ready drops his deferential way of speaking to Mr Seagrave, and takes it upon himself to upbraid his social superior directly. After Ready's death, however, as Mr Seagrave recounts Ready's many acts of self-sacrifice, he exclaims, "by his example, sinful as I must ever be, I have become, I trust, a better man" (III.129). As Claudia Nelson argues, "Ready's shielding of Tommy from guilt extends the lesson to the entire adult world" (*Boys* 16). But it also rejects the idea that the lesson can have relevance in the world of the child. For Tommy must never be told the truth of Ready's final sacrifice, and thus cannot learn to be a "better" child, as his father learns to be a "better man"; he must remain, the recalcitrant, mischievous boy who cannot change, a safe repository for the sins of the adult world that Ready's sacrifice works to banish. Limiting sin, renamed "mischievous behavior," to the realm of the boy constructs such behavior as only natural, if often to be regretted, thereby taming sin by restricting it to the world of the relatively powerless child. Marryat thus simultaneously rejects the "grisly Sherwoodian principles of infant accountability" common to evangelical children's fiction (Nelson, *Boys* 16) and embraces a vision of childhood characterized by aggressive, selfish impulses, impulses that, by being restricted to childhood, make the adult world safe from sin.

Yet to confine bad behavior to childhood in this way is also to open up a yawning gap between the adult and the child. This gap forms the crux of the vision of the Romantic poets' child—his self-sufficiency depends on his isolation from the social, particularly from the family. But in Marryat's text, such a gap is not celebrated, but mourned. The adult Ready knows that his childhood behavior gave great pain to his mother, yet also recognizes that when a he was child, as the text constructs that child, such knowledge was explicitly denied him:

> "I've often thought since, how selfish and unfeeling I must have been. I was too young to know what pain I was giving her, and how anxiety was preying upon her, all on my account. Children cannot feel it; if they did, they would do otherwise, for our hearts are seldom hard until we grow older."

> "I agree with you, Ready," said Mr Seagrave. "If children really knew how much their parents suffer when they behave ill, how alarmed they are at any proofs of wickedness in them, they would be much better."

> "We never find that out, sir, till it is too late," continued Ready (II.21–2).

Even while the text constructs the child within it as "unfeeling," as unable to "know," however, the suffering of the adults around them, it attempts to construct a child *outside* the text who does feel, who does know. If Tommy must be kept in the dark about Ready's sacrifice, the reader just as surely must be told of it. Though the text's overt message seems to suggest to its reader, who, presumably, will be closer to William's age than Tommy's, to act more like the idealized elder Seagrave child than the younger ordinary one, Marryat's construction of Tommy invites us, no, demands that we occupy both positions simultaneously: to know and to not know, to be naturally inquisitive, venturesome, adventurous *and* to accept the text's message of piety and self-effacement. Ready himself was transformed from a mischievous child and young adult into a mature Christian only by being continually abused and abased: suffering the death of his mother, being whipped and beaten, deprived of food and water, and repeatedly incarcerated whenever his pleasures were becoming too paramount. Ready's textual sacrifice suggests that there is another way; by experiencing the sufferings of another vicariously, through a text, the child reader may be able to leap over the gap between unthinking, unfeeling child and rational, feeling adult that his own text has constructed.

But the text itself cannot depict its own characters making the leap over such a gap; we never see Tommy learning to change his ways, as we saw Ready. Instead, the text itself makes the leap, over time, telling us in the "P.S." that concludes the book, "Tommy, notwithstanding all his scrapes, grew up a very fine fellow, and entered the army. He is now a major, and is said to retain his juvenile tastes so far, that, among his many arduous duties, he is still a very sedulous and efficient young officer at the *Mess Table*" (III.135). Tommy's childhood aggression has been rechanneled into the military, put to productive social use; his bodily desires are no longer constructed as sinfully greedy, but as the trace of "juvenile tastes" that, in the adult, become the objects of laughter rather than anxiety. Tommy may still be making a "mess," but he's no longer creating chaos, danger, or peril. He has "grown up," a process which Marryat's novel demands of its readers but cannot portray in its narrative. By consigning bad behavior to the realm of the pre-rational child, then, Marryat can deploy the constructions of the ordinary child and the innocent Romantic child, while simultaneously ensuring that ordinary childish mischief will never be transformed into adult rebellion or sin.

The Utter Impossibility of Empathy: Gothic Invades the Island in Jefferys Taylor's *The Young Islanders* (1841)

> "Are father and mother yet alive, and little Sally; and do they ever dream about poor George? Did the people put on mourning for us; and do they feel certain we are all dead?"[5]

While those who, like Martin Green, expect a "myth of Protestant and progressive triumph" in their robinsonades, may find the death of Masterman Ready shocking, for readers familiar with early and mid-Victorian conventions of literary deaths, the pious seaman's passing would seem all too familiar. The convention of the "good death," found in devotional literature known as the *ars moriendi*, or the art of dying, in late medieval and early modern England, had been in decline during the Enlightenment, but reappeared in the fervor of the Evangelical revival. Pat Jalland describes four characteristics of the good death: death should take place at home, with the dying person making explicit farewells to each family member; the dying person should retain his or her physical or mental capacities, in order to beg God for forgiveness and prove his or her worthiness for salvation; the dying should have time enough to set his or her final affairs in order; and death should be met with fortitude, and even welcomed. As Jalland notes, the evangelical concept of the good death influenced not only those who belonged to evangelical congregations, but also a majority of the nineteenth-century English population (17–19, 26, 20). While in actuality few could achieve all four of its requirements, the good death flourished in literature, from the evangelical tracts to the most popular novels of the day, particularly those of Charles Dickens.

---

[5]   Taylor, *The Young Islanders*, 245.

Masterman Ready, like his contemporaries little Nell or Paul Dombey, dies the sentimental good death, providing religious consolation to his spectators both within and outside the text.

The evangelical good death proves impossible to achieve in another juvenile robinsonade published shortly after *Masterman Ready*: Jefferys Taylor's *The Young Islanders: A Tale of the Last Century* (1842).[6] In Taylor's novel, not just one, but dozens of inept, confused, and panic-stricken schoolboys lose their lives on a far from beneficent deserted isle. Kevin Carpenter, who describes Taylor's novel as "one of the most morbid stories offered to early-Victorian children," suggests that the novel is best read in the context of evangelicalism: on the island, the marooned schoolboys "learn quite literally that 'the wages of sin is death'" (106). But the book's horrific, rather than sentimental, view of death suggests another model may be in order. The novel, in fact, seems closer to William Golding's twentieth century anti-robinsonade, *Lord of the Flies* (1954), suggesting that Taylor's work will reject the innocent Romantic child in favor of a darker vision of the young as inherently uncivilized, bestial, murderous. Taylor's novel, I will argue, performs similar cultural work to Golding's, but has a far different feel, a far different tone, than either the stern retribution found in early nineteenth-century evangelical novels or the bitter disillusionment in Golding's post-World War II rejection of Enlightenment liberal humanism and benevolence. Taylor's novel evokes a profound dis-ease with the construction of the Romantic child, particularly when that child is confronted with the task of making the transition between childhood and adulthood. In Taylor's robinsonade, three cornerstones of the construction of the Romantic child—his connection to a nurturing natural world, his isolated self-sufficiency, and his creative, generative imagination—are unceremoniously yanked from the foundation, bringing the entire vision crashing down around the reader's ears. Nature leads to loss, not life; separation from the world of adults is endlessly mourned; imagination creates not life or freedom, but danger and death. The result is a novel pregnant both with mourning and horror, a robinsonade in which decay, not progress, is the dominant note. For in Taylor's robinsonade, the Gothic has invaded the island.

---

6   Jefferys Taylor's robinsonade was not reprinted as often as Marryat's, not unsurprisingly given Marryat's enormous popularity as an author for adults. Yet Taylor's book was not simply an oddity, published only to disappear after a single edition. The novel's original publisher, Tilt and Bogue, later known for importing the American practice of issuing inexpensive editions of classic works, was recognized during the 1820s and 1830s for the wide variety of books it published for children (Mock 57; Browning 296). Taylor's novel was reprinted twice by Tilt and Bogue (in 1844 and in 1849), and was later reissued in 1853 and 1859 as *The Young Islanders, and What Came of Their Adventures* by Simpkin, Marshall & Co. (Carpenter 106). WORLDCAT also lists 10 American editions published between 1842 and 1910. In its first decade, it would seem, Taylor's novel proved more popular than Marryat's, although the tide would shift in *Masterman Ready*'s favor soon after. The illustration featured in this volume was taken from the 1842 New York Appleton edition.

The Young Islanders opens with an introduction in which the book's purported author accounts, slyly and ironically, for the genesis of the tale that will follow, an account that prefigures many of the obsessions of the subsequent narrative. Initially, it seems as if the narrator is attempting to validate the truth of the story by telling the reader that he is not its author; in its original form, it consisted of "a musty, worm-eaten coil of papers, enveloped in dusty and cobwebs" (v). Taylor appears to be deploying the trope common in eighteenth-century fiction of pretending that a novel is not in fact a novel at all, but a "true history." But we hear no details about the source of the papers, where the author found them and or why they are to be believed, suggesting that something different from validation is occurring here. Instead, this discovery of papers suggests a connection with the genre of the Gothic, whose novels often featured opening frame narratives in which their narrators both account for the fantastic and/or supernatural components of the tale that follows and distance themselves from it by attributing them to another author. Though in the introduction Taylor's narrator does not discuss the horrific components of the story that will follow, he does "attribut[e] to the Islanders the entire value and interest of their adventures" (vii). Yet this distancing is not as stable as it initially seems.

The author of the introduction tells us that he has taken the dusty collection of papers outside, to "give the YOUNG ISLANDERS the threshing they long ago deserved" (vi); as the singular of the novel's title shifts to the plural "they," the characters and the manuscript of which they are the supposed authors become conflated, a cleaning of one shading into a punishment of the others. Yet such attempts at chastisement backfire: a spider, "not thinking himself entitled to that discipline, issued, with all speed of terror, from the dark interior of the scroll, and sought, what he contrived to be, the unappropriated and more tranquil retirement of my coat sleeve" (vi). The identity of the adult authority figure, the discipliner (the narrator) remains stable here, but the identity of the disciplined shifts once again, from islanders to manuscript to spider; such instability of identity prefigures the novel's subsequent invocation of and play with different constructions of the child. In its new guise, the disciplined child/spider flees from terror by seeking comfort, sanctuary, in the arms of the adult authority figure, yet that authority figure "know[s] not" what becomes of it. The safety promised by a turn toward adult authority is questioned; what kind of sanctuary does the authority figure offer, when he himself is the author of the very discipline that terrorized the child/spider in the first place? The spider's act causes the narrator to drop "the precious bundle" and to kick it as he dances a "tantivy" in his efforts to rid himself of the eight-legged interloper. Child identity shifts once more, the manuscript once again conflated with its purported creators; like the "truant subjects of their pages, they eschewed all control," scattering in the wind. Physical discipline, rather than inspiring self-control, leads only to greater chaos. The failure of anything else that might take the place of "threshing" in an attempt to control recalcitrant youth is a central obsession in the novel that follows.

The manuscript's "truancy" means that the author must play editor, "arranging, numbering, and deciphering the multitudinous collection" (vi). The editorship suggests that such deciphering is possible, that order can be restored. But the editor's task, although termed "delightful," is made difficult by the state of decay in which the pages consist: "scarcely a leaf of which was not stained, obliterated, or partly consumed, by rain, mildew, sea-water, or some such casualty of time and travel" (vi). The decay of the pages purportedly written by the young islanders foreshadows not only their own decline and decay, a decay that the following narrative will play out in harrowing, melancholy detail, but also the difficulties of restoring order to adult-child relations in the wake of the new construction of the Romantic child.

The introduction takes a final twist with its author refusing to "play the part of Daniel Defoe" with the reader, a part which, "if the report of his day be true," would require the author to "plume" himself in the "ill-spared feathers" of another (in Defoe's case, Alexander Selkirk's) and "figure away with the writings" of another "as his own" (vii). The originary robinsonade which appears to be the model for Taylor's own narrative is itself a displacement, a "figuring away" that makes the original writer disappear, the truth of his story hidden in the plumes of the fictional. Yet Taylor's aim is clearly not to recover a truth that is now lost, but to question the potential for such a recovery project at all. Taylor concludes his introduction with a sly joke: "Rather by far, would I reverse [Defoe's] plan, and place magnanimously to the account of others, the very labours that I performed myself" (vii). Of course, Taylor himself *has* reversed Defoe's plan; a knowing reader will understand that the "labours" that follow were clearly "performed" by Taylor, and not by the novel's purported narrator, 14-year-old schoolboy Miles Selwyn. Just as adult readers have learned to question the assurances of the "editor" of *Robinson Crusoe* when he reports that "The Editor believes the thing to be a just History of Fact; neither is there any Appearance of Fiction in it" (3), so, too, Taylor suggests, child readers must learn to see behind the "truth" to the performer who constructs it. The "truth" that Taylor wishes his readers to see beyond are the multiple, conflicting, impossible constructions of childhood present in his culture, constructions created not by children, but by adults; to force his readers to see these "truths" as performances, Taylor will disrupt the conventions of the robinsonade, estranging us from its story of progress by turning it into a Gothic tale of horrific proportions.

Given Taylor's witty preface, a reader might expect to turn to the adventure that follows to discover amusement, humor, or even parody in the story, set 100 years in the past, of 52 schoolboys who, one by one, disappear or succumb to death via accident and suicide, starvation and illness, on a deserted island. Such an expectation would only be reinforced by the author's reputation for being the "wag" of the Taylor family (Field 323), a literary clan well-represented in the annals of children's literature: Taylor's father, Isaac, a dissenting minister and line-engraver, who wrote (with Jefferys) juvenile informational books such as *Scenes in Europe* (1818), *Asia* (1819), *Africa* (1820), and others; mother Ann, author of conduct literature and children's stories; and, most famously, sisters Ann and Jane Taylor, authors of some of the earliest poetry for children, published in collections such as *Original Poems, for Infant Minds* (1804, 1805) and *Rhymes for the Nursery* (1806). Jefferys Taylor's own previous work for children, including *Harry's Holiday* (1818), *Aesop in Rhyme* (1820), and *The Little Historians* (1824, discussed in Chapter 3) is characterized by a sense of humor and play similar to that found in this novel's preface. Yet F.J. Harvey Darton's brief description of this later novel—"a lively series of adventures, but not entirely free of moralization" (186)—seems the epitome of understatement when one turns to the dark tale that follows, a story haunted by bodies, decay, and death.

The novel proper opens with a long description of Seaward-house, the home of the "ancient foundation school" in the parish of St Runwald, founded during the reign of Edward VI[7] (9). Though the former abode of nobility, the property is now, in 1754, "gloomy" and in "a ruinous and unsafe condition" (10). The house itself sits atop a chalky knoll, land that has been gradually worn away by the "constant encroachment of the sea" (15); the stone dug from the chalk pits behind the house, in an attempt to form a breakwater, only makes it easier for the sea to do its damage. Storms "rocked [the house] to the foundation and, at such times, threatened its instant demolition" (11); work to repair the "frightful" cracks in the walls is to no avail. Such descriptions place us clearly in the realm of the Gothic, an oppressive physical space demarcated by decay and decline. Indeed, our narrator, 14-year-old Miles Selwyn, makes explicit the house's link, in his mind, to death: "There was, I remember, a neat crack in one of the towers, reaching from a window on the staircase to the next above it, and so on to the top. In high winds, this crevice would gape and gasp like the lips of the dying" (22), while the booming of the sea "impressed my youthful imagination, as with the groans of deep voices, sobbing murmurs of distress, or the half suppressed whispers of secret discourse" (16). Child imagination here leads to visions, but not the visions of unity or wholeness that characterize the Romantic child; instead, the decaying Seaward-house evokes fragmentary images: whispers half suppressed, unintelligible groans and murmurs, the "unspeakable" common to the Gothic.[8]

---

[7]   Edward VI, the boy king who did not live to rule in his own right and was continually subject to the dictates of his adult male advisors, seems a deliberate choice here, his early death foreshadowing the multiple boy deaths to follow in the novel.

[8]   Literary Gothic points to something quite different than architectural Gothic, a discourse that Elizabeth Gargano evokes in her analysis of Victorian debates about school design in *Reading Victorian Schoolrooms*: "… architectural styles took on a symbolic resonance as embodiments of pedagogical styles … the century's contest between ornament and utility played out in the struggle between classical education, linked with traditional Gothic structures, and a new scientific pedagogy associated with a modern rectilinear architecture" (15). Taylor's text is more concerned with social than with pedagogical reforms; the Gothic structures of Seaward-House are linked not to a call for a traditional classical education, but to the horrors of the literary Gothic.

Yet if Taylor draws upon some conventions of the Gothic, he transforms others. For in the Gothic for adults, as Ellen Moers, Sandra Gilbert and Susan Gubar, and Michelle Massé have all observed, the threat of violence against women plays a central role. In Taylor's novel, violence remains, recast in the opening chapters as discipline: Seaward-house "gave the idea of some dismal edifice—half castle, half prison—erected or reserved for the restraint or discipline of some sad delinquents within" (22). Yet the bodies upon which this violence is played out are those of adolescent boys, not young women. The discipline at St Runwalds is "rough and peremptory," its "routine and regiment … harsh, and manifestly injurious" (24). The rules of the trust that established the school, written centuries earlier, dictate the treatment of its students; any attempt to change its "routine and regiment" would endanger the school's very existence. Post-French Revolutionary fiction, including gothic fiction, often portrayed ancien régime-style laws or will provisions that continued to reach out to cripple the present as corrupt and corrupting. But the rules themselves are not the focus in Taylor's text; we hear little about the specifics of the routines and regimens of the school, only that they are "harsh, and manifestly injurious" in their required "rough and peremptory discipline" (24). Thus, the school sits atop a foundation of violence, a foundation more difficult to undermine than the decaying school building itself. This violence is indicative not of repressed sexuality, or the repression of male-female relations under patriarchy, as in many Gothic novels for adults in the period; instead, it points to a disturbing relationship between adult males and the boys in their charge.

Initially, this perverse adult-child relationship seems to be positioned as something in the past, a relationship engendered by the construction of the child as marked by original sin, a construction that progressive contemporary adults reject. Public schools for boys before the nineteenth century, primarily populated by sons of the landed classes, were famous for their harsh or indifferent teaching, their uncomfortable and often immoral living conditions, and their tolerance of bullying. But during the 1830s and 1840s, many public schools, following the example of Thomas Arnold at Rugby, undertook reforms focused on order and character-building (Frost 46). Certainly, the adults who run Seaward-house— Dr Poynders, the headmaster, and his chief assistant, Mr Baldrey—initially seem closer to the Arnoldian model than to that of the strictly punitive, authoritarian model encoded in the school's trust documents. When Mrs Whiskin, the "ubiquitous … grim gliding housekeeper of the establishment," who embraces an original sin construction of childhood, catches the boys carving couplets that lament their troubles into the oak-paneled walls of the school, she drags them to the breakfast parlor of the headmaster, almost breathless and screaming in her excitement.[9]

---

[9]   Elizabeth Gargano points out that the teacher's room is typically constructed by novelists as a "nurturing annex to the classroom," a place that "evokes the less regimented space of home" in school literature of the period (48, 49). Gargano, however, argues that the teacher's room can be more accurately read as a demonstration of the "link between home space and institutionality," a site that "reveals the provisionality of domestic attachments, the

But her glee at impending physical discipline is immediately undercut by Dr Poynders, who "took the paper, read it with alternate expressions of gravity and mirth, and dismissed both accuser and the accused with this general assurance, that 'he would do what was proper'" (24). Instead of physical punishment, however, the boys are vindicated, their physical complaints lessened: "The only result, however, was a decided improvement in the domestic management from that time; our cabbage broth was exalted into pea-soup; matting was laid in our bed-rooms; we were never pumped upon again; and Mrs Whiskin disappeared altogether from Seaward-house" (24). As in Hofland and Tytler's robinsonades, Taylor's story invokes a newer model of adult-child relations, one that requires that the adult give up the role of violent enforcer of discipline. It also suggests that instead of viewing misbehavior solely as a sign of sin that must be eradicated through punishment of the body, the adult can take pleasure, can respond with "mirth" to what is now viewed as ordinary mischievous, rather than sinfully evil, behavior, and can work to meliorate conditions that formerly would have been viewed as salutary, but which are now seen as oppressive.

This new model also emphasizes the role of emotional connection between adult and child. Dr Poynders and Mr Baldrey are not only firm in their guidance of their students; they are also characterized by a "habit of tenderness," an amiability, a "benignity," towards the schoolboys in their charge (27, 30). The narrator suggests that the two men not only think about their charges, but that they also feel for them. Just as in *The Young Crusoe* and *Leila*, Taylor's text takes issue with those who would restrict the new influence-based disciplinary model to women only; instead, Taylor constructs men, and men only (remember the oppressive Mrs Whiskin!), as the repositories of parental feeling. In *The Young Crusoe* and *Leila*, such a shift toward feeling in the adult is replicated in the child characters in the text—the father's love of his son or daughter leads to a reciprocal return of love of father in the child, a reciprocity that binds the child all the more closely to the desires of the parent. Dr Poynders clearly believes in this new model; one morning, after the schoolboys have behaved particularly well, he announces an afternoon off, explaining

> "Boys ... you have not vexed us this morning; you have considered our cares and feelings and we thank you for it." We looked at each other; "Yes," he said, "Mr Baldrey and I *thank you*, at this time, and at all times when you appear to regard our happiness by remembering and performing your own duties; when you do not *punish us*, by requiring correction *from* us. You have been true to yourselves, and just and kind to your tutors." (31)

Yet in Taylor's novel, the reciprocity envisioned by Dr Poynders is doomed to failure; the "appearance" of regarding the happiness of the adults is just that, an

---

germs of institutionality located at the very heart of home" (49). Though Gargano does not discuss them, scenes such as this one, in which students are taken to the room of the head in order to be disciplined or punished, seem particularly relevant to supporting such a claim.

appearance, not a reality. While adults may feel for children, the child can never feel for the adult in the same way, Taylor's text asserts. Dr Poynders's habit of tenderness *ought to*, the adult narrator states, have "won all our hearts" (27). Yet their charges, "perverse and ungrateful," are not won; instead, the entire school is plagued by "a spirit of disobedience and of *plotting* that was never really at rest" (27). The name of the parish in which the school is located—St Runwald—signals the character of the boy scholars themselves, "run wild," out of control. The eyes of the adult[10] narrator, looking back on his earlier years, may "fill with tears of affection for [his teachers]" (27); yet the adolescent Miles and his fellow classmates are completely unable to "regard the happiness" of the adult men around them, to see from their emotional point of view, to empathize with them as they are able to empathize with their charges. The shift in the model of child discipline in juvenile literature, from an older model of physical punishment to a model of reciprocal affection and love, is doomed, Taylor suggests, by the competing demands of the two new constructions of childhood, the ordinary mischievous child and the innocent Romantic one. For while the ordinary mischievous child forges a connection between the child and adult through the pleasure the adult takes in observing his "naughty" behavior,[11] the Romantic vision of the child demands that the child be self-sufficient, unconnected to the world of adults. Adults may be allowed to feel for this new type of child, but the child cannot return the emotion.

It is also doomed by the specter of the older construction of the child and the disciplinary model that accompanies it, a specter which, at least at Seaward-house, even the kinder, gentler adults cannot escape. Dr Poynders's wishes to "remodel [the school] on a plan dictated by his own kindness and wisdom" (24), and spends 30 years trying; yet the rules of the trust stand in the way of any real progress, any meaningful change. Violent discipline may be mitigated, but Dr Poynders must still "sway the iron sceptre," even if he does it with a "gentle hand, concealing its very form as much as possible" (25). Miles and his fellow students "dreaded the school"; merely the sight of it as they return from Christmas holidays strikes them "with a sickening qualm; an undefined feeling of dismay, arising from the consciousness of a penal state of things then and there existing" (25). Even empathetic adults cannot mitigate the feeling of dismay: "nor could the bland, urbane smile of the Doctor, who always received us with careful and paternal kindness in the hall, nor the duly and truly reflected complacency of his demure, melancholic assistant, Mr Baldrey, banish the pervading sensation of punishment, toil, and privation, which the very shade and atmosphere of the place occasioned" (25).

---

[10]   Miles later tells us that his account was written during his time on the island. Yet in these opening chapters, he reveals information that he could not have known while stranded, suggesting that they were penned by an adult looking back rather than an adolescent in the midst of experience.

[11]   See James Kincaid's provocative *Child-Loving: The Erotic Child and Victorian Culture* for a discussion of the ways in which the "naughty child" functions to fulfill adult desires (246).

Not surprisingly, a desire to escape the confines of the oppressive Seaward-house form a significant part of the boys' imaginative lives. As Elizabeth Gargano notes, the grounds and gardens of the Victorian school "minimizes or obscures the role of adult authority figures, allowing children to interact in allegedly 'natural' ways—to run, shout, fight, work, and play" (89). Yet even the playground and gardens of Seaward-house are "dull ... gloomy and forlorn," enclosed as they are by a wall that has been deliberately heightened "to keep even truant eyes" from wandering outside the school grounds (16). The boys, thus, are drawn to the chalk pits and saltwater ponds beyond the school grounds, from which they are forbidden to tread by the school rules. "There we imagined the performance of unheard-of achievements of agility and adventure, might we but be let loose in the spot for one half day" (17). Here, fears that Gargano suggests school gardens might also inspire—"adult fears about children's 'natural depravity'"—are displaced to the grounds outside the school (90).

The adult Miles, looking back on the imagination that characterizes his schoolboy days, echoes this fear. The narrator immediately undercuts imagination's power by ironizing the "achievements of agility and adventure" that a realization of their desires would have led to: "But no, we were absolutely denied the privilege of buffeting live crabs and breaking our necks in that unexplored region at all" (17). Though posed as a wry adult commentary on childish ways, Miles' choice of images suggests something darker: underlying the promises of imagination are the hauntings of death.

But the pleasures of horror, of listening to stories of death, are part and parcel of the spot's appeal. The boys' desire to play at the chalk pits, Miles surmises, is "no doubt enhanced by sundry traditions of death and deadly doings there," tales of bandits and smugglers (18). But their desires to trespass are "quietly cured" by the sight of real death: "when we saw the sodden, attenuated body of a pedlar man, drawn out of pit near the wall-door, the cracks of which afforded us a glimpse of his ghastly visage, half consumed by the crabs we had longed for!" (18). Even when alive, the pedlar, Giles Grimsby, was an "image of posthumous emaciation" (18); in death, he becomes a ghostly presence, sending the boys scrambling indoors when "the hint went round that Grimsby was whispering through the door, or showing his white head and empty eye-sockets above the garden wall" (19).

Yet for the imaginative child of Romanticism, death cannot be a reality. Unlike the evangelical children dying the good death, or their later sentimental counterparts Little Nell and Paul Dombey, each of whom acknowledges the reality and inevitability of her or his mortality, the Romantic child (as in the Wordsworth epigraph to this chapter) does not admit the possibility. And so, as Miles recounts, "Time, however, unfortunately for us, effaced those impressions. Grimsby became a joke in a year or two—by daylight at least,—and the old desire to transgress revived and ripened in the minds of the worst of us" (19). The schoolboys get their chance to indulge their desire when Jacob "Crab" Crawley, a village boy and former student at Seaward-house, tempts them to leave the school grounds and board a ship in the nearby harbor.

A reader might surmise that to board that ship, to escape from the oppressive physical surroundings of Seaward-house, would be to escape from the threat of violence and death that seem to haunt the school. Yet when Crab Crawley sets Miles and his 51 fellow schoolmates adrift, he is not setting them on a course of freedom. Instead, they are captured by pirates, and endure weeks of physical privations before being marooned on a deserted South American island. And the robinsonade that follows, far from being an island idyll, presents a life far more horrific than that the boys experienced at Seaward-house. There, what the boys thought was privation and punishment is nothing to the grim realities of subsistence survival. At home, dread was primarily in the mind; away from home, violence is visited, over and over again, upon the bodies of the straying boys.

The death count begins almost immediately, long before the boys reach the island. In their first hours on *The Golightly*, "as much her own manager now as her wild young crew ever desired to be," the ship catches on "The Hook," an angle of rock in the harbor. The ship seems to come to life: "as *The Golightly* struggled with this entanglement *she shook from her sides 13 of her fated young intruders!*" (52, emphasis in original). While in later asides the adult narrator will blame the boys' deaths on their misbehavior, or their disobedience, here, and at all other moments of child death, there is no such moralizing; instead, the narration works to describe the horror of Miles, and to evoke a similar sense of horror in the reader: "Their shriek rings in my ears even now; yet it was soon hushed, and nothing was heard but the hissing of the recumbent wave, which crouched for an instant, ere with renewed fury it mounted the ship's side for its further prey, and, sweeping over the deck, carried away nine more of our number, without time for a prayer, or even for a cry" (52). Both nature (the rock, the waves) and civilization (the ship) seem malevolent, bent on destruction; the binary hierarchy of positive nature/corrupt culture constructed by Rousseau and by Romanticism is undercut, both dealing death with equal abandon. While in later narrative asides such death is often linked to the boys' initial disobedience, it is never connected to divine retribution, as it would have been in Sherwoodian evangelical fiction, fiction invested in the construction of child as marked by original sin. Instead, death seems detached from the moral lesson the adult narrator would have his reader take from the text, a force unto itself, a force designed to make both the child within the text and the child reader outside the text feel horror.

This horror extends to the construction of nature throughout the novel. Taylor continues to undercut the Romantic construction of nature as beneficent, life-giving, a safe haven for the child, during the boys' initial months on the island. Though the pirates who maroon them tell them they will find turtles, eggs, sheep, goats, fowls, fruit and forage "all for the taking" (81), the boys spend their first months struggling to feed themselves. Water is initially inaccessible, falling from a "frightful precipice, and lost again in an abyss below, where the eye almost feared to follow" (94); when they do find a quieter stream, one boy falls in and is retrieved only with difficulty. The animals are plentiful, but with no weapons with which to kill them (and lacking the ingenuity that is almost *de rigeur* in the typical robinsonade, ingenuity to make their own weapons, or to design a trap), the boys are reduced to eating the rotten meat left them by the pirates. The very food that, to most shipwrecked characters, would be sustenance, is to these boys an object of horror: a turtle is deemed "loathsome"; yams, with no means to cook them, are deemed unpalatable; any substances not already familiar to them are rejected for eating. The narrator specifically rejects the Romantic construction of the child as a being at one with nature: "The fact is, that man, and the young of his race especially, suddenly thrown for support on mere natural instinct, and animal efforts, are the most destitute and helpless creatures in the world" opines the narrator (106–7).

But the boys' lack of ingenuity or Romantic imagination is not the only problem; Taylor constructs nature itself as aggressive and horrifying, a force aligned against the boys. In what would have been a scene of amusement in *The Family Robinson Crusoe*, monkeys pelt the boys with cocoanuts; in Taylor's novel, the scene is one of violence and pain—each boy receives "a thump and a bump apiece ... with many a gushing wound beside" (105). Another potentially humorous scene—in which a boy falls asleep on what he thinks is a rock, only to awaken on the back of a moving sea turtle—inspires not laughter, but crawling flesh (109). Taylor's fear is that the adolescent is all too close to this violent, horror-filled nature, and that such closeness points not to freedom, but to a dangerous devolution of the human: "But we were not only sinking in health, but in intellect: we were literally becoming wild *animals*, burrowing and groveling in the soil for shelter, and using our hands very much as our feet, through the weakness of our legs" (116). The boys talk in monosyllables and eat like pigs; only a handful can give "any account of our past history, that could have been understood" (116). Devolutionary fears, though often veiled in humor, are repeatedly invoked in Taylor's text. The boys' tattered clothes wouldn't entitle them "to the name of human beings, could we so have appeared in England"; instead, "we should probably have occupied the monkeys' ward in any menagerie in London; and one or two of us might have enjoyed the distinction of being presented to royalty as new species of the tribe, like apes imported by the East India Company" (144). Their reaction to a discovery of a store of supplies, left by previous (now mysteriously disappeared) settlers on the island is animal, not human: "If dogs, wolves, or monkeys had slipped in there, they would have done as well" (173).

Horror is linked not only to a dangerous devolution of the human when set apart from society, but also to the powers of the imagination, those so celebrated in the construction of the Romantic child. For Taylor, the adolescent imagination does not function primarily as a generative, creative force; instead, it inspires its opposite: terror, violence, death. During an early night on the island, the sounds of the animals "almost unsensed the most sensible of our distinguished company. The more fearful buried their faces in the herbage, and, huddling together, spoke or sobbed with fluttered breath" (101). This "unsensing" may close down rational thought, but it leaves imagination all too free:

> There was a rustling of the thickets continually, a padding of feet, noises near
> and distant, and a fitful murmuring of the wind through the unknown forest, that
> kept our imagination in constant exercise; and we strained our eyes to see things
> which we did not see, and listened for sounds which we did not hear. (101)

Imagining threats in nature immediately leads the narrator to envisioning those
who have already succumbed to them: "the upturned white visage of Philip
Aylmer seemed to pass before my eyelids. I involuntary muttered his name, and
was sharply rebuked by Prout; who, however, soon after, in the same mood I fancy,
talked to himself of Grant and Wyatt." (101). Aylmer, Grant, and Wyatt are all
boys who died before their fellow students were stranded on the island. Imagining
the horrors of nature leads immediately to imagining the horrors of death.

What is the purpose of learning to feel horror? Why should the schoolboys,
and, through them, the reader, need to experience the terrifying other side of
generative, creative imagination? If this were an evangelical novel by Mary
Martha Sherwood, the purpose of horror would be to inspire a turn to religion,
to embrace God out of fear of the horrors of the sinful. Taylor gestures in this
direction when one boy urges the others to pray to God for their survival after the
boys are first shipwrecked on the island, and later in the text, when Nat Prout,
the boy who becomes the leader (of sorts) of the islanders, says he will not continue
to live with them unless they adopt Christian habits and keep the Sabbath. Yet
just as divine retribution plays so little role in this text, so too is an embrace of
the divine notably lacking. The boys' praying leads to no moment of evangelical
conversion, no permanent shift away from the sinful to the spiritual; the Christian
habits the boys later agree to adopt are far from lasting.

Taylor's construction of the boys' disobedience, a disobedience linked to their
inability in the opening school scenes to empathize with their adult caretakers,
suggests instead that to feel horror may be the first step in learning to feel empathy.
The shipboard death of the crippled younger boy Philip Aylmer is linked directly to
empathy and its lack. Back at school, both Miles and Nat Prout had defended the boy
against the taunts of fellow schoolmates (sympathy among boys apparently being
easier to achieve than child-to-adult empathy). When Miles awakens after a night
aboard the ship, he hears the "weakly child" cry out, calling for "his parents amid
broken sobs, then his brothers, and his sister Amy" (53). But instead of responding
to Philip with comfort, Miles can only ask him if he knows where they are. Philip's
response—"some reply that was inarticulate"—suggests a breakdown of that
sympathy that marked their earlier relationship, a relapse into the unspeakable
of the Gothic. With a "tempest of horror" beating upon him, Miles doesn't move
to help the boy, but crawls upon the deck (53). When Nat Prout asks him where
Aylmer is, Miles responds, "Where I left him, and dead by this time, I fear" (55).
Morbid, melodramatic expostulation, a reader may surmise—how could one night
adrift at sea kill a boy? Yet when Miles and Prout return to the hold, the crippled
boy lies stiff, cold, dead. Aylmer becomes a ghostly presence: his coffin "bobbed
against the vessel several times before it left us, and we thought we heard it do

so again during the night; but we must have been mistaken, I suppose" (64). Yet his presence is elusive, its message of empathy shrouded, forgotten: "Sometimes even now, his expressive upturned face will glide across the shadowed scenery of a dream," Miles tells us, "but I scarcely can recall it, otherwise, by any effort" (58).[12] Nat Prout is the only boy who seems to understand the message, nursing Miles during their first weeks on the island, and rallying his fellow schoolboys throughout their years of isolation and want to think of one another, rather than solely of themselves.

Yet the idea that horror can lead productively to empathy, offered up here as a tantalizing possibility, is subsequently denied, over and over again, as the tale of the schoolboy islanders unfolds. When, a few weeks after being marooned, the wasting boy Tayspill confesses that he knew that Crab Crawley had pushed the pedlar Grimsby into the chalk pit to his death, and immediately dies himself, the horror of the story and of Tayspill's demise sends the boys fleeing from the hut. In their "haste and perturbation," they forget the two other deathly ill schoolmates who remain in the hut, and return only to find them dead, too. Five boys who fled into the forests in terror disappear, and are presumed lost.

Initially, this killing off of the "Crawleyites," those who were earlier labeled "the wicked example and corrupt influence of three or four profligate youths, and other bad persons at hand" that led the "good" boys to disobey (27), suggests that once the good have been purged of the bad, their goodness, their humanity, can reassert itself. And initially, this is what occurs. The remaining "16 or 17" boys find a store of goods left by previous (now mysteriously vanished) settlers; they organize themselves into a community, with each boy performing the work he is best suited for; and the narrative finally gives the reader the Robinson Crusoe-like account of how the boys build their huts and plant their crops he or she would expect from a juvenile robinsonade. But even during this "idyllic" period, there are hints of trouble, of discord, of underlying horror. Some boys will not adhere to the Christianity Nat Prout imposes; others slack off from their work, or grow "discouraged, listless, idle, and unreasonable" because of lack of progress (172). Their settler efforts, far from being endlessly ingenious and creative, are far more often marked by failure. Five boys split off into their own group; months later, two return, "[b]lackened, distorted, and wasted by want and suffering, their countenances seemed to resemble not the dead, but tenants of the grave" (192). Other deaths haunt them as well: digging to find the original entrance to their storage cave, "as we were pulling with all our might at the vegetation which grew from under a block of sandstone, and between the beams, a skeleton hand came away" (153). Its owner, and his fellow settlers, had been buried under tons of fallen earth, their bodies fragmented, decaying. If adult settlers could not escape death, how then can the adolescents?

---

[12] Taylor's depiction of Aylmer becomes even more horrific when one finds, from sister Ann Taylor's note about her poem "Crippled Child's Complaint," that it was "suggested by the suffering and lameness of my brother Jefferys" (Armitage 166).

The discovery of the two emaciated boys initially suggests that the message of empathy embodied in Philip Aylmer's death can transform the boys: "We were now doctors, nurses, and servants of all work, and enjoyed the refreshing change of an interesting and arduous employment, exercised not for ourselves, but on account of others" (193). Yet when Nat Prout attempts to extend this empathy, by going to search for the three other missing boys, only horror ensues. Prout urges his mates to accompany him on a rescue mission into the caves where the boys are purported to be, but they protest, rejecting his urge to empathy. Prout understands their reaction: "I don't much wonder that these lads dislike such an errand, which I dare say we none of us enjoy very much: we all would rather fight for our lives in open daylight, than grope there for bodies, dead or alive, in the very darkest chamber of death itself." But he also sees a darker alternative: "but then, again, we would rather do that, and run all hazards, than wake in the night, after DREAMING that our fellows called for help and we would not answer" (200–201). The terrors of the real are outweighed by the horrors of the imagination, Prout argues. Yet their mission of mercy, inspired by empathy, goes horribly awry; they hear one boy in the cave, and call to him, but their voices do not save him, but instead drive the crazed boy over a precipice to his death: "'Jermyn, is that you?' 'Yes, yes mother! I am running down the stairs so fast!' O my dear readers, think of it; we heard a rattling scramble, a tumble, a scream, and a plunge, and all was over!" (205). A similar mission of mercy later in the book, once again to search for missing companions, ends almost as horrifically. Spying what they think are monkeys, they shoot; one of the wounded turns out to be not a monkey, but a missing schoolmate. "I suppress the name of the poor fellow who, in a moment of mere thoughtlessness, had discharged his piece. He uttered a wild cry of horror when he saw what he had done" (257). The most horrific act of empathy may be the suicides of two of the boys who earlier refused to be abandoned on the island: "without uttering a word, [Grant and Wyatt] writhed themselves out of the pirates' grasp, and plunged, headforemost, into the water! We saw—yes, so clear was the lucid wave—we saw them slowly descend, still embracing each other, and revolving as they went down" (79). Grant and Wyatt, communicating without words, choose an empathetic "embrace" of death over a life of community on the island, a horrific distortion of the message of empathy the text initially seemed to support.

If feeling horror is not about teaching children to become more religious, and not about teaching them to empathize, what purpose, then, does it serve? If there seems to be no good answer to this question, perhaps it is because we are wrong to ask it. Our expectation in reading children's literature of the early nineteenth century is that it will contain, by definition, a didactic message. But as David Punter notes in regards to adult Gothic, "Gothic fiction is almost never didactic, it is too tentative, too hesitant about its own perceptions." Instead, he argues, Gothic "points implicitly and constantly to the insupportability of the accepted alternatives" (411). Taylor repeatedly invokes both an older conception of the child as marked by original sin, and a newer conception of the Romantic child, self-sufficient, connected to nature and the imagination, only to reject each as insupportable,

Fig. 2.2   "A mission of mercy goes gothically awry": a St Runwald's pupil, shot by another when mistaken for a monkey. Courtesy of the author.

untenable, horrific. But the third alternative that begins to emerge in the literature of the early decades of the nineteenth century, the ordinary mischievous child and an child-adult relationship based on mutual affection, regard, and empathy, is equally untenable, Taylor's text asserts, particularly when it is a relationship of son to father, or adolescent boy to adult male mentor.

For the most common thread running through this text, besides the thread of death, is that of longing for connection to home and to school, and to the adults connected with those places of comfort. When the boys are first left alone on the island, Miles tells us "Our hearts were now, I think, for the first time, sensibly touched" (83). To be sensibly touched initially seems to be to turn to a forgotten religion: as described earlier, one lad exclaims that they should pray to thank God for their salvation. But their prayers turn quickly away from God, from thanks and requests for forgiveness, and towards their sorrowing families. They pray not only that God will "comfort our dear— dear fathers and mothers, and brothers and sisters," but also "the dear and good and kind Dr Poynders, and poor Mr Baldrey," the teachers they continually failed to empathize with during the early scenes of the novel (83–4). Throughout their time on the island, the boys are haunted far less often by the imagined ghosts of their dead companions than by dreams of the home and school they have left behind. These dreams initially give comfort: "Yes, we slept and dreamed—not of future joys and adventures, but of the past … We dreamed of SCHOOL, as happiness restored!" Miles reports after their first night on the island (90). "Our companions were soon occupied by the only visions that really blessed our thoughts—those of happy dreams, that transported us to the cliffs of England, to our homes, and the dear towers of St Runwald's school. The wakers knew by the sleepers' muttered breath what scenes were occupying their brains, and longed to share their imagined joys" (112). "I have said before, that our fondest thoughts by day, and dreams by night, led us to the homes we had, at times, little valued, and to the towers of Seaward-house, whose very shadows we once both dreaded and hated" (236). Relating to one another their dreams of home and school are "the chief solace we had" (123).

Such dreams would, in a typical juvenile novel of the period, serve to teach the novel's protagonists (and its readers) the empathy for adults that the text constructs children as so terribly lacking. Yet while Miles continues to assert that these dreams give the boys comfort, more disturbing visions connected to home and school soon erupt in the night. One boy reports "I thought … that I had been all day on my knees before Dr Poynders, and he wept, and promised to forgive me; and held out his hand to raise me up, and yet I could *not* rise, nor get near enough to touch him" (90). Nat Prout attempts to mitigate the horrors of dreams of home gone awry by instituting an imaginary post-office, in which the boys write letters to their loved ones back home, letters which he himself answers. Yet we rarely are allowed to read the comforting letters from "home"; instead, Miles reprints the boys' letters, in which we hear more of the boys' dreams, dreams in which the inability to return home continually turns the comforting dream into a vision of terror:

… the old dog stood upon his legs, but he did not know me; his eyes flashed fire, and he had the mouth and mane of a lion! Then I wanted to pull the bell, but could not find the handle; and I tried to call, but my breath seemed to be gone, and I could only mutter; but in another moment, I was indoors, in the small parlour; the shutters were closed, and I could find nobody. Then I was back here again, and dreamed that you all stood before me in black, and mother beckoned me, but nobody spoke a word; then I tried to go to her, and fell into a pit, and that woke me. (245–6)

Even the rational leader Prout cannot resist the horror: "We slept, and dream'd that we were thrust—to rest, / Outcasts, beside the thresholds of our home!" he writes in a poem to Dr Poynders (249). Such continual eruptions of images of being outcast, barred from home, seem to point to a punishment for the sin of disobedience, of failing to empathize with the adult who loves you; significantly, none of the images depict an adult rejecting the child, only the child's inability to reach the adult, or an unnamed agent which "thrusts" the boy from home. Yet other letters more frighteningly suggest that the responsibility for the rejection of the child-adult relationship may not lie solely with the child. The one letter to which Miles prints the response is meant as a joke:

> "August (I suppose), Moco (I think)
> "Dear Unkey Rob,
> "Here I am, and I can't help it.
> "Your nephew,
> JOHN ROUSE."

Yet the humor of its reply ill-masks the horror behind it:

> "Nephew John Rouse,
> "There you may keep, and I don't care.
> "Your unkey,
> "ROB. ROUSE." (244)

Readers are clearly meant to respond to one boy's plaintive epistle—"Are father and mother yet alive, and little Sally; and do they ever dream about poor George? Did the people put on mourning for us; and do they feel certain we are all dead?" (245)—with a definitive "yes"; yet the openness of the question, and the lack of textual response to it, suggests the horrific possibility that the answer may in fact be "no." Adult-child connection may be impossible not only because the child is unable to empathize with the adult, but, more frighteningly, because the adult forgets or rejects the child. The island thus functions as an exaggerated version of the public school to which the boys had initially been abandoned by their purportedly loving families, signaling anxieties about the increasing numbers of Victorian boys of the middle-class who would be similarly sent away to school over the course of the nineteenth century (Tosh, *Man's Place* 117).

The island idyll section of the novel, during which the boys worked cooperatively to build, hunt, and grow crops, begins to fall apart after perhaps the strangest episode in this immensely strange novel, an episode which again undercuts the idea that the adult-child relationship can be fixed if only the child can learn empathy for the adult. Instead, the parent-child relationship is recast as mysterious, shrouded, horrific. Now that their settler successes have given them more leisure time, the boys turn to explore the trunks of the mysterious previous settlers. Reading the name "Augustus Prout" in a book long-overlooked amidst more immediately helpful stores, Nat Prout "gazed at it with a fixed eye for a moment, turned deadly pale, and crying out 'My father!' fell senseless from his seat" (225). The skeleton hand pulled by the boys from the ruins of the cave belongs to Nat's own father, as the initials "A.P." engraved upon a ring taken from it reveal. The horror that continually "unsenses" the boys throughout the novel here attaches itself to the father-son relationship, a relationship irretrievably broken by distance and death. We are given no information about Nat's mysterious father, no account of why he and Nat were separated; in fact, the narrator specifically withholds such information from us: "He passed from fainting into sleep of a disturbed and delirious kind, during which I learned particulars of his father's history, and of his own, which otherwise would, I know, have been buried with him in the grave; and they shall be buried in mine" (226). Nat later gives us a brief, mysterious history of his family, one that echoes not the story of the boys who, through disobedience, rejected the loving adult, but rather the melodramatic horrors of the Gothic:

> I have been surrounded and followed by calamity from my birth, and, as far as I know, it has been the lot of our race to be hunted into the grave—no, I must not say that, for several of our family never occupied a tomb delved by human hands—I say, then, we have been chased out of the world by misfortune, one after another; and, because a fatal history must have a signal close, I, the last of my race, have been borne hither, that I might lay my bones beside my father's. Mountains must fall, that he might be crushed; and 50 families must be torn with anguish, that I might perish still more wonderfully than he! (227).

From this point on in the narrative, Nat is "no longer the lad he had been, in cheerfulness and activity. He took, indeed, more than his full share of the various thoughts and labors connected with our situation, but the lively interest, the bright intelligence, which used to point and actuate his suggestions, were wanting, and the gloom which hung about him, overshadowed our whole party, more or less" (230). Nat's fall into melancholy and mourning signals the impending disintegration of the island community.

This disintegration occurs not through death, but through yet another perversion of the adult-child connection. A friendly native tribe, the Kimboes, returns to the island, bringing along four of the boys who had run away from their schoolmates after the death of the boy Tayspill. But the adult Kimboes are not in charge; one of the boys has used the power of his gun to force himself on the tribe as their leader, titling himself "Thewma, king of the Kimboes" (280). He has returned to the island, he says, so that the other boys can be "great folks" among the Kimboes, but he has ulterior motives: he wants their help (and firepower) in wars against a neighboring tribe. Nat Prout, who has taken on a paternal role among the boys, rejects "Thewma's" offer on behalf of them all. One boy openly disagrees with Nat, desiring to join the Kimboes, but the others appear to acquiesce. Yet the appearance of sympathy with a paternal figure once again turns out to be just that—an appearance. In an eerie repetition of the opening of the novel, the boys disobey their leader, sneaking away without telling either Nat or Miles that they have decided to leave the island with the Kimboes. After a night passes and the boys have not returned, Nat and Miles are filled with a "feeling, amounting nearly to horror," a horror which leads to "a wild expression of suffering" (283). Five pages later, Nat is dead.

Unsurprisingly, Miles is rescued from the island within a paragraph; struggling in solitude on the island has never been the point of this strangest of robinsonades. A naïve reader might hope for a happy ending, a chastened Miles joyfully reunited with family, teachers, and headmaster. Yet the novel continues to resist any move to recuperate the death, mourning, and loss that haunted the boy on the island. The final chapter abruptly shifts from the first to the third person, as it follows an elderly man (clearly Miles) who returns to the site of St Runwald's school, only to find it long washed away by the sea; Crab Crawley, insane and animalistic, a ward of the abusive Mrs Whiskin; Mr Baldrey, a suicide; Dr Poynders, dead of sorrow. While the final page tells of Miles's reunion with his sister, its closing line—"he had the inconceivable happiness of reading and relating, in her ears, the adventures, as now published, of THE YOUNG ISLANDERS"—belies the joy promised by familial reunion. For who could gain happiness through reciting such horrors to a sister? True happiness lies not in a reunion with family, or a return to a home once lost. Nor does it lie in learning the overt message of the tale: "Hasten then, with generous promptitude, to surprise with joy those who may be weeping in despair of you. They have often forborne to chide: they will never forbear to pardon you. To-morrow it may be *too late*. Death may have closed their lips. Your conscience then will find them a tongue of fire!" (33–4). Rather, it lies in relating its impossibility, the Gothic horror of a child-adult connection desperately longed for, but forever unattained.

Chapter 3
Engaging The Ordinary Reader:
Fictionalized History for Children

The first thing to be done, is to seize the moment when curiosity is excited by the accidental mention of any historic name or event. When a child hears his father talk of the Roman emperors, or of the Roman people, he naturally inquires who these people were; some short explanation may be given, so as to leave curiosity yet unsatisfied.

—Maria Edgeworth, *Practical Education* (1798)[1]

I am aware I may be here reminded of the necessity of rendering instruction agreeable to youth, and of Tasso's infusion of honey into the medicine prepared for a child; but an age in which children are taught the driest doctrines by the insinuating method of instructive games, has little reason to dread the consequences of study being rendered too serious or severe. The history of England is now reduced to a game at cards. ... It may, in the meantime, be subject of serious consideration, whether those who are accustomed only to acquire instruction through the medium of amusement, may not be brought to reject that which approaches under the aspect of study; whether those who learn history by the cards, may not be led to prefer the means to the end ... .

—Sir Walter Scott, *Waverley* (1814)[2]

Even when presented as a tool to teach proper manners, morals, and mores, adventure fictions, including robinsonades, all fell under the suspect generic category "novel." And fears of the noxious effects of novel reading on the young (in particular, on girls) expressed in eighteenth- and early nineteenth-century conduct books continued far into the nineteenth century. For the children of parents still alive to the cautionary words of James Fordyce, John Gregory, Lady Sarah Pennington, Hester Chapone, Hannah More, Jane West and others who cautioned parents against letting their children read fiction, "amusement" would have to be gleaned from a more acceptable genre. For such children, literary adventure might still be found in a type of literature granted much higher status than that given to the novel during the opening decades of the nineteenth century: the genre of history.

---

[1] Page 200 in the Pickering Masters edition of *Practical Education*.

[2] Pages 46–7 in the Penguin Classics edition of *Waverley*.

The History of History for Children

As Gillian Avery notes, elite educated boys in the seventeenth and early eighteenth centuries often read classical histories intended for adult readers ("Beginnings" 18–19). For boys, the study of classical history—grand narratives of nations or empires, featuring a linear account of successive political events—served to prepare future leaders of the state for their roles in public life. By the mid-eighteenth century, history also began to be recommended for as a suitable subject of study for girls, albeit for different purposes. As Jacqueline Pearson, drawing upon Kathryn Sutherland, suggests, conservative educationalists viewed the reading of history by girls as "training in compliance to a male-dominated culture and its discursive practices." For girls, the function of history "would be primarily 'moral,' even 'religious,' since it provided 'the study of virtue' rather than 'the study of vice' to be acquired from novels, with which history was persistently contrasted" (50). But history, as Pearson argues, also offered women "opportunities for complex acts of resisting reading" (51). I would argue that history also offered those same opportunities to the young. Children thwarted in their desire to read adventure fiction could often mine histories intended for adults for derring-do plots of murders, battles, political wranglings, and sexual misdeeds in addition to (or instead of) their purportedly exemplary educative messages. In "The Uses of History," Anna Letitia Barbauld clearly recognizes such a desire in the child reader; writing to her niece, she reminds her: "You may recollect probably that the mere *adventure* was all you entered into, in those portions of it [history] which were presented to you at a very early age" (140, emphasis in original).

A desire to narrow the opportunities for children to "misread" their history, I surmise, was one factor that led British educators, publishers, and authors in the latter half of the eighteenth century to begin to write and to publish histories specifically intended for a juvenile readership, rather than a mixed audience encompassing both children and adults. Changing ideas about what it meant to be a child were clearly at the root of such a desire. Rousseau, an early proponent of the new vision of childhood, singled out the study of history for particular disdain. A true knowledge of history depends on an understanding of history's "causes and effects," its "moral bearings," which most children are not developmentally able to understand, he argued (*Émile* 88). Writing more than 60 years after Rousseau, Barbauld echoes his assertion, reciting as a commonplace what was once a radical notion: "… a child never fully comprehends what he is taught: he receives an idea, but not the full idea, perhaps not the principal of what you want to teach him. But as his mind opens, this idea enlarges and receives accessory ideas, till slowly and by degrees he is master of the whole. This is particularly the case in History" ("The Uses of History" 140).

Unlike Rousseau, however, Barbauld and other educators thought the solution to the problem of children's history reading was not to abandon the study of history altogether, but to carefully monitor the content of children's history reading. In *A Description of a Set of Prints of Ancient History* (1786), Sarah Trimmer writes

"In pursuing the plan at first proposed, of giving the outlines of UNIVERSAL HISTORY, great difficulties have occurred in respect to the choice of subjects proper to be exhibited to young children" (*Description* iii). Trimmer does not elaborate about the specifics of her difficulties, but they can be surmised from her practices as a children's literature critic. As Matthew Grenby notes, in her reviews of children's books in *The Guardian of Education*, Trimmer objected to works of fiction that included death scenes, mentally ill characters, and open sexuality ("Introduction" *Guardian of Education* xxxv). The descriptions that accompany the prints in *Ancient History* and other history books Trimmer crafted carefully omit material similar to that which she found objectionable in the works of other writers. For example, in her discussion of Semiramis, she leaves out any mention of the ancient queen's purported sexual exploits, or that she may have been murdered by her own son (5–6). Likewise, Barbauld, though she objects to those who would leave out "all that was vicious" from the history reading of "young people," agrees that "till the mind has gained some strength, so frightful a picture" as that presented by history "should hardly be presented" to younger children (136, 135). Instead, drawing upon a developmental model of childhood, Barbauld asserts that "chosen periods of history may be selected for youth, as the society of chosen characters precedes in well-regulated education a more indiscriminate acquaintance with the world" (135).

In the wake of changing ideas about the child and its relation to history, a new market for histories created specifically for an audience of genteel children emerged in the late eighteenth and early nineteenth centuries. Many such titles were simply abridgements or epitomes of, or extractions from, works of political or military history for adults, such as Oliver Goldsmith's *Dr Goldsmith's Roman History Abridged by himself* (1782). Works of biography (typically featuring male political or religious figures), modeled on the exemplary biography for adults, also proved popular well into the nineteenth century. Books of history intended for the schoolroom rather than the private library drew on established pedagogical models in their choice of form: question and answer, dialogue, and catechetical memorization. Such histories, biographies, and schoolbooks could easily weed out any material from adult histories deemed inappropriate for children, crafting their narratives to conform to contemporary constructions of childhood, whether they be grounded in a conception of the child as inherently evil, inherently good, or developmentally progressing.

Yet differences in content alone did not differentiate juvenile histories from those written for adults. As Karen O'Brien suggests, late eighteenth-century historians for children were particularly innovative, experimenting on the level of form (125). O'Brien points to works such as Goldsmith's *History of England, in a Series of Letters from a Nobleman to his Son* (1764) and similar books by Thomas Lewis and William Russell, all of which present their history lessons as conversations between adults and children, as examples of historical experiments in form. Letters and conversations, however, were just the tip of the innovative iceberg.

Writers and publishers also experimented with histories in verse,[3] drama,[4] historical prints with captions,[5] miniature editions, panoramas, even histories in hieroglyphics.[6] As Walter Scott's dismay at the current state of historical education (in the epigraph which opens this chapter) suggests, history could also be learned from sources other than the literary: dissected puzzles, table or board games, and games of cards.[7]

Though Scott fears that "reducing" the teaching of history from its lofty classical heights will lead not only to the intellectual, but moral, degeneration of the child, it is clear that the inclusion of "amusement" to accompany the "instruction" of history was not confined to works for children alone. In many ways, these experiments in historical form mirrored changes taking place in the writing of history for adults during the eighteenth and early nineteenth centuries. For readers before the eighteenth century, the word "history" most often evoked the famed works of Greek and Roman writers such as Livy, Tacitus, Herodotus, and Thucydides, histories that presented a linear narrative of the political and military events of a state or nation. With the concurrent rise of print culture and English nationalism in the eighteenth century, however, the scope of history gradually broadened; historians began to include information about civil and social life to histories written in the classical mold. Voltaire's *Age of Louis XIV* (1751), which depicted the cultural, as well as the military and political, achievements of Louis's reign is typically cited as the harbinger of "philosophical" history, history interested in linking the manners, mores, and cultural achievements of a nation to its political and military accomplishments. British historians such as David Hume and Edward Gibbon drew upon Voltaire's example by including such information

---

[3]   The titles of such books, including Louisa Brown's *Historical Questions on the Kings of England, in Verse. Calculated to Fix on the Minds of Children, some of the most striking events of each reign* (1815) and W.R. Johnson's *The History of England, in easy verse: from the Invasion of Julius Caesar, to the close of the year 1809. Written for the purpose of being committed to memory by young persons of both sexes* (1806) suggest the author's hope that committing to memory the facts of political history might prove easier for children in the form of rhythmical poetry than dry prose.

[4]   See for example, Barbara Hofland's *Little Dramas for young people, on subjects taken from English history: intended to promote among the rising generation an early love of virtue and their country* and the plays for children of Stéphanie Felicité, Comtesse de Genlis, *Théâtre a l'usage des jeunes personnes*. For more information about children's plays in this period, see Levy.

[5]   See for example Sarah Trimmer's series of "Prints with Descriptions," numerous editions of which were published for more than half a century, and Emily Taylor's *Historical Prints*.

[6]   See Mary Ann Rundall's *Symbolic Illustrations of the History of England from the Roman invasion to the present time* and *A History of England; in which the most remarkable events are illustrated by numerous symbolic engravings*.

[7]   See Jill Shefrin's excellent article on educational games for children for more detailed information on this topic.

in their broad-scale histories, while others (William Robertson, for one), moved away from extensive narrative overviews, focusing instead on specific periods, institutions, or rulers, a shift in scope that allowed them to delve ever more deeply into the manners and mores of an era. Simultaneously, European encounters with indigenous peoples led to the emergence of a very early cultural anthropology; the discussion of the cultural information about indigenous societies, in works such as Robertson's *History of America* (1777), only increased the appetite in European readers for similar cultural information about their own past. Such developments all contributed to the rise of what is today termed "social history." Though traditional linear histories of military and political events continued to hold the highest rank in the hierarchy of prestige within the genre of history, by the late eighteenth century, information about social and cultural life had become an increasingly important subject in historical writing.[8]

If the content of history broadened during the eighteenth century, so, too did history's audience. Expanding beyond its traditional readership of elite males to include women and non-gentry men, history now needed to satisfy different readers with different expectations and demands. Mark Salber Phillips suggests that because of this broadening of history's audience, "for the first time, evocation became an important goal of historical narrative, and sympathetic identification came to be seen as one of the pleasures of historical reading" (xii). Though the purpose of history still encompassed didactic, moral lessons, works of history increasingly came to be judged for their ability (or failure) to engage their intended reader.

In addition to this broadening of history's content and audience, a third change in historiographical practice emerged during the opening decades of the nineteenth century, a change that challenged the very purpose of history as understood by eighteenth-century readers: to provide models of moral exemplarity. The stadial theory of Scottish Enlightenment, and the technological developments, social changes, and political revolutions in America and France of the late eighteenth-century both challenged earlier historians' belief in the possibility of depicting a universal moral exemplarity, one equally suitable to classical Rome as it was to early nineteenth-century England. As discussed in detail in the Introduction, the historicism that emerged in the early decades of the nineteenth century increasingly came to view historical actors not as exemplars of universal moral lessons, but as human beings subject to both the restrictions and possibilities of the times in which they lived.

Though these three major historiographical shifts—the rise of social history, the need for readerly emotional engagement due to a broadening audience, and the awareness of the past as a space of radical alterity rather than of universal

---

[8]   This is a much-simplified account of the complex, uneven developments in historiographic convention in the period. For an overview of eighteenth-century historiographical changes, see O'Brien. For a detailed treatment of the same, see Phillips. For an overview of romantic historicism, see Chandler, "History"; for an extensive rumination on the same, see Chandler's *England in 1819*.

moral values—all began to emerge in England during the eighteenth century, it was not until the 1840s, with the popular acclaim given to the first volume of Thomas Macaulay's *History of England* (1848–1861), that what is today known as "historicism" became seen as the norm, rather than the experimental, in the writing of history, particularly in histories intended for children. Yet changes in historiographic practice register in several works of history for children written during the period 1820–1840, in an experimental genre that I will call "fictionalized history."

The need for readerly engagement with history emerges as a requirement in the work of Jefferys Taylor, whom we first met in Chapter 2 as the author of the gothic *The Young Islanders*. Written in a far lighter vein, Taylor's earlier work, *The Little Historians* (1824) has at its heart the purpose of clarifying what counts as "real" history in the face of eighteenth-century challenges to the narrow scope of traditional classical history.[9] Taylor attempts to create a bond of sympathy between the young reader outside the text and the two boys who both read and write history within it, in order to make the study of history more engaging for both groups. Greater engagement comes with its own dangers, however, and policing the boundaries of sympathy becomes just as important a project as maintaining the borders of history. Yet the agency granted to the boys in the name of engagement opens up a space for them, and for their readers, to resist such policing, or at the very least to call it into question.

Broadening the boundaries of history, rather than policing its borders, proves the central concern of Agnes Strickland. Strickland (whose work is also discussed in Chapter 4) appears to be one of the earliest writers for children to focus on social history, in the form of everyday material life, and to place children as central characters in the depiction of the past. In her *Historical Tales of Illustrious British Children* (1833), young readers are invited not only to sympathize with the emotions of children of the past, but also to identify with them by visualizing their physical, material worlds. In order to make these two innovations, however, Strickland must break the rule set down by the father of Taylor's little historians about what "counts" as history—that imagination should be used only to sympathize with known historical actors, not to extrapolate from the historical record in order to surmise what those historical actors must be feeling. Taking a page instead from the book of Sir Walter Scott, Strickland presents history in the form of a fictionalized story. But rather than denying her work's connection to the romance and sentimentalism of fiction, as Scott does so markedly in his preface to his first historical novel, *Waverley* (1814), Strickland deploys these genres to disrupt the "masculine" construction of linear political and military events as the only "true" history.

---

[9]   When I use the term "classical history," I refer to linear histories of political and military events written after the model of the ancients, not solely the famed Latin and Greek histories.

Though Strickland deploys social history and focuses on reader engagement, her historical characters still tend toward the ideal exemplar, a common trend in early nineteenth-century fictions for children. Writing less than a decade later, however, Harriet Martineau would experiment with the didactic exemplar, only to abandon it as ill-suited to the new goal of historicism: to suggest what might happen in the future of one's own society by understanding how radical changes occurred in the pasts of other cultures. In particular, Martineau wishes to avert the reoccurrence of the class warfare of late eighteenth-century France, as depicted in her two works—one a novella, one a history—published as one volume under the title *The Peasant and the Prince* (1841). To prevent a recapitulation of France's class warfare in England, Martineau asserts, her young readers must cross not only the boundaries of time, but also what for many might be an even more radical gap: that of class. Learning about the social and material conditions of both the peasantry and the nobility will lead young readers to sympathetic engagement with both classes; such engagement is the only guarantee that the violent class divisions of Revolutionary France will not repeat themselves on British ground. Yet Martineau, like Taylor before her, is keenly aware of the dangers of sympathy, and struggles to find a genre in which sympathy can function as a means to achieving the goal of social transformation, rather than as a solipsistic end in itself.

Lewis and Paul Write the History of England: Learning What Counts as History in Jefferys Taylor's *The Little Historians* (1824)

> I suppose you know all about the Wars between him [Henry VI] and the Duke of York who was of the right side; if you do not, you had better read some other History, for I shall not be very diffuse in this, meaning by it only to vent my spleen *against*, and shew my Hatred *to* all those people whose parties or principles do not suit with mine, and not to give information.
> —Jane Austen, age 15, *The History of England, from the Reign of Henry the 4th to the Death of Charles the 1st, by a Partial, Prejudiced, and Ignorant Historian* (1791)[10]

> … as we should think it a dreadful thing to be terrified, or forced, by the fear of punishment, towards the opinions of others, so we ought to think it as dreadful a thing to attempt, by terror, to force the opinions of others towards our own.
> —Father, in *The Little Historians* (1824)[11]

During the late eighteenth and early nineteenth centuries, writers of histories for children, drawing on a convention established in the earlier fictional moral tale, began to experiment with presenting history in the form of a conversation between an adult and a child. In the earliest of such histories, conversations were hierarchically constructed by age, by gender, and by social class. Gentry-class

---

[10] Page 4 of the Penguin Classics edition.
[11] From volume III, page 32.

fathers wrote letters to their sons, instructing them in the facts and principles of political histories, with the sons given no opportunity to reply (see Goldsmith, Lewis, and Russell).[12] Later writers sought to broaden the exchange by framing their histories as a lecture by a father to a group of children, with the children interrupting their parent to ask questions or to offer answers to questions posed to them. The earliest such history-as-conversation appears to be a translation of Joachim Heinrich Campe's *The Discovery of America; for the use of children and young persons* (1799); written in a style "somewhat more elevated" than his better known *The New Robinson Crusoe*, Campe's history features a dominant, all-knowing father similar to that found in Wyss's *Family Robinson Crusoe* (discussed in Chapter 1) (*v*). Campe's English translator, Elizabeth Helme, soon took up his model, crafting her own *The History of England, related in familiar conversations, by a father to his children, interspersed with moral and instructive remarks and observations on the most leading and interesting subjects* (1804) and its companion volume on the history of Scotland (also 1804). Eliza Constantia Campbell and Elizabeth Penrose, the latter writing as Mrs Markham, copied these earlier models in the 1820s and 1830s, with history presented as a story told by an adult, with digressions from children interspersed (or in the case of Mrs Markham, restricted to the end of each chapter). As Elizabeth Helme explains in her preface to *The History of England*, crafting history as a conversation between father and children, a conversation that includes "casual interruptions" and "domestic conversations," renders the study of history more engaging for youthful readers: such digressions make "the subjects lighter" and the "conversations more interesting to children" (qtd in St John II.783). History by itself, particularly when it is shorn of its more enticing moments, may prove simply too dull to appeal to the nineteenth-century child.

In his sole foray into the field of history for children, *The Little Historians: A New Chronicle of the Affairs of England in Church and State, by Lewis and Paul. With Explanatory Remarks, and Additional Information upon Various Subjects Connected with the Progress of Civilization; also, Some Account of Antiquities* (1824),[13] Jefferys Taylor follows this model of juvenile history as a conversation

---

[12]   Goldsmith at least pretends that the son actually exists, with the father commenting upon ideas brought up by his sons' letters, letters we never see. Russell makes few such efforts; although he refers to the son as "my dear Philip" we hear little about Philip's reaction to the history lesson his father imparts. Such epistolary histories, as Christopher Mayo points out, were clearly modeled on the example of Lord Chesterfield's *Letters to his Son* (written between 1737 and 1768, published after his death in 1774).

[13]   This early work of Taylor's is the least known, and the least popular, of all of the primary texts analyzed in this book. Its publisher, Baldwin, Cradock, and Joy, was active in London in the 1810s and 1820s, publishing a variety of novels and nonfiction; it was also one of the two principle publishers of works by the Society for the Diffusion of Useful Knowledge (S.D.U.K.) (Anderson 166). The company appears to have purchased the rights to several popular children's works originally published by John Marshall, reprinting works by Sarah Trimmer and Mary Ann Kilner as well as producing original works for young readers.

between a father and his children. Yet Taylor, whom we saw writing in a more dour vein in his 1842 *The Young Islanders* (see Chapter 2), here lives up to his reputation as the "wag" of the prolific Taylor family of Ongar by inverting the generic model: his history will not be written or spoken by a father, but rather, as indicated by the book's subtitle, by "Lewis and Paul," who prove to be two boys younger than fourteen.[14] By presenting fellow children as the active authors of, rather than the passive recipients of, their own national history, Taylor works to create a greater sense of identification between his readers and his subject; while there may be few children in conventional political history with whom readers can identify, Lewis and Paul function as surrogates, illustrating through their often emotional reactions to the events and personages of history how children might come to identify with historical adults through the bonds of sympathy. Thus Taylor follows the educational model set forth as early as the mid-eighteenth century by Frenchman Abbé Pluche, in the sixth volume of his *Spectacle de la nature* (1732–1751), when he urged parents to allow their daughters to write poems and perform in dramas about key historical events (Koepp 165).

Yet Lewis and Paul do not have complete control over the writing of their versions of history. Unlike the fifteen-year-old Jane Austen, whose irreverent *The History of England, from the Reign of Henry the 4th to the Death of Charles the 1st, by a Partial, Prejudiced, and Ignorant Historian* (1791), a parody of Goldsmith's popular history for children, shows little to no signs of guidance from or interference of a supervisory parent, Lewis and Paul's histories are carefully monitored by adults. The boys' learned father, and, to a lesser extent, their uncle and mother, initially allow Lewis and Paul to indulge in an Austen-like narration, one characterized by partiality, prejudice, and ignorance. But by depicting his parents reacting not with condemnation, but amusement, to such accounts, Taylor both establishes a bond of sympathy between adult and child within the text, and a similar bond between textual adult and child reader. By laughing along with the father at the history-writing foibles of his sons, and taking pleasure in the loving relationship established between textual parent and children, readers of *The Little Historians* become ready, like Lewis and Paul, to accept the guidance of a teacher-father, even while being granted the apparent agency to write history themselves. In his preface, Taylor suggests that his project's innovation is in its content: he will

---

Each of the three volumes of Taylor's history contains one frontispiece: a black and white engraving of a historical figure, which suggests that the publisher wished to present the book as a work of serious history rather than as the experiment in fictionalized history that Taylor actually produced. Unlike Taylor's robinsonade, *The Little Historians* did not go through more than one edition, and appears not to have been translated, suggesting that its mix of humor and history was far too experimental for its intended readers' comfort.

[14]   Taylor never tells us directly just how old his "little historians" are, yet he sprinkles hints throughout his text. They are younger than 14, the age of Edwy when he was crowned king of the Britons (I.124), but they are old enough to remember the battle of Waterloo in 1815 (III.211) and the death of princess Charlotte in 1817 (III.212). Given the book's publication date of 1824, we can guess that the boys must be between 10 and 13.

spend as much time on ancient as on modern history, so that young readers will
come to understand the real, albeit remote, causes of present conditions (I.v). Yet
Taylor's true innovation lies in his ability to make didacticism palatable to young
readers by clothing it in agency and emotion, and thereby teach children both
within and outside the text what truly "counts" as valid history.

> "There, Papa!" said Lewis, closing a large old book with force, and striking
> it with his hand, "I have done with this; what am I to have next?"
> "Done with it!" said his father.
> "Yes, Papa," said Lewis.
> "There must, I think, be some mistake here," replied his father …
> "Dear Papa," said Lewis, bringing it forward, and pointing with his finger
> to the last paragraph, "see, I have read that, and even the word *Finis*, and the
> printer's name." (I.1)

The opening chapter of Taylor's *The Little Historians* explains just what is wrong
with children attempting to read histories intended for adults. While Lewis may
have read *Finis*, and even the name of his book's printer, he has scarcely taken
in any of the lengthy history he and his younger brother Paul have selected from
their father's library to while away the long winter evenings. With a title that
runs nearly a page and a half when recounted in Taylor's book,[15] "Francis Fagg
Faithful's" immense folio volume can never by "done" by a child. Lewis admits as
much when his father quizzes him on essential points of history, and he can give
no answers. He has "finished" with the folio, he finally acknowledges, not because
he has finished reading it, or because he disapproves of it, but rather because of
its off-putting length and style: "it was so *dry*, and the tops of the leaves were
such a way off, and the lines were so long, and it was so heavy to lift about, and I
always used to go to sleep very soon after I began to read it" (I.8). Paul confirms
his brother's opinion: "some of it was rather tiresome; especially that about why

---

[15]   "A complete Chronicle of the Kings of England, from the Time of the Romans'
Descent, unto his sacred Majesty which now reigneth: containing all notable Passages of
Church and State, and other, the Sundry Observations proper for a Chronicle. To wit: of
each King's coming to the Crown; of its Battels, his Taxations, his Laws and Ordinances;
of his Works of Piety and other chief Acts; of his Wives and Children; of his Personage and
Conditions; of his Death and Burial. Also of the Affairs of the Church in each Reign; of Men
of Note; and strange Casualties. Likewise an Account of the Maiors and Sheriffs of the City
of London: A Record of the founding and endowing of the most chief Buildings, civil and
sacred, and of divers others, the Alms–deeds of pious Folk, proper to set forth. To which is
prefixed, a Commodious Digest of the History of Geoffrey of Monmouth, Ecclesiastick;
who wrote the Affairs of this Land in the Time of Abraham, Isaac, and Jacob. Also the entire
Text and Interpretation of the Prophecies of Merlin; for as many as take Delight in the same.
The whole plentifully interspersed with Suitable Reflections, and Sundry Pleasantries. By
FRANCIS FAGG FAITHFULL, *Esq.* of *Ponderwell Hall*, in the County of *Cumberland.
London: Printed by U. Blackitt*; for *A. Webb*, and *Posthumous Patience*, at the *Venerable
Bede*, in *Little Britain*. MDCLVI" (I.4–5).

people called this country *Britain*. There are 177 pages about that; and when I had read them all, I did not know the reason" (I.8). Also puzzling are references to what he thinks are real people and events, but which he cannot find in his copy of "Goldsmith's little History of England" (I.9). Their father explains that not only is Mr "Faithful's" volume stylistically ill-suited to young readers, but that its content, which includes "fables and nonsense," presents problems. Children interested in history, Taylor's text asserts, will be put off by dry, lengthy prose, and confused by the inclusion of undocumented history, for children cannot be expected to differentiate fact from fable.

What, then, should children want from their histories? What, in fact, do they actually desire from their history reading? Taylor proceeds to set forth some theories in the remainder of his opening chapter. When their father redirects the boys to the section of his library labeled "Juvenile Miscellanies," Lewis and Paul are attracted to different volumes. When asked what drew him to *An Old Story*, Lewis replies "Dear Papa ... because I suppose there is an account of a great many strange things, which happened to famous people who lived a long time ago, such as I always like to read, and am always sure to remember" (I.11–12). Paul, the more sober of the two boys, explains his choice of *A History of Two Thousand Years*: "Because ... I think there must be an account of a great many things which have happened, that I have never yet heard of, and that I should wish to know about and remember" (I.12). Though each boy dutifully concludes with the idea of memorization (history is that which one can remember about the past), other qualities prove equally, if not more, appealing: strangeness; novelty; the satisfaction of a desire to know; and, above all, the experience of pleasure ("such as I always like to read"). Children, Taylor thus asserts, want from their histories not a panoply of moral exemplars they can commit to memory, but rather what they want from their fiction—pleasure.

Yet the volumes the boys pick for their different titles in fact turn out to be the same book inside: *A New and Complete History of England, from the coming of Caesar, to the present time* (I.15).[16] Their father explains that although "the volume you wish to read is not exactly the kind of thing you think it is, and you will not probably be so much pleased with it at first as you expect to be," if his sons adopt the plan of study he suggests, they will not only take pleasure from their reading, they "will like [their history] better than any book [they] have yet read" (I.14). Initially, his plan sounds much like a schoolroom exercise: the boys will, on occasions appointed by their father, recount to him the key points from a specified set of chapters. Yet the plan soon shifts to something more engaging: the boys will not simply recite, but will write their own versions of history, and will read them aloud not only to their father, but to their entire family circle in the evenings. Granted the agency to craft their own histories and then to perform them

---

[16]   In all likelihood an edition of *A New History of England; from the Invasion of Julius Caesar to the Present Time*, first published by (and attributed to) John Newbery in 1759. The work went through multiple editions, and publishers, in subsequent decades.

for an audience, Lewis and Paul do not simply become the passive recipients of knowledge, but instead actively work to construct knowledge; though they may be "little," they are historians all the same. And as historians, they are free (at least initially) to include in their histories the very fictional elements that they find so lacking in their reading of histories written for adults.

Rife with humorous commentaries, digressions, and misunderstandings, Lewis and Paul's initial forays into the realm of history-writing suggest that their father's promise to "make every allowance that we can, and not laugh more than we can help" when listening to them may be difficult to keep (I.18). Certainly, the inclusion of material such as "O, had you been an Ancient Briton, / You'd not have had a stool to sit on" invites the reader outside the text, as well as the listeners within it, to laugh heartily at the boys' mistaken ideas of what constitutes serious history (I.20). Such humor, of course, allows the reader a delicious sense of superiority over those who are less well-versed in history-writing conventions. But it simultaneously functions to create a bond of sympathy between the boys and those readers who remember well their own misunderstandings when first learning history (or who are still in the midst of figuring out history's generic conventions). As with the protagonists of the family robinsonades discussed in Chapter 1, ideal exemplarity gives way to identification with a less-than-perfect role model.

Humor also forges a connection between the father and the reader, both of whom take pleasure in laughing at the same things. We chuckle together at Lewis's accidentally using one installment of his history as building material for a kite; we smile along with father as Paul, overlooking a footnote that points to the lack of historical evidence, asserts as truth the "tale" of Joseph of Arimethea converting early Britons to Christianity (I.93–4); we all laugh at Lewis's misreading of the term "papal bull" (King John "persuaded the pope to send him a *bull* to frighten the barons and make them give it up—as if all the great barons with their swords, and armour, and vassals, and horses, would be such cowards as to mind a bull!" [II.19]).[17] In each case, laughter functions to align the reader with the father, and thus makes readers open to his authority and guidance.

But such alignment does not come at the expense of identification with Lewis and Paul; the laughter the reader shares with the father, unlike that in Wyss's *Family Robinson Crusoe*, lacks an aggressive edge. Lewis and Paul's father may laugh at his sons, but he never subjects them to contemptuous ridicule to prove his own superiority. Concerned that their first attempts might contain "some errors which would cause more mirth than would be quite agreeable," he vets their drafts (I.21). And when "a sudden expression of mirthful astonishment" erupts in reaction to at Paul's "history" of Joseph of Arimethia, it is quickly "suppressed" when his family "perceived that Paul was not in the least entertained by merriment indulged at his expense" (I.93). His father even apologizes, and suggests that Paul's mistake results not from his childishness, but from a problem confronted by

---

[17]   Taylor's wit extends even further here, as those readers familiar with the term "Irish bull" (a ludicrous, incongruent, or logically absurd statement) would be well aware.

Fig. 3.1 "One of the 'Ancient Britons' without a stool to sit on: Egbert, the first King of England in mail armour." The caption makes no mention of the boy beside him, typical of the exclusion of children from classical history. Courtesy of the UCLA Charles E. Young Research Library Department of Special Collections.

all historians: "My dear lad we ought not to have laughed; for I confess that it was really neither ridiculous nor wonderful that you should have believed that which old men with long beards have believed before you" (I.93). Most tellingly, it is not only the reader, but also the boys themselves, who often recognize when they are being teased, and who join in laughing at themselves. For example, when father asks them "who was Lord Mayor of London, in the days of King Lud; and, who was Sherriff, in the time of Uter Pendragon; or describe to me the personage and conditions of Gogmagog?" Lewis recognizes that he is the subject of a joke, and takes pleasure in it: "Lewis had still nothing to say; but seeing a smile upon his father's countenance, he smiled too" (I.6). Instead of creating a narrator or a father who acts in collusion with the reader against the narrative's protagonists, Taylor instead creates a sense that all three parties—father, children, and reader—are in on the joke.

This sense of belonging, crafted both through identifying with the child protagonists, and participating both with the children and their father in the pleasures of humor, serves as the step requisite to the main goal of this text: teaching children the generic conventions of history. While their father asks them to completely rewrite their initial drafts, he does not discount what writing them has achieved: "I perceive, by what you have done, that some good is accomplished already: your attention is awakened to the subject" (I.23). Only now that their "attention" has been "awakened," can the real work have any chance of success: "I have now an opportunity of directing your minds accurately to the essential parts of it [writing history]" (I.23). Similarly, only now that the reader's attention has been awakened through identification with Lewis and Paul and participating in the shared community of laughter that the narrative invites him[18] to join, can his mind be opened to the less engaging task of learning the codes of history.

At the beginning of his first public reading, Lewis, who has been charged with the task of recounting England's political history, notes that no historians seem to know for sure when the Britons first arrived, or from whence they came. To fill in the gap, Lewis imagines how it might have been:

> "One day the people that lived in Gaul, which is now called France, standing upon the sea-shore, most likely somewhere near Calais, and looking toward England, said, perhaps, 'I wonder what sort of a country that is that we can just see over there? suppose we go and look at it.' Then some others might reply 'Suppose we do.' After that I dare say that a few of them got into a boat and sailed across; and finding it a pleasant country, and that nobody had found it out before, they came with as many more as liked it, and lived there themselves. That is how, I think, Britain was first peopled." (II.26–7)

---

[18]   I use "him" purposely here, as Taylor's novel suggests that the true audience for history is a male one. While Taylor himself had several older sisters, Lewis and Paul have only a much younger sister, one who enters the narrative only sparingly. Mother interjects comments occasionally, but their subjects—typically religious or moral—suggest that feminine participation in the project of writing or learning history is distinctly limited.

In response to Lewis's invented tale, his father tells him (and the reader) that although "it is very likely that Britain might have been peopled in the way you have supposed," such an imagined account "is not *history*, which is what I am waiting to hear" (I.28). For Lewis, history is a project of identification: a narrative constructed to bridge the gaps in the historical record, filled with the probable but imagined thoughts of unknown people of the past. By picturing what he himself might have thought when faced with the expanse of the English Channel, and then projecting those thoughts onto unknown people in the past, Lewis creates a connection between past and present, between the subjects of history and the historian himself. Lewis here does exactly what Abbé Pluche had recommended that parents encourage their daughters to do: create dialogues in which they imagined the motivations of figures from history (Koepp 165). While such historical play might be appropriate for girls, boys, who need a stronger grounding in history, must not indulge. For, as father points out, such narratives, though they might be probable, are not *histories*. Drawing on supposition rather than fact, narratives such as Lewis's prove instead to be history's opposite: fiction.

Insisting on the binary relationship between history and fiction, with history in the position of the privileged term, proved particularly important during this period, when the newly-emerging social history and the need for reader engagement that accompanied it led to the introduction in history writing of many forms and techniques more commonly associated with eighteenth-century narrative fictions than with traditional classical histories.[19] During the eighteenth century, such techniques—epistolary narratives; personal anecdotes; biographies that included information about domestic as well as political or military events; footnotes with detailed information about culture; historical accounts focusing more on conveying the emotional impact of historical events than on establishing a linear narrative of them—first emerged in the "minor" genres of history, such as biography or memoir, rather than in the central, most prestigious linear narratives of public events. Such innovations presented a challenge to the prestige of classical linear history, a prestige build in part upon the history reader's definition of himself as all that was opposite of the novel reader: a mature, active, rational, public-minded, and above all, male reader, rather than a young, passive, emotional, private female reader. By the early nineteenth century, the elite male reader could acknowledge the need for innovation in history writing, particularly the need for reader engagement, but still

---

[19] The majority of these "fictional" techniques can be found in works that pre-date the eighteenth-century novel, of course; collections of letters, portraits of public figures, and collections of anecdotes and sayings were all known to the ancients. During the eighteenth century, both history and fiction drew upon preexisting literary forms to meet the demands of their growing audiences; each also borrowed from the other. Yet a focus on the social and inner lives of public figures is far more commonly associated with fiction than with traditional classical history in the period. See Braudy and Phillips (Chapter 4) for information about the relationship between the two genres in the eighteenth century; see Ferris for a discussion of fiction and history in the early nineteenth century.

felt a clear need to insist upon strict boundaries between history and the novel, even while in practice these boundaries remained in flux (Phillips 81–102).

In *The Little Historians*, Father devises a plan by which the "not historical" can be differentiated from the true elements of history: a bottle of red ink sits on the table beside the little historians, and each must draw a line through any material of which father disapproves. Examining those moments when father calls out "red ink" (and those instances where we might suppose red ink will be called for, but is not) reveals father's interest in maintaining the binary hierarchy of history/fiction. Yet it simultaneously suggests that the project of crafting engaging juvenile history may depend on deploying certain elements more commonly associated with fictional discourse.

The most common cries of "red ink" result from mistakes in style and aesthetics, particularly issues of vocabulary. History, as the highest form of literary endeavor, demands formal language and accurate comparisons, not the informality of the vocabulary typical of a family discussion. Thus, one might also expect that the informality of using the first person might lead to a call for the red ink bottle; and indeed, several times during the boys' narrative, "I" statements are subject to deletion. But not all such statements suffer that fate, but rather, only those that lead the little historians to self-referential comments that have nothing to do with the history at hand. Lewis starts to talk about the Druids, even though Paul is in charge of relating ecclesiastical history, and soon veers humorously off topic: "I have seen a print of a Druid, that looked like an old woman in a long cloak. They used to live in woods and caves, and hollow trees, and ate nuts and acorns.—I like nuts very much, but acorns are exceedingly disagreeable. I am glad that I am not a Druid" (I.28–9). Digressions that lead authors into the realm of the personal, rather than back to the historical ("Margate and Ramsgate are in the Isle of Thanet, to which people go in the summer. I have been there myself"; "They chose for their generals, Caractacus and Togodumnus, two brothers:—what hard names! I am glad that my name is not Caractacus, and that Paul's is not Togodumnus: I would call him *Tog*, if it was" [I.86; I.34]) typically lead to calls for "red ink." Such self-referential uses of the first person, uses which bring the narrative focus back to the historian rather than to the history itself, have no place in the historical project.[20]

Yet many instances of Lewis and Paul's use of "I" pass without a call for the ink bottle. Examining these instances suggests that two types of first-person narrative may be included in the historical project. First, "I" statements that lead the historian (and his reader) to identify with the people of history, or to feel sympathy for them, prove acceptable to father. When relating the period of Roman occupation, Lewis asserts "I begin to be tired of the Romans, and to wish they were gone; for I do not like this part of the history at all; and I dare say, that the poor Britons did not like it much better" (I.35), and tells his auditors that "I shall

---

[20]   Such self-referential "I" statements do, of course, function in the project of creating reader identification, discussed earlier. Thus, the narrator slyly benefits from the very things he is purportedly teaching his readers not to do.

take some notice of *him* [Edwy]; for he being then only 14 years of age, was but a little older than somebody who is now writing his history" (I.124). Taylor even includes mention of extra-textual moments of identification: Lewis says "I think I shall dream about an Ancient Briton tonight, and, Paul, mind that you dream about a Druid" (I.81); later, Lewis and Paul recount their attempt to build their own "antiquities" in the backyard, and their play at being ancient peoples ("I made an earthen barrow ... that was quite a *tumulus*, and I wanted Paul to lie under it a little while, for the sake of being an Ancient Briton, but he said he would not, unless I would be a Druid, and eat acorns for my dinner" [I.154–5]). Bringing a sense of self to history helps the historian connect emotionally to history's participants; such connection, similar to the connection forged between Lewis and Paul, their father, and the reader, functions to create a sense of engagement and identification all too often lacking from the lengthy linear public histories written for an adult audience, but more commonly to be found in fiction.

"I" statements that function to connect historian to history appear throughout the three volumes of Taylor's work. But as the little historians become more practiced, more aware of the conventions of history as their accounts are commented on, corrected, or emended by their father and uncle, a second type of "I" statement begins to appear. This type stems from a prominent feature of classical historiography for adults: the portrait, a "final assessment of the balance of virtues and vices exhibited in the life of an important man" (Phillips 65). Such portraits typically appeared at the end of a historian's depiction of the events that occurred during his subject's life, and functioned not only to bring a sense of closure to the narrative, but also to underscore the moral lessons to be gained by studying the exemplary virtues and vices of famous men. Once the little historians reach the reign of William the Conqueror, their father begins to serve as the portraitist of classical historiography: after Lewis and Paul have completed their description of the events of a certain rule, father summarizes the character of each ruler. Soon, following his example, Lewis and Paul begin tentatively to enter their own moral pronouncements upon the men of history. But unlike their father, who deploys the second person plural, or, more commonly, gives no attribution to his judgments, the boys typically rely on the first person to couch their moral assessments. The boys must first create a sense of connection between themselves and their history before they can make the statements of valuation that come so easily to their learned father.

Intriguingly, the boys' first moral judgments focus on the domestic, rather than political, behavior of their subjects. Lewis knows that Athelstand was a good king, and a clever warrior, but finds his stranding his brother in a boat with no food in order to prevent his usurpation of the throne morally lacking: "I think this is the worst thing that I have had to mention in all my history. How different must Athelstand have been from Alfred, who, I dare say, so far from doing that, would himself have jumped over to have saved his brother, or any one else from drowning!" (I.122). Such a digression into the realm of the imaginative would seem a likely candidate for red ink, but their father does not ask that the passage be deleted. Paul, the more sober of the two boys, moves more easily toward judging political actions; in describing the fate of the Fifth Monarchy men, he comments, "In about three days, however, they were nearly all killed by the soldiers, and the rest were hanged. I do not think it was persecution to put to death such men as these" (III.127). By quickly responding "Certainly not," father indicates to his sons that their moral assessments of the men of history are just as important as their knowledge of the facts of their lives. And soon, following his brother's and father's model, Lewis begins to deploy this model, too: "I rather think that this king [Charles II] was one who liked, above all things, to enjoy himself, and be merry; and so long as he could get money enough for that, he did not seem to care much how other affairs went on" (III.118–19).

As Phillips notes, the "portrait" of classical historiography is not simply a hollow convention; it points to what classical writers believed to be the primary purpose of the study of history:

> Humanist and neoclassical tradition viewed history as preeminently a training for public life, and since public life was taken to be the highest sphere of moral choice, history's lessons were as much ethical as political. Thus history's concern with character is twofold. As mimetic narrative, history is largely the story of the revelation of character in action, while as instruction, it is an effective form of teaching that uses compelling examples to train readers to aspire to virtue and to shun the temptations of vice. (65)

For younger historians, however, Taylor's text suggests, the instruction of "compelling examples" will prove less efficacious if history's students do not begin first by identifying with the people of history. Only by first deploying "I" statements that function to connect, then "I" statements that judge historical actors own abilities to connect to individuals (a brother, a husband) around them, can younger readers progress to "I" statements that function to judge political actions that impact the citizenry as a whole. Identification thus functions more powerfully than ideal exemplarity to "train readers to aspire to virtue and to shun the temptations of vice." Only by first feeling admiration or disgust, love or anger, for the people whose lives they recount can Lewis and Paul, and by extension, the little historians outside the text, properly learn to apply their moral examples to their own lives.

Yet making the proper moral judgments—knowing when to admire and when to be disgusted—may not be as simple as this account suggests. When the boys finish their story of the reign of Charles I, their father finds he cannot provide a summarizing portrait, for "the fact is that neither historians nor people in general are at all agreed in their opinions concerning the transactions of those times" (III.105). Uncle Clement asserts that Charles's conduct in "domestic life" was "truly excellent"; likewise, father notes of Oliver Cromwell, "As to his disposition, we are still puzzled to understand it; for he was certainly guilty of the most atrocious cruelty, particularly in Ireland; yet he is known to have been a kind and tender father" (III.115). According to the norms of classical historiography, a man's character can explain his actions, both public and private; yet the glaring contradictions presented by Cromwell and Charles I suggest a more complex construction of identity, one far less open to definitive moral pronouncement than that promised by classical historiographic portraiture.

Additionally, as Maria Edgeworth, echoing Gibbon, points out in *Practical Education* (1798), the disconnect between historical fact and contemporary morality may present an ambiguous moral message to young readers:

> The simple morality of childhood is continually puzzled and shocked at the representation of the crimes and the virtues of historic heroes. History, when divested of the graces of eloquence, and of that veil which the imagination is taught to throw over antiquity, presents a disgusting, terrible list of crimes and calamities; murders, assassinations, battles, revolutions, are the memorable events of history. The love of glory atones for military barbarity; treachery and fraud are frequently dignified with the names of prudence and policy; and the historian, desirous to appear moral and sentimental, yet compelled to produce facts, makes out an inconsistent, ambiguous system of morality. (202)

Though Paul and Lewis are likely a few years older than the six- and seven-year-olds to whom Edgeworth applies the term "simple morality of childhood," her words suggest that all children not trained to throw a "veil" over the past might take the immoral for the moral, or, perhaps more damagingly, recognize the hypocrisy of adult narrators who commend in their descriptions but then condemn in their concluding portraits. To prevent such misreadings of history, Edgeworth suggests, albeit obliquely, that teachers would do best to curtail the scope of the written factual history they present to their pupils: "he will conceive, that it is of more consequence that his pupils should have distinct notions of right or wrong, than that they should have perfectly by rote all the Grecian, Roman, English, French; all the 50 volumes of the Universal History" (202).

In *The Little Historians*, Taylor puts Edgeworth's recommendation into action. Yet his concerns about what children should not read differ in many ways from Edgeworth's, in part because his text contains the very "judicious and honest preceptor" she calls for, in the form of Lewis and Paul's father (202). Father clearly conveys the message that glory should be regarded less than honor when he and Uncle Clement opine that Henry V's wars in France and Scotland, though surprising and remarkable, were "unjust in the extreme"; such battles contrast unfavorably with more recent British actions at Waterloo, for Napoleon's imperial graspings find their parallel in the actions of the earlier unjust English king (II.113–14). Few descriptions of the glories of battle occur in the work of the little historians, and father's interpretive interventions ensure that his sons do not fall victim to history-reading's potential for instilling the "inconsistent, ambiguous system of morality" feared by Edgeworth.

Yet even father's interventions cannot make all historical fact acceptable material for youthful ears, and Taylor, following Edgeworth, edits his account accordingly. Two areas of particular concern are those very events likely to appeal most to youthful readers hoping to mine history for its exciting, rather than edifying, stories: violence and sex. In describing the punishments meted out to the religious dissenting Lollards, Paul ends his account by noting that if a Lollard failed to recant, "he was to be burned alive!" (II.125). Uncle Clement proceeds to describe the violent punishment in dramatic, fiction-like detail:

> Suppose a man had said that he believed the church of Rome to be the wicked woman mentioned in Revelation; then suppose he is seized and brought into a strong room, in which he sees whips, cords, knives, iron screw-cramps, a spiked wheel, a large fire, and three or four of the most dreadfully cruel-looking men that could be found; then suppose one of these men says to him,—'Do you believe that the church of Rome is the wicked woman mentioned in the Revelation?' The heretic would say, perhaps, 'I do.' Then his judge might say, 'Give him the iron boot.' A case of iron would then be put upon his bare leg, and a wedge would be placed so as by a blow, to be driven in between the boot and the bone, and cause the most inconceivable agony. But, perhaps, before this was done the miscreant, as they would call him, might say, 'O, I RECANT! I RECANT.' But if he had strength of mind enough still to hold his opinion, his judge would say, 'Strike!' (II.125–6)

But just as it was inappropriate for Lewis to imagine what might have led the first Britons to cross the Channel, so too is it inappropriate for Uncle Clement to allow his youthful audience to "suppose" such pictures of torture in all their immediate, gory detail. Mother, who only speaks on rare occasions, interrupts Uncle Clement's dramatic account, calling for its curtailment: "I think this is enough for our present purpose" (II.127). Father later echoes her concern, prefacing Paul's account of the persecution of the Protestants during the reign of Queen Mary by proscribing such violent detail: "I hope you have not been very particular in describing the shocking scenes of the reign. I intended to have told you, that it is only needful to *mention* them, and to show what effect they had upon the Reformation" (III.42). Relating violent events in lavish detail may teach young readers to take vicarious pleasure in accounts of the violence of the past, rather than to read them as examples of negative behavior: as father opines, "I do not like to hear the sufferings of the martyrs described merely for the sake of relating what is shocking" (III.43).

The textual representation of sympathy in the late eighteenth century began to shift away from a vision of sympathy as an original spontaneous feeling, a vision undergirding the popular mid-century literature of sensibility, towards a conception of sympathy as a relationship of spectator to spectacle. Such a relationship had not only the positive potential inherent in the earlier vision of sympathy—to bind fellow beings more closely together—but also a negative potential, to distance the feeling spectator from the object of his sympathetic speculation. For this new type of sympathy, as theorized by eighteenth-century writers such as Adam Smith, entailed a spectator who adopts not the feelings of another, but his own image of what those feelings must be (Todd 27). As Smith famously writes in *The Theory of Moral Sentiments* (1759/1790),

> Though our brother is upon the rack, as long as we ourselves are at our ease, our senses will never inform us of what he suffers. They never did, and never can, carry us beyond our own person, and it is by the imagination only that we can form any conception of what are his sensations. ... It is the impression of our own senses only, not those of his, which our imaginations copy. (9)

By imposing one's own imaginative representation of suffering on the body of a real sufferer, the experience of sympathy becomes aestheticized; the danger of such aestheticization is that a spectacle of suffering will become a moment for taking aesthetic pleasure in a theatrical event, rather than a moment when identification between spectator and sufferer can occur (Marshall 21–7).

Uncle Clement's detailed depiction of the torture of the Lollards clearly evokes such an aestheticized theatrical spectacle. But unlike Uncle Clement, who appears to relish an imaginative engagement with scenes of violence, the little historians clearly reject the potential for taking pleasure in the spectacle of history's violent acts. For example, Paul quickly tells his father that he has "not said much about" Mary's religious persecutions, adding, "Indeed I was very glad to hurry over this part of my history, for I could not even bear to think of the things I read of" (III.43). By constructing his child in such a way, Taylor suggests that reading history for the shock-value of its violence acts, rather than for their moral lessons, is not simply unacceptable, but unnatural.

While Taylor states his messages about the dangers of experiencing vicarious pleasure through depictions of violence directly and clearly, he must disguise his strictures against the far more taboo subject of sex. The children term the Duke of Monmouth, Charles II's illegitimate son, "a certain son of the king's," the narrator unwilling to have his youthful historians even acknowledge the King's sexual life (III.125). Most strikingly, father interrupts his sons' story when they arrive at the figure of Mary Queen of Scots; the story of this Queen's sexual adventures proving far too risky to entrust to the hands of the boys, father takes it upon himself to write his own two-page history of Mary's reign, a history that he then proceeds to make Lewis read aloud.[21] Father terms Mary's actions "bad conduct," but only describes her liaisons as "making a favorite" of one man or another, and refrains from definitively asserting whether or not Mary was directly involved in the plot to murder her husband Darnley (III.53). Only after Mary's imprisonment at Tutbury are the little historians allowed to once again take up the thread of her story. Father offers no explanation of why he has taken the extraordinary step of inserting himself into his children's history, nor do the boys question his unprecedented action. That at no other point in the narrative does father give his sons a written account to replace their own suggests the disturbing power of Mary's story, a tale of female sexuality erupting into the masculine realm of politics. Children must be protected from such history, Taylor's work asserts, but, unlike in the case of violence, it is imperative that they not know from what they are being protected.

---

[21] See Vallone's "History Girls" for an account of Victorian girls' reactions to this controversial queen.

Taylor, through his father character, continues to cordon off additional areas as inappropriate to children. Throughout the narrative, father replies to questions about certain areas by explaining that his youthful historians are simply too young to understand them. Economics, religious disputes, and especially party politics are all labeled off limits to little historians. When he arrives at the reign of Charles II, Lewis notes that "people began to quarrel about politics, and called each other *Whigs and Tories*," terms that he does not understand. He wants to know what they mean, so that "I may know which I am" (III.121–2). But father resists Lewis's attempt to place himself in relation to history; when Paul asks father why he does not wish his sons to be either Whigs or Tories, father tells him that party men, no matter what their party, "are neither of them right in their conduct," something that "when you are a little older" father promises that Paul will be able to understand himself. For now, though, father wishes his boys not to "form any opinions upon these subjects. I have no objection to *little historians*, but have a great dislike to *little politicians*" (III.123). Father's objections stem in part from his belief that party politics lead inherently to prejudice: "As king William obtained the crown of England almost entirely by the management of the people called *whigs*, the people called *tories* were never very fond of him, and have given him a very indifferent character" (III.154). Party politics lead to a failure of the very objectivity that the study of history holds out as its greatest truth. Yet, as the boys discover, the majority of post-Restoration history consists of party politics; by labeling Whig and Tory "off limits," father severely curtains the ability of children to study contemporary history, or to form judgments about contemporary political issues. His sons internalize this lesson quickly; opening his account of the reign of George II, Lewis notes, "I find that a great part of the history of this reign, like the last two or three, is taken up with an account of the disputes of politicians upon public affairs, which I am not to say much about" (III.173).

Yet if the little historians, and through them, young readers, come to internalize many of the lessons of conventional historiography promulgated by Taylor through his father character, the very act of writing and speaking, rather than simply passively absorbing, history allows Lewis and Paul to express resistance to other historical conventions. For example, throughout their narrative, Lewis and Paul take issue with classical history's primary focus on warfare. Early in his history, Lewis grows tired of the continual accounts of Roman and Briton battles: "I begin to wonder that the Britons, as well as the Romans, were not tired of war and fighting: it seems as if the history of England would be nothing but an account of battles with the Romans, so long as they were here" (I.41). Later, Lewis expresses surprise at how little has been written about the peace-loving king Alfred besides descriptions of his wars with the Danes, an oversight Uncle Clement suggests results from the current construction of history: "There would have been more for you to have said about Alfred if he had not been so fond of peace; for history in general is an account of war and battles" (I.117). Lewis takes direct aim at this conventional construction of history in his account of the reign of George II:

> For some time, they say, that no event happened of any particular consequence; so historians call this '*an unimportant period.*' But I know a *little* historian who thinks it a very important period indeed; for all this time, I suppose, the people could go about their own business, without either fighting or being fought, which I think, was of more consequence to them than if the king of England had become king of France. (III.173–4)

Lewis here suggests that classical history's focus on war, and on the "great events" of history, teaches readers to value the wrong things: by granting importance only to battles, history ignores the importance of peace, and its impact on the day-to-day lives of the "people" who rarely feature in linear public history's annals.

Father seems to share in this critical analysis of the practice of history, never disagreeing when his sons suggest that "great men ... [should] settle their disputes amongst themselves like other folks" rather than engage in wars (I.211). Yet other objections raised by the little historians either pass without comment, or are sidestepped or suppressed by father, suggesting that the critique offered by Lewis and Paul may not always align so neatly with the opinions condoned by the adults. For example, Lewis calls attention to how even the smallest insignificant details about a famous person find their way into recorded history, while the events deemed most important to a less-renowned historical actor fail to register as true history. Lewis explains, "William the second was surnamed Rufus, by which we know that his hair was red. What little things are remembered in history if they concern people of consequence! If my hair was green, I dare say that nobody would know it a hundred years hence" (I.183–4). Lewis later suggests that Titus Oates, found guilty for his role in the popish plots during the reign of James II, probably "thought this [his imprisonment] to be the most important event in the present reign. But I now must speak of one which was by other people thought of much more consequence. This was the duke of Monmouth's rebellion" (III.139).

Taylor's tongue-in-cheek tone may be intended to lead readers to laugh at Lewis's historical inexperience, and at the presumption of Titus Oates in thinking his own concerns of more consequence than those of a rebellion. Yet Lewis's pronouncements also open up another possibility, one that dovetails with his earlier critique of history's focus on battles rather than on peace: that the conventions of classical history place emphasis on the wrong things. By ignoring what is deemed of vital importance to "unimportant" historical actors, and presenting only the actions and descriptions of "important" men, traditional linear history puts blinders on our ability to understand the lives of the people, rather than the rulers, of the past. Lewis thus aligns himself with modern social, rather than classical, historiography, historiography which during the opening decades of the nineteenth century began to see the value in studying not only monarchs, but manners, not only affairs of the state, but also the affairs of society. Taylor's sly humor makes it difficult to argue definitively that he aligns himself with Lewis and Paul's critique; he may merely wish readers to view it as a "childish," and hence comic, reaction to the study of history. But even if he intends us to laugh rather than question, the simple act of allowing his child characters to construct and critique, rather than simply listen and absorb the historical lesson suggests to young readers that they, too, might do the same. While Taylor's decision to create child history-writers may originally have begun as an effort to make the lessons of history more engaging, and thus to make child readers more likely to embrace its messages and its generic conventions than if it were presented directly, it simultaneously functions to open up a space (intentional or no) of resistance that even the "judicious and honest preceptor" cannot completely control.

The boys' most subversive critiques circle around the issues of race, nationality, and imperialism, critiques that Father is quick to repress. When Lewis attempts to apply contemporary Christian doctrine to the treatment of the Jews under Richard I and Edward I—"But the poor Jews were sadly used and persecuted"—father provides a brief explanation of usury, but then redirects his son's attention: "But there is so much to say about Edward, that we must not stay talking about the Jews" (II.52). Likewise, when Lewis describes the imperialism of France and England critically—"I rather think that they were all trying to take possession of countries that did not belong to them" (III.185)—Father intervenes, suggesting that Lewis's moral judgment stems from his lack of knowledge about the situation, and adding an explanation of the cruelty of the Indian *Nabobs* and the way they "took" Calcutta, which "belonged to the English" (III.185). The moral objection to unjust warfare raised earlier in connection with Henry V's invasion of France holds no weight when discussing more recent imperial projects; after noting England's victories in the Indian rebellion of 1745, Father additionally notes, "In America, also, we did great things" in "taking" Quebec which now, like India, "belongs" to England (III.186). Henry V's military prowess must not be glorified, but Father sees no hypocrisy in casting contemporary imperialistic efforts in terms of national pride. The boys seem to understand that such a double vision must be sustained, and veil subsequent critique accordingly. For example, this brief mention of Irish unrest finds its way into the longer account of Napoleon: "At this time, or a little before, there was a rebellion in Ireland, and a battle was fought before the folks there were quiet again. Then Ireland was joined to England, as Scotland had been, in order, I suppose, that it might be better taken care of" (III.201). Lewis here recites the line of the dominant culture—Ireland needs to be taken care of, and England is the country to do it—yet the doubt expressed in his "I suppose" hints at another, less flattering explanation, an explanation that active readers will recognize they are being called on to write themselves. Thus Taylor invites his readers, like his child protagonists, to become active participants in the project of critiquing history, even while demonstrating the need to veil their critiques to escape the scrutiny of authority figures who might repress more directly worded objections.

Taylor concludes his tale of the little historians with just such a critique hidden under a veil of humor. At the end of his history, Lewis imagines the historical actors who have peopled their account "standing in a row, all still, and saying nothing, in a very, *very* long, straight quiet road, so that one can hardly see whether those that are a *thousand years off* are there at all" (III.213). When Uncle Clement jokingly asks him "And suppose all these famous kings and warriors were then suddenly to come to life again, and draw their swords, what do you think they would do to you, for all the terrible things you have said of them?" Lewis deflects the potential critique, while simultaneously constructing a critique of his own: "I think they would fight a most terrible battle with each other, to see which should be king of England again. I do not suppose that they, or any body else, would think it worth while to be very much displeased with '*The Little Historians*'" (III.214). Rather than learn to throw an Edgeworthian "veil of the imagination" over the atrocities of the past, or to use history only as a ground upon which to construct a moral self, the perceptive little historian can use his imaginative, emotional engagement with history to present a critique of past *and* present. But Taylor simultaneously cautions such a little historian to veil his critique with humor, for children must not appear to be involved in contemporary politics. If he deploys a veil of humor, the little historian can take aim at contemporary political ideologies while protecting himself from the potential displeasure such a critique might evoke.

Expanding the Borders of the Historical: Sympathy, Invention, and Social History in Agnes Strickland's *Historical Tales of Illustrious British Children* (1833)

> "There is nothing to be said respecting the character of little Edward [V], since he was but a child, and never really reigned. His name appears amongst the kings of England, because for some months nobody else could take the crown; but that period was properly an *interregnum*, or space between two reigning kings"
> —Father to Lewis and Paul, in *The Little Historians*[22]

Jefferys Taylor attempted to find a place for the child in the historical project by allowing him to become a historian. But given the lack of success *The Little Historians* met within the marketplace (only one edition appears to have been published), and the lack of any later Victorian juvenile histories which follow its lead,[23] Taylor's model proved less than successful in opening up a space for the child in the realm of history. A far more promising experiment in juvenile history can be found in the work of another author writing less than a decade after Taylor: Agnes Strickland.

In the 1830s, Strickland, a popular and practiced writer of fiction for children, began to explore ways in which to transform the writing of history for a juvenile

---

22 Taylor, II.153.

23 The one exception I have been able to find, *The Students; or Biography of Grecian Philosophers* (attributed to Christian Isobel Johnstone, and published by John Harris in 1827) contains none of the irony or humor so characteristic of Taylor. Three schoolboys, known as the "Students," decide to spend their free time researching and writing biographies of the Grecian philosophers and share them with each other on their next half-holiday. What follows are fairly straightforward biographies, the frame narrative of child authorship serving more as pretext to present traditional history than an experiment in form.

audience. In her first experiment, *Historical Tales of Illustrious British Children*, published in 1833, Strickland does not position children as outside observers or even crafters of historical narratives, as does Taylor; rather, she brings them front and center, asserting that children have and did play meaningful roles in the course of British history. In order to do so, however, Strickland must first push at the boundaries of traditional classical history, not only in regards to what constitutes acceptable content, but also in regards to what constitutes acceptable form.

Ensconced, like their mothers and aunts, in the domestic sphere, children rarely feature in the annals of classical political and military history. Romantic constructions of childhood, which gained increasing influence during the nineteenth century, constructed children as "more than" adults (more imaginative, more idealistic, more self-sufficient) without displacing the earlier tradition that they were also "less than" adults: less rational, less able to reason. If humanist and neoclassical tradition held that history's most important function was to teach ethical behavior, children constructed as less-than-rational could hardly serve as the models of rational moral behavior integral to such a lesson. As the father of *The Little Historians* asserts, there is "nothing to be said respecting the character" even of a child king, "since he was but a child."

Yet if children rarely held center stage in works of history, they had long been at the moral center of a different type of writing: religious exemplary biography. The inclusion of children in this tradition began in the seventeenth century with the dissenting writer James Janeway's enormously popular compilation of spiritual biographies, *A Token for Children, being an Exact Account of the Conversion, Holy and Exemplary Lives, and Joyful Deaths, of several young Children* (1671–1672). The tradition of exemplary religious children continued in countless imitations of Janeway published in both England and America, well into the Victorian period, in both religious and secular forms. In the nineteenth century, the genre was re-envisioned in fictional form by Evangelical writers such as Mary Martha Sherwood, who introduced what would later become a favorite Evangelical juvenile literature theme—the conversion of an adult by a pious child—in *Little Henry and his Bearer* (1814) (Avery "Religion" 503–8). Gillian Avery suggests that such biographies, which portrayed adults awestruck at the exemplary lives and triumphant deaths of young boys and girls, "enthralled" readers from the seventeenth century well into the nineteenth. As William Godwin's description of his reading of Janeway— "I felt as if I were willing to die with them, if I could with equal success, engage the admiration of my friends and mankind"—demonstrates, child readers found the agency and power granted to children within these biographies immensely appealing (qtd in Avery, "Religion" 504).

Writers of history for children were slow to draw on the model provided for them by exemplary religious biography, but by the early nineteenth century, a few stray works of juvenile history began to feature the early lives of famous men (and occasionally, women). The anonymously published *The Juvenile Plutarch: Containing Accounts of the Lives of Celebrated Children, and of the Infancy of Persons who have been Illustrious for their Virtues or Talents*, which first appeared in 1801, attempted to draw on the youthful desire of engaging the admiration of others evinced by readers of religions exemplary biographies such as Godwin. As the author of *The Juvenile Plutarch* notes in the book's preface, "Examples of the progress of great and good men in the paths which led them to that glory which has rendered them objects of admiration to posterity, cannot but excite in the minds of ingenuous youths a desire to imitate them" (Preface). Featuring biographies of secular and learned children such as Blaise Pascal, Anne Baynard, and Alexander Pope, the *Juvenile Plutarch* suggests that a child need not die a martyr to become the object of attention; cultivation of the intellect, as long as it is accompanied by exemplary moral qualities, may do as well. A similar volume—*Buds of Genius; or, Some Account of the Early Lives of Celebrated Characters Who were remarkable in their childhood. Intended as an introduction to biography* (1816)—combines the form of fictional dialogue with historical portrait, framing its fifteen biographies as a conversation between a mother and her two children after they asked her what "great men ... did when they were little boys" (qtd in St John, II.779). Full-length biographies of adults for children, such as Elizabeth Sandham's *The History of Britannicus and his sister Octavia* (1818) and *Elizabeth Woodville: Or, the Wars of the Houses of York and Lancaster* (1822) began to include details about the youths of their featured characters, as did one early work of historical fiction for children, Clara Reeve's *Edwin, King of Northumberland* (1802).

Yet it was not until 1833, when the children's book author and soon to become popular woman's historian Agnes Strickland published *Historical Tales of Illustrious British Children*,[24] that child readers could find themselves depicted as individual actors in a book-length work of history. Strickland's collection of seven historical narratives all feature a child or children as primary characters. In order to construct the child as an agent in history, however, Strickland cannot rely on historical fact alone; as today's historians of childhood often lament, historical documents and artifacts that give insight into the actual experience of childhood,

---

[24] Strickland was well-known as an author of children's books when *Historical Tales* was published, having sold multiple manuscripts to children's publishers John Harris and William Darton in the 1810s and 1820s. She continued to publish with Darton, but later began a relationship with Nathaniel Hailes, known for his Juvenile Library (Brown 80), publishing *Evenings of Mental Recreation* with the company in 1828. Her collection of historical tales, originally published in 1833, was reprinted multiple times in the nineteenth century, according to WORLDCAT listings: by Hailes in 1837; by Hamilton & Co. in 1847; by Jarrold and Sons in 1850, 1858, 1862, and, under the title *Illustrious British Children: A Story of their Childhood*, in 1899. An American edition was published in the 1840s by Boston publisher Monroe and Francis. The collection's central story, "The Royal Brothers," later appeared as a stand-alone title, *The Royal Brothers: An Historical Tale*; WORLDCAT lists an 1876 edition published by Jarrold. The WORLDCAT listing notes that this is the "8th edition," although no other WORLDCAT listings appear for the volume.

The original edition of *Historical Tales* contains only one illustration, a beautiful black and white engraving of "Lady Lucy's Petition" by E. Chauvane SG, reprinted in this volume.

and individual children, are all too rare (Cox 3). Though Strickland's narratives are all "founded on some striking authentic fact in the annals of their own country, in which royal or distinguished children were engaged" (iv–v), they move far beyond the limits of the historical record. In her preface, Strickland asserts that the "pages of few works of fiction can offer anything so attractive" or "exciting" as history, yet she simultaneously suggests that in order for the "inexhaustible treasure of entertainment" that history contains to be accessible to the child reader, the writer of juvenile histories must offer something besides the "barren chronology of monarchical successions, bloody wars, and dry political intrigues" that typically form the contents of histories intended for children (iii–iv). What Strickland offers in place of dry, factual history is an experiment in combining discourses. To bring children into history, both as actors and as audience, Strickland suggests, she must first broaden the scope of what counts as "history." Only by opening up the realm of history to the social and the emotional experiences of those living in the past, experiences that she must extrapolate from the historical record and then creatively imagine through fiction, can Strickland find a form "agreeable" enough to convince the "reluctant student" of history not to turn away "with weariness and distaste" (iii, iv).

> We do assuredly lament that people should be found to write history who ought to be writing novels; and that the public require history to be written like novels in order to read it … . [We] must plead guilty to a great dislike for the growing tendency among women to become writers of history. These authoresses, often gifted as they are with a certain insight into character, a vivid appreciation of individual facts and a great facility of narration, have in our opinion no historical grasp—no powerful comprehension of events; and what they produce is at best but a pretty phantasmagoria of coloured figures. —J.M. Kemble, in a review of Dr Doran's *Queens of England of the House of Hanover*, 1855[25]

> To make the past present, to bring the distant near, to place us in the society of a great man on an eminence which overlooks the field of a mighty battle, to invest with the reality of human flesh and blood beings whom we are too much inclined to consider personified qualities in an allegory, to call up our ancestors before us with all their peculiarities of language, manners, and garb, to show us over their houses, to seat us at their tables, to rummage their old-fashioned wardrobes, to explain the uses of their ponderous furniture, these parts of the duty which properly belongs to the historian have been appropriated by the historical novelist. —Thomas Macaulay, *Miscellaneous Essays*, 1828[26]

In the Preface to *Historical Tales of Illustrious British Children*, Strickland points not to the novelty of featuring child characters, but to the inclusion of "useful and entertaining information illustrative of the manners, customs, and costume of the era connected with the events of every story" as her primary innovation as a

---

[25]   [J.M. Kemble], *Fraser's Magazine* 52 (August 1855), 149; quoted in Maitzen, 10.

[26]   *Miscellaneous Essays* 1:310; quoted in Phillips 346–7.

historian for children (v). In histories for adults written during the opening decades of the nineteenth century, names, dates, and descriptions of events had gradually begun to be supplemented by new information about the social and cultural, but these historiographical changes have made little impact on the writing of history for children, Strickland suggests. But children, like adults, want to know what people ate, what their houses were like, what clothing they wore, she asserts, and includes such details in her tales in abundance. For example, porridge is a delicacy during the reign of Alfred, when swine flesh and barley broth are the usual fare (6–7). The Sunday best of a Saxon thrall consisted of a "supertunic ... made of coarse homespun white linen, precisely similar in all respects to the long open frocks worn in the present day by waggoners," while that of the wife of a Saxon franklin included a kirtle, a surcoat, and a hood (28–9). The son of Edward IV sits in a "crimson canopied chair fringed with gold" in front of a "carved ebony reading table" to study books and illuminated manuscripts, including "a folio, printed on vellum, and bound in rose-coloured velvet, clasped and studded with gold, and emblazoned on either side with the royal arms of England" (81).

With her inclusion of such material details of life in the past, Strickland aligns herself with a new type of history: social history. By the mid-nineteenth century, social history referred not only to the greatest cultural achievements of a nation or period, but also to the depiction of the everyday lives of people and cultures of the past. Such a turn to the domestic and quotidian dramatically historicized the lives of women previously excluded by the generic constraints of classical history, Rohan Maitzen argues (23–4). In her *Tales*, we can see Strickland attempting to broaden historiography further, deploying social history to pry open a space for the inclusion in the realm of history not only of women (who feature prominently in many of her tales) but also of children.

But Strickland's inclusion of such information on the material, rather than the political lives of people of the past has a second purpose, I would suggest: to further the project of reader identification so central to many of the juvenile works of adventure fiction during this period. After reading such details of cultural life, young readers can imagine themselves wearing a supertunic, reading a velvet-covered folio, eating barley broth (or, if they were lucky, some of that porridge). By including what has typically been excluded as extraneous in histories written for children, Strickland thus draws her youthful readers closer to the past.

Yet the inclusion of such material details cannot accomplish this goal by itself, Strickland suggests, for they cannot give readers access to the component she deems central to reader identification: emotional interiority. As in the robinsonades discussed in Chapter 1, Strickland constructs the creation of emotional connection between her readers and her child characters as the key to the project of fostering reader identification. And in order to create such emotional connection, Strickland must give her readers access to the emotions of her youthful historical protagonists. But with no historical record of the feelings of these protagonists, Strickland must turn away from the documents of history to the genre long envisioned as history's opposite: fiction.

Although Strickland opens the first story of her *Tales* in a historical vein ("The tale I am about to relate, which is founded on an authentic historical fact of this nature, is an illustrative sketch of the manners and customs of the Anglo Saxons and Danes" [2]), she almost immediately shifts into a far different narrative mode:

> One bright autumnal morning, about eleven o'clock, the hour at which our Saxon ancestors usually took their principal meal, just as the family and serving-folk of the Saxon franklin, Selwood, were seating themselves at the well covered board, a loud barking from the watch dogs that guarded the homestead, answered by the low, but more angry growling of the household curs under the table, announced the approach of strangers. (2–3)

Instead of depicting history as that which has already happened, and thus a story with no suspense (for readers will of course already know the ending), Strickland transforms her "authentic historical fact" from the dry Saxon annals into the immediacy of fiction. Readers sit, alongside the family and serving-folk of the Selwood family, waiting to find out who the strangers are, what they might want, whether or not they will prove a threat. History as a process of emotional discovery, rather than as the memorization of that which has already been discovered, Strickland suggests, makes for far more entertaining, and thus far more involving, study.

Strickland encourages reader involvement not only through the immediacy of her storytelling, but also by granting her readers access to the interiority of her historical protagonists. We learn that the enslaved boy Guthred longs for his native Lethra, and curses his Saxon masters; that seven-year-old Ethelred weeps more for the separation from a beloved brother than from disappointed ambition when his half-brother Edward, rather than himself, is crowned king; that 14-year-old Edward Atheling yearns for the pleasures and freedoms of life before his accession to the throne (17, 41, 44). While the father of Taylor's little historians would discount such imaginative forays into the minds of the people of the past as not being true "history," Strickland follows Lewis's example, extrapolating from the known facts to imagine the feelings and motivations of her child protagonists. For in discovering not just what these historical children did, but also what they felt, readers can feel along with them, thus creating an emotional connection between child of the present and child of the past.

In championing the inclusion of material, domestic history, and the emotions of its protagonists, Strickland clearly positions herself on one side of the debate occurring among history-writers for adults in the early Victorian period, historians who wished to recapture those readers drawn away from the genre by the temptations of the novel, particularly the novels of Walter Scott and his many imitators. Some critics and historians, such as J.M. Kemble, fought to keep in place a binary opposition between dignified, objective, methodical, impartial, and impersonal "real" history and lively, personal, emotional, digressive, detailed imaginative fiction (a binary that often drew a link between genre and gender, as Kemble's epigraph to this section demonstrates). Others, such as Thomas Macaulay, argued for the broadening of history, both stylistically and content-wise, so that the playing field might be leveled between history and fiction (for history's, not fiction's, benefit) (Maitzen 5–10). Strickland, with her roots as a fiction writer, clearly aligns herself with the Macaulay camp, making a case through her own writing that emotional affect, far from being anathema to history, is in fact its most compelling characteristic, precisely that which makes history more vivid, and hence more memorable, particularly for children.

Yet, ironically, even as Strickland insists on the primacy of emotion in the historical project, her stories themselves continually depict the failure of emotion to effect historical change. Access to the emotional interiority of historical children functions to craft a sense of connection and community between reader and protagonist, but within Strickland's stories themselves, such connection and community prove nearly impossible to sustain. The central event of Strickland's third story, "The Sons of the Conqueror," exemplifies a failure repeated in more than half of the stories in the volume. In Strickland's account of William the Conqueror's clearance of the villages near the New Forest to make way for his own hunting ground, more than houses and churches are leveled; a "little community linked together by the strongest ties of love and neighbourhood; always ready to serve and assist each other" disappears, destroyed by the forces of history (68). So, too, in Strickland's stories, will the children of history be betrayed by a refusal by the adults around them to accept their offers of emotional connection, the invitation of fiction within the genre of history.

Rohan Maitzen suggests that female Victorian historians legitimized their scholarly work by constructing the agency of women of the past not as direct power, but as indirect "influence":

> The new historiographical emphasis on indirect agency, on effects stemming from diffuse causes rather than decisive acts, on an infinitude of tiny changes bringing about gradual revolutions, created a new model of historical explanation, one that was entirely consistent with women's accepted form of power: influence. ... Not direct, remarkable action but oblique, pervasive, beneficent sway over circumstances is the ideal for female behavior as well as an increasingly popular conception of historical significance. (40)

Through their roles as wives, mothers, daughters, and sisters, women of the past could leverage their emotional ties to the real political actors (the husbands, fathers, sons, and brothers) to exert a "feminine" spiritual, moral, and educational influence over political and military events (Maitzen 42).[27] But for the children of history, as portrayed in Strickland's tales, even such indirect agency proves inaccessible. Though several of her tales end on a happy note, Strickland's most powerful narratives conclude darkly—with the accidental deaths or murders of their child characters. But unlike the child martyr tales, these child deaths prove not a triumph, but a failure—a failure of the adult men (and in one instance, the

---

[27]   The lack of royal mistresses in Maitzen's list of those with feminine moral sway suggests that Victorian writers rarely considered their influence in a spiritual or moral light.

woman) who hold the reigns of political or military power to be "influenced" by children, to accept the connection, the community that active empathy with the emotions of the historical child would offer.

In her children's histories, then, Strickland participates in an ongoing debate about "distance" in the writing of history during the late eighteenth and early nineteenth centuries in England. During this period, according to Phillips, some historians began to "reconceive the reader's engagement with the historical narrative in more inward and sentimental terms" (103). Challenged not only by the inward turn of Romanticism, but also by the philosophical history of manners, the attractions of the novel, and literary sentimentalism, historians such as James Mackintosh (*History of England*, 1830–1832), Thomas Carlyle (*The French Revolution*, 1834), and Thomas Macaulay (*History of England* 1848), began to argue in the 1830s and 1840s for a historiography marked not by the aloof generality and distance they felt were characteristic of eighteenth-century linear political histories by Gibbon and Hume, but instead by the "evocative closeness" formerly associated with biography and memoir, the minor subgenres of eighteenth-century history (Phillips 199, 114, 28). By the mid-nineteenth century, this dispute had been definitively decided in favor of immediacy and closeness, Phillips suggests, but during the 1830s, when Strickland wrote, the issue was still the subject of much debate.

Thus, Strickland's moral critique of the behavior of her historical adults becomes aligned with her generic critique of the limits of traditional history. For it is not only the adults *in* history, Strickland suggests, but also the adults who *read* classical history and adopt its generic conventions—objectivity, rationality, emotional distance—who fail to accept the emotional connection offered to them by historical children. Rather than becoming agents of history, then, children are cast by Strickland as the victims of its generic dictates.

Strickland's combined moral and generic critique, and her proposed alternative, can be seen in two parallel stories in *Illustrious Children*, one which functions as the physical and emotional center of the collection, and one which concludes it. In the longest tale in the volume, "The Royal Brothers," Strickland depicts the lives and deaths of the Little Princes in the Tower, Edward V and his brother Richard, demonstrating the failure of emotional connection. In the volume's final tale, "Lady Lucy's Petition to the Queen," Strickland relates a far less well-known historical incident, in which nine-year-old Catherine Preston (whose name, for some undisclosed reason, Strickland changes to Lucy) saves her father from being executed for treason after the Glorious Revolution of 1688 by making a personal, emotional petition to the newly-enthroned Queen Mary.

Strickland introduces her readers to Prince Edward at a highly-emotional moment: in 1470, when the 12-year-old boy receives word of the death of Edward IV. His uncle, the Earl of Rivers, informs him of it not by telling him his father has died, but by offering him his obeisance as Edward the Fifth, King of England. When Edward, breaking into tears after understanding the implication of his unfamiliar salutation, upbraids his courtiers for their smiles, Edward's half-brother, Richard Grey, asserts that he has no reason to lament: the king's death was from natural, not violent, causes, and Edward, unlike himself, will not be economically or politically ruined by his father's death, but instead will be exalted. But Edward resists this insistence that he interpret the event politically, rather than emotionally, and politely but determinedly asks to be excused from homage that only brings him pain (87–91).

When Edward feels himself ready to accept a political, in addition to an emotional, role in the events that his father's death have set in motion, however, his attempts are continually thwarted by his other uncle, Richard, Duke of Gloucester, who would usurp his throne. Edward attempts to assert his political authority when Gloucester imprisons the Earl of Rivers, first pledging his royal word for Rivers's loyalty, then, when that proves ineffective, demanding that Gloucester release his uncle. But Gloucester insists that Edward, because of his age, has no place in political decision-making: "Tut! tut! tut! your grace is a child, and no competent judge of such matters ... it is, methinks, high time that persons of maturer age, and greater discretion than one can be expected at your tender years, should assist you in guiding the helm of state for a while" (100). When Gloucester soon arrests Edward's half-brother, Edward tries again to assert his authority, but again, Gloucester rejects it, advising his nephew that "Your grace, although nominally a king, would be wise to refrain from issuing commands which you have no power to enforce" (106). Children have no political power, for they have no access to the military power that undergirds political power, Strickland demonstrates; the adults who do have it can use the assertion of a child's inability to "judge" politically as a pretext to usurp what little political power he may by rights be entitled to.

Gloucester's thwarting of Edward's attempts to assert his political will lead the boy king to attempt a power play of a different sort, one typically associated with women: the assertion of emotional influence. Yet Edward has not learned the techniques of "oblique, pervasive, beneficent sway" that characterize the most effective wielders of feminine influence; instead, he gives free and unconstrained vent to his frustration and grief in passionate weeping. In contrast to a more oblique approach, which masks the power of the influencer and allows the one being influenced to continue to see himself as the one in charge, such an outpouring of emotions presents a direct challenge to the authority of the powerful. To accept Edward's invitation to empathize, and thus identify, with his nephew's outpouring of emotions would require Gloucester to give up his authority, something that not even "all the eloquence which [Edward's] affectionate nature had taught him," can move him to do (106).

In the early days of his imprisonment, Edward moves back and forth between masculine assertion of his political rights as sovereign and feminine attempts to establish influence, repeatedly offering his uncle the chance to forge a bond of emotional sympathy by responding to his repeated displays of tears and entreaties. But neither approach proves effective. Gloucester responds to the first with "cutting sarcasms" and "scornful contempt," and to the second by upbraiding his nephew for acting like a child (109). Edward attempts to turn this second criticism into an advantage, by hiding behind it to avoid his uncle's commands. When Gloucester demands that Edward write to his mother to insist that she turn over his brother, Richard, the Duke of York, to him, Edward replies: "It would ill become me, at my tender years, to presume to dictate to my royal mother in any thing … but especially in a matter that doth so nearly touch herself, and of which she must of necessity be a far more competent judge than myself" (121–2). But Gloucester will not have the logic of his own reasoning turned against him; instead, he responds to Edward's refusal by refusing to allow him to correspond with his mother at all. Edward, angered, tells him that he has no right to do so; his uncle ends the conversation by reminding Edward once again what really matters: "Ay, but I possess the power" (123).

Strickland's depiction of emotions here clearly draws on a specific genre of fiction: the sentimental. Though its heyday in literature for adults, in the form of the novel of sensibility (1740–60), had long passed, sentimental discourse could be found in much nineteenth-century popular literature, including juvenile literature, particularly in the mid and late Victorian periods. Characterized by its goal of arousing pathos in its readers and its use of stock characters and situations (in particular, an innocent, virtuous victim), sentimental literature demanded an emotional response from its reader (Todd 2). Claudia Nelson notes that books written for children during the Victorian period that feature acts of social injustice (such as Hesba Stretton's *Jessica's First Prayer* [1867] and Frances Hodgson Burnett's *Little Lord Fauntleroy* [1886]) typically portray sentimentally-constructed children softening "the hard hearts of their seniors" ("Growing Up" 78). Yet the social injustices of history, Strickland suggests, are far less amenable to emotional "softening" than those of fiction; history's emphasis on political and military power blinds it to the powers of emotion.

Intriguingly, what later juvenile sentimental fiction would portray as a value— the child whose innocence puts up no barriers between her interior emotional life and her external behavior—proves to be precisely the problem for the child of history. Bishop Ely, coming upon Edward in a bout of tears, speaks to him kindly; Edward, little used to such treatment, immediately embraces him as a friend. Yet the Bishop warns him to beware of trusting people based only on their "soft words and plausible appearances," for in the realm of politics, one quickly learns to hide one's real emotions (115). Edward, unable to learn the "courtly lesson of covering a heart of tears with a face of smiles," quickly finds that his direct expression of emotion, far from moving his uncle, leaves him dangerously exposed: even though he avoids talking with his new ally the Bishop in front of Gloucester, his unwonted cheerfulness and his inability to refrain from looking at the Bishop "with an expression of such affectionate regard" excites Gloucester's suspicions against the Bishop, and leads Gloucester to remove the boy from his care (114, 117).

Strickland's story, then, despite its sentimentally-iconic portrayal of Edward, seems more closely aligned with the adult fictions of childhood of the 1830s and 1840s, books such as Charlotte Brönte's *Jane Eyre* and Charles Dickens's *Oliver Twist*, in its anxiety about the ability of the child to influence through emotion.

Claudia Nelson argues that if many of the adults within such texts fail to be influenced, authors of such texts achieve emotional power because they can depend on their adult *readers* to provide the sympathy and understanding that the textual adults so striking lack ("Growing Up" 80). In the real world, Strickland's cross-written text functions to persuade the adult reader of the imperative need to respond to the emotional distress of the child victim, both the child of history and the children around them.

Yet Strickland seems to recognize that her message might well not be heeded by her adult readers in the real world, just as it is ignored in the historical one. And thus she suggests a second solution, one that centers not on changing the minds of adults, but on equipping the mind of the child. Rather than relying upon innocence, Strickland suggests, the child must develop historical awareness, must come to understand how those in the past have failed to respond to the emotional pleas of the innocent, and must protect themselves accordingly. At the opening of "The Royal Brothers," Prince Edward is so engrossed in his reading of the *Chronicles* of Sir John Froissart, and its tale of the "lively and chivalric details of the splendid reign of the third Edward" that he ignores the arrival of the courier who will announce his father's death (87). Written in the fourteenth century, Froissart's *Chronicle* of the Hundred Years' War featured "the honorable enterprises, noble adventures, and deeds of arms, performed in the wars between England and France ... to the end that brave men taking example from them may be encouraged in their well-doing" (qtd in Muhlberger). This work, according to Steve Muhlberger, served as a key text in the construction of the aristocracy's self-image in the period. In reading Froissart, and focusing on the chivalry and the splendid details of wise kings, Edward reads history traditionally: to discover the exemplar upon which he can model his own behavior. But such reading also leads him to ignore the real currents of political power and intrigue that surround him, an ignorance that proves his downfall. By the time Edward takes up the volume "The Various Fortunes of Kings," it is far too late; he, too, like several of the rulers featured in its pages, is immediately condemned to live (and later, to die) in the Tower (119). The only books allotted him now are those left behind by the murdered Henry VI.

The remainder of Strickland's tale depicts not a child who can move adults through the power of his innocent emotions, but rather a child preyed upon by Gothic horrors stemming from his very innocence. Strickland invites the reader both to be moved by the innocence of the young King, and to experience the horror of his victimization. We are asked to shudder with Edward as he spies bloodstains on the Tower floor; to pale with Edward and his brother as they hear the "portentous roll of the muffled drum and the measured tramp of armed men" that signals a forthcoming execution; to shriek with brother Richard at the sight of the executioner; to stop our hearts and our breath as we hear the crash of the axe that severs the head of Edward's one ally (156). At the end of her story, Strickland attempts to assert once again the power of sentimental innocence in her depiction of the royal brothers' murder:

And so touching, so beautiful was the picture of brotherly love and holy innocence which the gentle pair presented in their serene repose, their heads resting on the same pillow, in which laid the breviary book they had been so lately perusing, that, as one of the murderers afterwards confessed, 'it shook his guilty purpose,' and had it not been for the taunts and threats of his more obdurate companion, he could not have perpetrated the crime of crushing two such sweet and hopeful blossoms in the bud. (171–2)

In an ideal world, one in which adults are alive and open to the emotional connections offered them by the child, innocence can be valued, celebrated, sentimentalized. But even such an overly-sentimental vision of the young brothers fails to prevent their murder; in a world where such innocence leads only to victimization, embracing an innocent understanding of history can only lead to a life of "waking horror" (160).

It is far too late for young Edward to learn the proper way to understand history, Strickland acknowledges, but in the final story of her collection, "Lady Lucy's Petition to the Queen," Strickland suggests that such knowledge can and should be learned by other young readers of history. Unlike Prince Edward, Lady Lucy Preston is well aware of the emotional horrors of history. Since her father has been imprisoned for treason within the Tower for conspiring to return James II to the throne, her housekeeper has regaled her with stories of "the deeds of blood that have been perpetrated in this fatally celebrated place" (244). Edward's written history portrays the events of history as chivalric, exemplary; Bridget Oldworth's oral recounting constructs history as gothic horror. Thus Lucy knows from the very beginning of her story that the Tower is where not only the adult Henry VI, but also the children Edward V and Richard Duke of York, were all murdered. Such knowledge of history will be of great use to Lucy in her attempts to free her father.

Lucy does not yet recognize this, however, and instead turns to the method that worked so poorly for Edward: an appeal to the emotions. When her father tells her matter-of-factly that he has been condemned to die for high treason, and that he "shall not leave this place till they bring me forth on Tower Hill, where they will cut off my head with a sharp axe, and set it up afterwards over Temple Bar or London Bridge" (246), Lucy asserts that her emotional pleas will prevent such an outcome: "they shall not kill you, for I will cling so fast about your neck, that they shall not be able to cut your head off; and I will tell them all how good and kind you are, and then they will not want to kill you" (246). Lucy's father terms her reaction "simple talking," and initially dismisses her plan to plead directly with the queen to pardon him, but then accedes to her desire after she casts her act not as one of female self-assertion, but one of piety: "God would teach me what to say" (249).

Secreted into the palace, Lucy accosts the Queen as she returns from chapel. Mary is moved by the sight of Lucy's beauty, and especially by her tears. But when Lucy presents her father's written petition, the queen casts it aside. Lucy's words fail her; all she can utter is "Spare my father." Though Lucy's emotional display (and her sentimentally-described beauty) evokes pity in the Queen, Mary knows

Fig. 3.2   "Lady Lucy's Petition" to Queen Mary, with a portion of the portrait of King James II in the upper left-hand corner: emotional connection and historical knowledge working in tandem. Courtesy of the UCLA Charles E. Young Research Library Department of Special Collections.

her duty: those who break the law must die. The objectivity of the law must not be subject to the influence of emotion. Lucy's faith in the power of emotion alone to persuade the Queen proves unfounded.

Only when Lucy is able to combine the two discourses—emotional connection and knowledge of historical fact—is the child able to achieve her goal. Seeing Lucy's attention focused on a portrait of King James II, father of the current Queen, Mary asks the girl why she gazes so earnestly at the picture. "I was thinking," Lucy replies, "how strange it was that you should wish to kill my father because he loved yours so faithfully" (257). Lucy's words lead to a bond of identification between herself and the Queen; Mary views her own "filial piety" as markedly less than that displayed by Lucy, remembering that "whatever were his political errors as a king, [James] had ever been the tenderest of fathers to her" (257). Bursting into tears, Mary grants the asked-for pardon.[28] Lucy's emotional plea has worked—but only because she was able to use her knowledge of history to form a connection of identification between herself and the Queen, and thus make her emotional plea pointed, relevant. Strickland describes Lucy's reproof as both "artless" and "wise"; using both the power of emotion that stems from innocence, and the power of historical understanding that stems from experience, Lucy serves as an exemplary model of the youthful historical reader envisioned by Strickland, a reader who disrupts the generic boundaries of classical history both by insisting on the importance of emotion in the historical project, and simultaneously using the information conveyed in classical history to heighten the emotional plea.

The Child and the Historical "Other": Necessary but Limited Sympathy in Harriet Martineau's *The Peasant and the Prince* (1841)

Strickland's collection of stories clearly deploys what many writers in the Victorian period would term a "feminine" discourse to disrupt the "masculine" construction of classical historiography. Yet as Rohan Maitzen notes, gender was not the only issue behind the debates over the proper style, affect, and content

---

[28]   In her later biography of Mary for adults, in volume VII of *Lives of the Queens of England* (published in the mid-1840s), Strickland would present a far less sentimentalized portrait of the queen. Arguing that "the abilities of queen Mary, and the importance of her personal exertions as a sovereign, have been as much underrated, as the goodness of her heart and Christian excellences have been overestimated," Strickland presents a portrait of a ruler far more talented than her militarily-inclined husband, and a woman less virtuous than one would hope (315). Many eighteenth-century writers, Jacobite or no, reproached Mary for disloyalty for participating in the movement to overthrow her father, King James II. Strickland would clearly like to attribute Mary's participation in the Revolution of 1688 to her Christian subservience to an ambitious husband, yet the evidence of letters between Mary, her sister, and her father force Strickland the historian to acknowledge Mary's interest in diverting the succession away from her newborn half-brother. The vileness and coarseness of Anne's behavior towards her father, as Strickland characterizes it, comes in for far more condemnation, leaving Mary somewhat free from the taint of disloyalty.

of history that emerged during the early Victorian period. Political structures, as well as gender structures, were believed to be at risk. Those who, like Macaulay, argued for a more emotionally appealing history concomitantly seemed to desire a more widely disseminated history. Before the eighteenth century, the extensive study of history had been restricted to the ruling classes, and served as a marker of gentlemanly identity. But with the rise of print culture, particularly the magazines of the latter eighteenth-century, accessible histories became available to a wide mass of readers. Radicals of the 1760s and 1790s liked to print their versions of history in periodicals and pamphlets; such publications, when added to the rising rate of laboring-class literacy, led many in the ruling elite of the landed gentry and the professional and business classes to regard a mass reading public, particularly one well-read in history, as a threat to the traditional social order. The spread of literacy and the dissemination of knowledge might spark political awareness and activism among plebeians, and lead to the social disruption seen in France during the Revolution and its aftermath (Maitzen 11; Altick 66–77). The cultural capital signaled by the knowledge of history, once the singular province the ruling elite, might, through the "feminization" of historical practice, be taken from its hands.

While Strickland, a writer of conservative political inclinations, may imagine her youthful readers of history as in need of greater emotional identification than that required by adults, her portrayal of "illustrious" children hardly suggests that expanding the *class* of her audience was a prime motivation for her experiment in history. But another writer for children, one with far different political affiliations, would attempt a similar experiment less than a decade later, an experiment that would draw upon the new historiography to disrupt the class assumptions not only of classical history, but of children's literature.

In 1840, while debilitated by illness, Harriet Martineau decided to take on "the light and easy work (for which alone I was now fit)": a series of novels for children (*Autobiography* 159). Martineau, famed as an essayist and political commentator, was at that time best known for her *Illustrations of Political Economy* (1832–1834), a series of 24 tract tales intended to teach economic principles to the working classes. She undertook the project of writing for children at the request of Charles Knight, the publisher most closely associated with the Society for the Diffusion of Useful Knowledge (SDUK), which printed reasonably priced books such as *Illustrations* with the intention of helping those whose economic means were limited improve their lot through increased access to education. From Martineau's description of her juvenile books' genesis in her *Autobiography*, however, it becomes clear that the primary audience for her four juvenile works—*The Settlers at Home*, *The Peasant and the Prince*, *Feats on the Fiord*, and *The Crofton Boys*, published under the series title *The Playfellow*[29]—was not a working-class one.

---

[29] Knight initially published each volume of *The Playfellow* separately, once per quarter; the books were later printed together in one volume (in 1841, and again in 1845). After his retirement, it appears that Knight sold the copyright for Martineau's books to Routledge, which reprinted *Peasant* (either as a separate edition or in a joint edition with

In fact, despite *The Peasant and the Prince*'s success with "poor people, who read it with wonderful eagerness," Martineau terms it "the least successful of the set" (161). Although Martineau reports that working-class readers term her narrative of the French Revolution "the French Revelation," and that the "copy in Lending Libraries was more thumbed than the others," she asserts that "among children and the general reading public, there was less interest about it than any of the rest" (161).

Critics and historians of children's literature have tended to take Martineau at her word when she terms *The Peasant and the Prince* "a failure," reserving their praise for the other three books that comprise *The Playfellow* (*Autobiography* 161).[30] Critics who focus on Martineau's writing for adults tend to concur, either ignoring her children's novels altogether or finding all of them lacking the same political protest found in her political essays and nonfiction. No one seems to have made the connection implicit in Martineau's comments—that *The Peasant and the Prince*'s very popularity with the poor may in fact be the cause of its failure with a "general reading public" constructed as a collection of genteel readers. Valerie Pichanick goes as far as to assert that even though Martineau believed these novels to be her "final contribution to literature," she did not invest them with any political consciousness, deploying "conventional sentiments" for the "conventional genre of the children's story" in order to secure a safe stream of income (127). Yet if twentieth-century critics fail to see the radical nature of *The Peasant and the Prince*, Martineau's contemporaries were far more aware; an anonymous[31] article on the state of books for children, published in 1844 in the conservative *Quarterly Review*, praised Martineau's three other *Playfellow* volumes, but "purposely omit[ed]" *The Peasant and the Prince*, because of its "reprehensible purpose and tendencies" (21).

Martineau's treatment of the peasants and artisans of revolutionary France, whom Martineau implicitly compares to early Victorian English workers, apparently proved much too sympathetic for the comfort of the landed gentry and the professional and business classes. In 1841, unrest among the English

---

the other three *Playfellow* titles) in 1856, 1857, 1885, 1895, and 1905. The novel also found an audience in America; Boston's Ginn & Company issued it in 1886, 1889, 1894, and 1917, with a Houghton edition issued in1902. The Knight editions that I've seen were not illustrated; the 1895 Routledge joint edition contains 171 black and white line drawings as well as several colored plates.

[30]   Each of the other three *Playfellow* novels fits comfortably within generic boundaries—*The Crofton Boys* within the school story, *The Settlers at Home* within historical fiction and the robinsonade, and *Feats on the Fiord* within both the travel narrative and the adventure story—making each intelligible to the critic familiar with the typical genres of Victorian children's fiction. *The Peasant and the Prince*, with its multiple and shifting generic affiliations, is far less easy to categorize, and thus to discuss in the broad historical overviews of children's literature which are the only places in which Martineau's works for children are mentioned.

[31]   Attributed to Elizabeth Rigby in the *Encyclopedia of Children's Literature*; reprinted in Haviland.

working classes, who were frustrated by political inequities remaining after the Reform Act of 1832, was on the rise. Members of the Chartist movement had collected more than a million and a quarter signatures in 1839 for the "People's Charter" it presented to Parliament demanding radical parliamentary reform, including universal suffrage; calls for a general strike and mass demonstrations protesting the imprisonment of many of their leaders followed in the wake of the Charter's rejection by Parliament. For many genteel Englishmen and women, such agitation evoked visions of French revolutionary mobs and their "Reign of Terror." To preach understanding of the people who made up those faceless mobs, as Martineau does in *The Peasant and The Prince*, is, for the *Quarterly Review*, to extend an invitation to the mob violence characteristic of late eighteenth-century France onto unsullied British ground.

Martineau had little patience for such genteel fears, firmly believing not only that an English transformation to democracy was inevitable, but also that it could and would occur without disorder or violence. This conviction stemmed not from any sense of the inherent superiority of the English working classes over those of the French, but rather from her belief in the ability of the people to govern themselves—if they were empowered through proper education. Martineau, through her work with publisher Charles Knight, became one of the major proponents of the extension of secular, rather than religious, education to the English working classes via inexpensive literature; such popular education would serve to create productive working-class citizens, ready to participate in the new forms of self-governance proposed by political reformers (Pichanick 151–3). As Shelagh Hunter argues, Martineau, through her writing, constructed herself as the instructor of this rising citizenry, a "governess to the nation," eager to edify her "*great pupil*, the public" (38–9).

In her experimental work *The Peasant and the Prince*, Martineau strives to extend the reach of her political pedagogy to the realm of childhood, for, as her tale suggests, it may be too late to teach adults constructed by constraining and oppressive social forces and institutions how to be proper citizens. But Martineau struggles to articulate just what such a progressive childhood pedagogy might look like, and in what genre it might be best expressed. Initially, Martineau's solution suggests an alignment with the Utilitarian doctrines of her day—greater knowledge will lead to greater historical understanding. Yet Martineau's definition of appropriate knowledge is not one which focuses on dates, or places, or historical events; rather, it points to the impact such events have on the lives of individuals. The ability to understand, and to empathize with, individuals subject to political events and political structures, particularly individuals of a different social position than oneself, prove a motivating force behind Martineau's work. Yet the emotion evoked by such a vision of history proves problematic for Martineau, for several reasons. First, because the pleasure evoked by such emotional connection can prove an end in itself, rather than a catalyst for change; second, because emotional connections to individual fictional characters may lead children to focus on individual solutions to social problems, rather than on the larger social forces that would change the lives of the many rather than of the few; and finally, because such emotional access can break down the proper boundaries between public and private selves so central to an emergent Victorian middle-class identity. Ultimately, Martineau suggests, the best way for children to learn to be sympathetic citizens is not to engage with the social "other" directly, but rather to educate themselves about that "other" through the mediation of text.

> If it be true, as some say, that the labourer's life-long toil demands a return, not only of sufficient food, and domestic shelter for his old age, but of intellectual and spiritual culture, what can we say to the working classes? ... we ought to put ourselves in their place, ... and then we shall understand how suspicious they must be of promises of unseen and future good when it is offered as better than the substantial good which they see others enjoying, and feel to be their due ... . They will not acquiesce while they see that those who work less are more comfortable; and they are not told why. This is what remains for us to do;—to find out the why, and to make everybody understand it. —Harriet Martineau, *The History of England during the Thirty Year's Peace (1816–1846)*[32]

While published under the single title *The Peasant and the Prince*, Martineau's novel actually consists of two separate tales. The text opens with *The Peasant*, a four-chapter narrative of the hardships experienced by a French peasant family, and their fairy-tale rescue by the charitable intervention of the future queen, Marie Antoinette, traveling through their village on her marriage journey from Austria to Paris. But this fictionalized portrayal of peasant hardship quickly gives way to a much longer narrative, *The Prince*, a nonfiction account of the French royal family during the Revolution. Gillian Thomas suggests that this divided narrative structure is a problem in a work purporting to be fiction, and, by implication, the cause of this volume's relative lack of popularity (103). Rather than judge Martineau's divided narrative a sign of her lack of skill as a writer, however, I would argue that it is a sign of her struggle to find an adequate genre in which to convey the new type of fiction, and the new type of history, her divided text strives to articulate.

In its broadest outlines, the plot of *The Peasant* conforms to generic conventions of the romantic stage comedy. Two young lovers, Charles Bertrand and Marie Randolph, prevented from marrying, endure multiple setbacks before a providential intervention removes all obstacles; the story ends with their happy union. But Martineau draws upon these conventions only to subvert them: Charles and Marie, unlike the typical protagonists of romantic comedy, are not members of the sophisticated ruling class but of the peasantry; the obstacles in the way of their marriage are far from the mistaken identity, comic misunderstandings, or stodgy interfering parents common to comedy, but rather the grinding poverty imposed upon them by the ancien régime. Despite the text's deployment of what Ainslie Robinson terms "fairy tale" tropes (396), *The Peasant* ultimately has more telling affinities with the emerging social realism of Martineau's contemporary Charles Dickens and his portraits of underprivileged children than with stage comedy or fairy tale.

---

[32]   [2:715–16]. Quoted in Pichaneck 144.

Pichanick argues that despite Martineau's liberal, often radical politics, the conventions of juvenile literature prevented her from making "any significant final radical gesture" in the volumes of *The Playfellow* (127). Yet, when read in the context of the juvenile literature of the period, it is obvious that in *The Peasant* Martineau's politics are markedly more radical than those of her fellow children's authors. Laboring-class or impoverished characters rarely take center stage in such literature; more often, they appear on the periphery, functioning to validate the gentility of the literature's protagonists. In eighteenth-century juvenile literature, working class characters appear most commonly in the form of a domestic servant, typically corrupted and corrupting of juvenile protagonists' moral virtue. Two other tropes—the contented agricultural laborer, and, less commonly, the industrious urban poor—while presenting the laboring classes in a more flattering light, also functioned ideologically to construct the poor as the "other" against which the landed gentry and the professional and businesses classes could then construct themselves as "the moral and productive center of English society" (O'Malley, *Making* 43–7; 39).[33] The chapbooks of Hannah More's Cheap Repository, published during the opening decades of the nineteenth century, intended for working-class adults but often featuring working-class children, continually assert that poverty results from the "idleness, folly, bad management, and mistaken attempts to emulate their betters" of the working classes rather than any institutional or social cause (Kelly 151). In books intended for genteel children during the early nineteenth century, such as Priscilla Wakefield's *Family Tour through the British Empire* (1804) and Ann and Jane Taylor's *City Scenes; or, a Peep into London for Children* (1818) and its companion volume, *Rural Scenes* (1806), the poor were portrayed more sympathetically, but the underlying message was similar: "Pitying the poor was encouraged, but so too was an acceptance of the unbridgeable gap between them and the more fortunate" (Avery and Kinnell 75). Not until the mid-Victorian period, with the vivid portraits of the urban poor presented by "Hesba Stretton" (Sarah Smith) in her bestselling tearjerker *Jessica's First Prayer* (1867) did the "Condition of England" question emerge as a major topic in fiction for children. Even then, however, writers, influenced by Romantic visions of childhood, typically constructed their juvenile characters sentimentally, as innocents amidst the vice and degradation of their surroundings. The poor child became a paragon, sentimentalized and idealized, able to transcend morally if not materially over her impoverished state (Briggs and Butts 132–3).

---

[33]   O'Malley uses the term "middle class" to describe the reader constructed by these texts. In contrast, as noted earlier, I prefer to use the terms "genteel" or "landed gentry and professional and business classes," to acknowledge that a dual conception of class identity (genteel vs. plebian) continued to exist long into the nineteenth century, even after a tripartite conception of class identity grew more common as the century progressed, and that the dual, rather than the tripartite, view was the more common one in children's literature written before the first Reform Bill.

In *The Peasant*, Martineau rejects each of the constructions of the poor
presented by earlier children's literature. As her title indicates, her protagonists
are not genteel children who observe or offer succor to grateful dependents,
but rather the poor themselves. More significantly, Martineau's peasants do not
function as negative "others" against which an emergent middle-class identity can
be constructed; Charles, Marie, and Marie's family are characterized by the same
virtues of hard work, thrift, and moral uprightness increasingly being attributed
to the middle class. Charles works hard—so hard that "he did not allow himself
sufficient food and rest, and was now almost as sallow and gaunt-looking as his
older neighbours"—but no matter how hard he works, he cannot earn enough
money to rent the cottage which would provide a home for his would-be bride
Marie (8). Charles's case is not exceptional, the text argues; Marie's parents, too,
work endlessly, but "no toil, no efforts on the part of the family, could keep them
above want" (9). Martineau's peasants espouse and practice what English society
would increasingly label middle-class values, yet they remain sunk in poverty.

Rather than embrace class hierarchies as natural, as do so many other juvenile
texts of the period, Martineau strives to "find out the why" behind class divisions.
If personal morality is not a "why," Martineau suggests we may do better to
look to the political for a cause: the social and political institutions that prop up
France's ancien régime at the expense of the dependents the patriarchal nobility
supposedly supports. *The Peasant* opens with an apparent celebration: the town of
St Menehould bustling with activity to prepare for the arrival of the Dauphiness,
traveling on her bridal journey to Paris. Yet there is a dark underside to the joy; the
roads over which the Dauphiness will travel must be repaired, and those who must
repair them are not "hired laborers," but "peasants, who were obliged by law to
quit the work of their own fields or kilns when called upon, to repair the roads for
a certain number of days" (7). The peasants must also feed and shelter the soldiery
quartered upon them for the Dauphiness's visit, staying up all night to wash their
uniforms. Most outrageously, after the arrival of the Count and his family from
Paris, each peasant on the Count's estate must supply two men to flog the ponds
all night, for the nobles, accustomed to the sounds of the city, cannot sleep amidst
the croaking of the amphibians. For all of their work, the peasants receive nothing.
Martineau, who supported *laissez faire* economic principles, believes that forcing
the peasantry to work, and to work without pay, violates the fundamental right of
the worker to "trade in the only commodity he possessed: his labor" (Pichanick
159). This, surely, is one of the "whys" she wishes to teach her readers.

A second "why" focuses on the dark side of the traditional paternalistic gentry/
peasant relationship, a relationship being newly espoused as the solution to the
"Condition of England" question by the "Young England" movement in the 1840s.
As Martineau described it, "the idea of the Young England party, in regard to the
condition of the people, was that all would be well if the ancient relation between
the rich and the poor could be restored—if the rich could, as formerly, take charge
of the poor with a protecting benevolence, and the poor depend upon the rich in a
spirit of trust and obedience" (*History of the Peace* 2:519–20). But the vision of

a just, beneficent aristocracy ruling over an agricultural society is just that—a vision, a fantasy, Martineau asserts through her depiction of the nobleman who controls the peasantry of St Menehould. The Count, regardless of his peasants' need to work, summons Marie and her father to him in order to discuss his arrangements for greeting the Dauphiness. The sumptuousness of the Count's life stands in marked contrast to the poverty of his dependents, so much so that even the Count remarks upon it, unable to believe that someone so wretchedly poor as Randolphe could be one of his principal peasants. Yet the sight does not move him to pity or to shame, or a desire to ameliorate the condition of his dependents. Instead, he sees it as only natural; as his bailiff reveals, "Randolphe is wretchedly poor, my lord, as you say; but there is no one of your people hereabouts who is less so" (30).

Despite the Count's lack of paternal interest, the patriarchal feudal structure requires that the Count have charge not only over the economic state of his peasantry, but over their personal lives as well. Before she can marry, Marie must have the Count's permission. The Count, who "evidently cared nothing about the matter," would have given his consent, but his son, who catches sight of the pretty peasant girl earlier, urges further investigation, and ferrets out that Charles and Marie have not the means to support themselves (30). Though another, kinder son protests at the interference—"Do leave these poor people to make themselves happy their own way. It is no concern of yours"—his brother urges the Count to refuse permission for the marriage, hiding his own sexual attraction to Marie under the guise of economic interest: "My father cannot look to them for anything. You see, sir, you can depend upon them for nothing in their present circumstances, and I do not see how you can consent to their marrying yet" (31). Martineau indicates the utter lack of empathy of the purportedly paternalistic Count by suggesting that the Count's decision has less to do with the feelings of Marie and Charles and more to do with the completion of his toilette: "the Count discovered that the valet had arrived at the last bow of the pig-tail, and that he must make a decision and conclude this interview" (31). Marie and Charles must wait to marry; Charles must serve three years in the military first. The Count adds insult to injury by suggesting that the prevention of the marriage is the fault of Marie's father, rather than his own: "He then bade good-day to his peasant dependent, and hoped he would see better times, and do the best he could for the young people before their wedding-day, as he would now have a considerable interval in which to meditate his duty as a parent to so pretty a daughter" (31).

As Martineau would assert in her later *History of the Peace*, the return to the "protecting benevolence" of a golden-age agrarian feudalism promised by the Young England movement is both false and impracticable (*History* 2:519–20). For the peasantry must submit not only to the control of their local landlords, but also to the imposition of the laws of the state, laws that contribute to their impoverishment. Though game is plentiful in the woods that surround their cottages, the law constrains the hungry peasants from hunting or even keeping game as pets. Marie's father cannot afford to apprentice his sons, not because of the apprenticing fee, but because of the "great sum to be paid to the King upon the indenture, and another and a larger before the lad begins his trade" (23). Most upsetting to the *laissez faire* Martineau, the law compels each peasant over the age of eight to purchase a set quantity of salt, even if he does not need it, and to pay an exorbitant tax on said purchase. When Marie's brothers were younger, the family got by, but now that the children, too, must purchase salt, the family is "brought down to a state of want" (9). Instead of giving his children "a chance of a better living than their father had before them," the burdens placed upon him by the state mean that Marie's father can only make them "poorer peasants than himself" (24, 23). Poverty, rather than something natural or resulting from the deficient management of a stray bad landlord, is endemic to the political system.

If *The Peasant* is intended to teach its readers about the institutional causes of poverty, it seems clear that for the poor within the text, no such lesson is needed. Charles, Marie, and Marie's parents are only too aware of that their economic difficulties, far from being natural or ordained by God, stem largely from the social and political structures of ancien régime France. Martineau makes this quite clear in the novel's second chapter, which features a conversation between the adult Randolphes and the three soldiers that have been quartered upon them. Though their conversation begins with a discussion of the impending arrival of Marie Antoinette, it soon shifts from talk of the luxuries the Dauphiness enjoys to the financial straits of the people. When one soldier opines that "there must be an earthquake somewhere in France, swallowing up all the money; for nobody could tell where it all went to," Randolphe protests: "How can you say that … when you think of the numbers of idle people that are feeding upon those who work." (20–21). Another soldier agrees with Randolphe's assessment: "there were the nobility, sitting heavy upon the people throughout the land, like the nightmare upon the sleep of a wearied man. These nobles must all be rich,—must all be pampered in luxury, though not one of them would work with his head or hands. If a nobleman had five sons, they must all be pampered alike; and the sons of five hundred peasants must be oppressed to supply the means" (21). As Andrew O'Malley notes, earlier literature for children often deployed the trope of the profligate and degenerate nobility in parallel with that of the immoral and work-eschewing poor; both tropes functioned to construct an emerging middle-class identity as normative by comparison to these unnatural "others" (*Making* 39). Martineau clearly draws upon such a tradition in her depictions of the Count and his family; their indulgence in luxury and their refusal to work construct them as the opposite of the normative middle class. Yet by refusing to align the aristocracy and the agrarian poor, *The Peasant* breaks the typical equation of noble and peasant as equally endangering to middle-class identity. Instead of desiring to ape the betters with whom they had once shared traditional social bonds, the poor, Martineau's text asserts, recognize all too well that such emulation can never be possible given the social structures that consign them to the role of the oppressed.

Unsurprisingly, this rejection of social stratification as natural, or divinely ordained, simultaneously leads Martineau to reject the stock depiction of the humble and contented poor so characteristic of earlier juvenile literature. As the poor receive little to no assistance from their social betters in this text, there is little for which they can or should be grateful. Instead, each peasant, to varying degrees, expresses frustration, fear, and even anger about the patently oppressive social arrangements that structure their lives. Rather than being thankful for the paternal interest of the Count, the Randolphes feel the need to perform the role of grateful dependent, a role that they know all too well is false. Similarly, when Charles tells Marie's younger brothers that they should not capture game from the Count's estates, he does not argue that they should respect the Count's property, but that they should fear being caught and punished by laws which they had no role in making, and for which they have little liking. And when her sons attempt to protect themselves by lying about the rabbits and pigeons they keep as pets, Marie's mother protests to the bailiff that it is not the boys' bad morals, but the oppressive conditions under which they live, that lead them to consider telling an untruth:

> … you see, sir, how trickery and falsehood come. If there were no reasons why my boys should not do such an innocent thing as bring up a brood of pigeons, the thought of an untruth would not enter their heads; but you see what you tempt them to, by driving them so very hard about almost the only pleasure they have. (27)

When she worries that her husband's talk to the soldiers might lead to trouble, Randolphe asserts, "It is no treason to say that in this land there are swarms of idle folk living upon the toil of us who work" (21). Martineau's peasants may be uneducated, but they are not ignorant; they can see all too clearly the institutional roots of their oppression.

Having identified the "whys" of social inequality, and demonstrated that those oppressed by the whys are far from content, what solutions does Martineau's text propose to ameliorate them? At first, it seems as if knowledge might be enough; once the oppressed give voice to their oppression, and those in power are made truly aware of their horrific situation, things might be different in the future, one soldier asserts. Yet the Randolphes' assumption that others will correct the situation— "How? Where? When? Why? Is anything going to be done for the poor?"—is belied by another soldier, who instead asserts that it is the poor themselves who will act: "Those that have looked into the matter say that the country people (those who really do the work of the land) possess only one-third of the country, and yet pay three-fourths of the taxes. One does not see why this should go on, when once they choose that it shall not" (22). Such a choice may have dire consequences for those currently in power, however; when one soldier suggests that the peasants poison the noisy frogs instead of beating the pond to quiet them, another opines that "that if they wanted to get rid of a nuisance, the aristocrats were fewer than the frogs" (26). If the rich "choose" not to do anything for those suffering in poverty, the nobility must "look to themselves"; the choice will be made for them by the poor (22). "The oppressed do get to speak out sooner or later," suggests the soldier; but speech might all too easily turn to action (21).

Martineau, like so many other early nineteenth-century writers, might have used her tale to point to the differences between a corrupt France and a just, egalitarian England. Yet instead of constructing France as England's negative Other, Martineau works to draw attention to the parallels between them: "It is not only France that has been ignorant, and guilty, and miserable. Every country is full of blessings given by the hand of God: and in every country are those blessings misused, more or less, as they were in France" (179). The rise of Chartism in England, a movement which to many genteel Englishmen and women appeared eerily reminiscent of the protests before the French Revolution, lent urgency and force to Martineau's comparison. The key to avoiding a descent into a Reign of Terror in England, Martineau argues, is for "every child, as he grows up" to be "taught this truth,—taught to reflect how all men may have their share of these blessings who are willing to work for them" (79). While this lesson sounds suspiciously similar to other contemporary literature for children, with its insistence on the embrace of values increasingly being associated with a middle-class identity, the concomitant lesson Martineau would teach—how "impious … it really is to call God the author of sufferings which need never happen"—suggests that her solution moves beyond personal moral training and toward institutional and social change (179). After learning this two-part lesson, Martineau argues, "there would be no more danger of such wo[e] as we have been contemplating" (179).

Yet while such lessons may be imparted through the medium of the novel, the generic imperatives of juvenile fiction—that all good children be rewarded, that all stories end happily—means that for Martineau, concluding *The Peasant* by leaving the Randolphes with no hope, with Charles and Marie unable to marry and Marie's brothers deprived of their pets, is simply untenable. And so, the short tale concludes not with the act of insurrection threatened by the soldier's muttered desire to be rid of the oppressive aristocrats, but with the very act of upper-class charity benevolently bestowed upon the deserving and grateful poor so common to depictions of the peasantry in earlier children's literature. Significantly, the benefactress is the Dauphiness, Marie Antoinette, who, having stopped in St Menehould to greet her future subjects, is moved by the sight of the swollen faces and the tears of Marie's brothers. After inquiring into their circumstances, the Dauphiness asks the Count, as a favor to her, to settle Charles advantageously upon the land and to allow Marie's brothers, by "special permission," to break the law and keep their rabbits and pigeons.

After the Dauphiness departs, the entire village celebrates the Randolphe's good fortune. Yet the story concludes not with celebration, but with doubt; a soldier, leaving the village, points to the limitations of the future Queen's act of charity:

> "It is all very well, and I am glad this one family is saved, but it is only one of many hundred thousand miserable families. What is to become of all the rest, who may not have the luck to see a royal bride pass their way? It is not a few royal smiles and gold pieces here and there that will save the royal, or the noble, or the poor, while the law and the customs of the great oppress and destroy a hundred to pamper one. If this young Dauphiness were to do this deed over again every hour of the year, she could not do more than put off for a little while the storm that will burst upon her and all of us when the poor can endure no more." (39)

Fig. 3.3   "The bailiff now put himself forward to explain": the Dauphiness makes a personal intervention to abate the suffering of the poor. Courtesy of the author.

As a genre, the novel, with its focus on individual characters, tends inherently toward individual, rather than institutional, solutions to social ills. Such solutions rarely address problems that have their roots in widespread, rather than individual, causes. Thus, the constraints of the genre make Martineau's attempt to politicize children's fiction stillborn. Fiction presents individual cases, and though things may turn out well for a lover, or a family, fiction is far less likely than other forms of writing to lead to changes in laws or customs that rule the lives of many hundred thousand miserable families. It is at this point that Martineau abandons her fictional tale, and begins the much longer second part of her volume: *The Prince*, a nonfiction account of the last years of the reign of King Louis XVI. But just as Martineau attempted to push (albeit not entirely successfully) beyond the boundaries of fiction in *The Peasant*, in *The Prince*, too, she attempts generic experiment; by opening up the field of juvenile history to the social, and to the idea of reader identification with character which was emerging as the cornerstone of fiction for children in the period, Martineau attempts once more to teach the lessons that will allow her country to progress to democracy, rather than devolve into anarchy. Yet constructing sympathetic citizens through history, rather than through the novel, introduces new difficulties and drawbacks.

> Another favourite was a story about the French Rev[n] in 'Mrs Hurry's Artless Tales,'—a book w[h] I had a burning desire to possess at nine years old,—so much so, that tho' a very shy child, I hinted as much to every body that I thought had money, & looked kind. It did not take, how[eve]r. —Harriet Martineau to Anna Jameson, June 15 [1841], recounting her childhood reading.[34]

In the opening chapter of *The Prince*, Martineau identifies what she views to be the root causes of the excessive violence of the French people against their aristocracy, and, by implication, what steps the English ruling classes should take to avoid a similar fate. Her first story, *The Peasant*, functioned to "show how poor and how oppressed some of the country people were"; but poverty and oppression alone do not create such violent feelings. Only when poverty and oppression are coupled with ignorance, Martineau asserts, do "passions of fear and hatred which [are] then terrible to witness" emerge (41).

Martineau begins to define the different types of "ignorance" that stand in the way of social justice during the final scene of *The Peasant*, in her descriptions of the young Dauphiness, 15-year-old Marie Antoinette. The first type of "ignorance" is a belief in the naturalness of class distinctions. When the Dauphiness offers Marie's younger brothers money to replace their confiscated pets, the bailiff explains that it is not money, but the law, that stands in their way; only nobles are allowed to keep game. Rather than take exception to such rules, as did the peasant Madame Randolphe, "The Dauphiness supposed this was all as it should be, for she was apt, through life, to believe that the nobles were by nature entitled to all things, and might give only such leavings as they did not wish for to inferior people" (38).

---

[34]   Martineau, *Selected Letters* 61.

This belief, Martineau later asserts, stems largely from the poor education Marie Antoinette received as a child, with indulgent governesses doing the lessons for an Archduchess little inclined to hard work. Such an education leaves the young Dauphiness in a state of knowledge little better than that of the French peasantry: "when this young girl entered France a bride, at 15 years of age, she knew next to nothing" (47). Such ignorance, especially of "men and common life," Martineau asserts, is "an irreparable evil," for Marie Antoinette, surrounded by sycophants and those who believe in the divine right of royalty, has no understanding that her education is lacking, and thus has "no means of repairing" such a fault (47).

A further fault lies in a different type of education the Archduchess received: the socializing messages of dutiful daughterhood. Such socialization teaches that good girls do not ask questions, but rather, in the words of Marie Antoinette's mother, Empress Maria Teresa of Austria, are "born to obey" (qtd in Fraser, *Marie* 13). Martineau points to the blinders that such socialization enforces on the Dauphiness when Marie Antoinette makes an attempt to see beyond her own sphere during her brief stop in St Menehould:

> The Dauphiness asked whether such poverty as she witnessed was not a thing hitherto unheard of—whether such misery could be common in the country she had just entered? The bridling of some of her ladies, and the annoyance in the faces of some of the gentlemen of her suite, showed her that she had asked an imprudent question. Yet she was only 15, and was to be hereafter the queen of this country; and if she had never done worse things than asking such questions, she might have lived beloved, and died lamented in a good old age. (532)

To ask questions, to look critically beyond one's own narrow sphere, and to try and find out the "whys" behind "unheard of" misery, is the first step toward knowledge, Martineau argues. Yet thinking critically is a skill far from encouraged by the members of the Dauphiness's court.

Finally, Martineau suggests, rational knowledge is not the only type of knowledge needed to bridge the gap between rich and poor. Emotional knowledge, too, will also be required. The sight of the tearstained faces of Marie's brothers forges an emotional bond between the peasant boys and the royal Dauphiness: "These traces of tears carried back her thoughts to her own weeping, some days before, on leaving Vienna; and she suddenly beckoned the children" (35). Emotion leads to empathy, and thus to identification; only when the rich can come to see the poor as people, as human beings subject to the same emotions as themselves, as individuals rather than as undifferentiated parts of an unruly mob, will they truly be moved to ameliorate their plight.

To be educated; to think critically; to be moved by the emotions of others and thus to identify with them—these are the three types of knowledge that Martineau insists are required in order to avoid the chaos of class warfare experienced in eighteenth century France and in mid-nineteenth-century England. In *The Peasant*, such lessons are directed primarily at the genteel reader; in *The Prince*, Martineau continues to highlight their necessity through her depictions of their lack in her main characters, Marie Antoinette and Louis XVI. But in the opening of this nonfiction section of her work, she simultaneously insists that such learning is a two-way street: if the members of the ancien régime need to recognize, analyze, and empathize with the daily life conditions of the poor, so too do the poor need to be educated about the actual conditions of life of those above them. For far too many of the peasantry, servant classes, and children replace actual knowledge of the lives of the genteel with dangerous fantasy. Believing "that to be a king, or one of the king's family, is the same thing as to be perfectly happy," they cannot imagine that "royalty does not exempt from sickness and death, and from the troubles of the heart and mind" (41). Such false information, Martineau asserts, will lead the poor to false belief: "such persons may go on for the greater part of their lives envying royal personages," an envy that, when added to severe oppression and poverty, is all too likely to flare up into "fear and hatred … terrible to witness … the most brutal rage, towards all the wealthy and noble" (41, 42).

Martineau, then, sets herself a double task: educating the ruling classes into an awareness of their lack of knowledge, understanding, and empathy for the poor; and, simultaneously, educating the working classes into a greater knowledge, understanding, and empathy for those who seemingly live lives of fairy-tale-like perfection and ease. To achieve both of these goals, Martineau eschews the names, dates, and political events common to the majority of histories written for children in the eighteenth- and early nineteenth centuries. Instead, she follows the practice of the new historiography for adults taking shape in the eighteenth and in particular during the early nineteenth century, a historiography which strove to expand the norms of classical history, which focused primarily on linear accounts of political events and public men, by pushing in two new directions: inward, to an attempt to evoke identification and capture the inward feelings of historical figures; and outward, beyond politics, to capture the broader life (art, literature, manners, culture) of past societies (Phillips). Thus, instead of offering her child readers a dry account of the key dates, events, and actors in the downfall of the French monarchy, Martineau instead presents her readers with a view of the monarchy from inside the palace,[35] a view which simultaneously functions both to create reader identification with the tragic prince and his family while also pointing to the "broader life" of manners and culture which have shaped them.

---

[35]   Martineau tells her readers that "we happen to have full accounts of the way of living of this royal family in the days of their prosperity, as well as of their adventures when adversity overtook them" (42), but cites no specific authors or texts. Her main sources appear to be the memoirs of Marie Antoinette written by Henriette Campan, the Queen's First Lady of the Bedchamber, first published in 1823; and the memoirs of Hanet Cléry (published in 1798), the valet who became the effective manager of the royal household during its time in the Tower. The memoirs of the Duchess de Tourzel, Governess of the royal children from 1789 to 1795, another potential source, would seem to have been published too late (1883) to have been used by Martineau.

Though political events are of obvious concern,[36] it is their impact on the family of Louis XVI that the text is at greatest pains to illustrate. The text proper opens with a chapter entitled "Royal Ways," which describes not the political events in which this royal family is enmeshed, but rather what the king, his aunts and sister, the queen, and the royal children do on a typical day. We hear of the king's penchant for hunting, and his secret love of lock-making; of the toilette, pocket-money, and charity of the queen; of the distance imposed between the royal children and their mother by the plethora of ceremonial attendants and their jealous guarding of their royal prerogatives. Thus Martineau encourages her readers to understand not the public actions of these most public of figures, but to see them as private individuals who, like themselves, experience the life quotidian.

Martineau's introduction to the royal family focuses not just on their actions, but also on their characters. In these depictions, Martineau works hard to steer a different course than those offered by the three available tropes of royal French portraiture: monarchs as happy, carefree, and indifferent to the plight of the poor, the view held, according to Martineau, by the ignorant, oppressed peasantry; the heroic martyred innocent construction promulgated by supporters of monarchical privilege (such as Edmund Burke in *Reflections on the Revolution in France*); and the corrupt, promiscuous, and perverse visions, particularly of Marie Antoinette, commonly espoused by the late eighteenth-century radical French press.[37] Instead, Martineau attempts to present balanced portraits, portraits that both acknowledge the positive characteristics of her subjects and the limits imposed on them by both their lack of education and their particular, individual character faults. The King, though too dull and indecisive to rule effectively, is not evil; he "might have been better and happier in many places than in his own palace" (44). The King's aunts lead "dreadfully dull lives," constrained by their royal rank and duties from developing intimate friends, pursuing gardening or walking freely about Paris. Yet their deprivations do not teach them to be less self-centered, or to feel empathy for their social inferiors (43). Marie Antoinette may be poorly educated, but "she was very clever, notwithstanding"; she may have been "careless and selfish, but

---

[36] Martineau's narrative begins shortly before the storming of the Bastille in July 1789, and concludes with the death of the prince. The primary events Martineau depicts during her narrative are the family's unwilling return to Paris from Versailles in October 1789; the reluctant acceptance of the new Constitution by the King (July 1790); the family's botched attempt to flee the country (June 1791); the storming of the Tuileries and the subsequent imprisonment of the royal family in the Temple (August 1792); the executions of Louis XVI (January 1793) and Marie Antoinette (October 1793); and the death of the child Louis XVII at the age of 10.

[37] Martineau eschews not only descriptions of the more lurid details of the radical French press (charges of orgies and rampant lesbianism), but even the more historically documentable accounts of a probable liaison with the Swedish nobleman Count Axel Ferson, the affair of the Du Barry diamond necklace, and the accusations made at Marie Antoinette's trial that she had sexually abused son Louis. While Martineau clearly desires to break down some of the generic boundaries of literature for children, she has no interest in opening up this literature to the realm of the sexual.

she was not hard-hearted, for whenever she witnessed misery she hastened to relieve it, often sacrificing her own pleasures for the purpose" (47, 48). The queen grieves at the death of her baby daughter, Sophie; she behaves in a "thoughtless and undignified" way in choosing to act in private theatricals; she uses her power to restrict free trade (anathema to free market proponent Martineau); she spends a good deal of her monthly allowance on charitable projects. In the fullness and nuances of her depictions, particularly of Marie Antoinette (who, rather than the title's "prince" figures as the main character in this section), Martineau strives for the factual, clear-headed, and empathetic vision of another that she constructs as the key to the knowledge that, if taught and understood, will allow the children of England to grow up and avoid the terrors experienced by the children of France.[38]

Such a factual, clear-headed, and empathetic vision of the other is precisely what the King and his family lack, Martineau's text asserts, over and over again. What stands in the way of such knowledge, Martineau suggests, is distance: The King may look "for hours together" through his telescope, "spying at the people who thronged the palace courts, or who went to and fro in the avenue," but such distanced vision gives him no real understanding. Though he sees, he cannot know that "his people were starving by thousands, and preparing by millions to rebel" (46). Likewise, the dauphin, though probably told of the plight of the poor, has no context in which to transform such information into true knowledge, the narrator asserts:

> ... it is difficult to give an idea of what want really is to children who have half a dozen ladies and footmen always at their orders, and who are surrounded with luxuries which seem to them to come as naturally as the light of day, and to belong to them as completely as their own limbs and senses. We have all heard of the little French princess who, when told by her governess how many of the poor were dying of starvation, in a hard season, said she thought that was very foolish, and that, rather than starve, she would eat bread and cheese. She had no idea that multitudes never tasted anything better than the coarsest black dry bread; and that it was for want of this that many were perishing. How should she know? She had never seen the inside of a poor man's hut, or tasted anything but the most delicate food. (79–80)

Because the King and Queen "lived amongst, and were acquainted with, not the poor, but the noble and the rich," they cannot hear what the poor would say, cannot see how the poor live, cannot understand what the poor want (79). Such ignorance leads them to believe that the cause of the rebellion is, as Louis tells the Dauphin when his son asks him why the people all seem to hate them, "wicked persons" inciting the populace to react violently to a few recent events, rather than widespread outrage at centuries of ill usage.

---

[38] The one exception to this balanced character depiction comes in Martineau's portrait of the king's sister, the Princess Elizabeth, whom Martineau holds forth as a paragon of virtue ("a young lady of such sweet temper—so religious, so humble, so gentle—that she was a blessing wherever she went" [54]), giving little account of her conservative antidemocratic political views, views so at odds with Martineau's own.

How then, can such a gap be bridged? How can the distance between monarch and peasant be lessened? Martineau presents one possibility during one of many passages where she expresses regret at the King's notable passiveness. "If the King had been active, decided, and equal to the dangers of the times, he would have made use of this winter in Paris to go among his people, and learn for himself what was the matter, what they wanted, and how much could be done for peace and good government" (84). Yet when the King and his subjects actually do come face to face, during the people's invasion of the Tuileries in June 1792, such direct contact fails to live up to its promise: "Now, at last, the sovereign and his craving people met, face to face: met, too, that they might petition and he reply. But they were no longer fitted for coming to an understanding. They despised him as weak and a double-dealer, and he despised them for their ignorance, their tatters, and their dirt" (133). Their mutual ignorance and prejudices have "unfitted" each side for the task of understanding the other. Having raised images of each other based not on knowledge but on projections, on fantasies, neither party can move past the emotions such false images engender to attempt connection; neither one can hear what the other has to say. In what proves the climax of the text, "The monarch and his people had met at last, face to face; and it was only to find that there was, and could be, no agreement between them" (137).

At first, it seems as if the face-to-face contact that failed so miserably when Louis met his people can work for the more personable Marie Antoinette. For during the time the monarchs spend as virtual prisoners in the Tuileries, "everybody who talked with the Queen liked her; her bitterest enemies were heard to shout as these women did ['Long Live Marie Antoinette'], when once they had heard her speak; and soldiers who had spoken insultingly of her before they knew her, were ready to lay down their lives for her when they became her guards" (76). Marie Antoinette's influence stems not merely from her beauty, or from her realization that her treatment of others will influence how she and her family are treated, but rather from the contrast between the real, human woman and the grotesque caricature of a queen that has become common parlance: "the ignorant and angry people had fancied her a sort of monster, determined upon her own indulgence at all cost, and even seeking their destruction, and delighting in their miseries … . instead of this monster, they found a dignified woman, with sorrow in her beautiful face, and gentleness in her voice" (76). Yet such knowledge of the "real" Marie Antoinette leads not to insight, but to a different kind of misprision; meeting the queen face to face, all "forgot for the time the faults she really had, and the blameable things she had really done. When again reminded of these in her absence, the old hatred revived with new force; they were vexed that she had won upon them, and ended by being as cruel as we shall see they were" (76). When emotional understanding supercedes other equally important types of knowledge, Martineau suggests, it can be just as blinding as no knowledge at all.

But if neither the peasants nor their monarchs can understand the other, there is one man, Martineau suggestions, who can understand "both sides of the question"— her hero manqué of the Revolution, the Marquis de Lafayette. Though Martineau, a proponent of democratic political structures, praises Lafayette's politics, it is his

Fig. 3.4   "A perilous situation": the Queen attempting to appease the mob of
                women storming the Tuileries. Courtesy of the author.

ability to "know" both the peasants and the royals that make him the true hero
in Martineau's eyes. Lafayette has precisely those qualities that Marie Antoinette,
described in the final scene in *The Peasant*, lacks. He can connect emotionally to
each side: he "grieved for the hardships of the people" but also "for the sufferings
of the royal family" (64). Unlike the Queen's, his privileged background has not
prevented him from questioning the naturalness of class hierarchies; rather, his critical
thinking leads him to become an "enemy to tyranny," "a friend of the people" (71).
Neither has he been "ground down by poverty" or "reared in hunger and brutal
ignorance," conditions which lead the peasantry to equally false presumptions.
While the mob, ruled by "passion and prejudice," blinds its children by teaching
them to "hate proud and selfish oppressors with a cruel hatred," Lafayette's "eyes
were opened by knowledge and reflection" (71).

    When coupled with compassion and empathy, such knowledge and reflection
allow Lafayette to see how false are both the people's view that all would be right

if only Marie Antoinette and a few other corrupt leaders were out of the way, and Louis's view that if those few "wicked people" just stopped inciting the kindly poor, revolution would be averted. Lafayette understands that political institutions and the woes they inflict stem not from a single individual and his or her recent actions, but result from "the growth of many centuries" (71). Since political structures and institutions are far more complex than any single individual who is subject to them, or seemingly in control of them, "no one person, or dozens of persons, was to be blamed as the cause" (71). Placing the blame at the feet of one or several individuals, rather than on social structures, is to misunderstand history, to read history as if it were a novel. Intriguingly, then, the type of history Martineau attempts to create demands both a novelistic insight into the motives and characters of those who enact it, coupled with the realization that such insight is never sufficient in itself; only when coupled with the "knowledge" of how political and institutional forces affect those people with whom one has been taught to empathize can history be truly complete.

Yet if *The Prince* is meant to stand as an example of a new type of history for children, one that merges the discourses of traditional political history with those of the novel, Martineau's text proceeds to demonstrate the difficulties in realizing such a visionary project, and even a wariness of its very implications. The first difficulty is suggested by the disparity between the text's title—*The Prince*—and the level of information Martineau can impart to its reader about its purported protagonist. As noted earlier, Marie Antoinette, rather than her son, appears to be the star of the story, a shift in focus resulting not only from Martineau's desire to counter previous false constructions of the queen, but also from the fact that as a historian, Martineau has greater access to materials about the adult queen than about the child dauphin. Notable in the multiple but brief passages that Martineau devotes to describing the prince are the prevalence of narratorial qualifications about the limits of the insight she can share with her reader. "It is not known"; "it is probable"; "I should think"; "we must hope the children did not [see]"; "Louis could not have liked"—each qualification only adds to our feeling that the very access into the personal that Martineau espouses as the ideal is limited. Unlike a novelist, who has complete access to the interiority of the characters she writes, a historian is limited by the documents that survive.

In the absence of such documentary evidence, the historian can make educated guesses—"It is probable that [the dauphin] heard something of [what the poor suffer]; for his elder brother and sister certainly had, upon one occasion" (79)—yet such guesses can degenerate all too easily into the creation of the very fantasy figures this text works so hard to dispel. When a mob prevents the royal family from going to their summer retreat at St Cloud, Martineau, unable to know "poor little Louis's" real reaction, opines that he "must have been very sorry," then proceeds to put in the place of actual knowledge a construction which shifts seemingly unaware from qualification to assertion of fact:

He had seen the hay-making at St Cloud, last summer; and now he must have been pleased at the thought of the sweet fields and gardens of the country, and the woods just bursting into leaf. He knew nothing of armed nobles lurking there, to save him and his family. What he thought about was the violets and daffodils, and fresh grass and sprouting shrubs,—the young lambs in the field, and the warbling larks in the air. (93)

The child as innocent, the child as close to nature—here is a vision of Romantic childhood quite distant from that of indulged royalty Martineau describes in other portions of her text (and particularly contrasts her description of the childhood of Marie Antoinette). That Martineau so easily falls into the very practice she condemns in the "ignorant" suggests the difficulties inherent in her project to truly "know" the historical other when evidence of that other's interiority is simply not reflected in the documentary evidence available to the well-intentioned historian.

A second difficulty arises from the text's depiction of the gap between public identities and private ones. When the General Assembly prepares a new Constitution, one that strips the monarchy of much of its privileges and powers, the King sends a letter to the Assembly proposing to swear to the new Constitution. But while the King and Queen put on a public display of "approbation and pleasure," in the "privacy of her apartment" each expresses a far different view: "These people do not like having sovereigns. We shall be destroyed by their cunning and persevering management. They are leveling the monarchy stone by stone" (122). Martineau insists that "all thinking persons must have known" that such public displays were simply "playing false," that only the "ignorant and thoughtless" could have believed that the King would happily sign away powers he "considered as truly his own as the throne itself" (122). Yet her "must" flies in the face of the historical evidence: "The members [of the General Assembly] were highly delighted: all Paris appeared highly delighted" (122); the people cry out "Long live the king!" during a post-agreement royal drive through the city. Knowing the difference between public performance and private feeling proves far more difficult than Martineau would have her readers believe.

Martineau espouses contempt for a man, who, like the King, would play a dual role: "What man of spirit would not rather have taken one side or the other, at all hazards, than have played such a double part as this?" (129). Such "playing false" is simply not "respectable," and leaves Louis open to the contempt of those knowledgeable enough to see through his deceptive public pronouncements (129). Martineau appears here to espouse the breakdown of public/private identity: if only the "double-dealing" of the king and queen were replaced by a full disclosure of their private selves, then the public could truly know them (129). Yet those very moments when the new political forces break down the boundaries between public and private in the lives of the royals prove to be the moments when Martineau espouses the most sympathy for Louis and his family. When the monarchs are brought back to the Tulieries after their attempt to flee the country, the National Guards receive orders to "never lose sight of the royal family" (120). Such scrutiny means a complete lack of privacy for Marie Antoinette and her family: with the guards "having their eyes upon the royal party all day, and upon their very beds at night," what little private domestic space this very public family ever had is taken from them (120). One soldier even goes so far as to harangue the sleepless queen in her very bed, an act which, ironically, leads not to greater communication, but to the performance of the public persona in the midst of the most private of spaces: the queen "then used the smooth and flattering tone which she always appeared to think her enemies would be pleased with" (121).

Even a sympathetic observer cannot remove the sense of violation that the opening of the private to the scrutiny of the public engenders. For when Madame Campan, first lady of the bedchamber, observes the king, sobbing after his false public declaration of approbation of the new Constitution, the queen exclaims "'Go! go!' in a tone which conveyed 'Why do you remain to witness the humiliation of your king?'" (123). Witnessing such private emotion, the text implies, even if you are a sympathetic observer, is to subject the object of your scrutiny to a form of violation, even of abuse.

Yet Martineau, despite her distaste for what she terms an "extreme of insulting rigor" in the level of observation the royal family must endure at the hands of their gaolers, cannot omit such scenes from her written history (121). In fact, her very program of engendering emotional connection between her readers and the people about whom she writes depends precisely on this same intrusion of public scrutiny into private lives. Her goal of bringing the domestic lives of the French royal family to vivid life for her readers subjects the monarchs to far broader scrutiny than they ever experienced at the hands of their gaolers. Yet it is a scrutiny at one remove; never in contact with the actual bodies of those with whom they would forge a bond of empathy, readers can be allowed access to the private lives of those they wish to understand without directly violating their private space. Face-to-face meetings with actual "others" continually produce failures in this text; yet text-to-mind meetings, Martineau suggests, can prove far more efficacious. Without a mediating teacher such as Harriet Martineau, direct contact with the other whom children are trying to understand can all too easily lead to misunderstanding, stereotyping, and a disturbing breakdown of the realm of the private. But if children pursue knowledge of that other through reading, then Martineau, the "governess to a nation," will ensure that they learn the lessons of emotional connection without destroying the realm of the private that would play so great a role in the construction of Victorian middle-class identity throughout the nineteenth century.

Chapter 4
"Men in Petticoats" and Girls in Pants: Contesting Ordinary Femininity in Historical Fiction for Girls

> Since the Men being the Historians, they seldom condescend to record the great and good Actions of Women; and when they take notice of them, 'tis with this wise Remark, that such Women acted above their Sex. By which one must supposed they wou'd have their Readers understand, that they were not Women who did those Great Actions, but that they were Men in Petticoats!
>
> —Mary Astell, *The Christian Religion* (1705)[1]

> And therein lies the difficulty I find with these—and many other—historical novels of the last 20 years. They evade the common realities of the societies they write about. In the case of novels about girls or women, authors want to give their heroines freer choices than their cultures would in fact have offered. To do that, they set aside the social mores of the past as though they were minor afflictions, small obstacles, easy—and painless—for an independent mind to overcome.
>
> —Anne Scott MacLeod, "Writing Backward: Modern Models in Historical Fiction" (1998)[2]

The Gendering of Sentiment

Just as Harriet Martineau in *The Prince* envisioned the process of sympathetic engagement as one in which not only girls, but also boys, could participate, so, too, had eighteenth-century British philosophers of sympathy and sentiment theorized the sympathetic act as one open to both sexes. Lord Shaftesbury, David Hume, and Adam Smith all used the general "he," not the specific "she" in their influential essays exploring the functions of emotion in the process of engaging with another; as Shaftesbury notes, "there is naturally in every Man such a degree of social Affection as inclines him to seek the Familiarity and Friendship of his Fellows" (255). Sentimental literature during the high period of the cult of sensibility (1740s–1770s) often featured male protagonists: both Henry Mackenzie's *The* Man *of Feeling* (1771) and Laurence Sterne's *A Sentimental Journey* (1768) take the sympathetic act as central to male, not to female, subjectivity.

Yet by the end of the eighteenth century, sentimentalism, and the literary outgrowth of this philosophical fascination with sympathy, the sentimental novel, were more

---

[1] Quoted in Looser, 18.

[2] http://www.hbook.com/magazine/articles/1998/jan98_macleod.asp.

commonly discussed in derogatory, not laudatory, terms, due in large part to critics' increasing tendency to narrow sympathy's scope to the feminine, rather than seeing it as a characteristic of "Man." The number of novels, particularly novels of sentiment, published by women grew markedly in the period; denied the opportunities of a classical university education, women could not easily write history, but the genre of the novel proved amenable to their skills and resources. This increase in the number of women writers was one contributing factor to the backlash against sentiment during the late eighteenth century. As Janet Todd notes, "[t]o many in Britain the cult of sensibility seemed to have feminized the nation, given women undue prominence, and emasculated men" (133). In response, Ann Wierda Rowland argues, many major authors writing during the opening decades of the nineteenth century "staked their claims to distinction by disclaiming the conventions of sentimentality" (192). Despite recent critical work pointing to the continuing presence of sentimental discourses and tropes in the canonical literature of the period, it is clear that growing fears of the purported effeminacy of sentimentality led many elite writers to laugh at, rather than laud, the sentimental.

Openly sentimental discourse, however, continued to be employed by many women writers, particularly writers of domestic fiction, long into the nineteenth century. Such discourse, however, functioned differently than it had in earlier eighteenth-century male-authored sentimental works. As Claudia Johnson has shown, the canonical male-authored sentimental novels of the eighteenth century create their affect by disempowering the female, relying on a "spectacle of suffering womanhood to elicit the melting humanity of male onlookers" (5). In contrast, women writers who continued to deploy sentimental discourse in the nineteenth century found the new linkage of sentiment with femininity empowering. John Tosh suggests that the growing consensus in British culture that women were quicker at reading the feelings of others granted women "special qualities in the moral sphere," qualities that men were presumed not to share (*Man's Place* 44). And as Rowland notes in her discussion of sentimental subjectivity in domestic fiction by women written during the Romantic period, innate sentimental virtue (or, in some cases, a sensibility heightened by a proper sentimental education) often led female characters to draw on their newly granted moral superiority as justification for "exercis[ing] … their sentimental charity" outside of "the bounds or interests of the husband's family" (201–2). Sensibility also gave many domestic novel protagonists the "ambition" to pursue work outside the home. Domestic ideology, with its insistence on home as the woman's rightful (and only) sphere, Rowland suggests, grew in importance during the opening decades of the nineteenth century in part as a "check on the more expansive possibilities offered to women by the exercise of their faculties for feeling" (202). Women were, by nature, better at feelings than men were, domestic ideology acknowledged, but it simultaneously insisted that women would, by nature, only want to exercise such gendered emotional skills within the privacy of the domestic realm. Such separate spheres ideology would not reach its pinnacle until the middle of the century, however, and during the nineteenth century's opening decades, the newly feminized rhetoric of sympathy and sentiment pointed to a possible avenue for women writers to envision a new, positive role for feminized sentimentality; a role that, as I will discuss later in this chapter, the genre of historical romance for girls in the period takes advantage of.

In order for the above outline of gendered shifts in the cultural valuation of sentiment and sympathy occurring during the eighteenth and early nineteenth centuries to be intelligible to us, we as twenty-first century readers must call on our contemporary understanding of gender as a social construct. But if the observation that certain kinds of female behaviors were produced by specific historical circumstances, with some considered acceptable and others not depending on the historical moment in which they occurred, strikes today's reader as obvious, the concept of what Miriam Burstein terms "gender anachronism" was far from a given for pre-twentieth-century readers. From ancient times until the eighteenth century, British accounts of women of the past focused less on their historical accomplishments than on celebrating their "virtues," virtues which tended to remain constant across time and place. As Burstein notes, when "the role of the exemplary woman in the state came in for discussion, the state did not function as an explanatory context"; instead, virtue emerged from a woman's own self-will, a quality held up for admiration to all women (*Narrating* 12). For those who believed in the universality of female exemplarity over time, no room for the possibility of gender anachronism could exist.

But just as the gender affiliations of sentimental discourse shifted during the late eighteenth and early nineteenth centuries, so, too, did British readers' understanding of gender roles over the course of history begin to change. Burstein suggests that an understanding of the concept of gender anachronism began to emerge in the philosophical, economic, and historical discourses of both Britain and continental Europe only in the late eighteenth century, with 1770 as the date when a specifically historicist approach to women's roles became a general concern (13). Such a shift may be linked to the emergence of a social history in this period. Women of the past typically played minor roles in statecraft or military campaigns, and thus were easy to relegate to a role of stereotypical virtue. Yet when history expanded to include emotions and society, differences between women over time became increasingly difficult to ignore.

Mary V. Jackson points to the late-eighteenth century as the period in which books for children, previously constructed as for a genderless "child," begin to feature different codes of propriety for boys and for girls (139). Such a bifurcation may be read as a sign of an awareness of this new gender anachronism, and a concomitant need for literature for children to contain the threats it posed. For if a woman's virtue could be different in ancient Rome than it was current-day Britain, writers of conduct manuals and moral literature for children lost one of their most important arguments for validating the behaviors they wished their readers to emulate: that such behaviors were natural, universally regarded as good by all people at all times. To address the potential for undermining writers' calls for exemplarity that the new gender anachronism posed, writers turned away,

Burstein argues, from the potentially destabilizing idea that there is *no* nature outside of culture, substituting instead what she terms "soft constructionism": the idea that an "authentic femininity" really did exist, but only appeared in its purest form at certain times and in certain geographical locations (14). Using "soft constructionism" as a frame, writers of women's history crafted stories of a society's progress towards an "authentic femininity." Unsurprisingly, the proper gender roles urged upon nineteenth-century British girls by conduct literature and improving fiction of the day bear a striking resemblance to historical constructions of "authentic femininity," a femininity characterized above all by its historical "uneventfulness," its confinement to the domestic and spiritual, rather than the public and political, realms (*Narrating* 11).

In her study of Victorian middle-class girlhood, Deborah Gorham notes that before the late-eighteenth century, the enforcement of female subordination had depended primarily on physical force or appeals to Biblical decree. But the growing cultural consensus during the opening decades of the nineteenth century that women were by nature different from men, that certain qualities were naturally "feminine," allowed an ideology of femininity to displace force and religious dogma as the "major ideological agent[s] in enforcing the subordination of women" (5). Gorham outlines the key aspects of subordinated femininity as applied to girls in the Victorian period: dependence on men; submission to men; a preference for a quiet life at home to a life of activity in public; a disposition characterized by innocence, purity, gentleness, and, above all, self-sacrifice; and a rejection of all anger, hostility, and ambition (4–5). In her study of girls' culture in the eighteenth and nineteenth centuries, Lynne Vallone concurs, describing the ur-text of girlhood in similar terms: "Each girl must decide how to conquer and then channel her girlish nature—characterized by desire, hunger, anger, ignorance, and aggression—into valuable, beautiful, womanly conduct" (*Disciplines* 5). In the canonical and non-canonical texts that Vallone discusses, including both texts for adults and those written for girls, correct "womanly conduct" is typically equated with the very same "self-will" (in the sense of having control over one's own will) that earlier histories of exemplary women cited as the universal mark of the virtuous woman. Progress on the individual level thus mirrors progress on the social level: as each novel's protagonist achieves self-mastery, she brings her society closer to achieving the ideal of "authentic femininity."

Yet as Hugh Cunningham notes, there was a "brief moment" during the opening decades of the nineteenth century when progressive parents attempted not to enforce strict gender norms, but to deemphasize gendered child-rearing practices (*Invention* 141–2). While the majority of authors of early and mid-nineteenth-century fictions for children embraced the concept of progress towards a pure, authentic femininity promised by "soft constructionism," a handful of progressive writers saw in the new concept of gender anachronism a space from which to call contemporary gender norms, clothed in the mantle of authentic femininity, into question. For if, as Anne Scott MacLeod claims in the second epigraph to this chapter, late twentieth-century and twenty-first century writers of children's historical fiction often project current-day visions of empowered femininity onto the past,[3] women who wrote the earliest historical romances and fictions for children used this emerging genre for precisely the opposite purpose. Rather than historically depicting women in the past as embodying similar values and virtues to early nineteenth-century women, a handful of writers of historical romance and historical fiction for children envisioned the past as a place where their female characters could act in ways far different, and far freer, than the constructions of femininity held up as exemplary in their own day. At a historical moment when femininity in literature, and in upper- and middle-class life, was becoming increasingly confined to and defined by the domestic sphere, such writers used the genre of historical romance to contest the equation of domesticity and femininity characteristic of "authentic femininity" in its purest form. In this context, what Burstein terms gender anachronism might be better termed gender *chronism*. For the adolescent female characters discussed in this chapter prove subversive not because they act in ways at odds with the gender norms of the times in which they live, but rather, because they behave precisely as their age instructs them. For a period that has newly become aware of the perils of gender anachronism, the subversiveness of the heroines I discuss in this chapter lies precisely in the fact that they were *not* anachronistic. By exercising freedoms that would not be available to women during the opening decades of the nineteenth century, but that were not at all anachronistic for the times in which their novels were set, such heroines had the potential to call into question the story of gender progress put forth by advocates of "soft constructionism."

The historical novel or romance written with an audience of girl readers in mind was not a commercially-common genre, despite the popularity of historical fiction for adult readers that arose in the wake of Walter Scott's *Waverley* in 1814. This lack of popularity may be due to the potential for subversion that the newly articulated gender chronism of the period suggested. But I have found several intriguing examples of such works for girl readers, including some written by the most popular authors of juvenile novels in the period, each of which is well worth analyzing. This chapter, then, will trace an increasing engagement with the concept of gender chronism over the course of three such juvenile historical novels/ romances published in the first half of the nineteenth century. In the anonymous *The Beautiful Page* (1802), history functions as a backdrop for the deployment of satire, rather than as a space charged with a sense of difference from the present. Such a use of history points to the novel's alignment with the genre of romance rather than with that of history. In contrast, Barbara Hofland's *Adelaide, or the Intrepid Daughter* (1823) deploys the concept of gender chronism to explain why a purportedly "feminine" heroine must continually engage in behavior that by the standards of contemporary readers would be deemed "masculine." Hofland's anxiety about the masculine intrepidity of her protagonist points to a deep-seated cultural discomfort with the destabilizing force gender chronism poses. The final

---

[3]   For an intriguing counter-argument to MacLeod, see Chandra Power.

novel this chapter considers, Agnes Strickland's *Alda, or the British Captive* (1841), evinces the deepest investment in gender chronism, using the concept not only to explain why the ancient Briton Alda acts the way she does, but also to call into question the gender norms currently taken for granted as "authentic" in Victorian society.

In each of these novels, girl characters choose, or are forced, to leave the protective cocoon of home; in the world beyond the domestic, they find themselves fighting in wars, experiencing torture, rejecting marriage, and speaking up for themselves to figures of authority. The realm of history, whether it is used comically, apologetically, or with an appreciation for its significant differences from the present, provides the female protagonists of these novels with a place for feminine adventure, a space in which to explore possibilities not offered by fictions, or lives, which would become increasingly relegated to the domestic sphere as the Victorian period progressed.

The "Child of Romance" and the Play of Genre: Satirizing Gender in *The Beautiful Page* (1802)

> The Word Adventures carries in it so free and licentious a Sound in the Apprehensions of People at this Period of Time, that it can hardly with Propriety be apply'd to those few and natural Incidents which compose the History of a Woman of Honour.
>
> —Charlotte Lennox, *The Female Quixote* (1752)[4]

The Beautiful Page, or Child of Romance: Being the Interesting History of a Baronet's Daughter, Intended as an instructive Lesson for Youth is not a historical novel by contemporary definitions of the genre, although it is clearly set in the past. The novel initially aligns itself with the eighteenth-century moral tale, as its third subtitle, and its opening lines, clearly indicate: "It is well known, from woeful, and continued experience, that there are few children who are not more willing to indulge their own humours than the direction of their tutors; which, however, seldom fails to make them afterwards unhappy; and from this misery it is the duty of parents to exempt their children by timely correction" (1–2). The indulgent child who will be the subject of parental correction is Matilda Colvin, daughter of the rich and powerful baronet Sir Lancelot and Lady Colvin, and goddaughter to Queen Elizabeth I. Her behavior—haughty, proud of her rank, and abusive to the servants—is typical of the aristocratic child characters of eighteenth-century moral fictions. The text suggests that poor behavior follows naturally from an embrace of aristocratic values, particularly those which focus on display and ornament: "But as her age increased, so did her ill temper; and she took delight in nothing so much as ill-treating the servants, and dressing herself in all manner of finery" (9). Initially, Matilda's parents mistake her rudeness and contemptuous treatment of

---

4   Page 327.

the servants as a sign of "spirit," echoing a common theme in moral tale fictions that aristocratic parents are overly-indulgent parents and hence the cause of the poor behavior in their children (Pickering 126). But when Matilda's servants and tutors begin to resign in protest at her mistreatment of them, her parents quickly shift from indulgence to discipline.

Instead of teaching his daughter himself, in the safety of the domestic sphere, as would a parent in a typical juvenile domestic tale of the period, Matilda's father, Sir Lancelot, makes the mistake of punishing his daughter (now a year or two older than four) by sending her away from home. Thinking that by depriving her of her aristocratic trappings, he will school her into better manners, Sir Lancelot sends Matilda to live in an old, dismal-looking house under the protection of a severe governess and even more severe tutors. Given the conventions of the moral tale genre, and their invocation in the early pages of the novel, readers might expect that the years Matilda spends in exile will lead either to her death or, as in later moral tale fictions, to her reform. This initially appears to be the direction the novel will take. Matilda discovers part of a "little story or novel" written in French, "giving an account of a young lady being banished from her father's house, for her ill behavior, and suffering many hardships, such as she had never before heard or read of, and such as made her tremble to think of" (25–6). The ending of the book is missing, and when Matilda asks her governess how the story concludes, she tells her charge that the girl reformed, and reunited with her parents. This experience leads to a "wonderful transformation" in Matilda; the girl begins to "see the propriety of being meek, sweet-tempered, and gentle," and begins to act in ways that suggest she will shortly follow the ur-text of girlhood as described by Vallone and Gorham to its authentically feminine conclusion (28–9).

Matilda's parents are informed of the transformation in their now 12-year-old daughter, and Lady Colvin wishes her child to return home, but Sir Lancelot is reluctant. Lady Colvin must accede to her Lord's wishes, yet she resists them in secret, stealing away disguised as a poor woman to visit her exiled daughter. This moment of disguise suggests a very different genre than the didactic moral tale we thought we were in; instead, with its air of mystery, secrecy, and role-playing, it points to the genre of seventeenth-century French courtly romance. Initially, however, the daughter seems an unlikely candidate to follow her mother's generic lead; Matilda, firmly ensconced in the dictates of the moral tale which led to her "wonderful transformation," performs the role of the reformed child in front of her masquerading mother: "I wish I was with my parents, to convince them of my obedience in all things to their will" (37).

Despite Matilda's words, Lady Colvin still cannot convince her husband to take Matilda back. And thus the novel, true to its first and second subtitles ("*Child of Romance*" and "*Being the Interesting History of a Baronet's Daughter*"), takes an abrupt, and deeply comical turn away from the didactic when Matilda begins to read other novels to while away her exile, novels from which the endings have not been expurgated. Eighteenth- and early nineteenth-century commentators on education for girls, whether conservative or progressive, all argued vehemently that novels were "'utterly unfit' for young women because their indulgence in 'passion and pleasure' leads to corruption of 'both the head and the heart'" (Pearson 83). But Matilda's governess seems not to share their anxieties; convinced that her charge can "imbibe no bad principles" in her leisure hours, she does not supervise Matilda's reading, reading which includes "some Romances, both French and English, which treated of love, and the adventures of lovers, and which represented young ladies as being adored for their beauty, and though plunged in distresses, were relieved by gallant knights, and sometimes by the intervention of supernatural beings" (30). Now, instead of reforming her behavior, Matilda's reading leads her to "fancy herself a damsel in distress; a baronet's beautiful daughter, confined in a castle, and against her will" (46). While Matilda acknowledges her previous bad behavior, she rejects the idea that she should continue to pay for her mistakes: "she felt that she had suffered enough; and she thought it high time that she should be released from what she considered to be a captivity" (47). Shrugging off the role of the obedient daughter offered her by her earlier reading, Matilda eagerly embraces a new, more empowering one; leaving behind the conventions of the didactic moral tale, Matilda instead embraces the romance.

The appeal of romance as a genre for eighteenth-century women readers, Jane Spencer argues, is its focus on the importance of women and the power of love. It was a long accepted poetic convention that in romance, "the normal hierarchy of the sexes was reversed, and the woman reigned" (184). Romance writers of seventeenth-century France, however, began to pretend that the hierarchical inversion "had decisive power in real life. They related historical events with the stress on romantic love as the cause of actions that changed the world" (184). Spencer argues that the escape from male-dominated reality that such romances offered, an escape embodied in fantasies of female power, were compelling enticements for eighteenth-century woman readers (184). I would extend Spencer's thinking here to suggest that for Matilda, romance offers not just an escape from male-dominated reality, but from parental-dominated reality, an authority (embodied here in the text by the father, Sir Lancelot) that constrains the girl child as much as it constrains the female adult. As Spencer notes, seventeenth- and eighteenth-century moralists feared that romances "encouraged those who ought to be subordinate—men of the lower orders, and women of all ranks—to indulge in dangerous dreams of pre-eminence, imagining themselves kings and queens" (186). Surely children, too, are a subordinate group, their dreams of being kings and queens a reaction against the powerlessness they face every day when confronted with the dictates of a parent.

But if Matilda eschews the didactic, the authority of the parent, by embracing romance, the novel in which she appears does not. For the tale of Matilda's adventures that follows is not a romance, but a satire; shifting from a moral to a comic mode, the novel relates the misadventures that result from the disjunction between the codes of romance and the realities of everyday life as Matilda pursues the path of "adventure" rather than the more conventional course of submission to filial duty. In this regard, Matilda's story can best be understood in the context of the anti-romance, a genre that depends on the disjunction between continental romance values and the values of contemporary society for its comedic charge. Such novels engaged in the eighteenth-century debate over the propriety of the novel as a genre, a debate whose anxieties were focused on the emergence of women as readers. As Ian Duncan notes, "Women were the occupants of a newly charged semiotic space of private life and domestic subjection which also happened to be the space of novel-reading. Official cultural anxieties about the role of women and about an expanding constituency of readers coalesced" around the genre of the anti-romance (12).

Perhaps the most famous of the eighteenth-century anti-romances is Charlotte Lennox's 1752 *The Female Quixote, or the Adventures of Arabella*, in which a young woman influenced by her reading of romances attempts to impose their conventions on everyday reality, to comically absurd effect. Critics who have written about this novel disagree as to the level of empowerment it offers Arabella, and through her, its readers, some viewing the novel as subversive rebellion against eighteenth-century patriarchal strictures (Langbauer; Marshall, "Writing"; Thomson, "Novel Interrogation"), others seeing it as an attempt to discipline women who would embrace the empowerment offered to them by romance (Levin, Duncan). Most agree, however, that the novel's conclusion, in which Arabella rejects her former embrace of romance and settles down to marry the man of her father's choice, sits ill with a message of female empowerment. In turning away from romance, Arabella turns away from adventure; her life as a virtuous married woman being unnarratable by the conventions of contemporary realism, her story, and the potential for empowerment offered by it, must come to an end.

Matilda's story has many parallels with Arabella's. Matilda, like Arabella, constructs her identity by taking on the manners and values of the heroines of the books she reads. As we saw earlier, when reading a novel in the didactic mode, Matilda takes on its standards of femininity—"meek, sweet-tempered, and gentle" (29)—and enjoys performing these standards for an audience of her governess and her disguised mother. When romance becomes her reading of choice, she retains those standards of conduct-book femininity that are consistent with the role of romance heroine. Intriguingly, unlike Arabella, whose adoption of the role of romance heroine leads those around her to doubt her sanity, Matilda attracts no adult attention at all. The graceful manners that characterize both the dutiful daughter and the romance heroine mask Matilda's shift from one to the other.

Although her shift goes unremarked by the adults around her, it certainly registers with the reader, for even while Matilda maintains some characteristics of the didactic moral tale heroine, she simultaneously rejects those characteristics that conflict with her role as romance protagonist. In particular, she rejects the demand that obedience to parental authority be the centerpiece of her identity. Matilda speaks up for herself: she writes letters to her father (one in English, the other in Latin!) and once to her mother (in French) asking to be restored to her home (49). Her letters performatively display her accomplishments, accomplishments that, because they are congruent with the role of dutiful daughter, continue to mask her newly emergent identity as "child of romance." But her letters do not have the desired effect; her parents are still in didactic mode. Significantly, her mother, who first hinted at the genre of romance through her disguise, shifts strongly back to didacticism. Voicing the decisions of her husband, decisions that the narrator earlier informed us conflicted with her own desires, Lady Colvin enacts the proper role of a dutiful wife. In a letter, she writes that Matilda's most important duty "is an implicit submission to your father's directions, who desires me to say, that your coming home before the expiration of the allotted time, will entirely frustrate the plans he has in contemplation for your benefit, and of which I hope and entreat you to avail yourself by a patient acquiescence with his commands" (53).

But Matilda, unlike Arabella, does find a sympathetic audience for her performance of romance. Significantly, Matilda's audience is not an adult, but an adolescent like herself. In a sly inversion of didactic fiction, the author makes the daughter of a rector, typically the most upright and dutiful of children, into Matilda's co-conspirator. Harriet Montague, having read the romances passed along to her by her friend, becomes as invested in their vision of femininity as Matilda is. When she hears of Matilda's high-born parentage (formerly hidden to save Matilda embarrassment), Harriet exclaims that Matilda is "as badly off as a great many of the princesses which, you know, we read of in the charming books you lent me" (59). Matilda, practical for a moment, says that the princesses were rescued by knights and warriors, "and I don't think there are any in these parts" (59). Miss Montague rejects Matilda's reasoning, arguing instead that if she were in Matilda's position, she would "do as many of the princesses and great ladies, and distressed damsels have done, when they were shut up in castles: I would make my escape, and run away" (60). "What, without a knight coming to deliver you?" asks Matilda; Miss Montague replies with a vehement yes: "you know how many of those ladies were glad to get away by themselves; and if I were a Baronet's daughter, I would do the same; for you never read of any harm coming to those great ladies" (60–61).

Clearly, readers are meant to laugh at this interaction between Matilda and her all-too-gullible friend, just as readers of Charlotte Lennox's novel laugh at the comic disjunction between Arabella's romance-inspired beliefs and the mores of her society. We laugh not only at the girls' faulty reasoning, and their innocent belief that the conventions of the romance will of course play out in actuality, but also at the disjunction between the lofty style of romance language and the comic simplemindedness of Miss Montague, with her continued insistence that, "O, if I were but a Baronet's daughter, you should soon see what *I* would do!" (62). Yet even while we are invited to laugh at the absurdity of these two innocents, the text also invites us to consider the possibilities for empowerment that escape, particularly a self-directed escape, might offer to the adolescent girl. By misreading the romance, by suggesting that its heroine's goal might in fact not be the embrace of hero, but a desire to "get away by [herself]," Harriet Montague opens up the possibility for resistance not only of the didactic conduct-book novel, but also to the limiting aspects of romance itself.

And thus Matilda, unlike her predecessor Arabella, takes the step that Arabella never could: she acts on her desire to get away, to escape, to leave home. Though Matilda initially rejects Miss Montague's suggestion, the reading of yet another romance, one in which a girl flees from a cruel stepmother, gives her justification for action and resistance:

> In this book, it was made very clear to her, that a young lady is not bound to obey those commands of her parents which are cruel and unreasonable; a sentiment which instantly met with her concurrence; and she began to apply it to her own case. She presently concluded that she had been banished, as she called it, long enough; and that instead of staying another year, she ought to go into the world, and seek her fortune, as other ladies in romance have done, since her parents were so cruel and unjust as to keep her from it so long after she conceived she had a right to be in it. (67)

Unlike Lennox's Arabella, whose impulse to flee her father's house is curbed by "The Want of a Precedent, indeed, for an Action of this Nature … she did not remember to have read of any Heroine that voluntarily left her Father's House, however persecuted she might be" (Lennox 35), Matilda finds her justification in a book. Taking on the masculine role of "go[ing] into the world, and seek[ing] her fortune," she dons boys' clothes[5] and flies into the nearest wood. The masquerade first modeled by the mother is here adopted by Matilda, the romance-influenced daughter.

Thirteen-year-old Matilda expects at any moment that the fantasy of female romance will be fulfilled, although her fantasy differs slightly from that in the typical romance: "she walked pleasantly along, not doubting but she should meet with some courteous knight on horseback, who would suspect she was a princess in disguise, and conduct her to his castle, where she would be entertained with all sorts of dainties, and have pages to attend her" (73). Having a hero be a slave to her love is not of concern to Matilda. Removing the sexual component from the romance desire, Matilda's fantasy constructs the romance heroine as the opposite of the dutiful daughter; "entertained" and waited upon, given "dainties," indulged rather than constrained. But the sexual component returns, despite Matilda's rejection of it. In a joke understandable to adult readers, the disguised Matilda, asked for her name by a farmer from whom she begs shelter, terms herself "Fitzallen." While Matilda takes the name from one of the books she has read, knowing readers will laugh at the implications of royal illegitimacy associated with names beginning with "Fitz," as they will at Matilda's predicament when she is offered a bed to

---

[5]   In her analysis of cross-dressing in children's literature, Victoria Flanagan suggests that "[f]or females, the cross-dressing experience is liberatory. It exposes the artifice of gender constructions, permitting the female cross-dresser to construct for herself a unique gendered niche which is not grounded within a single gender category, but incorporates elements of both" (79). See Margery Garber's *Vested Interests* for a more detailed account of the ways in which the figure of the transvestite disrupts binary understandings of gender.

be shared with the farmer's son. "But Matilda could not recollect any distressed damsel of high degree, ever sleeping with a peasant boy," and so slips free of the potential sexual comedy by asking to sleep on a chair instead (81).

While readers familiar with romance conventions are clearly meant to laugh at these hints of bawdy comedy, the main source of humor, as in most anti-romances, stems from the ludicrousness of romance expectations applied to the Elizabethan/ modern world. We laugh at the absurdity of Matilda's expectations of a knight arriving at any moment, and her actions while she waits. To cite one of only many examples: Matilda hopes to draw a noble listener by singing in the woods, but instead only attracts a deer; when she approaches it, thinking it enchanted by the magic of her voice, it, like any wild animal, flees at the sight of her. We are also clearly to laugh at the disjunction between Matilda and a real romance heroine— "she now recollected that she differed from most of the princesses of romance, in not having a farthing of money about her," the narrator slyly comments (76).

Yet when, unsurprisingly, Matilda's knight fails to appear, she does not act the part of a patient romance heroine, for such a role has too many affinities to that of the didactic dutiful daughter. Neither does she, like Arabella, draft a decidedly non-heroic boy or man into the role. Instead, Matilda adopts Miss Montague's earlier advice, and stops waiting for her prince to come. After spending only two days in the woods, Matilda revises her plan, deciding to offer herself as a page to a lady at a nearby castle rather than wait for rescue. Significantly, the castle she approaches contains not a knight eager to succor a damsel in distress, but a woman in distress herself—the very real historical figure, Mary, Queen of Scots, imprisoned by her cousin (and Matilda's godmother) Elizabeth at Tutbury Castle.

Readers might expect another generic shift at this point, a shift into history, yet anti-romance remains the dominant genre. In what would have been improbable in a work invested in historical accuracy, guards allow Matilda to enter; charmed by the beauty of the "youth," the queen, and her warders, quickly accept "Fitzallen" as a page. Matilda spends her time not devising escape plots for the imprisoned Queen, but rather in beguiling the saddened prisoner with her tales of romantic derring-do recounted from the books she has read, and her fervent belief that an actual rescue is just around the corner. Matilda does not recognize that she, under suspicion due to a stray letter offering succor to the Queen that she picked up, unread, during her travels, is just as much a prisoner as is Mary. Instead, Matilda is in a perfect joy at finding herself at the center of a real romance:

> The wishes of Matilda were now completely gratified.—She was in a situation extremely befitting a damsel of romance. She was disguised as a boy, and acting as a page to a captive Queen, who gave her some rich dresses suitable to her character. The next thing she concluded must happen, of course, was, that a thousand knights would come and release the Queen; that in the rencontre, her own sex and name would be discovered; and that the boldest and the handsomest of all those knights, after releasing her from some imminent danger, would demand her in marriage of the Earl her father. She entertained no doubt on this subject, and was therefore as cheerful as her compassion for the Queen would permit her. (119)

Fig. 4.1   "Matilda's Interview with the Queen": a girl not only in pants,
                but garbed in the entire outfit of a male page. Courtesy of the
                UCLA Charles E. Young Research Library Department of Special
                Collections.

Yet Matilda's dream of a romance ending to her unconventional adventures is denied, at least at first. For Matilda is not a real romance heroine, but merely a girl performing the role of one; and unfortunately for Matilda, her performance is flawed. When Mary proposes writing to Elizabeth to ask for "Fitzallen's" freedom, Matilda lets slip that Elizabeth is her godmother, her boy's clothing a disguise. Her attempt to justify herself to Mary—"it is just what I read of other young ladies doing; and I thought I had a right to do so too; being kept so long, and so far from my parents, with a governess in an almost desolate house" (129–30)—falls on deaf ears; instead, Mary subjects her to a long lecture about the foolishness of her affair with romance, a lecture worthy of the best of the anti-romance moralists. For readers familiar with the historical Mary—in particular her reputation for sexual indiscretions—casting the Queen in the role of moralist (or as an enemy of romance) is dubious at best. Unlike the respectable patriarchal Doctor (commonly assumed to be modeled after Samuel Johnson) who finally convinces Lennox's Arabella to give over her foolish investment in romance, Mary Queen of Scots evokes the specter of a powerful, intriguing woman, one whose own disobediences make her pronouncements to Matilda on filial obedience more than suspect.

With such a tutor, it is not surprising that Matilda appears to reject the lesson that Arabella finally embraces. "Indeed, madam, … I should love to have my father's forgiveness; but I had rather stay and be a prisoner with your Majesty, than go any where" (134). Mary reads this as a personal compliment: "Dear, simple girl! … Your attachment affects me" (134), but it could just as easily be seen as Matilda's refusal to give up romance, adventure, and the escape from parental authority that both promise.

For when the text once again implies that a generic shift is imminent—Queen Elizabeth calls Matilda to London to be questioned by the privy council under suspicion of treason—romance continues to trump the reality promised by the ending of the typical anti-romance. When accused of lying, Matilda does not humbly accuse herself, or apologize; instead, she protests, then upbraids the counselors, blushing not from fear or timidity, but with "indignation": "My Lords! … it would better become you to send a thousand knights to conduct the suffering Queen to her own kingdom, and seat her on her own throne, than question the truth or loyalty of Sir Lancelot Colvin's daughter!" (139–40). Even after her father is arrested for high treason, Matilda continues to behave just as a heroine of romance would: she "shrieked, and sunk into the arms of the young Lord Howard, who being an elegant and fascinating young nobleman, had been sent to talk with, and sound her" before throwing herself on her knees in front of her father to beg his forgiveness (143, 144). When the councilors accuse Sir Lancelot, it is not he who responds, but Matilda, Matilda who becomes the center of attention not only of the novel, but also of the political body of the privy council. Although her performance suggests that she has seen the error of her ways, and is ready to adopt the role offered by the didactic moral tale—she relates "in a plain and simple manner … how she had been misled by books of romance, to act as she had done, with all the particulars of her conduct; the behaviour of the Queen of Scotland to her; the excellent advice she had received from her; and her final resolution always to submit to her father's pleasure, and, in future to prove his obedient and affectionate child"—the denouement of the novel suggests that such an espousal is as much of a performance as was Matilda's earlier enactment of the romance heroine's role (145–6).

For rather than being amused at, or disgusted by, Matilda's behavior, "[t]he council listened with attention and delight; and the young Lord Howard was enraptured" (146). The final pages of the text focus not on Matilda's reunion with her father, nor on her reformed behavior; instead, they depict the effect of her actions on Lord Howard, who, instead of laughing at her, as we as readers have been throughout the novel, responds to her as if he were a hero in one of the romances she has purportedly given up, and she the romance heroine who inspires admiration and devotion: "Lord Howard flew directly to the Queen, and recounted to her Majesty all that had passed, protesting, that Miss Colvin was something more than mortal" (147). Though she is 13 and he probably not much older, he begs the Queen to allow them to marry. When the Queen chides him, telling him that they both had better go to school, he replies "Your Majesty's court shall be my school ... and Miss Colvin my Goddess" (147–8). The Queen laughs, just as we have laughed at Matilda's romance-inspired behavior throughout the novel. Yet, with the caveat of a one-year waiting period, she grants the wishes of Lord Howard and Matilda, and the novel ends not with the silent retirement of Matilda into the domestic sphere, but with the pomp and majesty of her aristocratic wedding. Though the final lines of the novel state that the Queen left "the young Lord and Lady in the possession of every happiness, and patterns of every virtue," the lack of detail about just what "virtues" Matilda and her young husband embody leave open the possibility that the construction of femininity that both the anti-romance and the didactic moral tale typically enforce will not, in the end, be demanded of this "child of romance." For what 14-year-old need be subservient to a parent when she has taken on the adult role of bride? And what bride need be subservient to a husband who, like herself, has imbibed the tenets of the romance, who thinks his bride "a Goddess," "more than mortal"? What began as satire has turned back upon itself; *The Beautiful Page* is not an anti-romance after all, but an anti–anti-romance, a novel that laughs at a genre only to re-embrace it in a final burst of exuberant pageantry and display.

Private Lives, Public History: Gender Chronism in Barbara Hofland's *Adelaide, or, The Intrepid Daughter* (1823)

> [The study of history] gives us, and it only can give us, an extended knowledge of human nature;— not human nature as it exists in one age or climate or particular spot of earth, but human nature under all the various circumstances by which it can be affected. It shows us what is radical and what is adventitious: it shows us that man is still man in Turkey and in Lapland, as a vassal in Russian or a

member of a wandering tribe in India, in ancient Athens or modern Rome; yet
that his character is susceptible of violent changes, and becomes moulded into
infinite diversities by the influence of government, climate, civilization, wealth,
and poverty. —Anna Barbauld, "On the Uses of History" (1826)[6]

Given the popularity of the anti-romance genre in the late-eighteenth century,
publisher T. [Thomas] Hurst could be forgiven for thinking that a juvenile anti-
romance would prove popular with his readers. The appearance of a second edition
of *The Beautiful Page* in 1805 would seem to suggest that Hurst's investment had
paid off; yet this second edition was not issued by its original publisher, but by
the firm of Castleman and Tegg. If the "Tegg" of "Castleman and Tegg" refers to
Thomas Tegg, an early-nineteenth-century publisher who specialized in remainders
reissued with new title pages (St Clair 529), then we can assume that Mr Hurst's
assessment of the public taste was a bit behind the times.

The Beautiful Page's lack of success can certainly be attributed to its breaking
of the conventions of the ur-text of girlhood, its final rewarding of a triumphant
Matilda rather than the ending far more typical of the adult anti-romance, which
commonly featured a chastening of the romance-addled girl along with her
rejection of the powers of romance in favor of womanly self-control (Todd 135). It
might also be attributed to the text's deployment of satire, a genre typically at odds
with the dictates of instructing the young to respect, rather than to mock. While
children's satires proved briefly popular in the opening decades of the nineteenth
century, in books that Mary V. Jackson has termed "papillionades," or animal
satires modeled after William Roscoe's *The Butterfly's Ball and the Grasshopper's
Feast* (1806), and Catherine Dorset's *The Peacock 'At Home'* (1807), juvenile
books that featured satiric portraits of people rather than animals grew increasingly
rare under the pressure of Romantic ideology's antipathy to the form.[7]

But the most probable cause of *The Beautiful Page*'s lack of success in
the market is its failure to deploy the past as history, rather than simply as an
opportunity to bring famous characters from times gone by onstage for amusing
effect. In early nineteenth-century Britain, history stood near the top of the
hierarchy of literary genres, while the novel (and in particular the sentimental
and the romance novel) stood at culture's fringes, feared for its perceived
pernicious effects on its primarily female readers. History, a genre traditionally
written by gentlemen to inculcate other elite men in the principles of good
government and citizenship, only grew in prestige with the rise of nationalistic
feelings in the wake of the Napoleonic wars. The novel, linked not only to an
emergent middle class, but also to women, who, during this period, were its
most notable practitioners, drew the fire of critics who argued that novel-reading
would seduce a woman into sexual corruption, or pull her attention from her true

---

[6]   In *A Legacy for Young Ladies* 123–4.

[7]   See Ruwe, "Satirical" for a more detailed account of the papillionades, and of
Romanticism's anti-satiric ideology of the child.

womanly duties, the management of her house and family (Ferris 8; Pearson 87). For children's writers, deploying history in their narratives meant that they could also appropriate history's cultural authority and prestige, thereby deflecting any fears of the corrupting potential of their fictions.

But not just any mention of history would serve the purpose. For, as discussed in the Introduction, the period in which *The Beautiful Page* appeared was one marked by a complex revolution in historical practice, a change in how people in the present understood and related to the past, and this new conception of history had to be reflected in any fiction that hoped to claim history's authority. James Chandler suggests that this historiographical change, typically given the name "historicism" and associated with the years 1770–1830, manifested itself in the period's interest in "comparative contemporaneities," or the dominance of the practice of comparing one's own age with former ages—a new concern with anachronism (*England* 107). *The Beautiful Page* is filled with anachronisms, but anachronisms in our current sense of the word: things, ideas, or events out of their proper chronological place. Sixteenth-century Matilda suffers from the curse of the eighteenth-century woman reader, an overindulgence in seventeenth-century French romances; Mary Queen of Scots adopts a didactic role more suited to the eighteenth-century moral tale than to the intelligent, intriguing queen of historical record. The new nineteenth-century historicism, however, focused not on anachronism as "out of chronological order," but rather on the way that things, ideas, and events seemed to belong to a different time than its own, and the way that this difference might shape those who experienced it in ways that would make the people themselves different from those in the present. It is this sense of difference, this absence of concern with comparative contemporaneities, that seems so noticeably lacking in *The Beautiful Page*.

And it is precisely this sense of difference that characterized the newly emerging literary genre that would capture the adult reading public's admiration in the opening decades of the century: the historical novel. In his influential *Historical Novel* (1937), Georg Lukács presents Sir Walter Scott as the originator of and chief innovator in this new novelistic form, a move echoed by the majority of twentieth-century scholars who wrote about the genre. Reading Scott as the genealogical father of this new genre, later critics codified what "counts" as historical fiction by using Scott's *Waverley* novels as a template, suggesting that a true historical novel is not simply a story set in the past, but rather one that focuses on the depiction of a specific kind of anachronism: a story of historical process, one in which inevitable historical forces invade and disrupt the idyll of an organic, but anachronistic society, in the process shaping a new national community (Trumpener xii–xiii). Depicting society broadly, dramatizing disruptive but inevitable historical change, and crafting historically representative characters thus become, in the wake of Scott, the hallmarks of "real" historical fiction, fiction which shares its society's fascination with "comparative contemporaneities" (Trumpener 130).

Historians of children's literature tend to follow Lukács's lead, pointing to Scott as the precursor not only of the adult, but also of the juvenile genre of historical fiction (Butts, "Dogs" 3; Agnew, et al. 114; Townsend 43–4). Although children's literature critics tend to grant children's writers some leeway in conforming to the Scott-based definition of historical fiction ("historical novelists for children are less concerned with depicting major historical events and figures than those who write for adults" [Agnew 335]), they agree that historical fiction "is not merely a story set in the past," but rather "a story which attempts, with the aid of scholarly research, to reconstruct and bring to life the events, culture, and *Zeitgeist* of the period" (Agnew 335).

Yet, just as contemporary scholars of the Romantic period have begun to question Scott's place as the sole progenitor of historical fiction for adults, and the independence of his historical fiction from other contemporaneously written fictions set in the past, a definition of juvenile historical fiction based predominantly on the example of Scott's works may also be worth troubling, in particular when analyzing the second text this chapter addresses, Barbara Hofland's *Adelaide, or, The Intrepid Daughter* (1823).[8] For the breadth of social scope found in Scott's novels simply cannot be portrayed in the course of a far shorter novel for children; neither is there room for the scholarly apparatus, including documentary sources, footnotes, appendices, and prefaces outlining historical evidence, increasingly becoming required to legitimate the truth claims of the historical novel for adults. More problematic, the insistence on "historically representative" characters, ones which strike the reader as significantly different from themselves, is at odds with the emergent goal of fostering reader identification in the period, a project in which Hofland, as demonstrated in her robinsonade *The Young Crusoe*, clearly participated (see Chapter 1). If the gap between reader and child or adolescent protagonist proves too large, the goal of fostering exemplary behavior through identification cannot be achieved. Perhaps most importantly, the denigration of the genre of romance, the "masculinization" of fiction that Ina Ferris identifies as central to the establishment of Scott's historical novels as worthy of literary acclaim, occurs not at all in Hofland's work; instead, her novel resonates with the emotion and with the providential plotting that mark both the "feminine" romance novel and the novel of sentiment. Rather than distancing herself from the "stigma" of these earlier

---

[8]   *Adelaide*, like many of Hofland's other novels for children, was originally published by John Harris. The 1823 edition contained 24 half-page engravings, printed two to a page. Several of Hofland's novels, including *Adelaide*, were available in two editions: one "plain," or illustrated with black and white engravings; a second, more expensive edition, with colored engravings. The UCLA Library's Children's Book Collection includes a copy of the color-illustrated edition, from which the cover illustration of this volume was taken.

In his biography/bibliography of Hofland, Dennis Butts includes the following publishing history of *Adelaide*: "Moon cites a second edition in 1825, third n.d., and fourth, 1830, while *NUC* records a fifth edition published by Newman in 1830 (?) and a Boston edition of 1834. The book was advertised as part of 'The Hofland Library' in the 1850s, and Mrs Moon remembers reading a copy as a child in the early years of this century!" (*Mistress* 73). While such a reprint history suggests that *Adelaide* was not the most popular of Hofland's juveniles, it does suggest a book with an appreciative audience beyond Mrs. Moon … .

forms, Hofland strives to appropriate the validating discourse of history while simultaneously drawing on the female-empowering discourse of the romance.

These gendered underpinnings of definitions of "real" historical fiction clearly influence Dennis Butts in his overview of nineteenth-century historical fiction for children. Butts mentions Hofland as a potential originator of the genre only to dismiss her; in *Adelaide*, he argues, Hofland "is far more interested in telling her melodramatic and coincidence-driven story than in giving an accurate picture of the historical period" ("Dogs" 3). "Melodrama" and "coincidence" here seem to stand for bad writing; Hofland fails as a writer of historical fiction because she attempts, and fails, to adopt the model set forth by Scott, or, perhaps more accurately, the model promulgated by those critics who have taken Scott at his word, ignoring the ways in which sentimental discourse continues to be at play in his novels. But if instead of reading melodrama and coincidence as signs of poor writing, as a failure to follow the masterplot of Scott, we instead look back to their original generic connections, we can see that Hofland attempts to perform quite different cultural work than does the "father" of historical fiction. Instead of masculinizing the novel by aligning it with history rather than with romance, Hofland draws upon the tropes of romance to consider how masculine, public, political history impacts the lives of purportedly private, domestic women and girls. Though she, unlike the author of *The Beautiful Page*, deploys the new concept of historical chronism in her historical narrative, she also questions the validity of the myth of "progress" inherent in this new historicism, particularly when it comes to judging progress in terms of a society's treatment of women.

In her opening note "TO THE READER" of *Adelaide*, a historical novel set in France during the St Bartholomew's Day Massacre of 1572 and its aftermath, Hofland both explores the issue of reader identification and demonstrates her awareness of the new discourse of historical chronism. Hofland explains that her writing method involves "interweaving the imaginary history of a young person living in those disastrous times with the important and interesting detail of historic facts, which are never altered or perverted, either in time, place, or circumstance" (iii). Accuracy of facts, however, is not enough to ensure reader identification; instead, evoking emotion proves key: "The author may also add, that she was desirous of impressing on the ardent and ductile mind of youth the value of that religious liberty, that peace and plenty, enjoyed in this favoured country, and thereby awakening a spirit of thankfulness to God and good-will to man" (iii). Here Hofland revises the *tabula rasa* view of childhood. Added to the common Lockean idea of the child as "ductile" blank slate, ready to be "impressed" by the lesson the adult author wishes to teach, is the curious word "ardent," suggesting that mere ductility may not be enough for a lesson to take hold. Instead, Hofland constructs the child as a creature of strong feelings, feelings which contribute to the ease by which an adult's lesson may be pressed upon him or her.

This emphasis on emotions reappears in Hofland's discussion of her primary goal: to "awake," by means of intertwining fiction and historical fact, "a laudable curiosity for works of History and Biography, which, it is presumed, will be read with more diligence, and recollected to better effect, when they are combined with that species of individual attachment awakened in a sensible child towards a person of his own age, actuated by his own motives and affections" (iii). To become a better reader of History and Biography, Hofland suggests, a juvenile reader needs first to feel for those portrayed within it; such feeling is easier to evoke by creating a fictional "person of his own age" than in recounting facts and figures, no matter how historically accurate. Once a child reader's feelings have been "awakened," and attached to an object/character within the text, curiosity about the person can be re-channeled to awaken curiosity about the past. Such a process grants a degree of agency to the child reader, by granting agency to the child protagonist; the character has "his own motives and affections," which, rather than the desires of the adult author/teacher, "actuate" a new curiosity in the child reader toward History and Biography. Hofland, like Johann David Wyss before her, and like so many authors after her, strives to draw in her readers by creating characters with whom they can forge an emotional bond.

The importance that Hofland places on reader identification can also be seen in the dedicatory essay that follows her Preface. Hofland dedicated her novel to Mary de Harcourt, daughter of Charles Amedee de Harcourt, a French émigré who had fled Revolutionary Paris as a young adult (Robert). In her dedication, Hofland draws Mary's attention to the clear parallels between herself and her fictional counterpart. They are both noble; both daughters of French fathers and English mothers; both suffer from "political tempests" (v); and the "happiness" of each will arise "in a considerable degree, from the restoration of peace to your paternal countries" (v–vi).

Yet Hofland is deeply ambivalent about this project of creating reader/character identification through emotion. For, after drawing attention to the similarities between the fictional Adelaide and the real Mary, Hofland backtracks. While she is eager to evoke a connection between reader and protagonist, a connection forged through emotion, she also wishes to establish a line of demarcation between the two, a line that will function to protect the reader from the dangers of identifying *too* closely with the protagonist. She does this by insisting that beyond the similarities outlined by her, "comparison ceases" (vi). Her worry is that Mary (and her fellow readers) will not simply be actuated by emotion to turn toward history and biography, but that their emotional attachment will lead them in a more dangerous direction: toward a desire to *act* as her protagonist Adelaide does, even though their historical circumstances are quite different from Adelaide's. As Hofland instructs Mary, "the misfortunes which fell upon your father's house have not affected you, and the courage, heroism, and patience, practiced by Adelaide, are, happily, not demanded in your situation" (vi). Espousing "courage" and "heroism" as traits appropriate to girlhood in 1823 England is anachronistic, Hofland worries; thus, she feels the need to protect both her readers and herself from accusations that her novel, rather than leading readers to greater curiosity about the safe realms of history and biography, may instead lead to those dangerous traits associated with novel reading. Mary and the book's other girl readers need to feel for Adelaide, but not so much that they want to *be* her, for to act as Adelaide does would be to act in a way inappropriate to contemporary gender norms.

To compensate for taking away the possibility of a girlhood constructed by "heroism" and "courage," Hofland offers in its place social and moral superiority: "living in times far more enlightened … you will readily perceive that the virtues and attainments called for in *your* situation are, in fact, more important than *she* practiced" (vi). Here Hofland draws upon the new historiographical concept of gender chronism to assert that actions that in one period may have been condoned as feminine may no longer be considered feminine in another. Miriam Burstein suggests, however, that the opening two decades of the nineteenth century saw a backlash against historically specific conceptions of gender, even of the "soft constructionism" type. Under pressure not only from anti-Jacobin and anti-French feeling, but also from the evangelical revival, gender chronism lost its explanatory force; in conservative writings in particular, gender chronism gave way to a reemergence of exemplary Christian portraits in women's history (*Narrating* 14). Though Hofland's move to judge time periods hierarchically may strike us as conservative, by deploying the concept chronism as an explanatory category in 1823, Hofland aligns herself with a liberal, rather than conservative, historiography of women.

To further differentiate her reader from the actions of her heroine of the past, Hofland also offers Mary a long description of "correct" contemporary "virtues and attainments," a list of impeccably properly feminine traits:

> You will be aware, that active benevolence, self-control, the dignity of a generous mind, the humility of a religious spirit, the gentle demeanour of courteous manners, the cheerfulness of a placid temper, are more endearing, as well as more feminine qualities, than the exertions of courage or the endurances of fortitude … . (vi)

And yet Hofland is not ready to abandon courage and fortitude entirely, or assign them without exception to the realm of the masculine; to do so would invalidate the story that follows, would make her heroine, if not her reader, suspect. And so Hofland tacks on a qualification to the above list that transforms its hierarchy on its head: the feminine virtues may be "more endearing as well as more feminine" than "the exertions of courage or the endurances of fortitude, *which yet, when called for, are perfectly compatible with them*" (vi, italics added). In the appropriate historical circumstances, Hofland insists, a girl can be both feminine *and* brave.

Hofland's protagonist, Adelaide, must be brave because "political tempests" have wrested her from her proper sphere, that of the loving embrace of her parents; readers outside of the text, like Mary de Harcourt, will presumably be safely ensconced within the confines of the family circle, and hence will have no need to assume the courage, the heroism, required of her protagonist. Hofland thereby gives herself license to construct a vision of femininity within her novel at odds with contemporary gender norms while simultaneously insisting that such a construction is safely ensconced within a less "enlightened" past. Thus, the past becomes a safe space in which to enact a fantasy of feminine heroism, a fantasy in which Adelaide's bravery is always carefully contained by its motive: a desire to reunite with her family, to return them and herself to the domestic sphere from which they have been so cruelly expelled. Yet even while the text deploys heroism to support a return to domesticity, its detailed depiction of the "horrors" inflicted on the bodies of both men and women by the political tempests that have been constructed as outside the boundaries of the domestic call the idyll of the domestic sphere—not only that of the past, but that of the present—into frightening question.

Dennis Butts suggests that Hofland's interest in history takes a back seat to her interest in her "melodramatic and coincidence-ridden story." But the novel's opening passage indicates that what animates Hofland is an interest in how history and the personal intersect:

> In the evening of the 24th of August, 1572, a young couple, whom the duties of a military life had separated for a considerable time, were glad to escape from the merriment and gaiety which reigned through the palace of the Louvre, where they were lodged, to a small apartment where they could talk freely of their own affairs, and those of the kingdom of France, and worship God in the manner their own religion dictated, as they were both of the Protestant, or, as it was then called, the Huguenot persuasion. (1)

The young couple is the son of a Count, Charles de Soubise, an officer in the service of Henry of Navarre, and his wife, Maria Shirley de Soubise, an Englishwoman who fled to the Continent with her uncle to escape the persecution of the Protestants during the reign of Queen Mary. Their "own affairs" can be discussed freely only within a sphere separated from the public life of the court. But their discussion is not confined to their domestic or familial concerns; both Maria and Charles take a vital interest in the "affairs" of the state, affairs that, far from being separated from their domestic sphere, have a direct impact on it. The narrator embodies this impact in the brief description of Madame de Soubise's parents: "her father having suffered at the stake, and her mother died heart-broken for his cruel fate" (2). Politics takes a bodily toll on the family, although in this passage, the toll is clearly gendered: the state inflicts punishment upon the body of the male, and then, secondarily and indirectly, on the emotions of the female. But later in the novel, physical suffering stemming from the political situation will push beyond the boundaries of the male body into the realm of the female, troubling the gendered construction of the intrusion of the political onto the domestic.

If Hofland's text points to the fallacy of constructing the family as a safe private haven from public history, it also evinces, at least initially, a desire that the boundary be maintained between history and the child. Adelaide, the seven-year-old daughter of the de Soubises, interrupts their private talk of public matters. Educated in the country, secluded from the intrigues of court culture, Adelaide, the narrator asserts, is "too young to share the troubles, or understand the cares, which agitated those by whom she was surrounded" (5). But although Adelaide does not have the knowledge to understand the political machinations of the courtiers and royalty whose plaything she has become during her time in Paris, she can read the emotions of the players. For when the King of France jokes "That is your best present, my little heretic; be sure you take care of *that*!" (5) after Adelaide is given a cross by the new Queen of Navarre, she asks her father "What the King could mean by calling her a little heretic, and looking so odd, that although he smiled, yet there was something that terrified her in his looks?" (5). Despite Adelaide's nascent political instincts, her father denies her any explanation: "You are too young, my little maid ... to understand any explanation. ... at a proper time, I will tell you more; say your prayers, and for the present, forget ... ." (6). Although her parents cannot "forbear to comment" on the King's meaning, they do so only after Adelaide is safely in bed. If this text is all too aware that the assertion of a separation between the domestic and political is a sham, it simultaneously gives voice to a wish that such an intrusion of the political not extend to the youngest members of the family.

But for Adelaide, simply forgetting cannot avert the eruption of politics into the domestic sphere. For, as readers with even a smattering of knowledge of French history would certainly know, Hofland's opening invocation of "the 24th of August, 1572" is a portent: the horrors of the St Bartholomew's Day Massacre and its seven-month aftermath, during which at least 70,000 Protestant Huguenots were killed in France, are about to intrude into the domestic space of the de Soubise family. Intriguingly, it is Adelaide's mother, rather than her presumably more politically involved father, who suspects the intentions of the French; her personal attendance on Henry of Navarre's mother, who died mysteriously soon after arriving in Paris, has given her insight to which her husband, involved more directly in court culture, has no access. In her portraits of both Maria and Adelaide, then, Hofland clearly draws upon emergent domestic ideology that equated greater emotional sensitivity to the feminine.

Unsurprisingly, then, it is Maria de Soubise who is first awakened by the sounds of soldiers, and sees them dragging terrified families from the safety of their homes into the streets to be murdered. The sight of the soldiers, and the authority with which the words "Kill them all:—spare not:—kill all the Huguenots!" are uttered, prove to Adelaide's mother that the "assaults were no private murder" (8). The woman is witness to the state's brutal intrusion on the "private" domestic space, its actions transforming a safe sphere of domesticity into a site of public execution. Following a pattern common to many novels written by women in the Romantic period, Hofland structures this scene as an "inexorable repetition of experience across two generations" (Campbell 163); Madame de Soubise, like her mother before her, is struck by "phrenzy so terrible" at the sight of her husband being stabbed by French soldiers (12). The eruption of political violence into the purportedly safe sphere of the domestic leads to emotional breakdown in the woman who is supposed to be safely ensconced in its protective confines.

But if Adelaide's mother seems destined to reenact her own mother's narrative, Hofland suggests that such recapitulation need not extend to her own daughter. Hofland's solution does not lay in ensconcing her protagonist in a domestic haven even safer than that of her mother's, or grandmother's, for her story argues that such a safe haven is an illusion. Repudiating the assumption at the heart of separate spheres ideology—that the privacy of the domestic sphere can be truly separate from the public—Hofland's text asserts the domestic offers only a false hope of protection from the forces of history. Instead, the novel suggests, Adelaide must venture out into the world of the public, with all its violence and horror, rather than fly from it into insanity, as does her mother.

Awakening to find herself alone, Adelaide goes in search of her parents; instead, she stumbles over the corpse of her father, "her feet … bathed by the warm blood still ebbing from his wound" (13). Though she determines to stay with the body, men thrust her aside, until she finds herself "in the open street, in the midst of horrors still greater than those from which she had escaped" (14). Hofland is not loath to describe these horrors in gory detail:

> On one side might be seen the wretched Huguenots in the hands of the brutal soldiery, and not less brutal mob, suffering under every form which licensed cruelty and unbridled ferocity could adopt: some were poniarded, others were suspended, and the flying were shot from the balconies of the Louvre by the king himself and his brother. The body of Admiral Coligny, though beheaded, was suspended on a gibbet, and the indignities on every hand offered to the dead, rendered the living the more hideous spectacle. (14)

Hofland's violent description finds an echo in the color illustration of Adelaide fleeing amidst piles of bodies and attacking soldiers; like Adelaide, readers must visually witness the horrors of history. In her preface, Hofland assures parents that "It will be found that the scenes of distress are by no means exaggerated (since it was impossible to increase the horrors of the times depicted)" (iii); the claim of accurate history here functions to justify the depiction of violence far from common in the children's literature of the period.[9] Such violence surely functions to distinguish early-nineteenth-century British "religious liberty" from corrupt French tyranny, to construct a juvenile subjectivity invested in the belief of England's superiority over suspect Frenchness (note the inclusion of the apocryphal detail of the King shooting his own subjects here, and the footnoted comparison drawn between the military greatness of Henry and of the Duke of Wellington later in the novel [59]). It also functions to elevate Protestantism over suspect Catholicism, particularly in light of the debates over Catholic Emancipation taking place in England during the 1820s.

Yet such depictions of violence simultaneously register a protest of the construction of female novel reading in the period, a construction, as Ina Ferris describes it, characterized by a conception of reading as an act of the body rather

---

[9]   The earlier tradition of the children's martyr tale, such as John Foxe's *Book of Martyrs* (1563) and James Janeway's *A Token for Children* (1632) certainly included scenes of violence. Such books were still being read in the early nineteenth century, but newly published books for children generally excluded the depiction of extensive violence and gore.

than an act of the mind. In Romantic-era reviews of novels, and in conduct literature of the period, female reading is troped as ingestion, or eroticism; not simply the content of the novel, but the act of reading it, is viewed as a pleasure, a satiation of female desire. In reviews of novels and romances for adults in the period, Ferris argues, such a construction of female reading led to reviewer resentment, a "conventional charge that novel reading takes wives and daughters away from their domestic duties and diverts their emotional energies from their families" (41). By crafting a depiction of bodies, particularly female bodies, as objects of the violence of historical, political forces, rather than as subjects desiring pleasure, Hofland turns such constructions on their heads. The violence of political history is what takes women away from domesticity, her text asserts, not the pleasures of novel-reading.

Instead of pushing her into insanity, the horrors that Adelaide experiences force her to act, to move beyond the sphere of the domestic. In the aftermath of the massacre, Adelaide longs to leave the protection of a priest who found and sheltered her, to "go ... out into the city to seek" her missing mother (17). Later, after she flees to England in the company of a French family, the Crébillons,[10] she purchases the supplies they need to conduct their embroidery business, and also accompanies them to the houses of their employers. After years pass in exile, the adolescent Adelaide[11] hears that other Huguenots survived the massacre, and resolves to "devote her life to seeking" her mother (32), a plan she puts into action by speaking up, telling her story, to Queen Elizabeth, who has hired the Crébillons to embroider a gown. Adelaide "would many a time, with clasped hands and streaming eyes, exclaim, 'Ah! why was I not a boy? then would I have flown to my king, and beneath his standard have secured to my father's name that glory his premature death denied'" (32); though the text cannot literally grant Adelaide's wish, it does so figuratively, when, dressed as a boy, Adelaide returns to France and becomes enmeshed in the newly crowned Henry IV's campaigns against his rebellious subjects.

---

[10] Crébillon was the name of a famous French romance writer ("romans libertins"): Crébillion fils, Claude-Prosper Jolyot Crébillon (1707–1777). His novels were deemed "immoral" and "licentious," and he was imprisoned and exiled for their veiled political attacks (Levi). If Hofland was aware of the "immoral" French writer, her use of the name for her virtuous bourgeois French family may indicate both her debt to romance and her rejection of its libertine excesses.

[11] Adelaide is seven when the novel opens in 1572; Henry IV ascended to the throne of France in 1589, which, if Hofland were carefully hewing to historical accuracy, would make Adelaide 24 when she returns to France, far from a child, or even an adolescent. But the text clearly presents her not as a woman, but as a child; Queen Elizabeth calls her "child"; most of the other adults who encounter her during her return to France (when she is disguised) call her "boy." Hofland asks us to think of her as "a youth of 15" (51). Clearly, the details of history are not as important to Hofland as considering the impact of historical events on individual children. Such unconcern with historical accuracy is, perhaps, why historians of juvenile historical fiction tend to overlook or dismiss Hofland in their accounts of the genre (Butts, "Dogs and Cats"; Rahn).

Yet at each moment when Adelaide acts in a way that might be considered by early nineteenth-century British standards of gender to be heroically masculine rather than docilely feminine, Hofland's text is careful to justify her heroine's actions by continually attributing their motivating force to Adelaide's respect for, and desire to return to, a stable domestic sphere. Adelaide would brave the dangers of the violent Paris streets not because she longs for adventure, but because her "great anxiety for the fate of her mother was incessant" (17). She ventures into the market, purchases goods, and accompanies the Crébillons to the scenes of business not because she longs to escape the confines of home, but because they cannot speak English, and she must aid them, since she is now a part of their family. Her petition to Queen Elizabeth asking the ruler to send her back to France is not the result of a carefully thought-out plan, but an "uncontrollable" (i.e., feminine) emotional reaction. When Queen Elizabeth[12] would refuse her plea to be sent along with the Queen's soldiers to Henry IV—"thou art better at home; we will devise thee employment more suited to thy birth—be content" (45)—Adelaide openly protests; the danger of rejecting both a Queen and her dictate that a girl is "better at home" is mitigated only by the strength of Adelaide's daughterly devotion:

> "Oh! my liege, I will be contented to lose my birthright, to pass my life in the humblest obscurity, so your Majesty suffers me but to convince myself that I have no longer a mother—for her sake I know myself capable of high achievement and severe endurance, and I long to encounter even the hardship which may prove me worthy of her: when I cease to hope, then only can I submit to the fate which separates us." (45)

Adelaide may be characterized by courage and heroism, but the text continually insists that such traits stem not from any masculine desire to venture from the domestic sphere, but from the feminine desire to connect (or reconnect) with a domesticity unnaturally torn asunder. Hofland's vision of gender chronism, then, rests not in a definition of gender as solely a social construction; rather, she draws upon the "soft constructionism" described by Burstein, a sense that a pure, natural femininity exists, but it can appear only in certain times, under certain historical circumstances (*Narrating* 14).

---

12   Elizabeth's prominent role in Adelaide's story is surely significant. For, as Leonée Ormond and Rohan Maitzen note, Elizabeth was far from revered by the Victorians. Maitzen suggests the Victorians' preference for Mary Queen of Scots over Elizabeth stems from "Mary's much greater compatibility with both gender and genre conventions." Unlike Mary, who can be fit into the generic victim or villainess roles, Elizabeth "poses so many problems to a would-be narrator that she is almost unrepresentable. For a Victorian, writing Elizabeth as a villain was not really an option, but writing her as a heroine would require redefining all the relevant categories: gender, power, history, and heroism" (164). That Hofland portrays Elizabeth positively, and powerfully (she sends military aid to Henry IV, making her decision without the aid of any male counselors), suggests a willingness to push at the boundaries of at least some of the "relevant categories" that formed the basis of Victorian constructions of femininity.

That Adelaide may also be inspired by a desire for masculine family glory, a desire linked directly to her desire to "be a boy," must be suppressed if Hofland's narrative is to conform to the vision of "authentic femininity" promised by a "soft constructionist" interpretation of history. Thus, the text continually pulls in two opposite directions: on the level of plot, the narrative repetitively thrusts Adelaide into situations which require her to act, to be "our young adventurer" (51); on the level of narration, in contrast, the narrator must continually assert, or make Adelaide assert, that such traditionally unfeminine actions hold no pleasure for the "authentically feminine" Adelaide. For example, earlier in the novel, during their flight to England, Adelaide and the female Crébillons disguise themselves as boys. But instead of suggesting any possible pleasure from the freedom such garb might grant, the text emphasizes their pleasure at returning to feminine attire: "It was the first care of Annette, and Louise Crébillon, to exchange their clothes for those which were proper, and as Adelaide desired the same comfort, they indulged her in it as soon as they were able" (21). When Adelaide again adopts a boy's disguise, masquerading as a servant to a Captain Latimer upon her return to France, the text hints at the pleasures of such disguise, only to disguise those pleasures once again, the disguise strengthened by focalizing the narrative judgment through the eyes of Queen Elizabeth:

> … her royal mistress … expressed herself satisfied with the completeness of her [Adelaide's] disguise, and as she was naturally inclined to be romantic, it is probable that she experienced some pleasure in aiding the adventurous designs of a young girl, whose purity of motive she could not doubt, and whose affectionate anxiety and warmth of heart, alone led her to renounce for a time the appearance and the habits of her sex, and to subdue not only the selfish indulgences, but the natural vanity, her youth and beauty were so well calculated to awaken. (48–9)

By shifting the attention away from a masculine "pleasure" in "adventurous designs" that a girl or woman might take from cross-dressing to a moral lesson about giving up feminine "natural vanity," Hofland neatly transforms cross-dressing from a gender-transgressing danger to a gender-bound virtue.

Hofland herself does not seem entirely persuaded by her own attempts to disguise the potential for gender disruptions presented by Adelaide's cross-dressing. Adelaide adopts the persona of a sickly boy, one who spent long hours in the company of women, and who therefore desires to spend time with the Captain's wife rather than with him. Yet her plan backfires; Captain Latimer takes it as a personal challenge to "wean him from effeminate pursuits, and, what he termed, 'make a man of him'" (50), a challenge which he meets by taking Adelaide along with his regiment to Rouen, instead of leaving her behind with his wife. But placing her protagonist in such a masculine sphere drives Hofland to a strange narrative move: instead of calling her "Adelaide," the narrator insists on calling her "Jaques," the name her character has donned along with her disguise, and using the male pronoun "he" rather than "she" when referring to the disguised Adelaide. The reason for the shift becomes obvious when Adelaide, thrust into battle, does not cower in fear; instead, the wounding of Captain Latimer, "evidently awoke in him [Adelaide] a desire of vengeance, as he immediately drew his sword and ran forward with an impetuosity which indicated either courage or despair" (52). Such a desire is far too dangerous to attribute to a girl, and thus not just the name, but the pronoun used to refer to the re-gendered protagonist, shifts. The narrator herself seems to have lost a degree of omniscience—she can no longer say definitively what motivates Adelaide ("evidently" it is a desire for vengeance, but not positively so; is it "courage" or "despair" that motivates "Jaques"?). Placing herself inside the head of her female protagonist while she experiences such masculine desires strikes this narrator as far too dangerous· only by distancing herself and her reader from Adelaide as boy can the actions she takes next prove admissible. For Adelaide does act upon her desire for vengeance: she draws her sword and successfully defends a French officer from the attacks of several men (a scene depicted in vivid detail—see the cover of this volume, where this illustration is reproduced). Though "urged more by humanity than valour," and deploying "rapidity and agility" rather than "force," Adelaide nonetheless prevails in this most masculine realm (52).[13]

Given the pattern of the book, readers should not be surprised to find Adelaide quickly whisked back to more "feminine" activities—comforting the dying Captain Latimer, nursing the other wounded,[14] displaying feminine self-sacrifice to "relieve and aid her suffering brethren" (54)—nor to discover the narrator once again using "her" and "Adelaide" to refer to her protagonist. Neither will they be surprised to discover that the man Adelaide has rescued is a relative, the Count de Soubise, Adelaide's masculine action made somewhat more respectable by being, at least in hindsight, a defense of her own family.

Yet the text, reluctant to return its protagonist so quickly to the domestic sphere, does not allow a reunion between Adelaide and her relative; instead, the narrative continues to thrust her into the role of boy adventurer. Brandishing pistols to escape kidnappers, discovering hidden treasure, bargaining with smugglers to provide food for a sisterhood of Protestant nuns[15] in the midst of a siege—Adelaide must continually don boy's clothes and the active role they signify. Though the narrator continually asserts that Adelaide prefers the passively feminine to the actively

---

[13]   Intriguingly, the text never states directly whether Adelaide wounds or kills anyone with her sword: Adelaide "succeeded in rescuing him from the destruction which menaced him; and those who were not compelled to abandon their prey from their wounds, slunk from it in shame at being foiled by such an opponent" (52). The full-color picture is not quite so reticent: it shows Adelaide on the verge of plunging her sword into the chest of a soldier on his knees.

[14]   Adelaide's battlefield nursing contrasts markedly with the home nursing more commonly associated with the truly feminine. Might Adelaide be read as a precursor of Florence Nightingale?

[15]   A sisterhood strikingly familiar to the one imagined by Mary Astell in "A Serious Proposal to the Ladies" (1694).

Fig. 4.2   "The intrepid Adelaide brandishes her pistols to successfully ward off potential kidnappers." Courtesy of the UCLA Charles E. Young Research Library Department of Special Collections.

masculine, readers may be forgiven if they, like Adelaide at the sight of the King, "felt as if she could again enter on the glorious toils of war" (60).

It may appear that that the text's repetition of this pattern functions to wean Adelaide, and potential adventurous girl readers, from any desire to replace "authentic femininity" with the pleasures and glories of the active masculine; the horrors of what Adelaide endures are so appalling that no other girl would wish to experience them. Yet the violence and death of war that Adelaide encounters function instead to make explicit the connection, rather than the separation, of masculine history and female domesticity. Adelaide's active role forces her, and through her, the reader, to bear witness to the degradation of domestic bodies by the forces of political history. Hofland makes explicit the connection between domesticity and history by constructing the effects of the siege of Paris as a deep perversion of family ties:

> During her melancholy perambulations, she saw, with equal compassion and horror, the progress of famine in this populous city ... the dead, or dying, were no longer reverenced; the ties of nature were dissolved; and insatiate hunger arose to madness: the living first envied the dead, and then preyed upon them ... even mothers preyed on their own children. (92)

As the "ties of nature" linking one family member to another dissolve in the face of the physical toll of war, "praying" transforms into "preying"; the spiritual and emotional connections constructed as natural to the family turn animalistic, cannibalistic. The horrors of the passage build to a gruesome climax: the dissolution of the construction of motherhood as endlessly self-sacrificing for the good of the child. When "even mothers" prey upon their own children, the powers of femininity and domesticity to serve as a bulwark against the forces of political history come frighteningly into doubt.

Hofland's solution to this perversion is two-fold. First, on the level of the personal, her text must assert ever more strongly the power of the mother-child bond. In a scene reminiscent of Ann Radcliffe's *The Italian*, Adelaide discovers that a woman hidden by the Protestant sisterhood is none other than her long-lost mother, a mother who will become the object of her aid rather than her appetite. Family must be reasserted in the face of the horrors of war, horrors that disrupt so violently proper family laws. Intriguingly, while Hofland reasserts the power of family, she does not reassert the construction of a passive femininity that typically undergirds the patriarchal family. Adelaide's reunion with her mother does not lead to a resumption of Adelaide's dependent, feminine role; no men suddenly arrive to rescue the helpless women. Instead, Adelaide becomes the rescuer, leading her mother and the remaining sisters from their home, which has been set afire by the artillery of the besiegers. Lingering to gaze on a sight they expected to see no longer, two more of the remaining sisters perish, crushed under the falling ruins of their own home. The domesticity that once provided shelter and succor, a space safe from the violence of the public sphere, literally entombs those women who fail to see that the boundaries between public and private are no longer in place, that being "out in the world" is not a decision, but a necessity. Passive femininity, a rejection of the public and retreat to the private domestic sphere, is simply not an option for Adelaide.

Hofland's narrator never asserts that the community of women in which Adelaide finds succor is unnatural, or wanting, because it excludes men. Yet its destruction suggests that such a model of family, a family of one sex only, must prove untenable, even though the more "tender hearts" of that sex render it an appealing fantasy for Hofland. It is not surprising, then, that immediately after its destruction, its former inhabitants begin to dream of a different type of family: a restoration of patriarchal order. But to regain this more acceptably gendered version of the family, Adelaide must once again act beyond gender conventions: "Do not, do not die, dear mother ... I will go directly to the King's camp and demand an interview with this new Count," the Count who has taken on her father's title (106).

And at this point in the text, when Adelaide meets King Henry, when private meets public, Hofland's second solution to the perversion of the family becomes clear. Rather than simply reconstituting the private family, Hofland fantasizes a transformation of the political structure, by shifting its motivation away from power and toward emotional connection, a move that echoes not history but the novel of sentiment. The novel's narrator asserts that King Henry turns to war not out of a desire for power, or a wish for "his own aggrandizement," but rather out of his "attach[ment] to his people" (66). He winks at smugglers who bring goods into the cities he besieges; he wishes to "conciliate" rather than "subdue" his subjects; he calls off the artillery after witnessing the horrors it inflicts; he calls for provisions to be secretly sent to the suffering Parisians. When debating his decisions with his counselors, Henry declares "I am their father and their King, and I cannot hear the recital of their calamities without being pierced to my inmost soul, and ardently desiring to bring them relief" (111).[16] Hofland here draws upon a tradition of validating royal authority by constructing such authority in terms of the patriarchal family, but hers is a patriarch motivated not by power, but by emotion. Hofland fantasizes a political structure founded not on the model of an authoritarian patriarchal family, but a family constructed by its ties of sympathy and feeling. If the political were domesticated, Hofland urges, then the breakdown of boundaries between public and private would be transformed into a joy rather than a threat.

But such a transformation is fraught, Hofland suggests, by male figures of power who almost uniformly disagree with Henry's empathetic approach. Henry takes pity on smugglers; his generals, "less scrupulous than himself," would hang them (67). The governors in Paris take Henry's stoppage of the artillery not as a sign of his pity, but of his weakness, and, by determining to keep up their resistance, "risked the total ruin of its inhabitants, and beheld, unmoved, those horrors, which unnerved the hand, and melted the heart of their generous assailants" (101–2). Even those "generous assailants," Henry's counselors, advise him to keep up his attacks, rather than act on his sympathy. Significantly, it is at just this moment, when Henry must decide whether or not to heed their advice, to choose between power and sympathy, that he encounters Adelaide. The sight of her emaciated body, an embodied sign of the state of his own people, leads him to cry with compassion; her recital of her story leads him to remember his own experiences during the St Bartholomew Massacre, and at his description of its horrors, "a deep sigh of sympathy ran from breast to breast" (116). Unsurprisingly, Henry's interaction with Adelaide, who symbolizes all of his subjects, leads him to adopt the role of the emotionally connected father, "to act on the suggestions of his pity, and to raise the siege" (118). Again, unsurprisingly, it is during this interview that Adelaide learns that the mysterious Count de Soubise, the man whom she defended at the battle of Rouen, is not a distant relative but her own beloved father, mistakenly believed murdered. Melodrama, to be sure, but Hofland's melodrama does not simply ignore or belittle political history, as Dennis Butts would have it; instead, it functions to imagine the possibility of political transformation.

Just as the triumph of Henry signals not a triumph of power, but one of emotion, so too does the restoration of Adelaide's patriarchal family. For her wounded father

---

[16] Hofland, perhaps aware that her construction of royal motivation might strike readers as improbable or unrealistic, footnotes this piece of dialogue, citing as her source a work not of fiction, but of history: "See Sully's Memoirs."

is not an authoritarian figure, or one whose strength of action allows Adelaide to take a stereotypically feminine/passive role. He, like Henry, is characterized by his emotions, rather than his actions. Adelaide initially believes that he, unlike her mother, can hear the news of the survival of his spouse without becoming emotionally overwrought, but when she reveals it to him, his excess joy leads to "convulsive gaspings and violent agitations," to "overpowering emotions of his swollen heart" that must be given vent (130). In a delicious piece of conduct literature turnabout, it is the Count, rather than his daughter or wife, who must "learn the necessity of curbing his emotions" (131). Her mother explains to Adelaide what is most to be valued in her father: "Oh! Adelaide, poor girl, never can I convey to thee an idea of the excellence of the father thou hast lost; the sweetness of his temper, the kindness of his heart, admit no parallel—I speak not of his courage, his honour, for those qualities he shares with many" (125). Though Hofland may worry about constructing a too-active femininity, constructing masculinity as suffused by emotion causes no parallel anxiety. Feminizing the patriarchal authority of both the father and the state proves the ultimate fantasy of Hofland's historical fiction.

Yet Hofland herself seems to recognize the improbability of her fantasy to feminize the masculine political realm. A brief footnote that serves as the final words of the book relates that Henry IV, far from being loved like a father by all his subjects, survived multiple assassination attempts before succumbing to the knife of a final plotter. That Hofland felt the need to include such information, and at the very concluding moment of her text, suggests that her attempts to retell the political story in familial terms cannot survive the scrutiny of an emergent historicism.

Hofland's second goal, to decree courage and action compatible with femininity, proves equally daunting. Her novel itself ends with a scene between the two patriarchal figures, the Count and the King, with the King first joking about Adelaide's masquerade as a boy, then asserting in a graver tone "I have ever observed, that the firmest temper, and the gentlest spirit, are perfectly compatible; that sensibility and fortitude go hand-in-hand,—I therefore doubt not, that Adelaide will henceforward be as much an affectionate and obedient, as she was once an enterprising and Intrepid Daughter" (155–6). Linking the authority of the narrator to the authority of the King, Hofland attempts to assuage readers' doubts that having once acted the part of a boy, Adelaide can no longer participate in a femininity characterized not only by emotion, but by obedience to a patriarchal authority, be that authority father or monarch. Yet as the story of the father of Mary de Harcourt, *Adelaide*'s dedicatee, implies, the transformation of femininity has the potential to work in both directions. If Mary, rather than her father, had been in Paris during the Reign of Terror, then she, too, might have had to exercise the "firmest temper" and the "fortitude" shown by her fictional counterpart. For if the physical deprivations visited upon bodies by the forces of history can occur not only in feudal 1572, but also in commercial 1789, they cannot be so easily confined to an earlier stage of historical development; the historical forces that shaped Adelaide may prove not to be as anachronistic as those in 1820s England might wish.

Gender Chronism as Cultural Critique: Agnes Strickland's *Alda, The British Captive* (1841)

"Facts, not opinions," should be the motto of every candid historian; and it is a sacred duty to assert nothing lightly, or without good evidence, of those who can no longer answer for themselves.

—Agnes Strickland, *Lives of the Queens of England*[17]

I am happy that she has become a sister of the craft, and that she will do honour to the body.

—John Lingard[18]

There she is—behold her!—in the library of the British Museum, with her poke bonnet, her umbrella, her India-rubber overshoes; perhaps—most likely—some sandwiches in that pocket where weighty tablets and bits of antiquity alone were wont to be ... nobody blowing a trumpet to clear the way as she goes home through the dingy streets of Bloomsbury,—instead of her triumphal car, putting up with an omnibus and carrying her notes in a little bag like any ordinary womankind ... instead of a slow succession of elaborate volumes, full of style and pomp, accuracy and importance, it is a shower of pretty books in red and blue, gilded and illustrated, light and dainty and personal, that fall upon us from her hands. In short, it is not Edward Gibbon, but Agnes Strickland—the literary woman of business, and not the antique man of study—who introduces familiarly to our households in these days the reduced pretensions of the historical muse.

—"Modern Light Literature: History."
Blackwood's Edinburgh Magazine (1855)[19]

The author of *The Beautiful Page* had no need to cite historical sources, for she/he could assume that the brief bits of history included in the novel would be common knowledge for the book's readers. Hofland, in contrast, clearly saw herself both as a storyteller and as a historian; she gives details of the political and religious situation in France comparable to those to be found in a typical children's history of the country across the Channel.[20] Hofland's expertise, though, is not as a historian,

---

[17]   From the "Preface" of volume 1 of *Lives*, xiii.

[18]   Quoted in Delorme, 48.

[19]   Attributed to Margaret Oliphant (see Burstein, *Reduced* 232). *Blackwood's Edinburgh Magazine* 78 (1855): 437.

[20]   See, for example, the brief description of the Massacre in *The History of France, from The Earliest Period to the Present Time* (1786), commonly attributed to Richard Johnson:

As the admiral was going home one night from court, he was wounded in the arm by some ruffians, hired by the Duke of Guise to shoot him. This was followed with an agreement, that on the 24th of August, at the ringing of bells, for the first prayers, in the morning, the Hugonots should all be massacred, and the Duke of Guise took upon himself the execution of it. The admiral, confined to his bed by his wounds, was the first who fell a sacrifice, and the slaughter continued for seven days with the most unheard-of cruelty. (89)

but as a novelist; as a novelist, she felt it necessary to provide occasional source citations, particularly at moments when readers might be likely to question the veracity of the historical details that she includes. One footnote directs her reader to "see Sully and Brantone and other historians," who will confirm her story that the Queen of Navarre was murdered by means of a poisoned glove (4); another to "see Brantone and other historians" to prove that Margaret de Valois had no knowledge of the plot to massacre the Huguenots. Hofland, a novelist, must rely on the work of others to validate the accuracy of her historical facts.

Yet the rise of historicism in the early nineteenth century meant not only that the subjects that history treated had changed; the qualifications for writing history had changed as well. And the sources upon which Hofland relies no longer held the same authority that they would have a century earlier. At the start of the long eighteenth century, history was typically written by men involved in the events they chronicled, or by antiquarians; by the start of the nineteenth century, politically partial eyewitness memoirs and annals-saturated accounts had given way to histories based on new standards of scholarship, scholarship characterized by a scientific approach to the study of documentary remnants of a culture (Looser 2–3). The sources upon which Hofland relies—the memoirs of both Maximilien de Béthune, duc de Sully, the superintendent of finances for Henry IV, and Pierre de Bourdeille Brantôme, an intimate of the court of Marguerite de Valois—fall within the first, unscholarly category. Though Hofland clearly intends to engage her reader in history, as well as romance, the sources for that history would not stand up to the scrutiny of later nineteenth-century historical standards.

Unlike Hofland, who spent the bulk of her career writing novels, the author of the final text this chapter will examine gained fame as a writer not of fiction, but of history. Agnes Strickland (with her anonymous co-author, elder sister Elizabeth) wrote one of the best-selling works of nonfiction in the nineteenth-century: the *Lives of the Queens of England* (12 volumes, 1840–1848). Strickland was not simply a hack historian; as Burstein argues, she was one of only two historians of women who were taken seriously as *historians* in the mid-Victorian period (*Reduced* 220). During the 1830s, she and her sister spent mornings in the British Museum Library, reading historical manuscripts and taking lessons in paleography from the library staff. But Strickland went far beyond library research to discover previously unknown information for her biographies of the English queens. Strickland corresponded with antiquarians and scholars; borrowed or consulted manuscripts from ancient aristocratic family libraries; lobbied to be allowed to consult documents in the state paper office after being refused access by the Home Secretary because of her sex (1837); and successfully petitioned (along with 83 other historians, including Thomas Carlyle, Charles Dickens, Thomas Babington Macaulay, and Mary Ann Everett Green) that fees for consulting public records charged to those engaged in serious historical research be waived (1851) (Mitchell; Laurence 125). In the preface to the first volume of *Lives*, Strickland asserts that "facts, not opinions" should be the motto of the modern historian; while current-day historians may find Strickland's tone and approach outmoded, it is clear that by mid-Victorian standards, the work done by Strickland and her sister was "both pioneering and intensive" (Mitchell).

In choosing a subject for her one historical novel for young readers, Strickland again demonstrates her credentials as a historian of the scientific mold. Both Barbara Hofland and the anonymous writer of *The Beautiful Page* chose to write about historical events that took place in what scholars of the time termed modern history, that is, historical events dating from after the rise of Christianity. As Devoney Looser notes, during the early nineteenth century, "modern" functioned as the lesser term in the binary pair "modern/classical" history. The explosion of print in the late seventeenth and eighteenth centuries increased the public's taste for modern history, but knowledge of modern history did not provide the same cultural capital as knowledge of ancient history did (10). Though the audience for all types of history broadened during the course of the eighteenth century, studying the military and political history of Rome or Greece remained primarily the province of the sons of the British elite.[21] Modern history was far more accessible to women and men without a classical education, because it did not require knowledge of Latin or Greek. Modern history emerged as a popular, rather than a scholarly, genre, a genealogy that, along with the genre's links to romance, contributed to what Looser terms its "second-class, feminized status" (11). Historical facts about Elizabethan times, the period during which both *Adelaide* and *The Beautiful Page* are set, would have been easily accessible to women writers during the opening decades of the nineteenth century, but finding the requisite background information about classical times would likely have proven more difficult for a woman without a classical education.

The history of ancient women was additionally off-limits for Victorian writers of women's history because of the Victorian equation of "woman" with religion and morality. For writers interested in the history of women of the past, Miriam Burstein argues, pre-Christian women's lives were "unwritable not simply because they were missing from the historical archives, but more importantly, because they lacked Christian virtue" (*Narrating* 112). Both male and female writers of women's history linked modern historical practice with a refusal to recover or write the histories of pagan women, Burstein notes, although one suspects that the pressure on female writers to eschew such histories was far greater than those on males.

---

[21] Greek and Roman mythology, and exemplary biography such as Plutarch's *Lives of the Greeks and Romans*, would have been familiar to many upper-class women, who could read such works in translation. In her *Letters on the Improvement of the Mind* (1773), originally written for her fifteen-year-old niece, Hester Chapone recommends two French volumes of ancient history, Rollin's *L'Histoire Ancienne* and Vertot's *Revolutions Romaines* (165, 167). In a similar volume, Anna Barbauld's *A Legacy for Young Ladies* (1826), Barbauld gives no recommendations about what her "Dear Lydia" should read, but posits the study of ancient history as possible: "if a young person begin with ancient history … ." (141). Barbauld, however, demonstrates her own familiarity with such history throughout her letter as she discusses of the necessity of maps as aids in learning about Hannibal, Pharaoh Necho, Socrates, Alexander, and other ancient heroes and rulers (144–5).

Agnes Strickland and her sister Elizabeth followed the pattern of writing about modern, rather than classical, women in their popular *Lives of the Queens of England*.[22] But the Strickland sisters, whose father believed in schooling daughters just as one would sons, had learned both Latin and Greek as children, and they demonstrated their familiarity with classical history in the Introduction to the first volume of the *Lives*. Quoting the words of Tacitus, the Stricklands draw a comparison between Queen Victoria and the ancient British warrior queen Boadicea, who led a revolt against Roman rule in first century Briton. Victoria governs not only "by rightful inheritance," and by "the consent of the people," but also "in full accordance with the ancient British custom," a custom noted by Tacitus in his description of Boadicea: "Solent foeminarum ductu ballare, et sexum in imperiis non discerne" (*Lives* I, xvii, quoting from Tacitus's *Life of Agricola*).[23] Significantly, the Stricklands do not translate this passage for their readers, and fail to name the queen (Boadicea) about whom it was written. The Latin quotation thus serves a double purpose: first, to demonstrate the authors' scholarly knowledge and thus their authority; and second, to distance their female readers, and their female sovereign, from the taint of Boadicea's association with the masculine realm of "matters of military command." Unsurprisingly, in their portrait of Boadicea later in the Introduction (which serves to present brief thumbnail sketches of the pre-Norman queens), the Stricklands focus not on Boadicea's military prowess, but on both her failure and her femininity, citing a long passage from an "earlier historian" which describes her "remarkably picturesque" "dress and appearance" on the eve of her defeat by the Romans. Though the Stricklands laud Boadicea as "heroic," they evince little interest in the "warrior" aspects of this "royal amazon" (*Lives* I, xix–xx).

Though the "ancient British custom" of female rule was beyond the scope of her nonfiction project, it clearly fascinated Agnes Strickland,[24] who chose to return to it in her historical novel for girls, *Alda, The British Captive*, set in Rome just after the defeat of Boadicea. Published in 1841, shortly after the appearance of the first volumes of the *Lives*, the novel was clearly meant to

---

[22]   Antonia Fraser, Jayne Lewis, Rohan Maitzen, Lynne Vallone, and Elizabeth Burstein have all argued that the bulk of the *Lives* functions not as a proto-feminist justification of women's rule, but rather as an encomiastic exploration of the domestic and feminine virtues of the queens whom the Stricklands profile (Fraser 159; Lewis 181–6; Maitzen, Chapters 2, 3, and 6; Vallone, "History Girls"; Burstein *Narrating* 115–16). Alda makes for a striking contrast, then, to Strickland's deployment of femininity in her nonfiction.

[23]   Translation: "they do not discriminate against women in matters of military command." Antonia Fraser, not I, identified the source of this quotation (59).

[24]   Strickland collaborated with her sister, Elizabeth, on many of her writing projects, including the popular *Lives of the Queens of England*, despite the fact that typically only Agnes's name appeared on their books. The title page of *Alda* gives its author as "Miss Agnes Strickland, Author of the *Lives of the Queens of England*," suggesting that this juvenile historical novel, like *Lives*, might have been a collaborative project. Pope-Hennessy, however, attributes sole authorship to Agnes (103).

piggyback on the popularity of Strickland's adult work, with "Agnes Strickland" prominently identified as the "Author of the *Lives of the Queens of England*" on the novel's title page.[25] In setting her novel in classical Rome, Strickland clearly breaks with Victorian writers of women's history, who deemed the lives of early women unworthy of depiction. To provide cover for her unconventional choice, Strickland chooses a British, rather than a Roman, character to be her protagonist, and draws upon the respected tradition of the Evangelical conduct novel for girls, writing not of a pagan girl, but of a pagan girl's conversion to Christianity. Yet under the surface of conversion tale lays the story of a girl far less conventional than the feminized, domestic Queens who feature so prominently in the *Lives*, or than Hofland's reluctant adventurer Adelaide. For conduct fiction is not the sole genre Strickland deploys; by combining conduct fiction with the genres of history, romance, and martyr tale, Strickland constructs a girl protagonist who, under the cover of an emergent Christianity, is allowed a temperament, spirit, and courage far more typical of a Victorian adventure novel hero than of a domestic novel heroine. And rather than apologize for the gender chronisms that depicting a heroine from the distant past entails, as Hofland feels compelled to do, Strickland deploys gender chronism to call into question the limited constructions of gender in her own times.

At the opening of *Alda*, Boadicea, the warrior queen of the Britons, has been overthrown by the Roman general Paulinus; among the "illustrious captives" now doomed to slavery in Rome is 16-year-old Alda, daughter of the British prince Aldogern (1). Like the gender-non-conforming Boadicea, Alda manifests a character far removed from early Victorian norms of femininity: headstrong, indulged, haughty, and passionate, she refuses to do the tasks assigned to her by her Roman captors, and glories in her defiance and freewill. Again, like Boadicea before her, Alda's adoption of masculine traits, it appears, must be punished and reformed into a more docile femininity throughout the course of the novel. Through

---

[25]   Pope-Hennessy suggests that *Alda* was written before *Lives*: Strickland "laid aside her historical work for a few days to polish up an old story *Alda*" for "now that her *Queens* had been so well received publishers were eager to take her work" (103). R.M. Healey confirms Pope-Hennessy's assessment, noting that it was a "minor coup" for the "fairly undistinguished early Victorian printer-publisher" Joseph Rickerby to acquire the rights to Strickland's first post-*Queens* novel (260; 258). Rickerby did not believe in the book enough to have it extensively illustrated; the book contains only one small piece of inaccurate black and white spot art, reprinted in this volume.

Despite the popularity of her nonfiction, *Alda* sold badly, perhaps contributing to Rickerby's decision to give up on publishing books later in the year of its publication (1841) to focus exclusively on the business of printing. No later English publisher would take up Strickland's book, although the novel proved extremely popular in France; the online catalog of the Bibliothèque nationale de France lists nineteen editions issued between 1858 and 1896 by devotional publisher Alfred Mame et Fils of Tours. The tradition of a female French martyr in Joan of Arc may have made Strickland's novel more appealing to those across the Channel than to the author's fellow Britons.

her interactions with fellow-slave Susanna, a Judean convert to Christianity, Alda learns the value of Christian submission; her devotion to her new religion leads her not only to temper her behavior, but also to the ultimate act of submission: death.

Such a summary clearly places Alda in the category of what Lynne Vallone has termed the "conduct fiction heroine," a girl protagonist who, during the course of a novel, must be taught to redirect her selfish emotions and desires towards others rather than herself, and in particular, toward the private sphere of heterosexual domesticity (82). Vallone points to Jane Austen's Fanny Price, in her *Mansfield Park* (1814) as an example of one type of conduct fiction heroine, the "Christian girl," a heroine that emerged in the novel of manners during the opening decades of the nineteenth century. But with Alda's lesson centered on religious conversion, rather than just moral conversion, one might be tempted to place the novel in Vallone's second example of the conduct fiction heroine, the one found in context of turn-of-the-century Evangelical fictions for girls, such as Hannah More's *Coelebs in Search of a Wife* (1809) and Mary Brunton's *Self-Control* (1810), *Discipline* (1815), and *Emmeline* (1819) (*Disciplines* 82, 93).

Yet when one moves beyond brief plot summary to an examination of the details of Alda's story, it becomes clear that while Strickland's novel draws on each of these traditions of girl heroines, it, and its main character, cannot be comfortably contained within their boundaries of the religious, domestic, and private. For *Alda* contains deeply transgressive moments within the confines of a seemingly constricting plot of feminine submission to Christianity and to the private domestic ideal. Strickland, like Hofland before her, uses the site of history to question what Vallone terms "the configuration of a hegemonic female value" in literature for girls, but her protest is far less constrained, far less fearful, than Hofland's (82). Instead of taming feminine desire for adventure by linking it to a desire for the family, as does Hofland, Strickland eschews domesticity altogether, creating a heroine who, despite her conversion to Christianity, emerges as radically different from the conduct fiction heroine of the moral tale, the Evangelical heroine, or the "Christian girl" of early nineteenth-century fiction for and about girls. Instead of functioning as a bridge from these earlier forms of girls' fiction to the emergent genre of literature for girls in the Victorian period, the domestic fiction of Charlotte Yonge, Juliana Horatia Ewing, and their contemporaries, Strickland's novel serves as a protest against such a continuum. Rather than being "'blind' to any desires beyond ideologically conservative values of domestic happiness" (Vallone 69), Strickland's Alda rejects domesticity in favor of adventure, heroism, and sisterly, rather than romantic, love. That Strickland is able to write such a story depends in large part on her knowledge of historical facts, facts that allow her to assert the validity of gender chronism with the authority of a modern scholar of history.

Strickland's novel opens not by depicting Alda within the safe confines of a domestic sphere, but rather places its heroine in the most public of positions: first, on the plain of battle (although not as a combatant); then on the streets of Rome, being paraded as a captive. The narrator writes, "The giddy and unfeeling

Fig. 4.3   The frontispiece of *Alda* shows not its heroine, but what appears to
be her father, King Aldogern, pleading with his Roman captors for
the lives of his people. As such a scene never occurs in the novel,
might this illustration, with its supplicant females at Aldogern's feet,
be an attempt to distract potential buyers from the unconventional
femininity the text depicts? Courtesy of the UCLA Charles E. Young
Research Library Department of Special Collections.

multitude enjoyed the spectacle, and were loud in their plaudits, and pressed with
eager curiosity to gaze on the stern and silent barbarians" (2–3). Alda, "a show
and a gazing-stock" for Rome's "gaping mechanics and insolent patricians" (161),
embodies not the virtues of the private domestic girl, but instead serves as the
object of public consumption.

After encountering these opening scenes, a reader might assume that the novel's
task will be to recuperate Alda from this public display of what nineteenth-century
domestic ideology constructed as an essentially private femininity. The task will
be a difficult one, though, for Alda, unlike Hofland's Adelaide before her, is far

from embodying the central characteristics of hegemonic construction of girlhood in the period: a preference for home rather than public activities; submissiveness, particularly to men; and a character that embraced innocence, gentleness, religiosity and shunned any show of ambition or anger (Gorham 4–5; Vallone, *Disciplines* 96). In fact, the words that Strickland uses most often to describe her protagonist imply precisely the opposite: "untameable," "unconquerable," characterized by "wayward will," Alda is "wild, ardent, and impetuous" (62). Alda's body also transgresses the boundaries of passive, delicate femininity: "although she had scarcely attained her full height, [Alda] was already of a tall and commanding figure. ... Her complexion was fair and brilliant. ... Her eyes were blue and sparkling" (63). Most notably, Alda refuses to resign herself to her fate; instead of submitting to the orders of her new Roman masters, "[s]he positively refused to perform any of the daily tasks that were allotted to her, and opposed useless resistance and passionate taunts to the authority of those under whose absolute power she found herself placed" (11). When her fellow slaves pull her hair, "the enraged and insulted stranger became furious, and resented this personal attack in so prompt and fierce a manner, that her persecutors fled precipitately from the apartment, and hastened to lay a formal complaint of her conduct before their lady" (6–7). Alda speaks up for herself, refuses to submit to tyrannical authority, and physically defends herself from attack; her lack of feminine resignation, and in particular the anger with which she responds to her situation (she dreams not of escape, but of murdering her captors with her own hands), suggests a dangerous alternate construction of femininity, a femininity which must be tamed if Victorian gender norms are to remain comfortably in place.

Strickland knows that such norms dictate that she lead her reader to condemn Alda's unfeminine behavior; Alda's "resistance, passionate reproaches, and revilings," her narrator opines, serve only "to aggravate her already desperate case" (15) after she shatters the household gods of Marcus Laelius, the patriarch of the family who owns her as a slave. Yet even while condemning her heroine, Strickland cannot help but admire the very transgressive behavior that she has created as a negative exemplar: "It is true she endured with the most unshrinking fortitude the infliction of Marcus Laelius's vengeance; and refusing to make the slightest concession, she suffered sternly and silently" (15) when she is beaten for her behavior.[26] Readers might expect a qualifying "but" to follow this "It is true," yet none comes, and the narrator leaves open the possibility that readers may

---

[26]   Alda's willingness to endure physical pain and punishment, in this scene and others throughout the novel, may suggest links to the ascetic Catholicism that was so reviled by anti-Catholic novelists of the period. Such asceticism functions in these novels, according to Miriam Burstein, as a moral threat to evangelical Protestantism, in particular to its constructions of femininity (*Narrating* 132–4). Burstein suggests that asceticism posed less of a threat to High Church Anglicans than to evangelicals; given her High Church beliefs (and accusations that she was a Catholic sympathizer [Laurence, 137; Petersen, 374]), it is not surprising to find Strickland more sympathetic to this vision of spirituality than her anti-Catholic peers.

admire Alda's "unshrinking fortitude" more than they disapprove of her obstinate, aggressive, and, by Victorian norms, clearly unfeminine behavior.

Strickland shields herself from criticism for constructing such an unfeminine heroine by linking Alda's behavior to her place in historical time. Eschewing a construction of a trans-historical, universal femininity, and drawing instead upon the relatively recent historiographical concept of chronism in gender, Strickland suggests that Alda's unfeminine behavior stems from the culture in which she was raised. The ancient Britons, unlike the Romans, are "uncivilized"; as the narrator notes, Alda's "manners partook largely of the semi-barbarism of her country" (62). Alda acts the way she does because barbaric femininity is different from the femininity found in civilized societies such as Rome (and, of course, as her readers' contemporary England), Strickland asserts. Alda's behavior, readers may be expected to conclude, could never be tolerated in Victorian society, but it is perfectly understandable in a girl raised under far different conditions.

Yet this shield becomes complicated by the issue of British nationalism, a nationalism that takes pride in equating the ancient Britons with freedom from tyrannical rule. Throughout the novel, references to the Britons—whether by Alda or the narrator—inevitably include some version of the word "free." The narrator describes Alda's life before her capture as characterized by "freedom"; Alda describes her time in Briton as a period when she could exercise "my soul's free impulses" (18); Alda's fellow-slave describes her people as "your free-spirited, hardy, and valiant countrymen" (21). Alda makes the connection between Britishness and freedom explicit when she exclaims after escaping from captivity, "I am again a Briton, for I am free!" (152). Strickland here clearly links Alda with Boadicea, and earlier British interpretations of the Boadicea story, which, after disappearing from historical accounts during the Middle Ages, reemerged during the sixteenth century to function as a trope of British patriotism and a prefiguration of the rule of Queen Elizabeth I. Eighteenth-century poets such as James Thomson ("Liberty") and William Cowper ("Boadicea") extended the trope, crafting an idealized Boadicea who functioned allegorically, as a symbol of British national pride, rather than as an individual historical woman (Fraser, *Boudicea's* 324–5). Alda's "Britishness" may be viewed negatively, as the cause of her unfeminine behavior, but, with its links to British patriotism, it also has clear positive connotations, connotations which make it difficult for the reader to condemn Alda's behavior; to condemn Alda's outspokenness and rebelliousness would also be to condemn the tradition that equates Britishness with freedom.

Additionally, while freedom in these examples clearly refers to freedom from enslavement, and from a despotic political system, Strickland intriguingly expands the definition of "Britishness" to include the freedom of British women's bodies. In Briton, Alda followed the chase with her brothers, an activity that led not only to "uncontrolled" behavior and "unbroken spirits," but also to a "wild vivacity of health" (136). While such adjectives throw a degree of suspicion over the means by which such British female health is achieved, other descriptions, ones that contrast the physical condition of women in Rome with those in Briton, suggest that civilization may not in fact always be preferable when it comes to the health of women's bodies. After Alda's enslavement, the narrator notes, only the friendship of a fellow slave "lightened the weight of bonds, otherwise intolerable to the free-born denizen of a land where the restraints and sedentary habits *imposed* upon females in a civilized state of society were unknown" (135, emphasis added). Alda makes a poor nurse, inexperienced as she is "in any kind of sickness, especially those languishing disorders which are too frequent among delicate females whose constitutions have been enervated by sedentary employments and the indulgences usual in civilized nations, then perfectly unknown to the robust and active women of her own country" (100). The dictates of femininity that civilized society "imposes" on women are clearly detrimental to their physical well-being, Strickland opines. Strickland's celebration of active, physical female bodies here is far ahead of her time; the muscular Christianity of Charles Kingsley and Thomas Hughes, which argued for a commitment to physical health and manliness for Christian boys and men, would not appear until the 1850s, while similar support for girls' physical activity would not become common until the 1880s (Avery, *Best Type* 267–70).

Using her knowledge of the past, Strickland, like the "soft constructionists," takes issue with the construction of a universal, unchanging femininity; instead, she suggests that different societies construct different visions of femininity. But she differs from those soft constructionists by suggesting that changes in gender over time may not always be signs of progress for women. Yet Strickland writes not for the wild and free Britons of old, but for the Victorian Britons of her own day, Britons as "civilized" as the women of ancient Rome. And she writes for girls, or for those who would buy books in hopes of educating their girls. Writing a novel charged with the consciousness of the complete difference between past and present human nature, as one finds in the historical fiction of Walter Scott or Maria Edgeworth, becomes problematic when one's audience is not adults, but impressionable girls. Strickland must balance her commitment to historicism with her desire to appeal to her reading public (or to that reading public's parents). And thus Strickland makes her protagonist conform, at least in part, to Victorian constructions of femininity. Alda must change, must learn to be "civilized"; in particular, she must accept the civilizing principles of Christianity. In order to learn her proper role, Alda must first meet someone who already embodies it: a good Christian girl. That girl is Susanna, a fellow-slave in Marcus Laelius's household, the only one to befriend the brash, outspoken Alda.

Strickland constructs Susanna, a Judean convert to Christianity, as Alda's physical opposite; not tall and commanding, but "rather below the middle height, of a fragile and somewhat bending form, though elegantly proportioned. Her complexion was pale and 'darkly delicate.' Her features of the true Eastern cast, and her soft black eyes were full of melancholy sweetness whenever she raised them from the ground" (63). Susanna's meek demeanor reflects her mild, patient temperament: "Susanna was composed, dignified, and full of feminine softness and tenderness. ... [she] united all the graceful accomplishments and polished manners of an Eastern female of high rank, with great learning, deep reflection, and a benevolence and universal kindness which were founded on principle, and improved by religion" (62). She also embodies a key trait of Victorian femininity: selflessness. "Susanna looked for no other reward than the approbation of her own conscience, and the pleasure of doing good," the narrator tells us early in the novel (8), confirming her assessment later when Susanna, after nursing her apparently dying mistress back to health, asks not for remuneration, but only to be able to nurse Alda as a reward (60–61). Susanna, unlike Alda, eschews revenge; when she encounters the uncle who sold her into slavery, now a beggar on the street, she greets him not with opprobrium, but with pity: "I thought not of myself at that dreadful moment; I thought only of the wretched, wretched man before me" (125). Also unlike Alda, Susanna resists speaking up. Although she asserts that if it had been "of the slightest service to the cause of Christianity" she would have declared her commitment to its tenets once in Rome, she keeps her affiliation quiet. Above all, Susanna demonstrates the very resignation to her fate, and submissiveness to authority (even unjustified authority) that is so inimical to Alda. "Believe me, where no sinful compliance is required, submission is not only the wisest but the most dignified course of proceeding, especially in a case like ours, where resistance is perfectly unavailing," Susanna counsels Alda (32). The narrator aptly terms her Christian exemplar "a ministering angel" (28); the angel in this Roman house, Susanna embodies both the principles of Christianity and of "dignified" Victorian femininity that Alda so lacks.

Significantly, Alda first indicates that she is open to reform when her model of proper feminine Christian behavior is taken from her: Susanna, who has neglected her other duties in order to nurse the British captive, is forbidden to attend her further. Alda must undergo a near-death experience to prepare her for conversion. The Druidic belief in reincarnation, which once led her to wish for her demise, offers no comfort to one actually faced with death, the narrator insists; instead, the deathly-ill Alda, recalling Susanna's stories of Christian doctrine, terrifies herself by dreaming a Dante-like vision of Christian hell. When she awakens, Susanna is at her side, ready not only to nurse her back to health, but also to suffuse her with a desire for Christianity. Alda agrees to give up her Druid beliefs, beliefs that offer a multiplicity of futures, in favor of the binary construction of a future in either Heaven or Hell.

Alda's conversion to Christianity leads her to redefine anger; no longer just resistance to unjust treatment, anger is now seen as sin: "the whole tenor of her life now appeared to have been one course of pride, anger, hatred, revenge, obstinacy, and ingratitude" (45). Yet while Alda's beliefs may have changed, her behavior, significantly, has not; her religious conversion is not accompanied by a concurrent conversion to submissive, other-directed femininity. In fact, the first words in dialogue we hear after Alda's "conversion" are words of execration against her Roman mistress; her first desire is to pray to this newly discovered God to avenge her injuries, both on that mistress and on the Roman people for the "calamities with which they have afflicted my own country" (55).

In fact, what Alda finds most appealing about Christianity is not the submission to fate and circumstance that it demands from its believers, but rather the heroic role it allows a believer, in the midst of nonbelievers, to adopt. For, as readers familiar with early Christianity would surely know, Christians in the midst of pagan Rome could be called on at any time to defend their religious beliefs with their very lives. As the narrator notes, Susanna's proselytizing succeeds with Alda because the Christianity she professes can force even the meekly feminine Susanna to act with masculine physical courage: "Nor did the precepts of the Christian faith lose aught of their persuasive power in flowing from the lips of one who was willing not only to uphold them in her life, but, if required, to testify them to death itself unshrinkingly, and to seal the sincerity of her profession with her blood, if such a test should be demanded of her" (49). Though readers may at first draw the conclusion that it is the strength of Susanna's submissiveness that makes her proselytizing "persuasive"—she is ready to make the ultimate act of submission, sacrificing her life—the narrative makes clear that to Alda, raised in a culture that values physical courage and strength, the appeal is not submission, but the excitement of being tested, of performing a heroic role, of asserting rather than subsuming self. Susanna warns Alda against "presumptuous self-sufficiency," reminding her of Peter's betrayal of Christ despite his brave avowals of steadfastness, when Alda declares she is ready and willing to go to prison, or to die, for her religion (67). Yet Alda goes on to assert her sense of a heroic self even more strongly: "Peter feared tortures, and dreaded death," Alda opines, adding in a declaration that asserts her superiority to the disciple of Christ, "I should not hesitate to face both" (67). Susanna further tests the new convert by showing her the sight of Christians being burned alive; still, Alda does not shrink, instead linking such acts to a code of manly bravery: "Their choice would, I trust, have been my choice, for they have chosen gloriously" she tells Susanna (71). With their masculine martial connotations, "glorious" and "victorious," the words Alda invokes most often to describe her religious belief, suggest that the Christianity that makes her eyes "glisten" and her cheeks "glow" is not one of passivity, but an active declaration of heroic selfhood.

Alda's body conveys not only her heroism, but also her passion for Susanna. With no family members to rely on, the two captive girls turn to one another for both for emotional support and for physical comfort: "Kneeling side by side beneath the starry canopy of heaven, with their arms fondly entwined together, the young friends offered up their mutual praises to the gracious God" (71); "[Susanna] folded Alda to her bosom, and kissed her several times with great affection" (126); "[Alda] flung herself into the arms of her friend and declared she could not leave her" (131). Alda is Susanna's "beloved"; Susanna is Alda's "treasure," her "heart" (132, 138). Such passionate descriptions of friendship between girls/women may strike us today as signs of latent lesbianism, and hence a transgressive disruption of heteronormative Victorian femininity. But Sharon Marcus suggests that we should be cautious about jumping to such a conclusion when reading about female friendships in Victorian novels. In *Between Women*, Marcus argues that emotional and physical friendships between girls and women such as the one Strickland creates between Alda and Susanna were common in the life-writing of Victorian girls and women, and could coexist and even complement Victorian heteronormativity. Not only were passionate friendships between women tolerated by Victorian society, they were actively viewed as good training for wifehood (39). Intriguingly, while public displays of physical affection were deemed not respectable when performed by lovers or spouses, girl friends could "openly exchange material tokens of their affection and exhibit themselves giving and receiving the caresses and kisses of friendship" (58). Because the Victorians did not see homosexual and heterosexual desire as binaries, Marcus argues, they had little reason to repress a female homoeroticism openly expressed by girls and women in their diaries, biographies, autobiographies, and letters. While the physical and emotional affection that characterizes Alda and Susanna's friendship is not common in twentieth or twenty-first-century writing, Victorian readers would find little in it to object to, for, as Marcus argues, Victorians envisioned relationships between women as "central to lives organized around men" (19).

In her analysis of Victorian novels, Marcus suggests that in focusing on the prevalence of the marriage plot, critics have overlooked plot of "female amity" that accompanies it, a plot in which female friendship serves as both a precursor to, and a catalyst for one or both friends' heterosexual marriage plots (Chapter 2). If Strickland's depiction of Alda and Susanna's passionate connection to one another coexisted with a plot that saw one or both of them happily married to a fellow Christian by novel's end, Marcus's theory would suggest that the novel's depiction of female friendship functions not in opposition to, but in support of, heteronormative patriarchy. Yet instead of redirecting Alda toward heterosexual domesticity (the goal, as Lynne Vallone points out, of traditional conduct novels for girls, and as Marcus points out, of the majority of Victorian novels for adults), Susanna's Christianity links the two girls in Christian sisterhood, a sisterhood that for them takes the place of all family ties, past and future: "By degrees [Susanna] became so dear to the young Briton that she appeared to supply to her the place of all she had lost, and more than she had lost; for no tie of kindred that Alda had ever possessed had been so truly precious to her as the friendship of her generous fellow-captive" (30). Both girls' fathers have died, and their mothers are never mentioned. Most surprisingly, no British suitors eager to rescue Alda from her enslavement wait in the wings; Susanna's cousin, to whom she was betrothed, dies the death of a Christian martyr before the girls meet. Rather than functioning as a relationship congruent with Victorian heteronormativity, then, Alda and Susanna's relationship truly does function as a transgressive rejection of the Victorian marriage plot.

Given the strength of the bond of love between Alda and Susanna, and the dangerous alternative it presents to the dictates of heteronormative domesticity, readers will not be surprised to find that by mid-novel, Strickland kills off her protagonist's new "sister." Susanna's death is not the heroic martyrdom she once envisioned; though the narrator asserts that despite her fragility, Susanna would have been steadfast if tested, Strickland offers her embodiment of docile feminine Christianity a different fate—Susanna dies of a wasting illness. Thus Strickland appears to kill two birds with one stone: by taking Susanna away from Alda, she removes the temptation of an alternative to heterosexual domesticity, while simultaneously offering Susanna up as a model of a truly feminine Christian death, an Evangelical martyr whose "good death" functions to teach those who remain behind to change their wayward ways, and to follow her docile, submissive example.

Readers might be forgiven for expecting, then, to find an Alda tamed, transformed, and ready to meet a likely male mate after the death of her bosom friend. Yet Strickland evokes the genre expectations of Evangelical conduct fiction, and Christian girl fiction, only to confound them. Susanna's death leads Alda not to greater acts of self-abasement, but to the most obvious act of self-assertion: Alda, "resolved to submit to her injuries no longer," plans and executes her escape from captivity, fleeing into the Roman countryside alone and with apparent ease (147). Unlike Hofland's Adelaide, or *The Beautiful Page*'s Matilda, Alda wears no boy's disguise during her flight; to cover up her femininity would be to consign bravery, courage, to the realm of the masculine. And such a consignment is precisely the opposite of what Strickland strives to achieve. For Strickland works precisely to construct, under the guise of historical gender chronism, a space for female bravery, a bravery that looks remarkably like the bravery of a male hero of her own historical time: "Young, active, and vigorous as she was both in mind and body, accustomed to hardships, fatigues, and dangers, and regardless of them all, she pursued her course with the same sagacity, courage, and celerity that a North American Indian exerts when traveling in a country with which he is unacquainted" (151).

Susanna's death thus functions in much the same way that Helen Burns's does in Charlotte Brontë's *Jane Eyre*; by first evoking, then killing off, the Christian moral guide, each author opens up a space for her protagonist to resist many of the dictates of submissive feminine Christianity that both Susanna and Helen (and their texts) hold forth as exemplary. Alda follows her initial act of resistance—escape—by a second—rejection of domestic heterosexuality typical of the Victorian marriage plot. One day into her flight, Alda encounters a group of robbers, several of whom offer to marry her. One man tells her "I think I will take you to wife, for I have long been in need of a spouse to cook for me, make my garments, and perform a hundred other little services which I am weary of doing for myself" (157). But Alda refuses to adopt the role of subservient wife, even when a more likely suitor, the group's leader, Mainos, a Briton who, like Alda, has escaped enslavement, appears. A flight into forced domesticity is not the role Strickland has in mind for her heroine. Thus, Strickland transforms Mainos into a father figure rather than a lover (he was a friend of her father), and allows her protagonist to refuse both his, and a local Christian community's, offers of shelter. Instead, Alda asserts her power, her desire, her self: what she most wants is to live alone. Mainos agrees to build her a cottage, and to allow her to "enjoy perfect leisure and retirement, and occupy herself as she thought proper" (165). Alda's resistance, then, leads not to a demand that she submit to domestic subservience, but instead to the chance to decide her own fate, to choose her own course, to live and to think for herself.

In fact, heterosexual domesticity fails throughout the novel to serve the needs of women. Susanna was to have married Azor, her cousin, but after her father's conversion to Christianity and his death by stoning for espousing his beliefs, Susanna's uncle breaks off the engagement, steals Susanna's inheritance, and, in the ultimate perversion of domestic ties, sells his niece into slavery. Azor cannot rescue his betrothed, for he, like Susanna's father, is killed for his religious beliefs. Susanna imagines being "united" with Azor after death, but there is no earthly reward of domesticity for this Christian couple.

The same falling apart of heterosexual domesticity reappears in the story of Laelia, the headstrong Roman girl who "owns" Susanna and Alda. A "young, handsome, and victorious" Roman general asks for her hand in marriage, but then abruptly breaks off his suit after Laelia's father is denounced to the Emperor. In breaking his marriage contract, Laelia's suitor has not the "slightest consideration for the feelings of his intended bride"; instead of defending his bride-to-be and her father from a false charge, he "congratulated himself on his good fortune in not being irretrievably connected with the family of a proscribed man" (198–9). In the hegemonic construction of Victorian girlhood, as Lynne Vallone notes, "When the girl is 'successfully' integrated into the socially sanctioned place already prepared for her—'no place like home'—the story ends happily" (Vallone 156). Yet in Strickland's novel, the reward of a home, of heteronormative domesticity, continually proves inaccessible, even undesirable, to Strickland's three girl protagonists.

As an alternative to heteronormativity, Strickland once again holds forth a vision of sisterhood, the sisterhood that appeared to have been repudiated with the death of Susanna. For soon after moving into her pastoral retreat, Alda is greeted by the sight of her old enemies, Marcus Laelius and his daughter Laelia. The arrival of the ragged, disheveled, and terrified Romans allows Strickland to demonstrate that Alda has exchanged her desire for revenge for a true spirit of Christian charity; instead of killing her former "owners" with her own hands, as she had once longed to do, Alda offers them shelter and aid. Such a providential turn of plot thus allows Strickland to conform to the dictates of the conduct novel for girls—desire must be exchanged for duty. Yet simultaneously, this plot development provides cover for more subversive work, by allowing Strickland to present the alternative of sisterly, rather than spousal, devotion. Just as she killed off Alda's father in her novel's opening, she once again does away with the patriarch, allowing Marcus Laelius to die within a few pages of his arrival from wounds suffered during his escape. When Laelia laments that her father's death leaves her with no ties to any living person, Alda objects, telling her "you have a sister here…. Let us therefore love one another, even as He has loved us, and become united in his service" (212–13). Being "united in his service" encompasses not only spiritual connection, but also physical connection: "Laelia sunk onto her bosom, forgetful of every former difference between them, 'and wept, oh how familiarly!' … Alda folder her arms about her, and mingled her tears with hers" (213). Strickland constructs this sisterly connection as a triumph of Christianity over both ties to the self, and ties to country, ties that work to separate rather than unify: "from that hour these heretofore jarring spirits ceased to remember every hostile distinction of national animosity and wrathful feeling of pride and prejudice that had inflamed their hearts with mutual anger and hatred against each other, and became as sisters indeed. The ties of consanguinity never cemented a firmer bond of friendship than that which was formed between the twain" (213). God may be the ultimate patriarch of the Christian family, but in this narrative, no earthly patriarch stands in his place; sisterly bonds, not fatherly or husbandly ones, prove the strongest and most sustaining for adolescent girls.

Strickland attempts to avert the potential for readerly rejection of Alda's non-normative experience by suggesting that her heroine, despite her rejection of domesticity, has in fact adopted the construction of femininity that typically accompanies a conduct novel protagonist's "reward" of heterosexual domesticity: "Alda's heart had been softened by her own sufferings, and amended by the divine spirit of that religion which inculcates universal charity and goodwill to all mankind" (179–80). Yet despite Alda's purported "softening," her adoption of Christianity does not bar her from taking actions that are motivated by desires other than charitable ones. In fact, Alda's Christianity serves to function as an opportunity for Strickland's heroine to practice the very public heroism that her adoption of "authentic" femininity would seem to preclude. When Roman soldiers arrive at her cottage, looking for Laelia and her father, Alda is "[p]erfectly fearless of any ill consequence that might result to herself from the part she had taken" in hiding Laelia and her father (186). Instead of telling a lie, or engaging in subterfuge, unchristian acts both, Alda "boldly answers" when asked by the soldiers if she has seen Laelia and her father, "that she would rather die than betray the unfortunate objects of their pursuit" (188). That she answers in the "barbarous provincial dialect of the Iceni," her native tongue, makes her comment at once unintelligible to the soldiers and symbolic to the reader: Alda has not given up her courageous British spirit, despite her adoption of feminizing Christian principles.

Strickland continues to construct situations in which Alda must simultaneously demonstrate Christian submission and British courage. When Roman soldiers interrupt a Christian gathering of worship, Alda, unlike many of her co-religionists, refuses to flee, making her more heroic than Christ's apostles, the "terror-stricken 12" who "provide[d] for their own safety in flight, when they beheld their heavenly Master in the hands of remorseless and murderous men" (226). "Not insensible of the peril, yet perfectly unruffled by its terrors," Alda calls "Courage, my sister!" when Laelia shrinks from the sight of Mainos, slain while fighting off the Romans (227). When the soldiers force their Christian captives on foot back to Rome, Alda supports the body of the ill Laelia for miles. In one of the many parallels in the novel, the opening procession of British slaves through the streets of the capital is reenacted, this time with Christians, rather than Britons, as its featured performers. Laelia fears entering Rome as "public gazing-stock"; being put on public display is a degradation worse than death (232). But Strickland, through Alda, rejects such concern for public opinion and public scrutiny. Alda, rather than shrinking from her forced public performance, seems rather instead to glory in it: "This day I shall enter Rome a second time as a prisoner, and a public spectacle withal, and also in a triumph; but this time the triumph will be mine, for I go to obtain the high prize of my calling,—the glorious crown of a Christian martyr; and I shall tread her streets with the exulting step of a victor" (233). Alda's martial imagery evokes not an image of a submissive feminine Christianity, but rather the muscular Christianity that would emerge in texts for boys and men in the second half of the nineteenth century (Hall, Vance). A Christian commitment to health and heroism (typically constructed as manliness), Strickland radically asserts, need not be confined to boys, but should be open to adolescents of both sexes.

And not just to one exceptional adolescent girl. For Alda is not the exception who proves the rule, the woman who, by acting "above her Sex," suggests that she is no woman at all, but simply the "man in petticoats" common to male accounts of women's history, accounts that so angered Mary Astell in *The Christian Religion*. For Alda has a double, a sister: Laelia. At the beginning of the novel, Laelia, like Alda, was characterized by strong emotion, headstrong will, and imperious command. Laelia's fall from power into illness and slavery tempers her character far more than it does Alda's: "Laelia, whose recent illness and general delicacy of habit rendered her very unequal to the fatigue of performing such a journey on foot, suffered much," the narrator tells us, but goes on to construct a vision of courage that includes not only acting up and speaking out, but also a quieter fortitude: "she suffered silently, and endeavoured to bear up against bodily weakness with a degree of resolution that was almost heroic, unaccustomed as she had been to any sort of hardship or privation" (229). The qualifying "almost" here does not function to diminish Laelia's type of heroism, but rather registers the difficulty in classifying such typically feminine actions as "bearing up silently" under the rubric of the typically masculine label "heroic."

Laelia's heroism may be different in kind than Alda's, but in the novel's climax, both girls prove themselves equally worthy of the label.[27] While several

---

[27]   Strickland suggests the breadth of her definition of female heroism by her brief references to two other famed women of first century Rome: Agrippina and Pomponia Graecina. "The granddaughter of Augustus, the virtuous and unfortunate Agrippina" (87), the loyal wife of the murdered Germanicus, Agrippina the Elder embodied, according to Tacitus, *puducitia*, the combination of fertility and devoted motherhood valued by the Romans. But she also participated actively in her husband's military career, and assumed a leading role in Roman opposition politics after the death of her husband, actions which Tacitus, and many subsequent historians, looked upon with suspicion, but which contemporary feminist historians of classical women have highlighted. Given her characterization of Alda, it seems far from unlikely that Strickland found both aspects of Agrippina's character appealing.

Pomponia Graecina, the wife of Plautius, actually features as a character in the novel, a Roman convert to Christianity who befriends her fellow Christian Susanna. In Tacitus's account, Pomponia was accused of foreign superstition. According to ancient Roman precedent, she was tried in front of her husband and relatives; Plautius pronounced her not

of their fellow Christians cowardly accept the Romans' offer of life in exchange for apostasy, Alda and Laelia reject it with dignity, choosing instead the public death of a Christian martyr: being thrown to the lions in the Roman amphitheatre. Even when the sight of their loveliness moves Nero to ask if they will purchase their own deliverance by offering an act of adoration to his own statue, both Alda and Laelia spurn him: "'Vain and presumptuous fellow-mortal, no!' was the simultaneous reply of the intrepid friends" (249). No male force rides to the rescue of the two damsels in distress, as would happen in so many male-authored adventure stories in the second half of the nineteenth century; instead, unified by both sisterhood and Christianity, Alda and Laelia die the deaths of heroes, together, triumphant:[28]

> The young Briton surveyed the infuriated [lions] with a fearless look; then extending her hands toward Laelia, she exclaimed, "Shall we not die together, my friend?"
>
> Leila sunk upon her bosom, and buried her face among the folds of her garments.
>
> The next moment the life-blood of the British and the Roman martyrs flowed in a mingled tide, as those once bitter enemies expired in each other's arms united in the tenderest bonds of love, and their enfranchised spirits entered at the same moment into that joy which passeth all human understanding. (250–51)

In describing perhaps the most famous Evangelical novel for children in the early nineteenth century, Mary Martha Sherwood's *The History of the Fairchild Family* (1818), Lynne Vallone argues that the book's girl protagonists "... will travel toward piety and fragility as they grow into Christian wives and mothers, a condition that represses the general barbarity of the child, creating, ultimately, characters of feminine exaltedness" (79). Strickland surely constructs a vision of feminine exaltedness at the end of her novel of Christian conversion; yet by rejecting both the demand that girl characters must always be rewarded with heterosexual domesticity, and that growth in girlish piety must always be accompanied by a fall into becomingly feminine fragility, Strickland disrupts the normative narrative of Victorian literary girlhood, drawing on gender chronism to argue for a more expansive definition of femininity than the gender norms of her day would allow. That Strickland's novel of historical feminine bravery went

---

guilty. Like contemporary historians, Strickland reads Pomponia's "foreign superstitions" as an embrace of Christianity; she furthers Tacitus's account by suggesting that her husband, after her trial, requested that she practice her religion in secret. Pomponia is not only famed for her Christianity, but for her sisterly loyalty; she dressed in mourning for 40 years, not for a lost husband, but a lost friend: Julia, persecuted by Messalina and Claudius.

[28] The narrator presents Alda and Laelia's deaths as a triumph, but they also might be read in the context of nineteenth-century novels for adults that end with the deaths of their woman-girl protagonists, a pattern of killing off heroines for whom authors cannot conceive socially possible endings: think *Anna Karenina*, *The Awakening*, or *The Mill on the Floss*.

through only one English edition, while Barbara Hofland's far more constrained *Adelaide* was reprinted at least six times, suggests that the nineteenth-century British juvenile book market was far more open to a heroine only indulging in masculine heroism while wearing easily put-aside pants than to one who acted boldly, outspokenly, courageously while in full female attire. Young readers would have to wait more than a century before girl protagonists who could both wear their petticoats and embrace adventurous identities without restraint would become the norm, rather than the exception, in their historical fictions.

Epilogue:
The End of an Adventure?

Two lads, both aged 13, in different schools, accept as their favorite book, "The Swiss Family Robinson." One writes that he likes it best because "it informs you what to do when shipwrecked;" the other "because it shows you how to get on when shipwrecked, and have no civilized people to help you."

"My favorite book," declares a young lady of 16, "is 'The Scottish Chiefs' by Jane Porter. I like it best because it gives you such a good idea of what used to go on in the days of such heroes as Wallace and Bruce, and because it is so graphic a description, that you can imagine the scenes to yourself as you read."

—Edward Salmon's *Juvenile Literature As It Is* (1888)[1]

In 1884, Charles Welsh sent out a circular to schools for boys and girls in England, asking students to answer questions about their reading preferences. Though Welsh also asked about poetry and magazine reading, the bulk of his questions focused on the novel: "What is your favorite book, and why do you like it best?" "Who is your favorite author?" "Which of his books do you like best?" "What other writers of fiction do you like?" Welsh received responses from 790 boys and more than a thousand girls aged 11 to 19. His colleague, Edward Salmon, undertook the work of tabulating the results of what may be the first poll of child readers' tastes and interests, issuing his findings in the introduction to his book, *Juvenile Literature As It Is*, published in London in 1888.

Salmon's introduction includes not only statistics, but also many quotations from the letters written by actual children in response to the broader questions posed by Welsh's survey. As the quotations above suggest, two of the primary goals of early nineteenth-century children's book writers, goals which would have seemed novel to eighteenth-century readers, had by 1888 become taken for granted by young readers: the idea that ordinary, rather than ideal, characters, characters such as the young Swiss Robinsons, can function as examples upon which to model action and behavior, and the idea that history, or its counterpart, historical fiction, should give a reader not only historical facts, but also the opportunity to imagine "what used to go on in the days" of those who lived in the past. Sympathetic identification with ordinary protagonists, and with the people of history, are no longer novel literary experiments, but the very grounds upon which young readers make their decisions about what texts they find most appealing.

If, by 1888, sympathetic identification had come to be taken for granted as a requirement for youthful reader engagement, other innovations that accompanied its emergence had fallen by the wayside. The mediating presence of parents

---

[1] Salmon, 17, 26.

who function to defuse the threat of the ordinary, mischievous child, ensuring that amusing playfulness, rather than original sin, lay at the heart of this new construction of childhood, are rarely deemed necessary by the end of the century, at least in the realm of adventure. While parents still play a large role in popular domestic narratives cited as favorites by girls (such as Charlotte Yonge's *The Daisy Chain* and Louisa May Alcott's *Little Women*), the adventure novels favored by Welch and Salmon's respondents (with the one exception of *Swiss Family Robinson*) prove remarkably free from an adult mediating presence. With the wane of Evangelicalism by the mid-Victorian period, the misbehavior of the ordinary child no longer seemed as threatening as it had earlier in the century; instead, such behavior became accepted as natural. No longer a sign of evil, mischievous child behavior now did not require the mediating presence of adults to contain its subversive potential. The dictate that the majority of twentieth- and twenty-first century children's writers take as a given—get the parents out of the way so that adventure can occur—was made possible only because parent characters in children's adventure novels in the early nineteenth century had acted as midwives for the adventurous child's birth. Having now served their purpose, such parental guarantors could safely retire from the field.

While the connection between parents and adventure, as embodied in the early nineteenth-century family robinsonade, had disappeared by the end of the nineteenth century, the early adventure novel's investment in landed gentry class ideologies, questioned by Harriet Martineau in *The Peasant and the Prince*, continued well into the Victorian period and beyond. While novels featuring values that throughout the Victorian period increasingly became labeled "middle class" grew in popularity, middle class adventurers continued to compete for reader interest with protagonists of far loftier class affiliations: Scott's Ivanhoe; Kingsley's Amyas and Frank Leigh (*Westward Ho!*); Yonge's Sir Guy Morville (*The Heir of Redclyffe*). Though originally written for adults, adventure novels such as Scott's and Kingsley's had by the late Victorian period been consigned to the realm of "children's classics."[2] Like their adult counterparts, historical romances and fictions written specifically for a juvenile audience continued to feature noble adventurers and to assert the primacy not of middle-class, but of landed gentry values well into the twentieth century.

By relegating works that promulgated landed gentry values to the schoolroom, adults could disavow such values as "childish" while simultaneously ensuring that those very values would be the ones taught to the youth of England. Just as John Ruskin learned from Scott "a most sincere love of kings and a dislike of everybody who attempted to disobey them," so, too, would well-read British children imbibe a sincere regard for landed gentry hierarchies (qtd in Beiderwell and McCormick 167). Genteel adults who still longed for the dual class structure of benevolent gentry and the grateful peasantry they succored, a social structure that the growing industrialization of Victorian England would push aside, could both mourn its

---

[2]   See Beiderwell and McCormick for a discussion of the transformation of one such adult adventure writer, Sir Walter Scott, into a writer suitable for children only.

passing and reengage with it nostalgically through their own children's reading. Or the persistence of landed gentry ideologies may be a sign that children's fiction of the period might be markedly less "middle class" than earlier historians have acknowledged. Only with the appearance of Geoffrey Trease's *Bows Against the Barons* (1934), and *Cue for Treason* (1940), did juvenile historical fiction begin to follow Harriet Martineau's early lead, featuring peasants, farmers, and "ordinary folk," rather than nobles and gentry, as protagonists (Collins and Graham 10–11). Trease's motivation for writing—a "revulsion against the sentimental romanticism then pervading historical fiction"—was a charge that might just as easily have been leveled against historical fictions for children written a hundred years earlier as against those being written in his own day (qtd in Hunt 209). Significantly, Trease's first historical novel was published not by a conventional commercial publisher, but by the "left-wing" publishers Lawrence and Wishart (Hunt 209). Even in the 1930s, portraying the aristocracy as brutal and corrupt in a book intended specifically for children, as did Trease in *Barons*, would prove deeply threatening. Novels set in the present, or in the near past, such as Alcott's *Little Women*, Susan Warner's *The Wide, Wide World*, and Dinah Mulock Craik's *John Halifax, Gentleman*, might promote middle-class values safely within a domestic sphere, but within the genre of adventure, particularly the sub-genre of historical fiction, questioning gentry hierarchy and privilege in the way that Harriet Martineau did in *The Peasant and the Prince* would continue to seem radical within the realm of children's literature for nearly another century.

What also seems radical is to suggest that boys and girls might equally be attracted to the genre of adventure. In the early decades of the nineteenth century, as my analyses in the previous chapters suggests, the lines between girls' books and boys' books had not yet been so rigidly drawn; a Captain Marryat might write a deeply religious book, despite setting it on a deserted island, while an Agnes Strickland might write a historical novel, despite placing it within the generic context of conversion fiction. But by Salmon's time, the boundaries between girls' reading and boys' reading had become more pronounced, so much so that Salmon felt the need to tabulate the responses sent in by boys separately from those sent in by girls, presenting his results in separate sections: "What Boys Read" and "What Girls Read."[3] Though the top boys' vote-getter is Dickens, the

---

[3] **Boys' top 10 authors:**

C. Dickens (223 votes)
W.H. Kingston (179)
Sir W. Scott (128)
Jules Verne (114)
Captain Marryat (102)
R.M. Ballantyne (67)
H. Ainsworth (61)
Shakespeare (44)
Mayne Reid (33)
Lord Lytton (32)

Boys' top 10 books:

Robinson Crusoe (43)
Swiss Family Robinson (24)
Pickwick Papers (22)
Ivanhoe (20)
Boy's Own Annual (17)
The Bible (15)
Tom Brown's Schooldays (15)
Valentine Vox (13)
Vice Versa (12)
St Winifred's, or The World of School (11)

other top 10 vote-winners among boys (with the one exception of Shakespeare) are all what we today would term "adventure writers," or, at the least, writers of historical romances: W.H.G. Kingston, Walter Scott, Jules Verne, Captain Marryat, R.M. Ballantyne, Mayne Reid, Ainsworth, Lord Lytton (14). The most popular book, however, was written by none of the above, but rather, by their progenitor: Defoe's *Robinson Crusoe*, with 43 votes, tops the boys' list (15). In their explanations for why the boys like certain books, Salmon explains, the most frequent reasons focus on action: "because it is interesting" or "because it is full of adventures" (17).

Salmon finds the boys' responses rather predictable. Given Diana Loxley's work on the ways that imperialistic fiction had been championed as appropriate school reading in the latter nineteenth century, we, too, cannot but expect such responses (Loxley 83–5). But when Salmon turns to the girls' reading preferences, he finds the results "surprising" (21). Their list of favorite authors, far from featuring only the expected "girls" writers, includes four of the same authors who appeared on the boys' list, and few of the most highly regarded girls' writers. Dickens and Shakespeare appear, unsurprisingly, but so do Scott and Lytton. Girls, it would appear, are far more catholic than boys in their reading tastes, wanting not just domestic stories (Charlotte Yonge), but also fairy tales (Andersen), literary realism (George Eliot), and the adventures deemed suitable only for their brothers (Kingsley, Scott, Lytton).

Salmon attempts to account for the surprising prevalence of "purely boys' books" on the list of the girls' favorite books in a variety of ways. First, he suggests that they might think it "proper" to vote for such well-regarded writers as Dickens and Scott; then he notes that works by Dickens and Scott and their ilk are far more commonly found in school or family libraries, and thus more "easily get-at-able" by girl readers; finally, he surmises that girls do not take account of authors' names, and thus cite familiar authors rather than the writers whom they actually read (30). Yet despite his conjectures, he also allows that one of Welsh's girl respondents might be speaking for "the general feeling of English girls" when she writes

Girls' top 10 authors:	**Girls' top 10 books:**
Charles Dickens (355)	*Westward Ho!* (34)
Sir Walter Scott (248)	*The Wide, Wide World* (29)
C. Kingsley (103)	The Bible (27)
C.M. Yonge (100)	*A Peep Behind the Scenes* (27)
Shakespeare (75)	*John Halifax, Gentleman* (25)
Mrs Henry Wood (58)	*David Copperfield* (22)
E. Wetherell (Susan Warner) (56)	*Little Women* (21)
George Eliot (50)	*Ivanhoe* (18)
Lord Lytton (46)	*The Days of Bruce* (16)
Andersen (33)	*The Daisy Chain* (13)

(Salmon 14–15; 21–2)

A great many girls never read so-called "girls" books' at all; they prefer those presumably written for boys. Girls as a rule don't care for Sunday-school twaddle; they like a good stirring story, with a plot and some incident and adventures. ... People try to make boys' books as exciting and amusing as possible, while we girls, who are much quicker and more imaginative, are very often supposed to read milk-and-watery sorts of stories that we could generally write better ourselves. (28–9)

The "Sunday-school twaddle" that the above writer mentions suggests that ideal exemplar or flat character construction, and the overt didacticism that often accompanied it, were still to be found in Victorian children's books, particularly in books for girls, but that readers at the end of the period were increasingly finding both less than palatable. Despite his own caveats about the accuracy of the girls' list, Salmon concludes his introduction by noting that the lack of purportedly popular girls' writers or girls' books from the lists books most popular with girl readers suggests that their popularity may be due primarily to the fact that such books are being purchased not by girls themselves, but by their parents and friends. "If girls were to select their own books, in other words, they would make a choice very different from that which their elders make for them" (31).

Salmon suggests that such choices would mirror those made by boys. If Welsh's poll had been conducted nationwide, Salmon asserts, "we should find nearly as many girls as boys have read 'Robinson Crusoe'... and other long-lived 'boys' stories'" (28). Yet looking at his list of girls' favorite books, one is struck by the fact that while 43 boys cited Defoe's novel as their favorite book (the top vote-getter among boys), only two girls out of more than one thousand liked *Crusoe* more than any other. One might just as credibly surmise that their tastes in adventure would more likely run toward the historical romance than to the robinsonade, given that novels of historical fiction are the only adventure novels cited by girls as among their favorites. Did the lack of female characters in the typical Victorian robinsonade, in contrast to their common presence in the historical romance (at least as love interests, if not as adventurers themselves) contribute to this difference? If the girls of 1888 had had some of the female protagonists with whom twentieth-century girl readers were able to identify—characters such as Fiona of Rosalie Fry's *Secret of the Ron Mor Skerry*, Mary and Jean of Carol Rye Brink's *Baby Island*, Ann of Robert C. O'Brien's *Z for Zachariah*, or Karana of Scott O'Dell's *Island of the Blue Dolphins*—perhaps the robinsonade might have featured more prominently among their favorites.

Early twenty-first century readers certainly have less difficulty finding adventure novels with female as well as male protagonists than did their 1888 counterparts. Today's readers also are far more likely to find middle class, rather then gentry, ideology shaping the themes of their fictions of adventure. But the assumption that young readers should and do identify with a text's protagonist—that they believe a character in a book is somehow like them, and that they can and should sympathize with said character's feelings and learn from the actions said character takes—remains a central tenet both of the children's writer's craft and the reading teacher's instruction to her young charges. Just as juvenile readers of the early nineteenth century were asked to identify with the longing of Charles for his lost father, the struggles of Leila to strike a balance between feeling and self-restraint, the efforts of Adelaide to fight for the life domestic in the midst of the forces of history, so, too, are twenty-first century readers expected to identify with, feel the pain and joy of, adventure heroes and heroines such as Brian of Gary Paulsen's *Hatchet*, Nhamo of Nancy Farmer's *A Girl Named Disaster*, Mau and Daphne of Terry Pratchett's *Nation*. Though the lessons readers take away from these late twentieth-century and early twenty-first century fictions are far different than those conveyed by *The Young Crusoe*, *Leila*, or *Adelaide*, the means by which readers learn them—through bonds of sympathetic engagement forged by identification—remains the same.

The pleasures of such identification are numerous, as the previous chapters demonstrate. But pleasures are often counterbalanced by dangers, as children's literature critics such as Perry Nodelman, Mavis Reimer, and John Stephens have begun to point out. When children are encouraged to identify completely with a character, as Stephens notes, "at least for the duration of the reading time, the reader's own selfhood is effaced and the reader internalizes the perceptions and attitudes of the focalizer and is thus reconstituted as a subject within the text" (68). Such reconstitution makes a reader ripe for socialization, Stephens argues, or, in Nodelman and Reimer's view, for "manipulation" (68). That using identification as a socializing tool, which for Victorian writers and educators would be viewed with approval, has now come under suspicion suggests much about the shifts in the construction of childhood, as well as the construction of educators and parents, from the Victorian period to the present.

Both Stephens and Nodelman and Reimer suggest possible remedies against the dangers of readerly identification. Stephens points to textual remedies, ones that might be deployed by authors: using "shifts in focalizers; focalizers who are not 'nice people,' and hence do not invite reader identification; multi-stranded narration, which may play one significance against another; intertextual allusiveness, which may indicate the presence of more than one interpretive frame and require top-down reading; metafictional playfulness, whereby a text draws attention to its own status and processes as a fiction; and overtly inscribed indeterminacies" (70). Nodelman and Reimer focus upon readers, inviting scholars and educators to teach children other strategies besides identification for engaging with a text. By becoming consciously aware that each text invites readers to inhabit a subject position, by learning to identify such subject positions, even by refusing the invitation to identification outright, young readers can distance themselves from the manipulations of the text, and thereby become "freer to negotiate their subjectivity" (179).

These suggestions assume that identification will long remain the preferred reading strategy for young readers to use when they engage with a text. But as this study has shown, identification is not a natural, timeless way of approaching a text, but instead a historically-specific, culturally-determined one. Identification as a reading technique emerged during a period of extreme social, technological, and economic change, a period in many ways quite similar to the one we are currently experiencing at the start of the twenty-first century. Will our shift to a global economy create anxieties similar to those that rose in the face of the proliferation of the eighteenth-century marketplace, forcing elite readers to abandon identification in the quest to devise evermore complex ways of interacting with narratives? Will identification seem foolish, old-fashioned, when the holodeck of Star Trek becomes a reality? Will readers even need to identify with characters when they will soon be able to adopt an avatar and *become* a protagonist within a narrative? With an understanding how characters perfectly satisfactory to eighteenth-century readers became to be judged "flat" by nineteenth-century ones, how reading to discover timeless maxims of virtue and vice gradually gave way to identification as the preferred technique for engaging with a text, it should come as no surprise to us if the "round" characters with whom young readers today are encouraged to identify come to be seen as just as "flat" as their eighteenth-century counterparts, if identification itself gives way to another, as yet unarticulated, strategy for engaging and socializing the youngest of our readers.

Works Cited

Agnew, Kate, Suzanne Rahn, and Roie Thomas. "Historical Fiction." *The Cambridge Guide to Children's Books in English*. Ed. Victor Watson. Cambridge: Cambridge UP, 2001. 335–8. Print.

Altick, Richard. *The English Common Reader: A Social History of the Mass Reading Public 1800–1900*. Chicago: U of Chicago P, 1957.

Anderson, Patricia J. "Charles Knight and Company." *Dictionary of Literary Biography* vol. 106. *British Literary Publishing Houses, 1820–1880*. Ed. Patricia J. Anderson and Jonathan Rose. Detroit: Gale, 1991. 164–70. Print.

[Anonymous]. *The Beautiful Page, or Child of Romance: Being the Interesting History of a Baronet's Daughter, Intended as an instructive Lesson for Youth*. London: T. Hurst, 1802; London: Tegg and Castleman, [1805]. Print.

Ariès, Philippe. *Centuries of Childhood: A Social History of Family Life*. Trans. Robert Baldick. New York: Vintage Books, 1962. Print. Trans. of *L'enfant et al vie familiale sous l'ancien régime*. Paris: Librarie Plon, 1960. Print.

Armitage, Doris Mary. *The Taylors of Ongar: Portrait of an English Family of the Eighteenth and Nineteenth Centuries. Drawn from Family Records by the Great-great Niece of Ann and Jane Taylor*. Cambridge, UK: W. Heffer & Sons, Ltd., 1939. Print.

Austen, Jane. *The History of England, From the Reign of Henry the 4th to the Death of Charles the 1st, by a Partial, Prejudiced, and Ignorant Historian*. 1791. London: Penguin Classics, 1995. Print.

Avery, Gillian. "The Beginnings of Children's Reading, to *c*. 1700." *Children's Literature: An Illustrated History*. Ed. Peter Hunt. Oxford: Oxford UP, 1995. 1–25. Print.

———. *The Best Type of Girl: A History of Girls' Independent Schools*. London: Andre Deutsch, 1991. Print.

———. "Religion: Judeo-Christian Stories." *The Norton Anthology of Children's Literature: The Traditions in English*. Eds. Jack Zipes, Lissa Paul, Lynne Vallone, Peter Hunt, and Gillian Avery. New York: W.W. Norton, 2005. 503–10. Print.

Avery, Gillian and Margaret Kinnell. "Morality and Levity: 1780–1820." *Children's Literature: An Illustrated History*. Oxford: Oxford UP, 1995. Ed. Peter Hunt. 46–76. Print.

Barbauld, Anna. "On the Uses of History." *A Legacy for Young Ladies, Consisting of Miscellaneous Pieces, in Prose and Verse*. Ed. Lucy Aikin. Second edition. London: Longman, Rees, Orme, Brown, and Green, 1826. *Women Writers Online*. Web. 15 July 2007.

Bator, Robert, ed. *Masterworks of Children's Literature*. Volume 4: *1740–1836: Middle Period*. New York: Stonehill/Chelsea House, 1983. Print.

Beiderwell, Bruce and Anita Hemphill McCormick, "The Making and Unmaking of a Children's Classic: The Case of Scott's *Ivanhoe*." Ed. Donelle Ruwe. *Culturing the Child 1690–1914: Essays in Memory of Mitzi Myers*. Lanham, MD: Scarecrow, 2005. 165–78. Print.

Bernard, Claudie. *Penser la famille au XIXe siècle (1789–1870)*. Saint-Étienne: Publications de l'Université de Saint-Étienne, 2007. Print.

Bloch, Jean. *Rousseauism and Education in Eighteenth-Century France. Studies on Voltaire and the Eighteenth-Century* 325. Oxford: Voltaire Foundation, 1995. Print.

Bolingbroke, Henry St John Lord Viscount. *Letters on the Study and Use of History* (1735). *ELIOHS: Electronic Library of Historiography*. Web. 5 July 2006.

Braudy, Leo. *Narrative Form in History and Fiction: Hume, Fielding & Gibbon*. Princeton NJ: Princeton UP, 1970. Print.

Briggs, Julia and Dennis Butts. "The Emergence of Form: 1850–1890." *Children's Literature: An Illustrated History*. Ed. Peter Hunt. Oxford: Oxford UP, 1995. 130–65. Print.

Bristow, Joseph. *Empire Boys: Adventures in a Man's World*. New York: Harper Collins Academic, 1991. Print.

Brodhead, Richard H. *Cultures of Letters: Scenes of Reading and Writing in Nineteenth-Century America*. Chicago: U of Chicago P, 1993. Print.

Brown, Philip A.H. *London Publishers and Printers c. 1800–1870*. London: British Library, 1982. Print.

Browning, Logan D. Jr. "Charles Tilt." *Dictionary of Literary Biography* vol. 106. *British Literary Publishing Houses, 1820–1880*. Ed. Patricia J. Anderson and Jonathan Rose. Detroit: Gale, 1991. 296–8. Print.

Buds of Genius; or, Some Account of the Early Lives of Celebrated Characters Who were remarkable in their childhood. Intended as an introduction to biography. London: Darton, Harvey, and Darton, 1816. Print.

Burgon, John W. *The Portrait of a Christian Gentleman: A Memoir of Patrick Fraser Tytler*. London: John Murray, 1859. Print.

Burke, Edmund. *Reflections on the Revolution in France* 1790. Ed. J.C.D. Clark. Stanford: Stanford UP, 2001. Print.

Burstein, Miriam Elizabeth. *Narrating Women's History in Britain, 1770–1902*. Aldershot, Hants; Burlington, VT: Ashgate, 2004. Print.

———. "'The Reduced Pretensions of the Historic Muse': Agnes Strickland and the Commerce of Women's History." *Journal of Narrative Technique* 28.3 (1998): 219–42. Print.

Butts, Dennis. "The Beginnings of Victorianism: *c*. 1820–1850." *Children's Literature: An Illustrated History*. Ed. Peter Hunt. Oxford: Oxford UP, 1995. 77–101. Print.

———. "Dogs and Cats: The Nineteenth-Century Historical Novel for Children." *Historical Fiction for Children: Capturing the Past*. Eds. Fiona M. Collins and Judith Graham. London: David Fulton Publishers, 2001. 2–9. Print.

———. *Mistress of Our Tears: A Literary and Bibliographical Study of Barbara Hofland*. Aldershot, Hants: Scolar Press, 1992. Print.

Calvert, Karin. "Children in the House 1890–1930." *American Home Life 1880– 1930: A Social History of Spaces and Services.* Eds. Jessica H. Foy and Thomas J. Schlereth. Knoxville: U of Tennessee P, 1992. 75–93. Print.

"Cambridge Companions to Literature." *Cambridge University Press.* Cambridge UP. Web. 15 March 2009.

Campan, Madame. *Memoirs of the Private Life of Marie Antoinette, Queen of France and Navarre.* 2 vols. London: H. Holburn and Co. and M. Bossange and Co., 1823. Print.

Campbell, Jill. "Women Writers and the Trope of the Woman's Novel: The Trope of Maternal Transmission." Ed. Richard Maxwell and Katie Trumpener. *The Cambridge Companion to Fiction in the Romantic Period.* Cambridge: Cambridge UP, 2008. 159–75. Print.

Carpenter, Humphrey. *Secret Gardens: The Golden Age of Children's Literature, From Alice in Wonderland to Winnie-the-Pooh.* Boston: Houghton, 1985. Print.

Carpenter, Kevin. *Desert Islands & Pirate Islands: The Island Theme in Nineteenth-Century English Juvenile Fiction: A Survey and Bibliography.* Frankfurt: Verlag Peter Lang, 1984. Print.

Chandler, James. *England in 1819.* Chicago: U of Chicago P, 1998. Print.

———. "History." *An Oxford Companion to The Romantic Age.* Ed. Iain McCalman. Oxford: Oxford UP, 1999. 354–61. Print.

Chapone, Hester. *Letters on the Improvement of the Mind.* 1773. London: John Sharpe, 1822. Print.

"The Civil Code Index." *The Napoleon Series.* Ed. Robert Burnham. 1995–2009. Web. 5 Feb 2009.

Clarke, Norma. " 'The Cursed Barbauld Crew': Women Writers and Writing for Children in the Late Eighteenth Century." *Opening the Nursery Door: Reading, Writing and Childhood 1600–1900.* Ed. Mary Hilton, Morag Styles, and Victor Watson. New York: Routledge, 1997. 91–103. Print.

[Cléry, Hanet]. *Journal de ce qui s'est passé à la Tour du Temple pedant la captivité de Louis XVI par M. Cléry, valet du chambre du roi et autres mémoires sur le Temple.* London: Baylis, 1798. Print.

Collins, Fiona M. and Judith Graham. *Historical Fiction for Children: Capturing the Past.* London: David Fulton, 2001. Print.

Cox, Roger. *Shaping Childhood: Themes of Uncertainty in the History of Adult-Child Relationships.* London and New York: Routledge, 1996. Print.

Cunningham, Hugh. *Children and Childhood in Western Society Since 1500.* Harlow, England: Longman/Pearson, 1995. Print.

———. *The Invention of Childhood.* London: BBC Books, 2006. Print.

———. "Review Essay: Histories of Childhood." *American Historical Review* 103.4 (Oct. 1998): 1195–1208. Print.

Cutt, M. Nancy. *Ministering Angels: A Study of Nineteenth-Century Evangelical Writing for Children.* Wormley, Hertforshire: Five Owls Press, 1979. Print.

———. *Mrs Sherwood and her Books for Children.* London: Oxford UP, 1974. Print.

Darton, F.J. Harvey. *Children's Books in England: Five Centuries of Social Life*. Third ed. Rev. Brian Alderson. London: The British Library; Newcastle, DE: Oak Knoll Press, 1999. Print.

Davidoff, Leonore and Catherine Hall. *Family Fortunes: Men and Women of the English Middle Class, 1780–1850*. Chicago: U of Chicago P, 1987. Print.

Defoe, Daniel. *Robinson Crusoe*. 1719. Ed. Michael Shinagel. New York: Norton, 1975. Print.

Delorme, Mary. "'Facts, not Opinions': Agnes Strickland." *History Today* 38.2 (1988): 45–50. *History Today*. Web. May 6, 2009.

Demers, Patricia. *Heaven Upon Earth: The Form of Moral and Religious Children's Literature, to 1850*. Knoxville, TN: U of Tennessee Press, 1993. Print.

Demers, Patricia and Gordon Moyles, eds. *From Instruction to Delight: An Anthology of Children's Literature to 1850*. 3rd ed. Don Mills, Ont.: Oxford UP, 2008. Print.

De Mause, Lloyd, ed. *The History of Childhood*. New York: Psychohistory Press, 1974. Print.

Duncan, Ian. *Modern Romance and Transformations of the Novel: The Gothic, Scott, Dickens*. Cambridge: Cambridge UP, 1992. Print.

Edgeworth, Maria. *The Parent's Assistant*. 1796. *The Pickering Masters: The Novels and Selected Works of Maria Edgeworth*. Vol. 10. Ed. Elizabeth Eger & Clíona ÓGallchoir. London: Pickering and Chatto, 2003. Print.

———— *Practical Education*. 1798. *The Pickering Masters: The Novels and Selected Works of Maria Edgeworth*. Vol. 11. Ed. Susan Manly. London: Pickering and Chatto, 2003. Print.

Ferris, Ina. *The Achievement of Literary Authority: Gender, History, and the Waverley Novels*. Ithaca: Cornell UP, 1991. Print.

Field, E.M. (Mrs). *The Child and His Book: Some Account of the History and Progress of Children's Literature in England* 2nd ed. London: Wells Gardner, Darton & Co., 1892. Detroit: Singing Tree Press, 1968. Print.

Fielding, Sarah. *The Governess: or Little Female Academy*. London: A. Millar, 1749. London: Pandora, 1987. Print.

Fisher, Margery. *The Bright Face of Danger: An Exploration of the Adventure Story*. London: Hodder & Stoughton, 1986. Print.

Flanagan, Victoria. "Reframing Masculinity: Female-to-Male Cross Dressing" *Ways of Being Male: Representing Masculinities in Children's Literature and Film*. Ed. John Stephens. New York: Routledge, 2002: 78–95. Print.

Fraser, Antonia. *Boadicea's Chariot: The Warrior Queens*. London: Weidenfeld and Nicolson, 1988. Print.

————. *Marie Antoinette: The Journey*. London: Weidenfeld & Nicholson, 2001. Print.

Frost, Ginger. S. *Victorian Childhoods*. Westport, CT: Praeger, 2009. Print.

Fudge, Erica. "Learning to Laugh: Children and Being Human in Early Modern Thought." *Childhood and Children's Books in Early Modern Europe, 1550–1800*. Ed. Andrea Immel and Michael Witmore. New York: Routledge, 2006: 19–39. Print.

Gallagher, Catherine. *Nobody's Story: The Vanishing Acts of Women Writers in the Marketplace, 1670–1820*. Berkeley and Los Angeles: U of California P, 1994. Print.

Garber, Margery. *Vested Interests: Cross-Dressing and Cultural Anxiety*. New York and London: Routledge, 1992. Print.

Garside, Peter. "The English Novel in the Romantic Period." *The English Novel 1770–1829*. Vol. II. Ed. Peter Garside, James Raven, and Rainer Schöwerling. New York: Oxford UP, 2000. Print.

Gargano, Elizabeth. *Reading Victorian Schoolrooms: Childhood and Education in Nineteenth-Century Fiction*. New York: Routledge, 2008. Print.

Gauthier, Maurice-Paul. *Captain Frederick Marryat: L'Homme et L'Oeuvre*. 2 vol. Lille: Service de Reproduction des Thèses, Université de Lille III, 1973. Print.

Genlis, Stéphanie Felicité, comtesse de. *Théâtre a l'usage des jeunes personnes*. Paris: Michel Lambert, 1785. Print.

Gilbert, Sandra, and Susan Gubar. *The Madwoman in the Attic: The Woman Writer and the Nineteenth-Century Literary Imagination*. New Haven and London: Yale UP, 1979. Print.

Gillis, John R. "Gender and Fertility Decline among the British Middle Classes." *The European Experience of Declining Fertility*. Ed. John R. Gillis, Louise Tilly, and David Levine. Cambridge: Basil Blackwell, 1992. 31–47. Print.

Godwin, William. "Of the Study of the Classics." *The Enquirer: Reflections on Education, Manners, and Literature*. 1797. Edinburgh: John Anderson, 1823. Print.

[———]. "The Preface." *Bible Stories, Memorable Acts of the Ancient Patriarchs, Judges, and Kings, Extracted from their Original Historians*, by William Scolfield. 1802. Albany: Charles R. and George Webster, 1803. *Early American Imprints, Series II: Shaw-Shoemaker*. Web. 24 Mar 2010.

Golding, William. *Lord of the Flies*. New York: G.P. Putnam's Sons, 1954, 1955. Print.

Goldstone, Bette P. *Lessons to be Learned: A Study of Eighteenth-Century English Didactic Children's Literature*. New York: Peter Lang, 1984. Print.

Green, Martin. *The Robinson Crusoe Story*. University Park: Pennsylvania State UP, 1990. Print.

Grenby, M.O. "Adults Only? Children and Children's Books in British Circulating Libraries 1748–1848." *Book History* 5.1 (2002): 19–38. Print.

———. "Introduction: Children, Childhood, and Children's Culture in the Eighteenth Century." *British Journal for Eighteenth-Century Studies* 29.3, 2006: 313–19. Print.

Grenby, Matthew. "Introduction." Sarah Trimmer. *The Guardian of Education: A Periodical Work*. Ed. M.O. Grenby. Bristol, England: Thoemmes Continuum, 2002. *v xli*. Print.

Hall, Donald, ed. *Muscular Christianity: Embodying the Victorian Age*. Cambridge: Cambridge University Press, 1994. Print.

Hanawalt, Barbara. *The Ties that Bound: Peasant Families in Medieval England.* New York: Oxford UP, 1986. Print.

Hazard, Paul. *Books, Children, and Men.* 1944. Trans. Marguerite Mitchell. 5th ed. Boston: Horn Book, 1983. Print.

Heywood, Colin. *A History of Childhood: Children and Childhood in the West from Medieval to Modern Times.* Cambridge, UK; Malden, MA: Polity P, 2001. Print.

Higonnet, Margaret R. "Civility Books, Child Citizens, and Uncivil Antics." *Poetics Today* 13.1 (1992): 123–40. Print.

Hofland, Barbara. *Adelaide, or, The Intrepid Daughter: A Tale, Including Historical Anecdotes of Henry the Great and the Massacre of St Bartholomew.* London: J. Harris, 1823. Print.

———. *Little Dramas for Young People, on Subjects Taken from English History: Intended to Promote Among the Rising Generation an Early Love of Virtue and their Country.* London: Longman, Hurst, Rees and Orme, 1810. Print.

———. *The Young Crusoe, or the Shipwrecked Boy.* London: A.K. Newman, 1828. Print.

Horne, Jackie C. "The Power of Public Opinion: Constructing Class in Agnes Strickland's *The Rival Crusoes*." *Children's Literature* 35 (2007): 1–26. Print.

———. "Punishment as Performance in Catherine Sinclair's *Holiday House*." *Children's Literature Association Quarterly* 26.1 (2001): 22–32. Print.

———. "Settler Dreams: Reestablishing Landed Gentry Hierarchies in Catharine Strickland's *The Young Emigrants*." *Canadian Children's Literature* 31.1 (2008): 19–42. Print.

Hunt, Peter. *Children's Literature: An Illustrated History.* Oxford and New York: Oxford UP, 1995. Print.

Hunter, J. Paul. *Before Novels: The Cultural Contexts of Eighteenth-Century English Fiction.* New York: W.W. Norton, 1990. Print.

Hunter, Shelagh. *Harriet Martineau: The Poetics of Moralism.* Aldershot, Hants; Brookfield, VT: Scholar Press, 1995. Print.

Jackson, Mary V. *Engines of Instruction, Mischief, and Magic: Children's Literature in England from its Beginnings to 1839.* Lincoln: U of Nebraska P, 1989. Print.

Jaffe, Audrey. *Scenes of Sympathy: Identity and Representation in Victorian Fiction.* Ithaca and London: Cornell UP, 2000. Print.

Jalland, Pat. *Death in the Victorian Family.* Oxford: Oxford UP, 1996. Print.

James, Allison and Alan Prout. "A New Paradigm for the Sociology of Childhood? Provenance, Promise and Problems." *Constructing and Reconstructing Childhood: Contemporary Issues in the Sociological Study of Childhood.* 2nd ed. London: Routledge, 1997. Print.

Janeway, James. *A Token for Children.* 1671. *From Instruction to Delight: An Anthology of Children's Literature to 1850.* Ed. Patricia Demers and Gordon Moyles. Oxford: Oxford UP, 1982. 45–53. Print.

The Juvenile Plutarch: *comtaining [sic] accounts of the lives of children, and of the infancy of illustrious men, who have been remarkable for their early progress in knowledge*. 1801. Republished under the title *The Juvenile Plutarch*: *Containing Accounts of the Lives of Celebrated Children, and of the Infancy of Persons who have been Illustrious for their Virtues or Talents* 4th ed. London: William Darton, 1820. Print.

Johnson, Claudia. *Equivocal Beings: Politics, Gender, and Sentimentality in the 1790s*. Chicago: U of Chicago P, 1995. Print.

[Johnstone, Christian Isobel]. *The Students; or, Biography of Grecian Philosophers*. London: John Harris, [1827]. Print.

Joyce, James. "Daniel Defoe." Trans. from Italian manuscript and ed. Joseph Prescott. *Buffalo Studies* 1 (1964): 24–5. Print.

Kelly, Gary. "Revolution, Reaction, an the Expropriation of Popular Culture: Hannah More's *Cheap Repository*." *Man and Nature/L'Homme et la Nature* 6 (1987): 147–59. Print.

Kertzer, David I. and Marzio Barbagli. *The History of the European Family, vol. 2: Family Life in the Long Nineteenth Century 1789–1913*. New Haven and London: Yale UP, 2002. Print.

Kincaid, James R. *Child-Loving: The Erotic Child and Victorian Culture*. New York: Routledge, 1992. Print.

Koepp, Cynthia J. "Curiosity, Science, and Experiential Learning in the Eighteenth-Century. *Childhood and Children's Books in Early Modern Europe, 1550–1800*. Ed. Andrea Immel and Michael Witmore. New York: Routledge, 2006. 153–80. Print.

Kümmerling-Meibauer, Bettina. "Images of Childhood in Romantic Children's Literature." *Romantic Prose Fiction*. Ed. Gerald Gillespie, Manfred Engel, and Bernard Dieterle. Amsterdam: John Benjamins, 2007. 183–203. Print. Comparative History of Literatures in European Languages.

Langbauer, Laurie. *Women and Romance: The Consolations of Gender in the English Novel*. Ithaca: Cornell UP, 1990. 62–92. Print.

Laurence, Anne. "Women Historians and Documentary Research: Lucy Aikin, Agnes Strickland, Mary Anne Everett Green and Lucy Toulmin Smith." *Women, Scholarship and Criticism: Gender and Knowledge c 1790–1900*. Ed. Joan Bellamy, Anne Laurence, and Gill Perry. Manchester, New York: Manchester UP, 2000. 125–41. Print.

Laver, James. *Hatchards of Picadilly, 1797–1947: One Hundred and Fifty Years of Bookselling*. London: Hatchards, 1947. Print.

Lennox, Charlotte. *The Female Quixote, or, The Adventures of Arabella*. 1752. Ed. Margaret Dalziel. Introd. Margaret Anne Doody. Oxford: Oxford UP, 1970, 1989. Print.

Levi, Anthony. *Guide to French Literature. Beginnings to 1789*. Detroit: St James Press, 1994. Print.

Levy, Jonathan. *The Gymnasium of the Imagination: A Collection of Children's Plays in English, 1780–1860*. New York: Greenwood, 1992. Print.

Lewis, Jayne Elizabeth. *Mary Queen of Scots: Romance and Nation*. London: Routledge, 1998. Print.

Looser, Devoney. *British Women Writers and the Writing of History, 1670–1820*. Baltimore: Johns Hopkins UP, 2000. Print.

Lovell, Terry. *Consuming Fiction*. London: Verso, 1987. Print.

Loxley, Diana. *Problematic Shores: The Literature of Islands*. Basingstoke: Macmillan, 1990. Print.

Lynch, Deidre Shauna. *The Economy of Character: Novels, Market Culture, and the Business of Inner Meaning*. Chicago: U of Chicago P, 1998. Print.

McGavran, James Holt. "Introduction." *Romanticism and Children's Literature in Nineteenth-Century England*. Athens, GA: U of Georgia P, 1991. 1–13. Print.

MacLeod, Anne Scott. "Writing Backwards: Modern Models in Historical Fiction." *Horn Book* Jan./Feb. 1998: 26–33. Virtual History Exhibit. *The Horn Book*. Web. 27 July 2005.

Maher, Susan Naramore. "The Uses of Adventure: The Moral and Evangelical Robinsonnades of Agnes Strickland, Barbara Hofland, and Ann Fraser Tytler." *Jane Austen and Mary Shelley and their Sisters*. Ed. Laura Dabundo. Lanham. MD: University Press of America, 2000. 147–58. Print.

Maitzen, Rohan Amanda. *Gender, Genre, and Victorian Historical Writing*. New York and London: Garland, 1998. Print.

[Mallès de Beaulieu, Jeanne Sylvie]. *Le Robinson de Douze Ans: Histoire Intérresant d'un Jeune Mousse Français Abandonné dans une Ile Déserte*. Paris: P. Blanchard, 1818. Published in English as *The Modern Crusoe: The Life and Adventures of a French Cabin Boy, Who Was Shipwrecked on an Uninhabited Island*. Boston: James Loring, 1827. Print.

Marcus, Sharon. *Between Women: Friendship, Desire, and Marriage in Victorian England*. Princeton, NJ: Princeton UP, 2007. Print.

Mark, Jan. "From the Front Line." *Opening the Nursery Door: Reading, Writing and Childhood 1600–1900*. Ed. Mary Hilton, Morag Styles, and Victor Watson. New York: Routledge, 1997. 133–41. Print.

Marryat, Captain [Frederick]. *Masterman Ready; or, The Wreck of the Pacific*. 3 vols. London: Longman, Orme, Brown, and Green, 1841–1842. New York: D. Appleton & Co., 1846. Print.

Marshall, David. *The Surprising Effects of Sympathy: Marivaux, Diderot, Rousseau, and Mary Shelley*. Chicago and London: U of Chicago P, 1988. Print.

———. "Writing Masters and 'Masculine Exercises' in *The Female Quixote*," *Eighteenth-Century Fiction* 5: 105–35. Print.

Martineau, Harriet. *Harriet Martineau: Selected Letters*. Ed. Valerie Sanders. Oxford: Clarendon Press, 1990. Print.

———. *Harriet Martineau's Autobiography*. With Memorials by Maria Weston Chapman. Vol 2. 2nd ed. London: Smith, Elder, 1877. Print.

———. *The History of England during the Thirty Years' Peace 1816–1846*. 2 vols. London: Charles Knight, 1849–1850. Print.

————. *The Peasant and the Prince* (*The Playfellow*). London: Charles Knight & Co, 1841. Print.

Massé, Michelle. *In the Name of Love: Women, Masochism, and the Gothic*. Ithaca and London: Cornell UP, 1992. Print.

Mayo, Christopher, Ed. *Lord Chesterfield's Letters to his Son: A Critical Edition*. Diss. Brandeis U, 2004. Print.

Maxwell, Richard and Katie Trumpener. "Introduction." *The Cambridge Companion to Fiction in the Romantic Period*. Cambridge: Cambridge UP, 2008. 1–6. Print.

Michie, Allen. *Richardson and Fielding: The Dynamics of a Critical Rivalry*. Lewisburg, PA: Bucknell UP, 1999. Print.

Mitchell, Rosemary. "Strickland, Agnes." *Oxford Dictionary of National Biography*. Oxford UP. Web. 27 July 2005.

Mee, Jon. *Romanticism, Enthusiasm, and Regulation*. Oxford: Oxford UP, 2003. Print.

Mock, David. B. "David Bogue." *Dictionary of Literary Biography* vol. 106. *British Literary Publishing Houses, 1820–1880*. Ed. Patricia J. Anderson and Jonathan Rose. Detroit: Gale, 1991. 57–8.

Moers, Ellen. *Literary Women: The Great Writers*. Garden City, NY: Doubleday, 1976. Print.

More, Hannah. "Sensibility." 1798. *Eighteenth-Century Women Poets*. Ed. Roger Lonsdale. Oxford: Oxford UP, 1989. 328–29. Print.

————. *Coelebs in Search of a Wife*. London: T. Cadell and W. Davies, 1810. Bristol: Thoemmes Press, 1995. Print.

Morillo, John D. *Uneasy Feelings: Literature, the Passions, and Class from Neoclassicism to Romanticism*. New York: AMS Press, 2001. Print.

"Mrs Trimmer." *The Cambridge History of English and American Literature in 18 Volumes (1907–1921). Volume XIV. The Victorian Age, Part Two*. Web. Bartleby.com. 6 May 2009.

Muhlberger, Steve. "A Brief Introduction to Froissart and these Tales." *Tales from Froissart*. Department of History, Nipissing University. n.d. Web. 10 July 2008.

Muir, Percy. *English Children's Books, 1600 to 1900*. New York: Praeger, 1954. Print.

Müller, Anja. "Introduction." *Fashioning Childhood in the Eighteenth Century: Age and Identity*. Ed. Anja Müller. Aldershot, Hants: Ashgate, 2006. 1–10. Print.

Myers, Mitzi. "Impeccable Governesses, Rational Dames, and Moral Mothers: Mary Wollstonecraft and the Female Tradition in Georgian Children's Books." *Children's Literature in Education* 14 (1986): 31–60. Print.

————. "Little Girls Lost: Rewriting Romantic Childhood, Righting Gender and Genre." *Teaching Children's Literature: Issues, Pedagogy, Resources*. Ed. Glenn Edward Sadler. New York: MLA, 1992. 131–42. Print.

————. "Reading Rosamund Reading: Maria Edgeworth's 'Wee-Wee Stories' Interrogate the Canon." *Infant Tongues: The Voice of the Child in Literature*. Ed. Elizabeth Goodenough, Mark A. Heberle, and Naomi Sokoloff. Detroit: Wayne State UP, 1994. 57–79. Print.

Nadel, George H. "Philosophy of History Before Historicism." *History and Theory* 3.3 (1964): 291–315. Print.

Nelson, Claudia. *Boys Will Be Girls: The Feminine Ethic and British Children's Fiction, 1857–1917*. New Brunswick, NJ: Rutgers UP, 1991. Print.

———. *Family Ties in Victorian England*. Westport, CT: Praeger 2007. Print.

———. "Growing Up: Childhood." *A Companion to Victorian Literature and Culture*. Ed. Herbert F. Tucker. Malden, MA, and Oxford: Blackwell Publishers, 1999. 69–81. Print.

———. *Invisible Men: Fatherhood in Victorian Periodicals, 1850–1910*. Athens, GA: U of Georgia P, 1995. Print.

Nelson, Dana D. "Women and Gender in the State of Sympathy." *Feminist Studies* 28.1 (2002): 175–87. Print.

Nikolajeva, Maria. "Children's Literature as a Cultural Code: A Semiotic Approach to History." *Aspects and Issues in the History of Children's Literature*. Ed. Maria Nikolajeva. Westport, CT: Greenwood Press, 1995. 39–48. Print.

Nodelman, Perry. "Pleasure and Genre: Speculations on the Characteristics of Children's Fiction." *Children's Literature* 28 (2000): 1–14. Print.

——— and Mavis Reimer. *The Pleasures of Children's Literature*. 3rd ed. Boston: Allyn and Bacon, 2003.

Nussbaum, Felicity A. *Torrid Zones: Maternity, Sexuality, and Empire in Eighteenth-Century English Narratives*. Baltimore: Johns Hopkins UP, 1995. Print.

O'Brien, Karen. "The History Market in Eighteenth-Century England." *Books and Their Readers in Eighteenth-Century England: New Essays*. Ed. Isabel Rivers. London: Leicester UP, 2001. 105–33. Print.

[Oliphant, Margaret]. "Modern Light Literature—History." *Blackwood's Edinburgh Magazine* 78 (1855): 437–51. Print.

O'Malley, Andrew. *The Making of the Modern Child: Children's Literature and Childhood in the Late Eighteenth Century*. New York: Routledge, 2003. Print.

———. "Crusoe at Home: Coding Domesticity in Children's Editions of Robinson Crusoe." *British Journal for Eighteenth-Century Studies* 29.3 (2006): 37–52. Print.

O'Sullivan, Emer. *Comparative Children's Literature*. Trans. Anthea Bell. London: Routledge, 2005. Print.

Orme, Nicholas. *Medieval Children*. New Haven and London: Yale UP, 2001. Print.

Ormond, Leonée. " 'The Spacious Times of Great Elizabeth': The Victorian Vision of the Elizabethans." *Victorian Poetry* 25.3–4 (1987): 29–46. Print.

Pearson, Jacqueline. *Women's Reading in Britain 1750–1835: A Dangerous Recreation*. Cambridge: Cambridge UP, 1999. Print.

Petersen, Robert C. "Agnes Strickland (1796–1874)." *Nineteenth-Century British Women Writers: A Bio-Bibliographical Critical Sourcebook*. Ed. Abigail Burnham Bloom. Westport, CT: Greenwood Press, 2000. 373–5. Print.

Phillips, Mark Salber. *Society and Sentiment: Genres of Historical Writing in Britain, 1740–1820*. Princeton: Princeton UP, 2000. Print.

Pichanick, Valerie Kossew. *Harriet Martineau: The Woman and Her Work, 1802–1876.* Ann Arbor: U of Michigan P, 1980. Print.

Pickering, Samuel F., Jr. *Moral Instruction and Fiction for Children, 1749–1820.* Athens: U of Georgia P, 1993. Print.

Pinch, Adela. *Strange Fits of Passion: Epistemologies of Emotion, Hume to Austen.* Stanford: Stanford UP, 1996. Print.

Plotz, Judith. *Romanticism and the Vocation of Childhood.* New York: Palgrave, 2001. Print.

Pocock, Tom. *Captain Marryat: Seaman, Writer and Adventurer.* London: Chatham Publishing, 2000. Print.

Pollack, Linda. *Forgotten Children: Parent-Child Relations from 1500–1900.* Cambridge: Cambridge UP, 1983. Print.

———. *A Lasting Relationship: Parents and Children Over Three Centuries.* Hanover and London: UP of New England, 1987. Print.

Pope-Hennessy, Ina. *Agnes Strickland: Biographer of the Queens of England, 1796–1874.* London: Chatto & Windus, 1940. Print.

Power, Chandra L. "Challenging the Pluralism of our Past: Presentism and the Selective Tradition in Historical Fiction Written for Young People." *Research in the Teaching of English* 37.4 (2003): 425–66. *National Council of Teachers of English.* Web. 5 May 2009.

Punter, David. *The Literature of Terror: A History of Gothic Fictions from 1765 to the Present Day.* London and New York: Longman, 1980. Print.

Rahn, Suzanne. "An Evolving Past: The Story of Historical Fiction and Nonfiction for Children." *The Lion and the Unicorn* 15.1 (1991): 1–26. Print.

Richardson, Alan. "Childhood and Romanticism." *Teaching Children's Literature: Issues, Pedagogy, Resources.* Ed. Glenn Edward Sadler. New York: MLA, 1992. 121–30. Print.

———. *Literature, Education, and Romanticism: Reading as Social Practice, 1780–1832.* Cambridge: Cambridge UP, 1994. Print.

[Rigby, Elizabeth]. "Children's Books." *Quarterly Review* 74 (1844): 1–26. Print.

Robert, A. and Cougny, G. *Dictionaire des parlementaries François, etc.* 5 vols. 1889–91. Microfiche. *Archives Biographiques Françaises.* I.502.13.

Robinson, Ainslie. "Playfellows and Propaganda: Harriet Martineau's Children's Writing." *Women's Writing* 9:3 (2002): 395–412. Print.

Ross, Deborah. *The Excellence of Falsehood: Romance, Realism, and Women's Contribution to the Novel.* Lexington: UP of Kentucky, 1991. Print.

Rousseau, Jean-Jaques. *Émile.* 1762. Trans. Barbara Foxley. London: Everyman, 1993. Print.

Rowland, Ann Wierda. "Sentimental Fiction." *The Cambridge Companion to Fiction in the Romantic Period.* Ed. Richard Maxwell and Katie Trumpener. Cambridge: Cambridge UP, 2008. 191–206. Print.

Russell, William. *The History of Modern Europe, with an Account of the Decline and Fall of the Roman Empire, and a view of the Progress of Society from the Rise of the Modern Kingdoms to the Peace of Paris, 1763. In a series of letters from a Nobleman to his Son. A New Edition, carefully corrected.* 1789. New York: Harper, 1839. *Google Book Search*. Web. May 6, 2009.

Ruwe, Donelle. "Guarding the British Bible from Rousseau: Sarah Trimmer, William Godwin, and the Pedagogical Periodical." *Children's Literature* 29 (2001): 1–17. Print.

———— "Satirical Birds and Natural Bugs: J. Harris's Chapbooks and the Aesthetics of Children's Literature." *The Satiric Eye: Forms of Satire in the Romantic Period.* Ed. Steven E. Jones. New York: Palgrave, 2003. 115–37. Print.

St Clair, William. *The Reading Nation in the Romantic Period.* Cambridge: Cambridge UP, 2004. Print.

St John, Judith. *The Osborne Collection of Early Children's Books 1566–1910: A Catalogue.* Volume II. Toronto: U of Toronto P, 1958, 1966, 1975. Print.

Salmon, Edward. *Juvenile Literature as It Is.* London: Henry J. Drane, 1888. Print.

Salway, Lance. *A Peculiar Gift: Nineteenth-Century Writings on Books for Children.* Harmondsworth, Middlesex, England: Kestrel/Penguin, 1976. Print.

Schultz, James A. *The Knowledge of Childhood in the German Middle Ages, 1100–1350.* Philadelphia: U of Penn Press, 1995. Print.

Scott, Sir Walter. *Waverley; or, 'Tis Sixty Years Since.* 1814. London: Penguin Books, 1972. Print.

Scrivener, Michael. "M.J. Godwin and Company." Bracken, James K. and Joel Silver, eds. *The Dictionary of Literary Biography*, vol. 154: *The British Library Book Trade, 1700–1820.* Detroit: Gale, 1995. 143–9. Print.

Shaftesbury, Anthony Ashley Cooper, Earl of. "An Inquiry Concerning Virtue, or Merit." *Characteristicks of Men, Manners, Opinions, Times.* 1711. Ed. Philip Ayres. Oxford: Clarenden Press, 1999. 189–274. Print.

Shahar, Shulamith. *Childhood in the Middle Ages.* London: Routledge, 1990. Print.

Shefrin, Jill. "'Make it a Pleasure and Not a Task': Educational Games for Children in Georgian England." *Princeton University Library Chronicle* 60.2 (1999): 251–75. Print.

Smith, Adam. *The Theory of Moral Sentiments.* 1759. Ed. D.D. Raphael and A.L. Macfie. Indianapolis: Liberty Classics, 1976. Print.

Spencer, Jane. *The Rise of the Woman Novelist: From Aphra Behn to Jane Austen.* Oxford and New York: Basil Blackwell, 1986. Print.

Steedman, Carolyn. *Childhood, Culture and Class in Britain: Margaret McMillan, 1860–1931.* New Brunswick, NJ: Rutgers UP, 1990. Print.

Stephens, John. *Language and Ideology in Children's Fiction.* London: Longman, 1992.

Stone, Laurence. *The Family, Sex, and Marriage in England, 1500–1800.* New York: Harper and Row, 1977. Print.

Strickland, Agnes. *Alda, or the British Captive.* London: Joseph Rickerby, 1841. Print.

————. *Historical Tales of Illustrious British Children.* London: N. Hailes, 1833. Print.

————. *Lives of the Queens of England: from the Norman Conquest: with anecdotes of their courts, now first published from official records and other authentic documents, private as well as public.* Vol 1. 2nd ed. Philadelphia: Lean & Blanchard, 1841. Print.

————. *Lives of the Queens of England.* Vol. VI. London: George Bell and Sons, 1885. Print.

————. *Lives of the Queens of England.* Vol. VII. London: George Bell and Sons, 1885. Print.

Summerfield, Geoffrey. *Fantasy and Reason: Children's Literature in the Eighteenth Century.* Athens, GA: U of Georgia Press, 1984. Print.

Taylor, Jefferys. *The Little Historians: A New Chronicle of the Affairs of England in Church and State, by Lewis and Paul; with Explanatory Remarks, and Additional Information upon Various Subjects Connected with the Progress of Civilization; also Some Account of Antiquities.* London: Baldwin, Cradock, and Joy, 1824. Print.

————. *The Young Islanders: A Tale of the Last Century.* London: Tilt and Bogue, 1842. New York: Appleton and Company, 1842. Print.

Thomas, Gillian. *Harriet Martineau.* Boston: Twayne, 1985. Print.

Thompson, Helen. "Charlotte Lennox and the Agency of Romance." *Eighteenth-Century: Theory and Interpretation.* 43.2 (2002): 91–114. Print.

Thomson, Helen. "Charlotte Lennox's *The Female Quixote:* A Novel Interrogation." *Living by the Pen: Early British Women Writers.* Ed. Dale Spender. New York: Teachers College Press, 1992: 113–25. Print.

Todd, Janet. *Sensibility: An Introduction.* London and New York: Methuen, 1986. Print.

Tosh, John. "Authority and Nurture in Middle-Class Fatherhood: The Case of Early and Mid-Victorian England." *Gender & History* 8.1 (1996): 48–64. Print.

————. *A Man's Place: Masculinity and the Middle-Class Home in Victorian England.* New Haven: Yale UP, 1999. Print.

Townsend, John Rowe. *Written for Children: An Outline of English-Language Children's Literature.* 3rd rev. ed. New York: J.B. Lippincott, 1987. Print.

[Tourzel, Louise Elizabeth, Duchess de]. *Mémoires de Madame la Duchesse de Tourzel, Gouvernante des Enfants de France de 1789 à 1795.* Paris: E. Plon et Cie, 1883. Boston: Elibron Classics, 2001. Print.

Traer, James F. *Marriage and the Family in Eighteenth-Century France.* Ithaca, NY: Cornell UP, 1980. Print.

Trimmer, Mrs [Sarah]. *A Description of a Set of Prints of Ancient History: Contained in a Set of Easy Lessons.* 1786. London: Baldwin, Cradock, and Joy, 1817. *Google Book Search.* Web. May 6, 2009.

Trumpener, Katie. *Bardic Nationalism: The Romantic Novel and the British Empire.* Princeton, NJ: Princeton UP, 1997. Print.

Tytler, Ann Fraser. *Leila, or The Island.* 1839. Boston: Crosby, Nichols, Lee and Co., 1861. Print.

————. *Leila in England: A Continuation of Leila, or, The Island.* London: J. Hatchard and Son, 1844. Print.

————. *Leila at Home: A Continuation of Leila in England.* London: J. Hatchard and Son, 1852. Print.

Vallone, Lynne. *Disciplines of Virtue: Girls' Culture in the Eighteenth and Nineteenth Centuries.* New Haven: Yale UP, 1995. Print.

————. "History Girls: Eighteenth- and Nineteenth-Century Historiography and the Case of Mary, Queen of Scots." *Children's Literature* 36 (2008): 1–23. Print.

Vance, Norman. *The Sinews of the Spirit: The Ideal of Christian Manliness in Victorian Literature and Religious Thought.* Cambridge: Cambridge University Press, 1985. Print.

Watt, Ian. *The Rise of the Novel: Studies in Defoe, Richardson and Fielding.* Berkeley and Los Angeles: U of California P, 1957. Print.

————. "Robinson Crusoe as a Myth." Reprinted in Defoe, Daniel. *Robinson Crusoe.* Ed. Michael Shinagel. New York: W.W. Norton & Co., 1975. Print.

Webb, R.K. *Harriet Martineau: A Radical Victorian.* New York: Columbia UP, 1960. Print.

Wiss, M. [Johann David Wyss]. *The Family Robinson Crusoe: or, Journal of a Father Shipwrecked, with his Wife and Children, on an Uninhabited Island.* London: M.J. Godwin and Co., 1814. Print. Trans. of *Der schweizersche Robinson, oder der schiffbrüchige Schweizerprediger und seine Familie. Ein lehrreiches Buch für Kinder und Kinder–Freunde zu Stadt und Land.* 2 vols. Zürich: Orell, Füsli & Compagnie, 1812–18132.

Wollstonecraft, Mary. *A Vindication of the Rights of Woman* 1792. Ed. Carol H. Poston. 2nd ed. New York: Norton, 1975, 1988. Print.

Wordsworth, William. *Selected Poems and Prefaces.* Ed. Jack Stillinger. Boston: Houghton Mifflin, 1965. Print.

Zelizer, Viviana A. *Pricing the Priceless Child: The Changing Social Value of Children.* New York: Basic Books, 1985. Print.

Index